A Canoeing and Kayaking Guide to Florida

OTHER MENASHA RIDGE PADDLING GUIDES

A Canoeing & Kayaking Guide to Georgia

A Canoeing & Kayaking Guide to the Streams of Kentucky

A Canoeing & Kayaking Guide to the Ozarks

A Canoeing & Kayaking Guide to West Virginia

A Canoeing & Kayaking Guide to the Carolinas

OTHER BOOKS BY JOHNNY MOLLOY

A Canoeing & Kayaking Guide to the Streams of Kentucky (with Bob Sehlinger)

A Paddler's Guide to Everglades National Park

Beach & Coastal Camping in Florida

The Best in Tent Camping: The Carolinas

The Best in Tent Camping: Colorado

The Best in Tent Camping: Florida

The Best in Tent Camping: Georgia

The Best in Tent Camping: Southern Appalachian & Smoky Mountains

The Best in Tent Camping: Tennessee

The Best in Tent Camping: West Virginia

The Best in Tent Camping: Wisconsin

Day & Overnight Hikes in Shenandoah National Park

Day & Overnight Hikes: Kentucky's Sheltowee Trace

Day & Overnight Hikes: Great Smoky Mountains National Park

From the Swamp to the Keys: A Paddle through Florida History

50 Hikes in North Georgia

Land Between the Lakes Outdoor Recreation Handbook

Long Trails of the Southeast

Mount Rogers Outdoor Recreation Handbook

The Hiking Trails of Florida's National Forests, Parks, and Preserves

60 Hikes Within 60 Miles: San Antonio & Austin (coauthored with Tom Taylor)

60 Hikes Within 60 Miles: Nashville

Trial By Trail: Backpacking in the Smoky Mountains

Visit Johnny Molloy's Web site
www.johnnymolloy.com

A Canoeing and Kayaking Guide to Florida

Johnny Molloy, Elizabeth F. Carter, John Pearce,
Lou Glaros, *and* Doug Sphar

Menasha Ridge Press
Birmingham, Alabama

Published by Menasha Ridge Press
Distributed by The Globe Pequot Press
Printed in the United States of America
First edition, second printing, 2006

Library of Congress cataloging-in-publication data

Molloy, Johnny, 1961–
A canoeing and kayaking guide to Florida/by Johnny Molloy and Lou Glaros…{ ext al.},
p.cm.
ISBN: 0-89732-588-5
ISBN 13: 978-0-89732-588- 2
1. Canoes and canoeing—Florida—Guidebooks. 2. Kayaking—Florida—Guidebooks. 3. Florida—Guidebooks. I. Title.

GV776.F6M65 2005
797.122'09759—dc22

2005047991
CIP

Cover photo © Johnny Molloy
Interior photos © Johnny Molloy
Cover design by Bud Zehmer
Text design by Ann Marie Healy

Menasha Ridge Press
P.O. Box 43673
Birmingham, Alabama 35243
www.menashridge.com

DISCLAIMER

While every effort has been made to insure the accuracy of this guidebook, river and road conditions can change greatly from year to year. This book is intended as a general guide. Whitewater paddling is an assumed-risk sport. The decision to run a river can only be made after an on-the-spot inspection, and a run should not be attempted without proper equipment and safety precautions. The author and publisher of *A Canoeing and Kayaking Guide to Florida* are not responsible for any personal or property damage that may result from your activities. By using any part of this guide, you recognize and assume all risks and acknowledge that you are responsible for your own actions.

Table *of* Contents

part **two**

part **three**

part **four**

part **five**

part **six**

part **seven**

part **eight**

part nine

part ten

Maps

Dedication

This book is for all the paddlers of Florida—from those on the waters of the Everglades, to the kayakers on the crystalline spring runs of the Ocala National Forest, to the casual floaters on the Chipola, to the float fishermen on the Withlacoochee, to the canoe campers on the Peace, to those floating the entire length of the Suwannee River, to those on tidal waters of the Tomoka on a Sunday afternoon—may you keep floating the waters of the Sunshine State.

Acknowledgments

Thanks to all the people with whom I floated a Florida river while researching this book: John Cox and Karen Stokes for paddling the St. Marys, Chris Phillips on the Suwannee, Aaron Marabel on the Santa Fe, Brian Babb on the Tomoka, Kevin Thomas on the Shoal and the Yellow, Wes Shepherd on the Ochlockonee and Sopchoppy. A special thanks to Holly Berman for getting on too many rivers to mention, day after day after day, and camping out night after night after night. Thanks to Old Town for providing me a quality canoe and kayak, to Eureka! for their quality tents, and to Silva for a reliable compass. Thanks to Lisa Daniel and Steve "Devo" Grayson for hitting the Everglades on numerous occasions, and Tom "Take-a-Break" Lauria, too. And thanks to the fabulous firemen and all around he-men Hans Hollmann and Jeff Cochran of Miramar for accompanying me down the Peace River. Thanks to John and Barb Haapala for being great friends and the best campground hosts ever. Thanks to Miss Helen on Fisheating Creek, to the Clearwater Seven and all their offspring for floating the Weeki Wachee with me, and to Bill "Worldwide" Armstrong for floating Turner River. Thanks to Roger and Pete for floating down to and then giving me a ride on the Wacissa, to Jim Bob Cooter for floating the Estero, and to Vivian "Snook" Oliva for loving paddling places all over the country, and to Meredith for providing a refuge and a friendly face. Finally, thanks to all the outfitters who ran shuttles and answered a lot of irritating questions.

—Johnny Molloy

Introduction

Florida has a lot of sand, but it also has a lot of water—and not just for drinking. It's only natural that native Floridians and transplants alike paddle and ply the waterways of this waterway-rich state. Of course, Florida's native Indians and subsequent settlers used the creeks, streams, and rivers long before the first plastic kayak or fiberglass canoe took to this watery paradise. In the early 1970s, the state of Florida established a canoe trail system, which was born out of paddlers discovering the many destinations here. For various reasons, this state-sanctioned canoe trail system lost momentum. Building on the state's efforts and adding their own discoveries, paddling enthusiasts Elizabeth F. Carter and John L. Pearce brought together the rich and varied streams, creeks, and rivers of Florida. Together, they penned the original version of portions of this book, *A Canoeing & Kayaking Guide to the Streams of Florida, Volume I.* Their book covered the north central part of the state as well as the panhandle. I used this excellent book for years on almost every river it detailed, never dreaming I would get the opportunity to update and add to it. This was followed by *A Canoeing & Kayaking Guide to the Streams of Florida, Volume II,* written by Lou Glaros and Doug Sphar. Their book covered the southern half of the state, waterways not included in Volume I. Paddling grew steadily in Florida due in part to these excellent guidebooks, establishment of paddling clubs, positioning of outfitters on rivers, and population growth. More people explored new waterways, not only in new kayaks made of varied plastic but also ultra-lightweight canoes easy to paddle and transport. More recently, a rise in the use of recreational kayaks has led to a rebirth of paddling's popularity.

Paddling grew in importance with me as I began making regular excursions to the Everglades, ultimately seeing the need for and then writing the definitive book for those in self-propelled boats there, titled *A Paddler's Guide to Everglades National Park.* Later, I wrote several other hiking and camping guides to Florida, including an adventure narrative that detailed my paddling journey from the uppermost Suwannee River to the Gulf of Mexico, where I jumped into a sea kayak and paddled the Gulf all the way to the Keys. That book, *From the Swamp to the Keys: A Paddle through Florida History,* cemented in my mind the fact that Florida truly is a unique and nearly limitless paddling destination that deserves national attention.

In 2004, I grabbed the opportunity to revise and update volumes I and II of *A Canoeing & Kayaking Guide to the Streams of*

Florida into the single volume that you are reading. I refloated previously covered rivers, checking access points, and floated new waterways to highlight newer opportunities for Florida paddlers. And in the course of paddling, I eliminated some old paddle destinations, such as the Braden River, simply because the accesses had been eliminated and/or they were simply overwhelmed by urbanization. I subsequently added more wilderness-oriented rivers to the book, such as the Econfina River of Taylor County and the New River, which flows through Tates Hell State Forest. Other new destinations involved developed paddling trails such as Graham Creek and the East River, part of the Apalachicola Wildlife and Environmental Area, a preserved estuarine swath of the lower Apalachicola River in the Panhandle.

Along the way I got lost in the Jeep, lost in the boat, rained on, sunburned, scraped ice off the canoe in the morning, jumped in the water after a blazing afternoon in the kayak, got bit by no-see-ums near the coast and away from the coast, got bit by troublesome mosquitoes nearly everywhere, cut my foot on oyster bars, got stopped by headwinds in the Everglades, fell onto a cypress stump, crashed into logs, got stuck in shallows, knocked a fishing pole into the water, and couldn't find a campsite when I

The author fishes for dinner on the Santa Fe River

needed one. But I also saw azaleas bloom on the Sopchoppy, shot the shoals on Sweetwater Creek, turned a lazy bend on the New River and saw a bear, saw more springs than you can imagine on the Suwannee and other rivers, met new faces around every bend, making new friends along the way, saw smiles on the faces of those peering into the clear waters of the Weeki Wachee River, enjoyed a great campfire and a better dinner alongside the Peace, and came to understand why the Loxahatchee is a federally designated Wild and Scenic River. All in all it was a great experience, and I am humbled to be a part of this book that will, in its updated and improved state, continue to serve the worthy paddlers of Florida.

This guidebook is the product of paddling and scouting miles of river, more miles of driving, shuttling, loading and unloading boats *ad infinitum* and many hours of map work, researching, and writing. Along the way, many memories were made. I hope you will make some memories of your own, paddling the streams of Florida.

Using This Guide

First, an overview description of the river is given.

Second, a list of topo maps that can be used for that particular section of river. Topographic maps are listed in the order in which the river flows. Unless otherwise noted as above, all maps are located on the Florida Index of the United States Geological Survey. If there is not a local source for maps they can be ordered on the Web at **www.topozone.com.**

Third, the river section to be described is labeled and identified by the section put-in followed by the section takeout.

Fourth, in an at-a-glance list to the side of the put-in/takeout section, basic river data is given including class, length, time, gauge, level, gradient, and scenery.

Class, or river difficulty, is adapted from a system developed by American Whitewater and is rated Class I through VI. For detailed information on the rating system, refer to Appendix C. **Length** provides the river miles traversed between the put-in and takeout. **Time** provides conservative paddling times for the runs without allowing for lunch, fishing, playing, napping, or otherwise dawdling. Wind, currents, and tides can alter these times. **Gauge** indicates whether the gauge of the river is visual, by phone, or Web. In this case, the Web is used. If visual, you literally have to look at the river to determine whether it is runnable or not. Phone indicates you can call a number to find out if it is runnable, and Web means you can look on the Internet to find out whether it can be floated. **Level** indicates the flow rates at

which a particular river can be run. Most Florida rivers can be run year-round. Where we do not have a specific figure we list the level as "NA," meaning not available. Government agencies like the United States Geological Survey (USGS) measure river flows at gauging stations throughout the country. This information is collected and recorded hourly. You will find Web sites and phone numbers listed in the discussion of river gauges below. You will also encounter "paddler's gauges" painted on bridge piers and rocks. Although not reported on Web sites, they remain in use. **Gradient** is the average drop of the river in feet per mile. For example, 2 means that the river drops at an average rate of two feet per mile. *Remember:* The difficulty of a river's rapids is not determined only by gradient. Some rivers drop evenly over continuous rapids of roughly the same difficulty. Others alternate between long pools and drops that are steeper than the gradient would indicate. Many Florida rivers have swift currents that sweep through fallen trees around unseen bends, adding to difficulty. **Scenery** is ranked on an A to D scale: A—remote wilderness areas with little sign of civilization, B—more settled, but still beautiful pastoral countryside, C—lots of development (cities or industry), D—pollution, phosphate mines, rundown buildings, and other forms of landscape abuse. The quality of the scenery along a river often changes. For example, the Hillsborough River within Hillsborough River State Park is considered A, but becomes C on its lower reaches where houses are common.

Fifth, the specific section of the river is described.

Sixth, **Shuttle** lists the exact takeout and put-in with directions to a particular highway or secondary road bridge. Detailed directions have been given to find the put-in and the takeout. Where there are several sections of a particular stream included, only the put-in on the first section and the takeout on the last section are described.

Seventh, and last, **Gauge** tells readers exactly which gauge(s) are needed to determine river runnability.

Finally, maps detail each river included in this guidebook. The maps include put-ins, takeouts, and features of interest such as bridges, landing areas, rapids, and confluences with other rivers, creeks, and streams. These maps will aid paddlers in finding their way but are no substitute for detailed USGS topographic maps, county maps, or map books such as the DeLorme *Gazzeteer.*

USING RIVER GAUGES

The Water Resources Division of the United States Geological Survey measures water flows on most rivers in the United States

at frequent intervals. The U.S. Army Corps of Engineers and various power companies collect similar information. These flows are recorded in cubic feet per second (cfs) and are available to paddlers.

The key variable is the height of the river at a fixed point. Gauge houses, situated on most rivers, consist of a well at the river's edge with a float attached to a recording clock. The gauge reads in hundredths of feet. Rating tables are constructed for each gauge to get a cfs reading for each level.

This information can be useful for paddlers who are planning a trip. However, in Florida, most rivers can be paddled year-round, since they are spring-fed or tidal, or simply have slow rates of fluctuations, a product of being fed by low-lying, swampy drainages, rather than faster-draining hills and highlands of other states. But droughts and excessive rainfall occur in Florida, and gauges can be useful. This gauge information can be obtained quickly at various Web sites, along with recent rainfall information! Make use of this information. Gauges are listed for Florida rivers where they exist. In most instances, minimum and maximum runnable flow rates have not been established for a particular river. However, if you float your favorite river time and again, you can record the flow rates and river levels each time you paddle the river and establish your own flow rates and levels at which you like to paddle the given waterway.

WATER LEVEL SITES

USGS—Real-time water levels for Florida; **http://waterdata.usgs.gov/fl/nwis/rt.**

The USGS has compiled an in-depth Web site. Hundreds of gauges for the entire country are updated continually, and graphs showing recent flow trends are now available at the touch of a mouse. This is the greatest thing for paddlers since dry bags were invented.

FRIENDLY ADVICE

Hurricane Damage

The hurricanes of 2004 wrought great damage and dumped incredible amounts of water on Florida. The local infrastructure experienced incredible damage that we all remember seeing on television. However, Florida has endured hurricanes as long as the peninsula has separated the cold Atlantic from the warmer waters of the Gulf of Mexico. For Florida paddlers, the resilience of Mother Nature means that the Sunshine State's waterways generally endure, although many waterways were stripped of their riverside vegetation, trees fell into and blocked riverways,

and banks remained underwater for extended periods, especially the Suwannee and Peace Rivers. Most damage of concern to paddlers occurred to landings and river outfitter facilities. Ultimately, hurricanes and storms are the stuff of which Florida's natural landscape is made, and, in a short period of time, the rivers have returned to their "normal" state.

Weather

Florida is known as the Sunshine State, and it has plenty of that, but paddlers will need to consider other facets of Florida weather, especially seasonal variations. General weather patterns may be discussed for three geographic regions: the Panhandle, Central Florida, and South Florida. The Florida Panhandle has four distinct seasons, though the climate is very long on summer, where highs regularly reach the 90s and thunderstorms pass through on most any afternoon. Nights can be uncomfortably hot. Fall finds cooler nights and warm days with less precipitation than summer. Winter is variable. Highs push 60 °F. Expect lows in the 40s, though subfreezing temperatures are the norm during cold snaps. There are usually several mild days during each winter month. Precipitation comes in strong continental fronts, with more persistent rains followed by sunny, cold days. Snow is very uncommon, though not unheard of. The longer days of spring begin to warm into the 70s, often straying into the 80s, and can vary wildly.

Central Florida is drier and warmer than the Panhandle. It is far enough south to attract snowbirds escaping the cold of the north. Winter is generally pleasant and dry. Daytime highs push 70, yet it is far enough north that a cold snap can bring afternoon highs down to the 50s and occasional temperatures below freezing.

Spring is an excellent time to enjoy waterways of the central state. The days are warm and clear, often topping 80 °F, yet nights remain cool enough to enjoy a campfire. Mornings are still crisp and insects are not bothersome. Then the days really warm up and frequent thunderstorms result, beginning in June. Daytime highs can exceed 90 °F during the long, humid summer, although temperatures will be a little lower at the nearby coastline. Fall is very nice, too. The thunderstorms subside and cool fronts clear the skies.

South Florida has a near tropical climate with two distinct seasons, wet and dry. Snowbirds flock to this area during winter. Winter temperature readings at Fort Myers and other cities can register as the nation's warmest, though cold fronts will punch down this far south, cooling things down. Rain occasionally accompanies the fronts, though infrequent storms will drift in

from the Gulf. But, overall, winter is also the dry season. The rainy season starts in May and lasts through September. Brief but heavy downpours inundate the area, adding to the extreme humidity. The Gulf region does not get as strong or frequent breezes as the Atlantic, resulting in some sweltering summer days.

Insects

During the warm months, mosquitoes, sand gnats, and yellow flies can be a source of discomfort. Mosquitoes are usually confined to shady, wooded areas and are at their worst just at dusk and in the early morning. Commercial insect repellents containing 30 percent Deet are effective in discouraging them. Yellow flies are usually present on hot, still days. They are rarely a problem after dark. They, too, are repelled by most commercial Deet products, but it may take a stronger formula and every piece of exposed skin must be treated. Sand gnats, or no-see-ums, are a great reason why quality tents have fine netting on the doors and windows. The bothersome gnats are most common in marshy areas near the coast, but are occasionally encountered inland. Insect repellent does not deter them as easily, but application of something oily to the skin sometimes will. Some cosmetic bath oils or baby oil mixed with repellent is useful for this purpose.

Reptiles

Six species of poisonous snakes are found in Florida. They are the Southern copperhead, cottonmouth, coral snake, and three varieties of rattlesnakes—timber rattler, pygmy rattler, and Eastern diamondback rattler. The cottonmouth frequently lounges on deadfall trees, and its coloration makes it difficult to spot. Paddlers should exercise caution when negotiating downed trees or making portages. The coral snake and diamondback are most apt to be found near campsites, especially around logs and thick brush. Use common sense when walking in the woods, never climb on or step over logs without checking for snakes, and avoid walking through stands of palmetto palms or dense underbrush.

Alligators maintain a serious presence in Florida waterways. They have made an excellent comeback here in the Sunshine State. If you are reasonably quiet, your chances of seeing alligators on most Florida streams are excellent. Usually as soon as they see you, they will slip into the water and swim away. If they do not, avoid approaching or annoying them in any way. In some more populated areas where the alligators have become accustomed to people, they are no longer shy and may be more daring than you would like. Needless to say, do not swim in areas where alligators live and do not feed or harass them.

Camping

Minimize your impact as much as possible when camping on Florida's rivers. Sandbars are the campsites of choice when they are available.

They have fewer insects, no poison ivy, and they generally help avoid the possibility of camping on private property. If no sandbar is available, look for a clearing in the woods on high ground. Camping in the swamp is definitely not acceptable. Bugs and/or rising water could make you miserable. If possible, avoid camping at boat ramps or other access points. A quiet dirt road leading to the river may turn into the local party spot after dark. Either carry along all drinking water or purify stream water to make it safe to drink. Filters, such as those manufactured by Katadyn, that use a ceramic element along with a charcoal pre-filter result in the safest and most palatable water. Mosquitoes can be fierce at night, so a bug-proof shelter is necessary for a good night's rest. Obtain camping permits where necessary, such as Everglades National Park.

Knowing Your Rights on the River

Florida's navigable rivers, lakes, and tidelands are held in a public trust, which imposes a legal duty on the state to preserve and control them for public navigation, fishing, swimming, and other lawful uses. The Public Trust Doctrine protects the public status of "navigable" water bodies in Florida. A waterway is navigable if at the time of statehood in 1845, it was used or was capable of being used (by canoes as well as other boats), as a highway for waterborne trade or travel conducted by the customary modes of that period. Navigability does not require year-round capacity for navigation, but does require capacity for navigation in the water body's ordinary state. Artificial water bodies or waterways rendered navigable through improvement by dredging are not legally navigable.

In Florida, the boundary of navigable freshwater lakes and rivers is the ordinary high water line. The public has the right to make all lawful uses of sovereignty lands up to this boundary line, including use of the shore or space between ordinary high and ordinary low water marks. By the same token, landowners' rights to prohibit trespassing on their land along creeks, if they so desire, are also guaranteed. Therefore, access to rivers must be secured at highway rights-of-way or on publicly owned lands if permission to cross privately owned lands cannot be secured. In granting you access to a river, landowners are extending a privilege to you. In Florida, many streams pass through populated areas, with houses and docks and such. Don't betray landowners' trust if they extend to you the privilege to launch canoes or kayaks or even camp from

Sandbar campsite on the St. Marys River

their riverbanks. Don't litter, drive through newly planted fields or climb on a dock or into someone's backyard. Tenure of land, landholding, and the right to do with it what you want, is serious business to landowners. Some landowners don't feel any compulsion or responsibility toward the paddling community or their legal rights. In some cases they might even resent people driving hundreds of miles for the pleasure of floating down a river. They may even feel that they "own" the river you want to paddle. Whether it's right or wrong, just be aware.

On the other hand, it may be that the landowner from whom you seek permission is intrigued with paddling and correspondingly quite friendly and approachable. Value this friendship and don't give cause for this landowner to deny you or others access to the river at some time in the future.

In general, paddlers may be trespassing when they portage, camp, or even stop for a lunch break, if they disembark from their boats on the water. If you are approached by a landowner when trespassing, by all means be cordial and understanding and explain your predicament (in the case of a portage or lunch break). Never knowingly camp on private land without permission. If you do encounter a perturbed landowner, don't panic. Keep cool and be respectful.

Landowners certainly have the right to keep you off their land, and the law will side with them unless they inflict harm on you, in which case they may be both civilly or criminally liable. If you threaten a landowner verbally, and physically move toward

him or her with apparent will to do harm, he or she has all the rights of self-defense and can protect him- or herself in accordance with the perceived danger that you impose. Likewise, if the landowner points a gun at you, fires warning shots, or assaults, injures, or wounds you or a boater in your group, you are certainly in the right to protect yourself. The landowner has no right to detain you as if holding you for the sheriff. If you fear for your own life at the hands of the landowner, you do have the right to protect yourself.

The confrontations between belligerent paddlers and cantankerous landowners are to be avoided, that's for sure. Although the happenstance of such a meeting may be rare, paddlers nonetheless should know their rights, and the rights of landowners. Judges don't like trespassers any more than they like landowners who shoot at trespassers.

Roads

Access roads used to reach the waterways in this guidebook range from congested interstates cutting through big cities to potholed sandy swaths snaking through sloppy swamps. Others, such as national forest roads, will be somewhere in between. Generally speaking the more urbanized a stream is, the higher likelihood you will be traveling paved roads on your shuttles. Consider weather in your shuttle process. Poor access roads may have deep sand pits in dry weather and wet bog holes during the rainy times.

Looking for wildlife along the Ocklawaha River

Leaving Cars Unattended

In writing this book I parked all over the state of Florida, often for days at a time. Use your intuition when leaving your vehicle somewhere. It is always best to arrange with someone to look after your car, and a small fee is worth the peace of mind. I once had my computer stolen from my car in a national forest north of Florida. National, state, and county parks with on-site rangers are a good choice for leaving your vehicle overnight. Also, check with fish camps and liveries, as many of these provide shuttle service and a safe place to park. Private businesses sometimes allow overnighters to park in their lots. Be sure to ask permission and offer to pay. When parking for day trips, it is better to leave the vehicle near the road rather than back in the woods out of sight.

Paddling Skills

Don't assume that the paddling skills you have developed will qualify you for everything Florida waterways have to offer. Many streams here are twisting, fast, and loaded with obstructions. They may also be miles from a road through sand hills or swamp. Five miles on a straight, spring-fed river is very different from 5 miles on a narrow, cascading stream with 15 pull-overs, or in a sweeping current pouring through a fallen tree. Read the trip descriptions carefully before you set out. Other waterways in this guidebook are tidal. Be aware of the tides before you set out! Otherwise, you may be paddling against a very strong current, or worse yet, get stuck trying to paddle where there is no water.

Exertion brings vital physiological reactions when there are worthwhile goals to achieve. Without weariness there can be no real appreciation of rest, without hunger no enjoyment of food, without the ancient responses to the harsh simplicities of the environment that shaped mankind, a man cannot know the urges within him. Having known this during a period of life when I could satisfy the needs, I think I understand what wilderness can mean to the young men of today.

—Sigurd F. Olson

Florida Rivers and Creeks

GEOLOGY

The state of Florida is a landmass that occupies a minor portion of the Florida Plateau. This plateau is attached to the continental United States and is a partially submerged platform about 500 miles long and varies from 250 to 400 miles wide. It has existed for millions of years and is one of the most stable places on the crust of the earth. Over the millennia, Florida has submerged and resurfaced from a series of ancient seas. The Coastal Lowlands are the most recent landmasses to have emerged from the sea. They are those areas that surround the hills of the highlands in the northern and western sections of the state, and they make up the flatlands that are known as south Florida.

The Highlands of the north and west are geologically much older than the Coastal Lowlands, and they reach their highest point at about 345 feet above sea level in the greater Yellow River watershed. Since the Florida peninsula is narrow, especially in the northwestern panhandle, it is often less than 50 miles from a high point of 300 feet above sea level to the Gulf of Mexico. The resulting gradient, combined with the terraces and ledges that have been left on the landscape with the recession of the seas, has produced the unique geological phenomena that have made north Florida rivers a paradise for canoeists.

North Florida includes the Western Highlands, the Marianna Lowlands, the Tallahassee Hills, and the Central Highlands. In geographic terms, this includes an area beginning at the Perdido River west of Pensacola and continuing south to an imaginary line drawn from New Port Richey on the west to Orlando on the east.

For the purposes of this book, the lower half of the Florida peninsula has been partitioned into four regions: the Atlantic Coast, the Southwest Gulf Coast, the Central Highlands, and the Everglades. Among these areas, less than a day's drive separates the beauty and solitude of the Everglades from the stretches of whitewater on the Hillsborough River. Dark and mysterious cypress forests, high pine-covered bluffs, and the open expanse of a coastal marsh can all be experienced in a single day of paddling. The unique natural history of the lower half of the Florida peninsula makes this enjoyable paddling possible. The rivers and streams within each of these regions share generally similar geology and natural communities.

The streams of the Atlantic Coast drain a long, narrow region that was ocean floor before glaciers covered North America. An ancient dune line forms a ridge that isolates the coastal drainage area from the St. Johns River drainage. The low elevation of this

Cypress swamp on Fisheating Creek

region—less than 50 feet above sea level—means generally sluggish stream flow. As these streams approach the ocean, they develop broad, funnel-shaped mouths known as estuaries. In estuaries fresh water mixes with salt water and ocean tides assume control of the water dynamics. The estuaries of Florida's central Atlantic Coast feature grassy marshes, whereas mangrove swamps are characteristic of the southern Atlantic Coast. The upstream plant communities are often hardwood swamp forests with cypress, oaks, and maples, or cabbage palm hammocks with palms, oaks, and wax myrtles. Alligators and otters are frequently seen upstream, but the manatee enjoys the estuary. The estuaries also provide great birding. The heron, egret, anhinga, and osprey are at home here. Ducks fly in when the weather turns cold up north.

The Southwest Gulf Coast has a number of major stream systems that pierce the interior of the peninsula. Tampa Bay alone is the terminus of four major streams: the Hillsborough, Alafia, Manatee, and Little Manatee. The nearby Peace River constitutes one of the largest drainage basins of Florida. A notable feature of the streams of the Southwest Gulf Coast is an underlying layer of limestone. On streams such as the Hillsborough and Alafia, this limestone spices up a day of paddling with stretches of Class II whitewater. Streams of the region typically have origins in interior highlands and upland plains. These areas are generally characterized by pine flatwoods and palmetto prairies; however, hardwood swamp forests with oak and cypress often are found in the immediate stream valley. A diverse selection of wildlife

unfolds along the way. The distinctive call of the pileated woodpecker is frequently heard, as is the knocking noise it makes pecking for insects. The shadowy form of the owl is seen fluttering through the forest canopy. Limpkins and ibis feed in the marshes and swamps that the streams pass through.

A region of highlands and upland plains lies north of Lake Okeechobee and inland between the two coasts. The streams in this region drain lands that in some places exceed 150 feet above sea level—stratospheric by Florida standards. This beautiful countryside presents a completely different image of Florida from the palm-studded beach scenes of tourist brochures. Central Highlands forests are comprised mostly of southern pines, but there are areas where oak and hickory predominate. Fleeting glimpses of deer darting through brush are not uncommon, and wild turkey can sometimes be seen. Curious raccoons and playful otters, as well as alligators, make a living along these streams. Groups of turtles basking on downed tree trunks slide into the water as a canoe glides by.

There is only one Everglades. A unique combination of ancient events created this wonderful ecosystem—an environment that exists nowhere else on this planet. In fact, the Everglades is an International Biosphere Reserve and a World Heritage Site. The Everglades is a sheet of water that flows imperceptibly south from Lake Okeechobee into Florida Bay. The underlying base of this drainage is a plain of oolitic limestone, which was formed from the sediment of an early sea. The gradient of this plain is so gentle that water only drops 15 feet over the 100-mile journey to Florida Bay. The limestone is covered with peat soils that support the vast freshwater saw grass marshes for which the Everglades is famous. Along the coastal extreme of the Everglades, grass prairies give way to mangrove forests. The western extreme of the Everglades has vast stands of cypress forest known as "strands." The Everglades is justly famous for bird life, and early in this century the Everglades supported a plumage industry that decimated many wading bird species. Fortunately, enlightened regulations and changing fashions brought this practice to an end. The Everglades is home for rare and endangered animals. The crocodile and Florida panther are making a last stand here. This unique habitat also supports the Everglades kite, reddish egret, roseate spoonbill, Florida mangrove cuckoo, and Everglades mink.

WATERSHEDS OF FLORIDA

Florida's watersheds are generally small compared to many other states. Think about the shape of Florida. It is 465 miles at its

widest, and 447 miles at its longest. Florida encompasses 54,090 square miles, making it the 22nd largest state by area. Its highest point, 345 feet, in Walton County, is the lowest point anywhere that borders the Atlantic Ocean. The maximum width of Florida is deceptive, however, as it actually runs in an east–west line across the Panhandle to the Atlantic. And its maximum north–south length can be deceptive, too, for anywhere one stands in Florida, they are never too far from the ocean. This fact is important in analyzing Florida's watersheds. In most parts of the state, there simply isn't enough land to drain before any given waterway hits the salty sea. The largest river by volume in Florida is the Apalachicola. But this river primarily drains Georgia and Alabama, not the Sunshine State. In length, the St. Johns is the longest riverway that flows entirely in Florida. The Suwannee, which originates in Georgia, is the longest river included in this guidebook, and actually has a larger drainage acreage than the St. Johns.

Most streams of the Panhandle form their own drainages extending from their sources in Alabama and Georgia to the Gulf, or meet in bays just before the Gulf, such as the Yellow/Shoal/Blackwater river complex. Moving east, the Choctawhatchee captures the panhandle west of the Apalachicola. The rivers of the Big Bend, such as Ochlockonee and Econfina, form their own watersheds. Northeastern Florida has an interesting phenomenon: two rivers draining one great swamp with one river heading to the Gulf and the other to the Atlantic. Here, the St. Marys leaves the Okefenokee Swamp and heads to the Atlantic Ocean, additionally forming the boundary between Florida and Georgia, while the Suwannee heads southwest to the Gulf, absorbing other rivers in this guidebook, such as the Santa Fe and Withlacoochee. Heading into the peninsula of the state, we begin to see rivers with drainages located entirely in Florida, all heading to the coast. An especially interesting drainage layout starts in the Green Swamp of central Florida. Here, the Ocklawaha, Withlacoochee (south), Hillsborough, and Peace Rivers head their respective ways, with all but the Ocklawaha aiming for the Gulf. The Ocklawaha flows into the St. Johns, which flows into the Atlantic Ocean.

Farther south, the Everglades extends its huge influence despite development of the entire eastern Everglades that is now part of the south Florida metroplex. Most rivers here flow into the Gulf or join the slow sheet flow of the Glades, on its inevitable southern and westerly flow. Rivers of the lower Atlantic Coast, such as the Loxahatchee, break east through the Atlantic Ridge of the East Coast and meet the Atlantic Ocean.

OUTSTANDING FLORIDA WATERS

An Outstanding Florida Water (OFW) is a body of water designated as worthy of special protection because of its natural attributes. This designation is applied to select waters and is intended to protect existing good water quality. Most OFWs are areas managed by the state or federal government as parks, including wildlife refuges, preserves, marine sanctuaries, estuarine research reserves, certain waters within state or national forests, Wild and Scenic Rivers, or aquatic preserves. Generally, the waters within these managed areas are OFWs because the managing agency has requested this special protection.

OFWs in this guidebook include all or parts of the Aucilla River, Blackwater River, Chipola River, Choctawhatchee River, Econlockhatchee River, Estero River, Hillsborough River, Myakka River, Ochlockonee River, Ocklawaha River, Perdido River, Rainbow River, St. Marks River, Santa Fe River, Shoal River, Silver River, Spruce Creek, Suwannee River, Tomoka River, Wacissa River, Wakulla River, and Wekiva River.

SPRING-FED RIVERS

Many of Florida's waterways are spring-fed or their flow is aided and enhanced by springs. Paddle trips included in this book that begin at a spring source include Salt Springs Run, Juniper Creek, Ichetucknee River, Weeki Wachee River, and Rock Springs Run, to name a few. In other places, springs will flow into or on the edge of the river, as occurs in many places on the Suwannee River. Florida's springs are among the most beautiful and unique phenomena that the paddler is privileged to see. There are over 300 springs in Florida, more than any other state in the United States and more than any other country in the world. They are the natural outflow of water from the underground water system and vary from tiny rivulets trickling from the ground to deep caverns far below the surface of crystal clear pools.

Most of Florida's springs are located along major rivers and are concentrated in the western part of north Florida. Some of the springs have been incorporated into state parks, national forest recreation areas, or privately owned tourist attractions. Over time, the state has acquired springs for protective and recreation uses, such as Weeki Wachee Springs and Rainbow Springs. Many more of them remain hidden away in areas not yet touched by development. These secluded gems of blue and green and silver are the special reward for those who paddle a boat.

For the paddler, spring-fed waterways are a reliable boating bet. Spring-fed streams offer a constant or slightly variable flow

that can be counted on during dry and wet weather. In these situations, there is little need to call ahead or check flow rates on Web sites to see if the riverway can be paddled.

When springs occur on the waterways described in this guide, every effort is made to describe their location, appearance, and the name by which they are most commonly known. Springs do change; high water may obscure them and extreme dry weather may reduce their flow. Some have been purchased privately and are fenced from public access—even from navigable water. In many cases the land around a spring may be private property, but canoeists may enjoy the spring from their boat. It is usually unwise to camp beside a spring unless permission has been obtained from the landowner.

TIDAL RIVERS

With so much coastline, it is only natural that many of Florida's streams and rivers would have a tidal component. This aspect where freshwater ecosystem changes to saltwater adds to the biodiversity of your paddle on such waterways as Pellicer Creek and Turner River. These tidally influenced destinations are governed both by the changing flow of water into and out of their estuarine regions and the absolute flows heading downriver. Take the time to learn the tides before you set out on your trip! A good Internet resource is **www.freetidetables.com.**

Tides can be your enemy or friend. Low tides can leave you stranded in the tidal mudflats, and high tides can make your return paddle to the put-in a strong-arm battle. Tides may cause discomfort or delay, but they can be dangerous in other situations. Be careful around manmade canals; a strong pull will take you where you don't want to go or ram you into a tree lying half submerged in the water. The biggest problem with tides comes when cutting corners in rivers. You will be paddling in one direction and the tide will be flowing perpendicular to your direction, catching the nose of your craft and turning you over before you know what happened. Watch for direction flow in the water ahead of you, such as ripples and eddy lines, and adjust your speed and direction. Tides can be a directional indicator as well. If you know the general times of tidal variation in your given area, you can tell in which direction the ocean lies and vice versa. Use the tides to your advantage while traveling the rivers described in this guidebook.

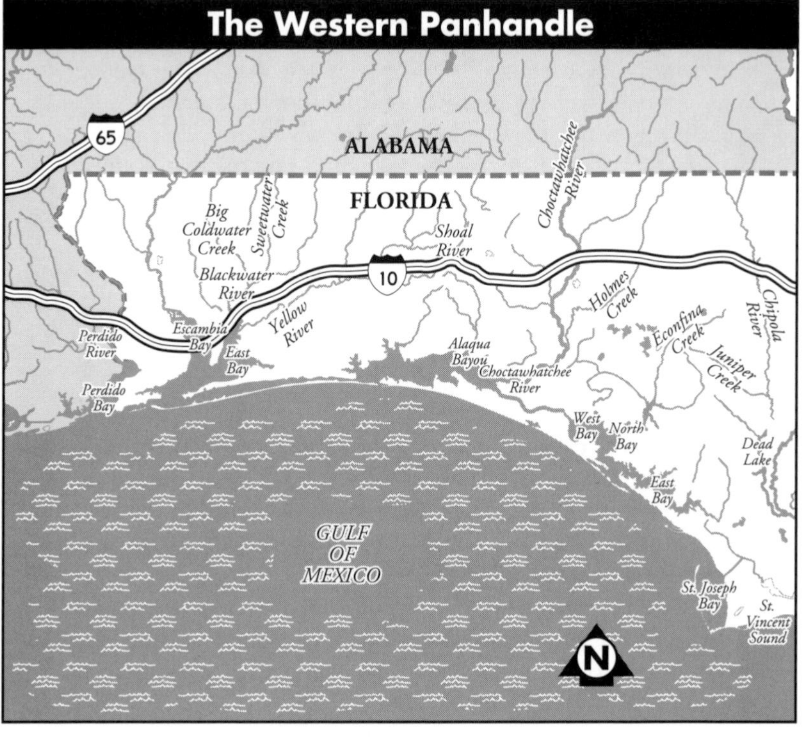
The Western Panhandle
65
ALABAMA
FLORIDA
Big Coldwater Creek
Sweetwater Creek
Choctawhatchee River
Shoal River
Blackwater River
10
Holmes Creek
Chipola River
Perdido River
Escambia Bay
Yellow River
East Bay
Alaqua Bayou
Choctawhatchee River
Econfina Creek
Juniper Creek
Perdido Bay
West Bay
North Bay
Dead Lake
East Bay
GULF OF MEXICO
St. Joseph Bay
St. Vincent Sound
N

part **One**

THE WESTERN PANHANDLE

PERDIDO RIVER

The Perdido River originates in south Alabama with the confluence of Dyas Creek and Perdido Creek. It runs along the state line separating Alabama and Florida to the west and is about 15 miles from Pensacola. The Spanish name, which means "lost," probably resulted from the hidden nature of Perdido Bay, which is formed by the Perdido River before it reaches the Gulf of Mexico.

Except for the upper section near Dyas Creek, a very strenuous trip, the Perdido is considered an easy and relaxing canoeing river. It is located in a remote area and runs through deep forests with banks of juniper and cypress trees as well as other upland hardwoods. The stream alternates between straight sections with modest banks 3 to 5 feet high to long curves with generously sized gravel and sandbars on the insides of almost every bend. Hurricane Ivan blew many trees into the river in 2004, so expect more strainers.

In periods of normal rainfall, the Perdido is a shallow river and the water will vary from being very clear to a tannish yellow color in areas where there is more siltation. There is no industrial development of any kind on its banks and very little agricultural activity. There are a number of excellent swimming holes as well as ample white sandbars for sunning and picnicking.

There are a number of small streams that drain into the Perdido; its major tributary is the River Styx that flows in from Alabama. The Alabama side of the river is primarily the property of private hunting clubs. On the Florida side, La Floresta Perdido Wildlife Management Area, a cooperative public hunting area managed by the Florida Game and Fresh Water Fish Commission, runs for many miles. Guns and dogs should not be taken on the river, and the canoe camper should be careful to observe posted no trespassing signs.

Because of the limited access and protected wildlife areas, the forests along the Perdido are heavily populated with deer and turkeys as well as wild hogs and bears. Local people also report an occasional sighting of a Florida panther along with the usual raccoons, opossums, and beavers. The observant canoeist may also see otters and alligators and the angler may catch bream and catfish.

MAPS: Seminole, Barrineau Park, Gateswood, Enon (USGS)

class	I
length	24
time	Varies
gauge	Phone
level	Call outfitter
gradient	2.8
scenery	A

THREE RUNS TO MUSCOGEE LANDING

DESCRIPTION: Unfortunately, access on this section is limited by rough roads or lack of public landings. Barrineau Park, 15 miles from Three Runs has been closed, but the state is working to get a launch in the area. Until then paddlers can travel 5 miles to Old Ferry Landing, but a four-wheel-drive vehicle is needed to access Old Ferry Landing. Closed Barrineau Park is 10 miles distant from Old Ferry Landing, and Muscogee Landing is 9 miles from old Barrineau Park.

The Three Runs area is the recommended uppermost put-in for the Perdido. Above there, from Dyas Creek to Three Runs, is very remote and inaccessible. It is also almost unnavigable because of the many logjams and resultant pull-overs that occur. These logjams are caused by the somewhat unusual characteristics of the red cedar tree, which is abundant in this area. These trees have a multitude of closely spaced branches that break off with stiletto sharpness. Furthermore, with its shallow but widespread root system, the juniper tree is easily blown over; both tree branches and tree roots become buried in the sandy banks on either side of the river. Since the red cedar is noted for its durability in contact with the soil, once down, they tend to stay there forever. Hurricane Ivan added to the troubles.

Starting at Three Runs, the river is 50 feet wide with heavily forested banks 6 to 8 feet high. The water tends to be shallow, and there may be some obstructions, but it is an easy section and maneuvering is not difficult. There are large gravel bars on the insides of most of the curves. The forests on either side are hunting preserves, and it is a remote area with no public access. Schoolhouse Branch enters from the east about midway between Three Runs and Old Water Ferry Landing.

The river continues to be remote beyond Old Ferry and varies between straight sections with clearly defined banks to gentle curves. Several creeks, including West Fork of Boggy Creek and McDavid Creek, flow in from the east, and the river becomes wider. The hunting preserves continue on both sides, and there are frequent sandbars and gravel banks. Barrineau Park is closed, due to unruly behavior of unthoughtful visitors. Hopefully the state will establish an access in the general area in the future.

The Perdido retains its shallow, winding characteristics with sandbars on the insides of turns and alternating straight sections

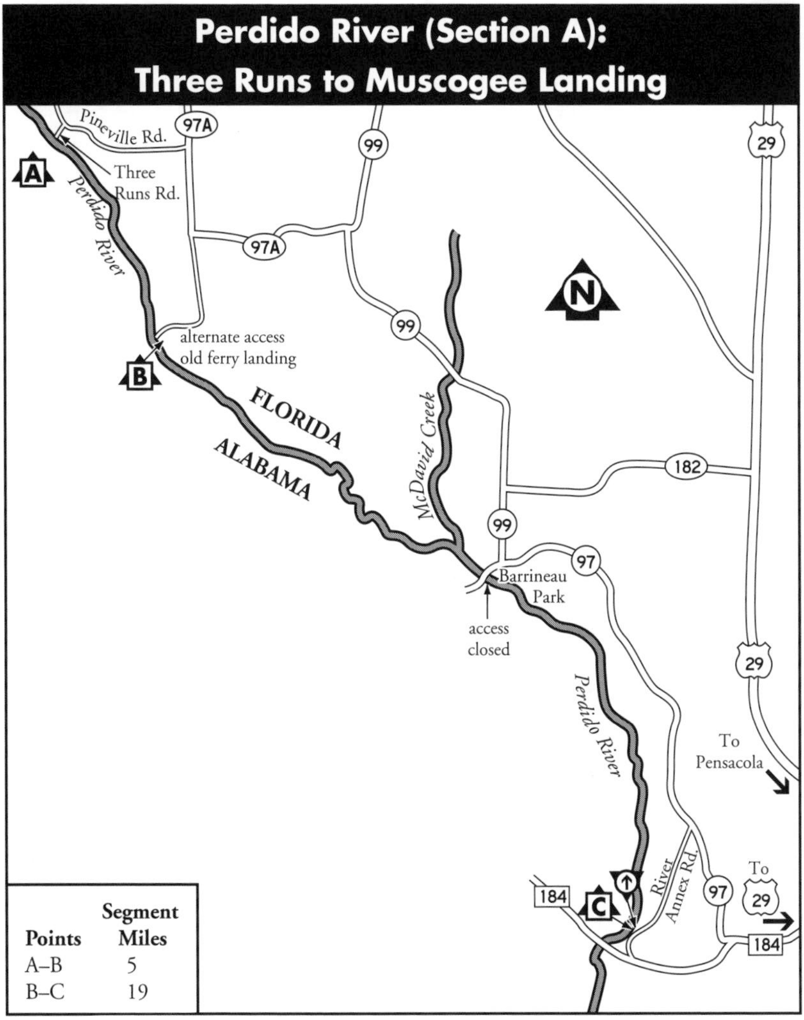

Perdido River (Section A): Three Runs to Muscogee Landing

Points	Segment Miles
A–B	5
B–C	19

with deeper water. There is more frequent private access to the river from the east side, a popular section for canoeing and fishing. There are a number of places where the presence of old pilings in the river indicates the location of former bridges. Just before reaching Muscogee Landing, there is an island in the river and a series of closely spaced pilings. The river narrows at this point and runs swiftly through the pilings, giving a touch of excitement to the run.

SHUTTLE: To reach the uppermost access from Pensacola, travel north on US 29 to the junction with FL 182. Turn left, west, on FL 182 and proceed to FL 99. Turn right, north, on FL 99 and

continue to the junction with FL 97A. Turn left, west, and continue for 3 miles until the paved road makes an abrupt turn to the right, north. Turn right, and travel for 1.5 miles to the first intersection with a graded road, Pineville Road. Turn left, west, on Pineville Road and continue to the river beyond the bridge at 2.3 miles. Look for a left turn onto sandy Three Runs Road to reach the Perdido River. To reach the Muscogee Landing takeout from Ensley, take US 29 north to CR 184. Turn left on CR 184 and follow it west to River Annex Road, just before the bridge over the Perdido River. Turn right on River Annex Road to reach the outfitter with a private launch and pay access.

GAUGE: Phone. Call Ruby's Fish Camp at (850) 944-2537 for the latest river conditions.

class	I
length	10
time	5
gauge	Visual
level	Call outfitter
gradient	1
scenery	A

MUSCOGEE LANDING TO US 90

DESCRIPTION: There is a very large sandbar on the north side of the river at Muscogee Landing, which is a popular swimming and sunbathing area for local people. This is the last of the campsite-sized sandbars, as the river becomes deeper and wider with either clearly defined banks or swampy areas on either side. There are some sites that will provide space for two or three tents, but they are scattered along this 10-mile section.

From Muscogee to I-10 is just over 2 miles. Just below the south lane of the interstate is a drop where water rushes through a group of old stumps and pilings. An exception to the generally wider and deeper nature of the river occurs about 0.5 miles below the interstate highway. Logjams sometimes occur here, as the river narrows and flows swiftly through the more confined area. An island divides the river just below this point, and it is possible to paddle on either side. Below the island, the river becomes much wider, the obstructions disappear, and the current slows considerably. Motorboat traffic increases with the advent of the deeper water and lack of obstructions. Hardwood forests line the banks with some swampy areas and small sloughs making an appearance.

Below US 90, the Perdido becomes tidal and begins to finger off into sloughs and bayous. This area is frequented by large motorboats as well. The east bank along the lower Perdido from US 90 to Hurst Landing, an 8-mile trip, is now owned by the Florida Conservation Association and offers attractive scenery. Hurst Landing is the last public access before reaching Perdido

Perdido River (Section B): Muscogee Landing to US 90

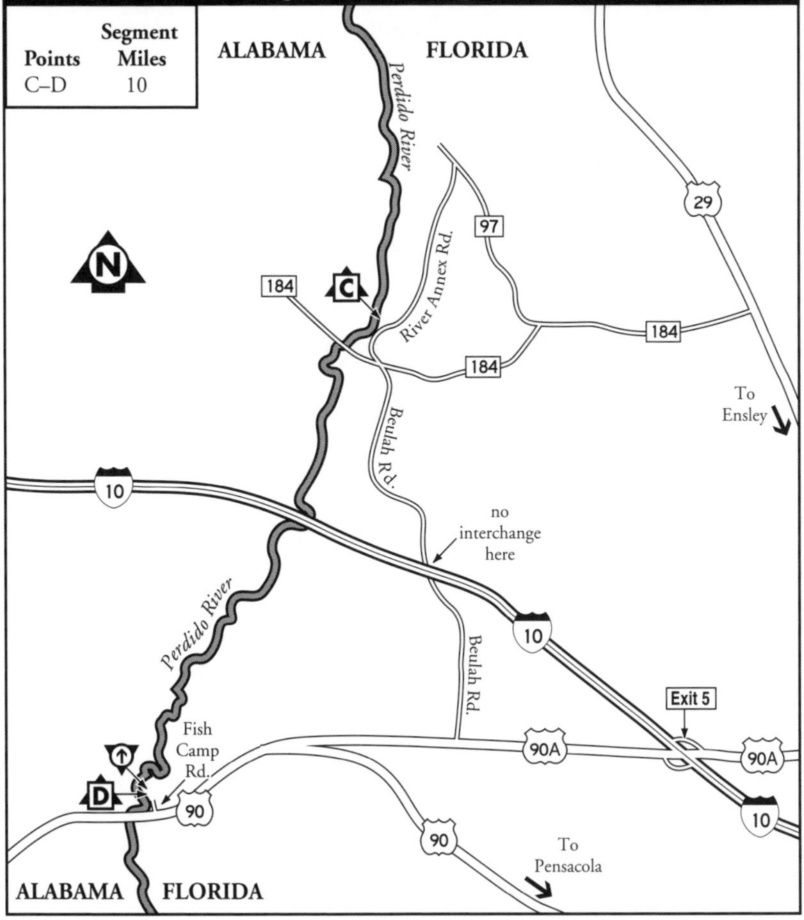

Points	Segment Miles
C–D	10

Bay, a large body of water that is subject to waves and high winds and not recommended for canoeing.

SHUTTLE: To reach the takeout from Exit 5 on I-10 near Ensley, take US 90A west until it merges with US 90 west. Keep on US 90 until you reach a right turn onto Ruby's Fish Camp Road, just before the bridge over the Perdido River. Ruby's Fish Camp, a private landing, offers parking and launch facilities. To reach the put-in from Ensley, take US 29 north to CR 184. Turn left on CR 184 and follow it west to River Annex Road, just before a

bridge over the Perdido River. Turn right on River Annex Road to reach the outfitter with a private launch and pay access.

GAUGE: Phone, visual. Call Ruby's Fish Camp at (850) 944-2537 for the latest river conditions.

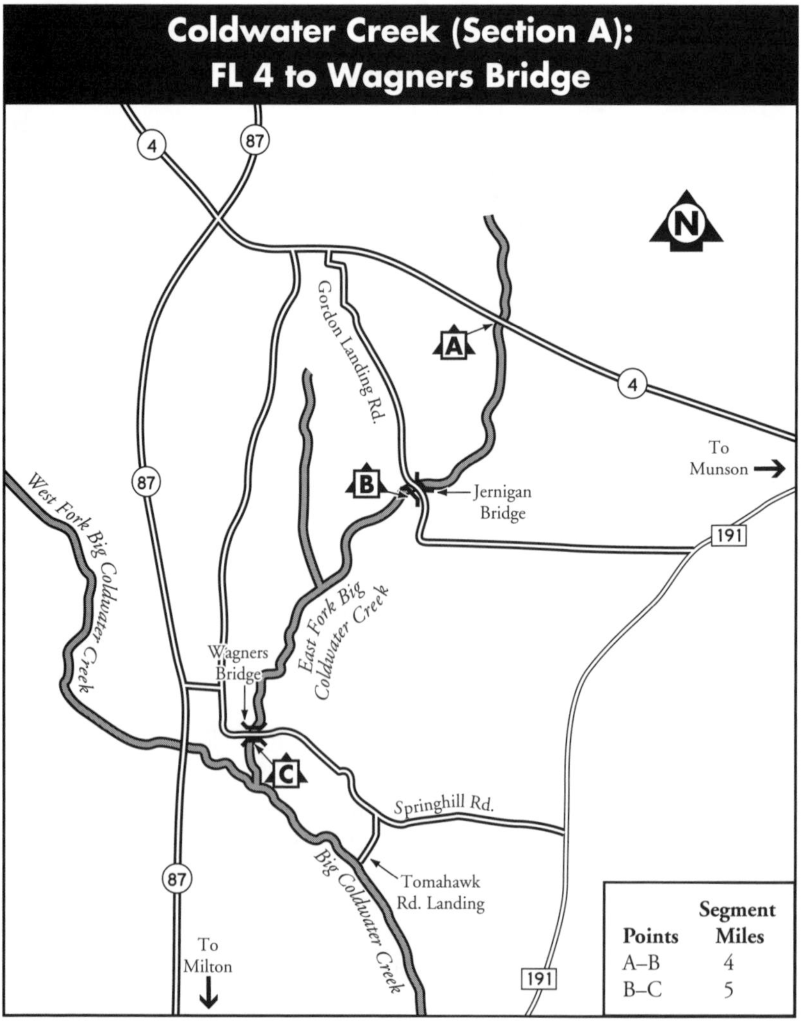

Coldwater Creek (Section A): FL 4 to Wagners Bridge

Points	Segment Miles
A–B	4
B–C	5

COLDWATER CREEK

Coldwater Creek is the most western of the streams in the Blackwater Forest and is said to be the swiftest. Flowing for some 20 miles through undeveloped land, it is very narrow in spots and has a steep gradient. Obstructions include stobs, cypress knees, logs, and wide gravel bars that extend into the stream from the sandbars. As a result of the swift water and the presence of obstructions, some maneuvering skill is needed to stay in the main channel. Lack of such skill leads to frequently running aground, an aggravating but harmless occurrence in the shallow water. Expect more blowdowns from Hurricane Ivan.

MAPS: Blackwater River State Forest map, Mclellen, Spring Hill (USGS)

FL 4 TO WAGNERS BRIDGE

class	I–I+
length	9
time	4.5
gauge	Phone
level	Call outfitter
gradient	4.5
scenery	A

DESCRIPTION: The upper part of this waterway is technically East Fork Big Coldwater Creek, but is simply known as Coldwater Creek. Name aside, this is a beautiful and remote section of Coldwater Creek. The stream varies from 25 to 30 feet wide at the beginning to 40 to 60 feet wide further down. The banks are up to 8 feet high and some have colorful variations of pipe clay. There are some obstructions in the water, but they are not hazardous.

Pass under the Jernigan Bridge and an alternate access at 4 miles. The access is the site of the Coldwater Horse Stables and Field Trial Area. There is an improved campground with tables, running water, and restrooms. This is also the spot where most of the liveries start their canoe rentals, and this section may be crowded from late May to early September.

As the creek flows downstream from the Jernigan Bridge, it occasionally narrows to 20 to 30 feet wide and may be somewhat deeper in these spots. For the most part it is wide, shallow, and clear, with many large sandbars. There are also two or three places where the stream runs over slight drops caused by cypress roots or rocks in the waterway. This adds a touch of spice to an otherwise leisurely trip.

SHUTTLE: To reach the put-in from Munson, travel west on FL 4 for 5 miles to the bridge across the East Fork of Big Coldwater Creek. (This will be the second bridge, the first having been the

bridge across Juniper Creek.) The access road is on the southwest side of the bridge. To reach the takeout from Munson, take CR 191 south to Springhill Road. Turn right on Springhill Road and follow it west to the Wagners Bridge over Coldwater Creek. Parking here is limited to just a couple of cars, as the adjacent land is owned by outfitters.

GAUGE: Phone. Call Bob's Canoe at (850) 623-5457 for the latest river conditions.

B

class	I–I+
length	9
time	5
gauge	Phone
level	Call outfitter
gradient	2.5
scenery	B+

WAGNERS BRIDGE TO CR 191

DESCRIPTION: The upper part of this section is heavily populated by tubers and on warm summer days may be congested. Fortunately the confluence with the West Fork of the Big Coldwater occurs less than 1 mile downstream, resulting in a much wider waterway with room for all. The West Fork is canoeable from FL 87, a distance of just over 1 mile.

Shortly below the confluence of the two creeks is Party Island, a large, white sand island in the middle of the river. This is a favorite stopping place for picnicking and swimming. At the southernmost end of the island, the river branches, with the widest part flowing right, and a small stream flowing almost due left.

An outfitter is located at Tomahawk Landing, 4 miles below the put-in for this section. Tomahawk Landing has a privately owned campground, launch area, and boat rental outfit. Canoes and equipment may be rented and shuttles arranged for a fee. There is also a fee for launching private boats and for parking.

Having left the state forest, this lower section of the Coldwater begins to lose its feeling of remoteness. It is also wider and shallower and there are areas where saw grass grows along the banks as it becomes more influenced by saltwater. Coldwater Creek continues for 3 more miles beyond CR 191 to its confluence with the Blackwater River. It is an additional 10 miles down a broad, tidal river to the city of Milton.

SHUTTLE: To reach the put-in from Munson, take CR 191 south to Springhill Road. Turn right on Springhill Road and follow it west to the bridge over Coldwater Creek. Parking here is limited to just a couple of cars, as the adjacent land is owned by outfitters. To reach the takeout, keep south on CR 191 to the bridge over Coldwater Creek.

Coldwater Creek (Section B): Wagners Bridge to CR 191

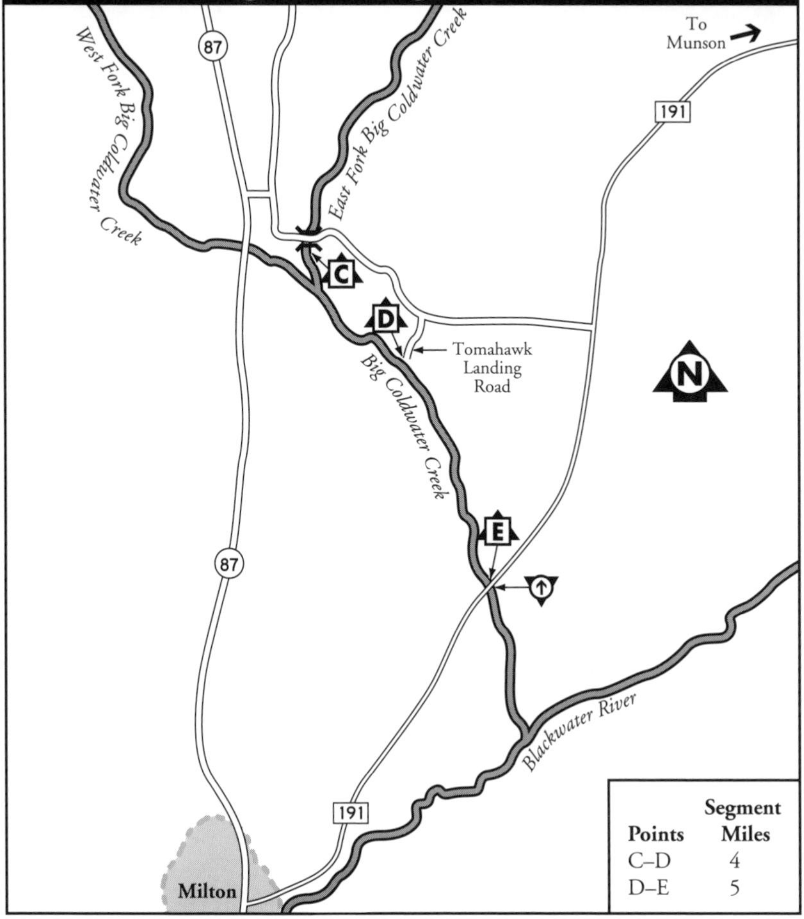

Points	Segment Miles
C–D	4
D–E	5

GAUGE: Phone. Call Bob's Canoe at (850) 623-5457 for the latest river conditions.

SWEETWATER CREEK AND JUNIPER CREEK

These two tributaries of the Blackwater River are usually canoed together, beginning on the Sweetwater. Trips of varied lengths can be undertaken, with access points on the creeks as they flow through the Blackwater River State Forest. It is possible to put in a canoe on Juniper Creek above FL 4, but it is an arduous trip and is not recommended. The stream is very narrow at that point, is canopied by trees, has high banks and many, many pull-overs. There is no access to Juniper Creek at the FL 4 bridge, but it is possible to put in at the FL 191 bridge and paddle the Juniper for less than 2 miles to its confluence with the Sweetwater.

The best starting point on the Sweetwater is at Sandy Landing Road, a little over 2 miles downstream. The paddler still has the experience of the canopied stream for the 2 miles above the confluence with Juniper Creek without the ordeal of pulling over a number of logjams.

Because these are swift streams, some caution should be exercised. Do not paddle on the upper sections when the water is very high or flooded, watch carefully for logs and other obstructions in the water and for overhanging trees. A moderate degree of skill and the ability to read moving water is helpful and will make a more enjoyable trip.

MAPS: Blackwater River State Forest map, Munson, Spring Hill (USGS)

class	I–I+
length	13
time	6
gauge	Phone
level	Call outfitter
gradient	3.3
scenery	A–A+

FL 4 TO INDIAN FORD BRIDGE

DESCRIPTION: Beginning at FL 4, the Sweetwater is narrow, shallow, swift, and may have a multitude of pull-overs, depending on water level. There is a beautiful canopy of hardwoods, clear, cascading water, and a few small sandbars. It is 2 miles from FL 4 to Sandy Landing Bridge. The canopied effect and the narrow stream continue below Sandy Landing Bridge for 2 miles to the confluence with Juniper Creek. At that point, the stream widens and there are large, white sandbars on either side. This is a popular spot for swimming and sunbathing and may be heavily populated on summer weekends. Red Rock Recreation Area is located 5 miles below Sandy Landing Bridge.

Red Rock is aptly named for the 40-foot-tall sandstone bluff on the east bank just below the bridge. It is the most impressive of several red-rock bluffs that are found along these streams. The clay found here is used in the making of pottery. Some of the

Sweetwater Creek and Juniper Creek: FL 4 to Indian Ford Bridge

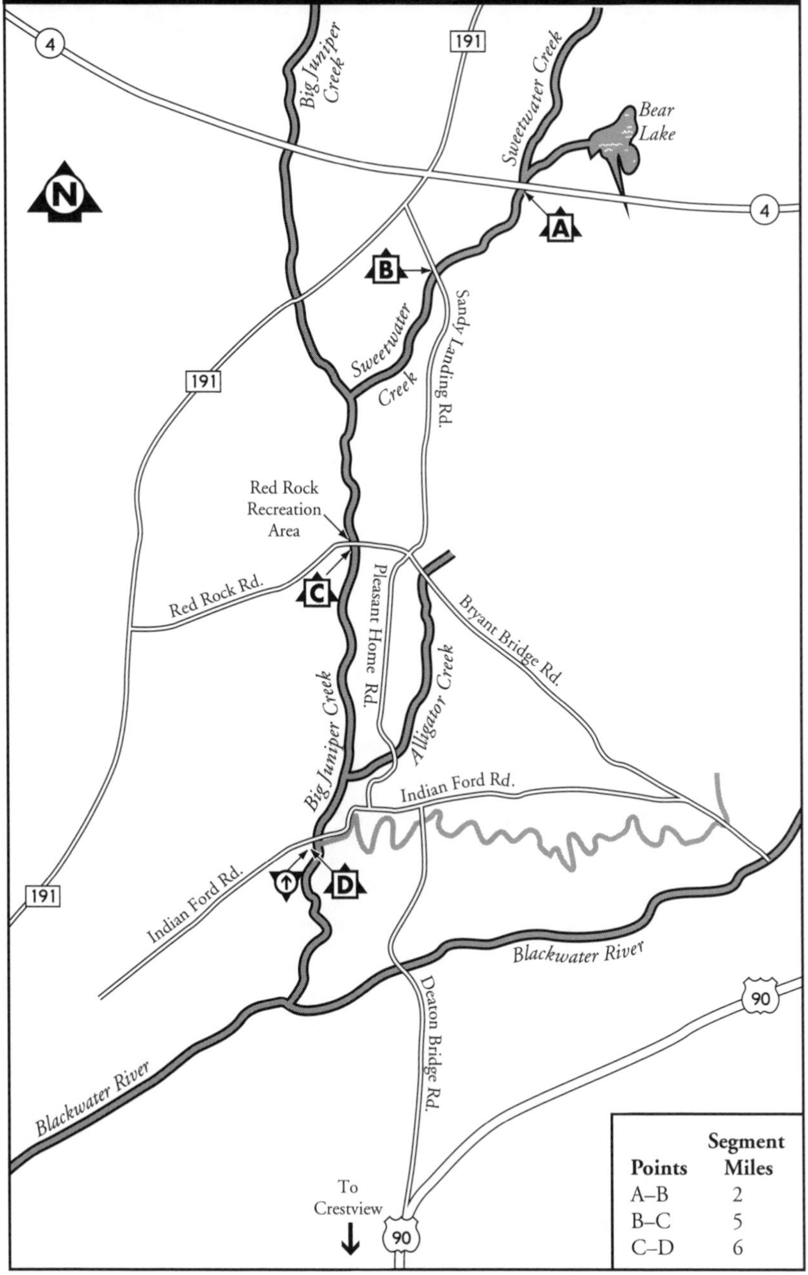

4
191
Big Juniper Creek
Sweetwater Creek
Bear Lake
N
4
A
B
Sandy Landing Rd.
Sweetwater Creek
191
Red Rock Recreation Area
Red Rock Rd.
C
Pleasant Home Rd.
Bryant Bridge Rd.
Alligator Creek
Big Juniper Creek
Indian Ford Rd.
Indian Ford Rd.
D
191
Blackwater River
Blackwater River
90
Deaton Bridge Rd.
To Crestview
90

Points	Segment Miles
A–B	2
B–C	5
C–D	6

bluffs have been turned into slides, adding another dimension to recreation on the river.

The stream continues to be wide and swift with very large sandbars on either side. It is 6 miles from Red Rock to Indian Ford Bridge. Within a mile of the Indian Ford Bridge, Alligator Creek flows in from the east bank. This is a shallow, canopied creek that can offer a shady spot for a last dip on a warm day.

SHUTTLE: To reach the put-in from Crestview, take FL 4 west to the bridge across Sweetwater Creek. This access is about 1 mile east of CR 191. To reach the takeout from Crestview, take US 90 west to Harold and turn right on Deaton Bridge Road, crossing the Blackwater River to reach Indian Ford Road. Turn left on Indian Ford Road and follow it to the bridge over Juniper Creek. Access is on the west side of the bridge. To reach the FL 4 put-in from the Indian Ford takeout, backtrack east on Indian Ford Road, then turn left and head north on Pleasant Home Road. Keep north as Pleasant Home Road becomes Sandy Landing Road, which reaches CR 191. Turn right on CR 191 to reach FL 4. Turn right on FL 4 and reach the put-in at 1 mile.

GAUGE: Phone. Call Adventures Unlimited at (850) 623-6197 for the latest stream conditions.

Setting up camp near a put-in

BLACKWATER RIVER

The headwaters of the Blackwater River originate primarily in south Alabama's Conecuh National Forest. As a result, there is virtually no development or agricultural activity to spoil the purity of the water. There are no real springs in the area, but some of the tributaries flowing into the Blackwater have such clarity that they look like spring runs.

Like its tributaries, Coldwater, Sweetwater, and Juniper creeks, the Blackwater is characterized by swift, shallow water and beautiful sandbars. The color of its water is more tannic than those of neighboring streams, hence the name, Blackwater. This is somewhat of a misnomer because the water is actually a clear, slightly red color that is far from black. The Blackwater River flows through almost 50 miles of remote and undeveloped terrain, much of it in the Blackwater River State Forest, making it an excellent choice for an extended canoe trip. In addition to sandbars, there are designated campsites at Blackwater River State Park. The red cedar is the predominant tree found near the streams, with red maple, cypress, oak, and a mixture of other hardwoods. Stands of planted longleaf pine are frequent on the higher ground. Fishermen occasionally catch black bass and small catfish from the streams, but the lack of aquatic vegetation greatly limits the fish population. A quiet canoeist may see raccoons, skunks, opossums, perhaps even a turkey or deer. But the scarcity of fish leads to fewer sightings of turtles, otters, or wading birds.

MAPS: Blackwater River State Forest Map, Blackman, Baker, Munson, Floridale, Harold (USGS)

CHESSHER BRIDGE TO COTTON BRIDGE

class	I–I+
length	15
time	8
gauge	Phone, visual
level	2–3
gradient	3.3
scenery	A+

DESCRIPTION: The river itself is characterized by being clear, shallow, and swift with a fine sand or gravel bottom. The uppermost section of the Blackwater may have many pull-overs. The banks are 5 to 6 feet high and heavily wooded with occasional small sandbars on bends in the stream. At low water this can be a strenuous trip, but it is a remote and undeveloped area that is very attractive to the wilderness paddler.

Kennedy Bridge is 5 miles below Chessher Bridge. Kennedy Bridge is the beginning of the Florida Canoe Trail for the Blackwater River and is an easy and leisurely trip. It is primarily wide and shallow, with about a third of the distance made up of narrow, deeper sections. There are numerous sandbars large enough

Blackwater River (Section A): Chessher Bridge to Cotton Bridge

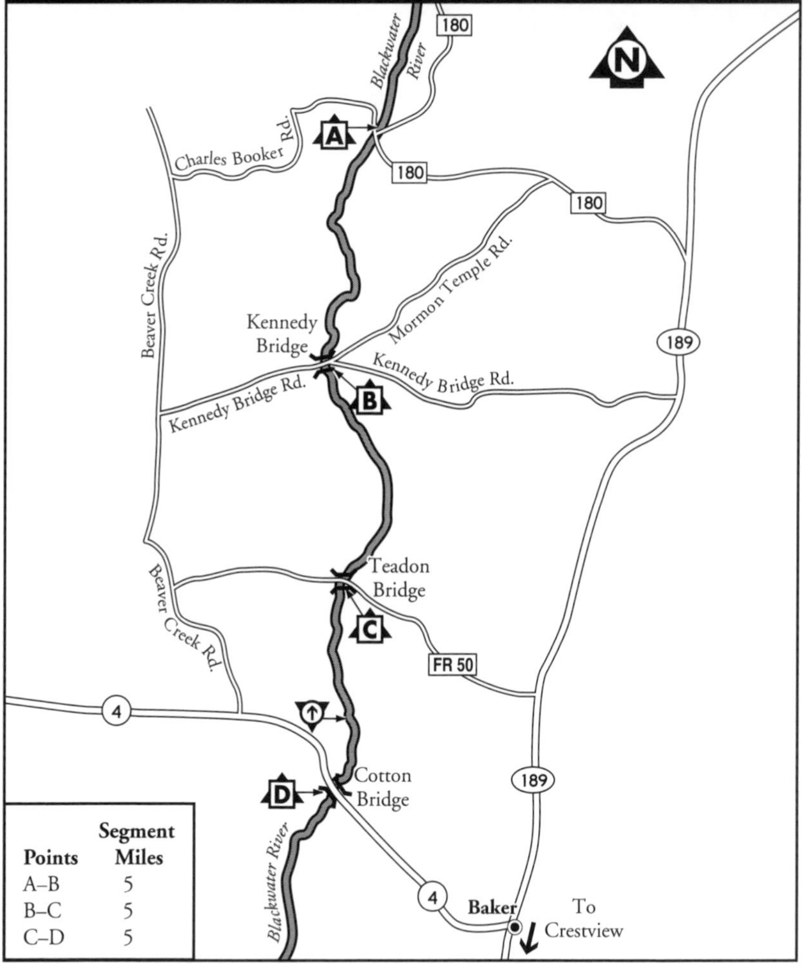

Points	Segment Miles
A–B	5
B–C	5
C–D	5

to accommodate campers. Hurricane Ivan dropped more trees in the water, so watch out for strainers.

Teaden Bridge is 5 miles below Kennedy Bridge. Below that bridge, the river has fewer of the deep, narrow sections and becomes generally wider and shallower. It is still remote and wild.

SHUTTLE: To reach the uppermost put-in from Crestview, take FL 4 west to Baker. Turn right onto FL 189 north and follow it to CR 180. Turn left on CR 180 and follow it to Charles Booker Road. Turn left on Charles Booker Road a very short distance to reach the Chessher Bridge over Blackwater River. To reach the

takeout, stay on FL 4 west of Baker for 4 miles to reach Cotton Bridge. A developed public boat landing is on the west side of the bridge, and a private outfitter is located on the east side of the bridge.

GAUGE: Phone, visual. A gauge is located on Deaton Bridge, on the downstream side of a piling. A reading of 2 feet is considered safe, with 3 feet the maximum safe runnable level. Or call Adventures Unlimited at (850) 623-6197 for the latest river conditions.

class	I–I+
length	20
time	Varies
gauge	Phone, visual
level	2–3
gradient	2.5
scenery	A

COTTON BRIDGE TO DEATON BRIDGE

DESCRIPTION: The river is very broad and shallow at this access and continues to widen as it flows toward Bryant Bridge. The banks vary from huge white sandbars to yellow clay banks from 3 to 8 feet high. Below FL 4 the river occasionally flows through private property but generally maintains its wild character. A number of small creeks flow into the Blackwater.

Bryant Bridge, 12 miles below Cotton Bridge, is a popular picnicking and swimming spot as well as being a put-in and take-out site for canoe liveries. As a result, it may be congested on summer weekends. Shortly below Bryant Bridge, the river begins to turn to the west and change in character. Small streams flowing in create little sloughs that in turn feed into the river. These little sloughs become more common as the river nears the state park. Deaton Bridge is a common day-use area, so it may be crowded here as well on weekends.

From Bryant Bridge, it is 8 miles to Deaton Bridge at Blackwater River State Park. This state park has a full range of facilities, including a very nice tent camping area. Florida state parks close at sundown, so those wishing to leave their cars inside will need to make arrangements with the ranger ahead of time. Cars are not allowed to overnight in the parking areas near Deaton Bridge.

Below the state park, the Blackwater continues to widen with more frequent sloughs that are now covered with saw grass. It is 2 miles to the confluence with Sweetwater–Juniper Creek and 7 miles to the confluence with the Coldwater. It is 14 miles to the roadside park at the city of Milton. The broad, slow nature of the river and the advent of motorboat traffic usually discourages canoeists from proceeding below Deaton Bridge.

SHUTTLE: To reach the take-out from Crestview, take US 90 to Harold and Deaton Bridge Road. Turn right on Deaton Bridge Road and follow it north to Deaton Bridge at Blackwater River

Blackwater River (Section B): Cotton Bridge to Deaton Bridge

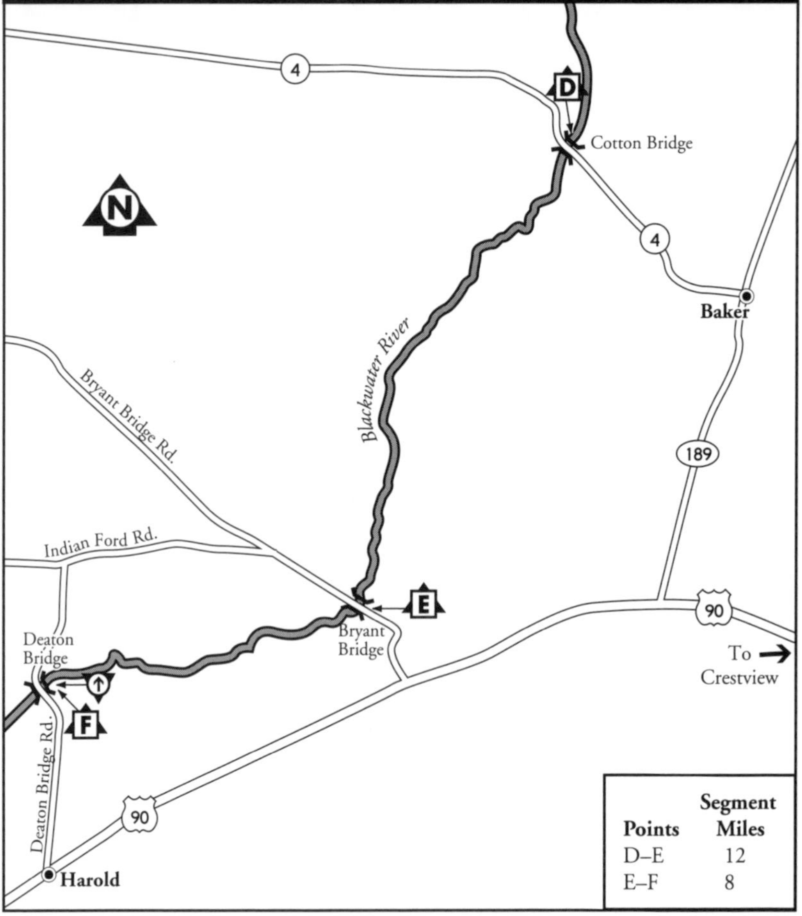

Points	Segment Miles
D–E	12
E–F	8

State Park. There are accesses on both sides of the bridge. A fee is required to park here. To reach the put-in from the takeout, backtrack on Deaton Bridge Road to US 90. Proceed east on US 90 to FL 189. Turn left on FL 189 to reach FL 4. Turn left on FL 4 and follow it through Baker to Cotton Bridge. A developed public boat landing is on the west side of the bridge and a private outfitter is located on the east side of the bridge.

GAUGE: Phone, visual. A gauge is located on Deaton Bridge, on the downstream side of a piling. A reading of 2 feet is considered safe, with 3 feet the maximum safe runnable level. Or call Adventures Unlimited at (850) 623-6197 for the latest river conditions.

YELLOW RIVER

The Yellow River drains the highest point in Florida and is fed by nearly 100 small streams and creeks as well as the Shoal River. It begins in south Alabama in the Conecuh National Forest and ends on the boundaries of the Eglin Air Force Base.

It is a swift flowing river that traverses a thinly settled area, providing over 50 miles of wilderness canoe camping and touring. The Yellow is generally not as clear as the neighboring streams in the Blackwater Forest. The sand along the banks and the river bottom has more of a tan hue than white, resulting in the yellowish appearance of the water. There is also more aquatic vegetation than in the rivers to the west so that fish are present, along with alligators, turtles, and waterbirds.

Other wildlife that may be encountered includes deer, turkeys, raccoons, and bobcats. Beavers are extremely active on this river, and evidence of their handiwork is everywhere. The trees along the river include river birch, willows, spruce pines, and many varieties of hardwoods. Lush vines, some with flowers, are frequently seen woven among the tree limbs.

With the confluence of the Shoal River, the Yellow turns almost due west and becomes much wider. It continues to flow for another 30 miles to Blackwater Bay but is broad and heavily used by motorboats and is of little interest to most canoeists.

MAPS: Watkins Bridge, Wing, AL, Oak Grove, Crestview North, Baker, Holt (USGS)

WATKINS BRIDGE TO OAK GROVE LANDING

class	I–I+
length	23
time	Varies
gauge	Visual, Web
level	N/A
gradient	2
scenery	A

DESCRIPTION: AL 55 is the furthest point at which the Yellow River can be canoed with any degree of ease. This section is winding with occasional banks up to 20 feet high. There are numerous sandbars on the curves and the deeper water on the outside of the bends provides good swimming holes. About 6 miles downstream, a large creek enters from the west bank and the river widens considerably. It soon narrows again; there is a rocky shoal below that point that can create a diversion at low water. Less than a mile from the AL 4 bridge, the river narrows, picks up speed, and flows through a series of strainers that may require a pull-over or carry-around. The strong current, deep water, and lack of maneuvering space make this a potentially hazardous spot for the

Yellow River (Section A): Watkins Bridge to Oak Grove Landing

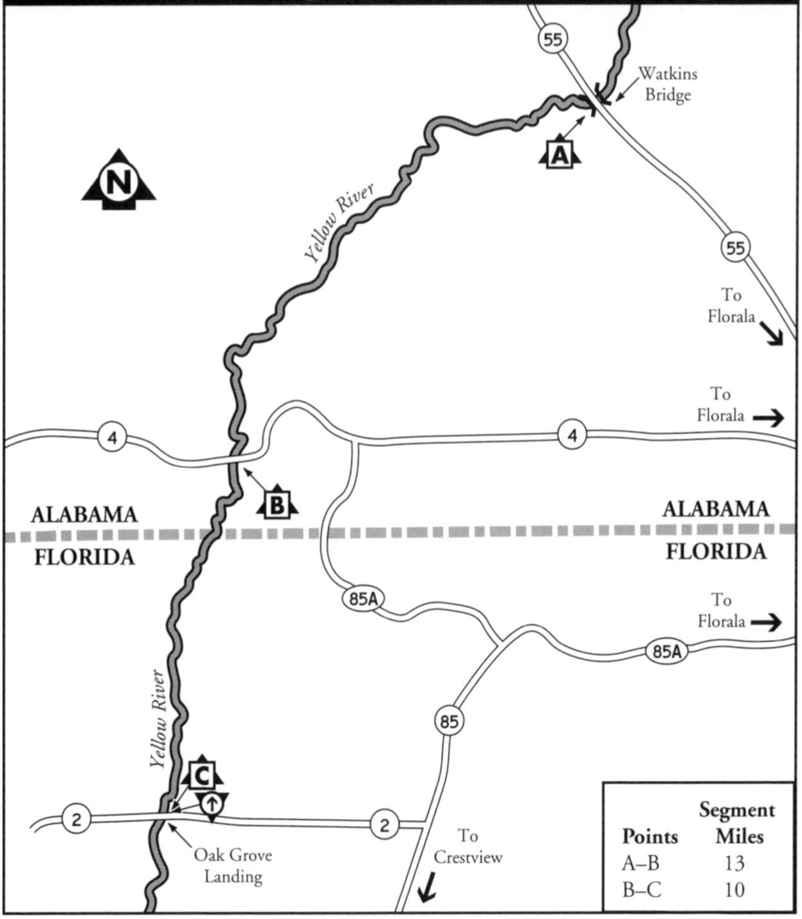

Points	Segment Miles
A–B	13
B–C	10

novice paddler. This section can be divided into two shorter paddles, as there is an access at AL 4. It is 13 miles from AL 55 to AL 4, and 10 miles from AL 4 to CR 2.

Just below the AL 4 access are several fishing and hunting camps. These buildings are some of the few seen on the river from AL 55 to CR 2. In this section the winding nature of the river continues with many bends, sandbars, and some high banks. The strong current lends assistance to the paddler, but some maneuvering skill will be needed to manage some of the tighter curves. There are numerous wooded roads—just tracks through the woods made by vehicles—that come down to the

river; these are used by fishermen and locals for swimming and picnicking. There is no public access along this run, and, overall, the river retains a remote atmosphere.

SHUTTLE: To reach the takeout from Crestview, travel north on FL 85 to the junction with CR 2. Turn left, west, on CR 2 and continue to the bridge across the Yellow River. Access is from the Oak Grove Landing boat ramp, complete with a picnic area. To reach the put-in from Crestview, keep north on FL 85 to Florala, Alabama, and continue northwest on AL 55 to the Watkins Bridge over the Yellow River. The access road, just before the bridge, may be potholed.

GAUGE: Visual, Web. The best way to determine water level is in person. However, the Yellow River is normally floatable year-round. But to check the river to see if it is at normal levels for any given time period, the USGS gauge is Yellow River in the town of Milligan, FL.

Oak Grove Landing to Gin Hole Landing

class	I
length	27
time	Varies
gauge	Visual, Web
level	N/A
gradient	1.5
scenery	A

DESCRIPTION: This is the beginning of the Florida Canoe Trail. The river becomes deeper and cloudier as it flows toward US 90. The variation from steep banks to low sandbars with some swampy areas continues, with the sandbars becoming smaller and less frequent during the first 15 miles. Bluffs up to 40 feet high are occasionally seen on the east side and may continue for 0.25 miles or more along the bank. There are myriad streams feeding the river from both sides, and campsites are scarce until a few miles above US 90.

Silver Lake Landing, an improved access off of a private road, occurs just over 8 miles down this section. There are several houses along the east bank at this point. About 2 miles above US 90, the large sandbars resume, and there is ample camping space available on most of them. The Yellow divides immediately south of the US 90 bridge at a large island. At the southern end of the island is the Louisville and Nashville Railroad trestle, which crosses the river. At one time the Yellow River was considered a navigable stream from Blackwater Bay up to this point, which was called Barrows Ferry.

The sandbars decrease again below US 90 as the riverbanks become much lower and more heavily wooded. I-10 crosses the river about 4 miles below US 90; there is no access. From I-10 it is less than 3 miles to the confluence with the Shoal River. Just

Yellow River (Section B): Oak Grove Landing to Gin Hole Landing

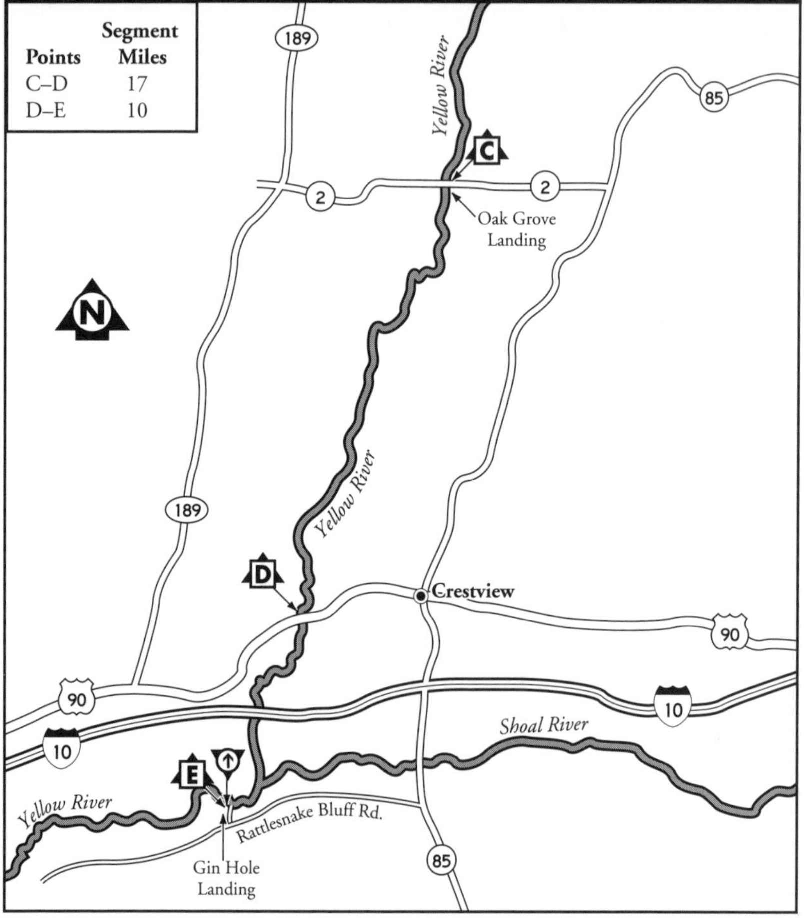

Points	Segment Miles
C–D	17
D–E	10

above this confluence, the Yellow River splits into several swift-flowing runs, and the Shoal, flowing in from the east, is not easily identifiable. After the Shoal joins the Yellow, it turns west and becomes much broader.

From this point on, the left (south) bank of the river is the property of Eglin Air Force Base and usage is restricted. Much of the property on the right bank is privately owned and posted. Groupings of houses and cabins occur on the north bank at regular intervals from this point to the takeout, but the roads that lead to them are not open to the public. With the advent of the deeper

water and broader river, paddlers encounter an increasing number of motorboats, and the trip becomes less interesting. The last access point, Gin Hole Landing, is on the military reservation, however, and requires a permit for access (which may be closed in the future). To obtain a use permit, call (850) 882-4164. If you do not feel like getting a permit but want to canoe this lower section, simply take out at the nice boat ramp on US 90, 17 miles below FL 2. It is 10 miles from US 90 to Gin Hole Landing.

The 9-mile stretch on the Yellow River from Gin Hole Landing to FL 189 is easily accessible to motorboats and is not particularly desirable to the canoeist. The Yellow River Delta, the 30-mile section from FL 189 to Blackwater Bay, is a maze of saw grass and tidal flats. It is often difficult to locate the main channel of the river. Blackwater Bay is a large body of water subject to high winds and waves.

SHUTTLE: To reach the takeout from Crestview, take FL 85 south across the Shoal River, then turn right on Rattlesnake Bluff Road. Follow the road about 4.5 miles and look for a two-track sand road leading right, which heads 0.3 miles down to the river. There may or may not be a sign on a tree at the turn. To reach the put-in from Crestview, travel north on FL 85 to the junction with CR 2. Turn left (west) on CR 2 and continue to the bridge across the Yellow River. Access is from the Oak Grove boat ramp, complete with a picnic area.

GAUGE: Visual, Web. The best way to determine water level is in person. However, the Yellow River is normally floatable year-round. But to check the river to see if it is at normal levels for any given time period, the USGS gauge is Yellow River in the town of Milligan, FL.

SHOAL RIVER

The Shoal River is the major tributary of the Yellow River and, like the Yellow, drains out of some of the highest land in Florida. It flows west for the first 15 miles, then turns southwest and almost parallels the Yellow for 7 miles until the confluence with Titi Creek. At that point, it flows west again until its confluence with the Yellow, just above Rattlesnake Bluff.

The Shoal is a swift, sandy waterway with tan-colored water that is seldom more than a few feet deep. It is narrow and twisting and, except for an occasional logging bridge or isolated county road, is a fine example of north Florida wilderness. Campsites are not plentiful, but there are occasional sandbars that are large enough to accommodate a small group.

MAPS: New Harmony, Dorcas, Crestview North, Crestview South, Holt (USGS)

A

CR 1087 TO US 90

class	I
length	18
time	9
gauge	Visual, Web
level	N/A
gradient	2.5
scenery	A

DESCRIPTION: This section of the Shoal is narrow, shallow, and characterized by high sandbanks, some sandbars, and many twists and turns. It can be broken into two segments, using an access site at FL 393, 10 miles downstream. There are over a dozen small streams and rivulets that feed into the river, most of them clean and shallow, but some make little sloughs that are covered with greenery. About 4 miles downstream, Crowder Cemetery Road bridges the river. The river is narrow at this point with steep banks, and there is usually a logjam against the pilings under the bridge. At high-water levels this situation can be hazardous, and it should be approached with caution. There is a similar situation 2 miles downstream at the Pond Creek Road bridge. The banks are lower, but there is often debris trapped under this bridge as well.

After passing under Pond Creek Road bridge it is 2 miles to the confluence of Pond Creek. This is a wide creek, as large as the Shoal at their confluence. The Shoal becomes broader below this point and it is only 1 mile to the access at FL 393.

Myriad small streams continue to feed into the Shoal, keeping the current lively. It is broader and there are several good campsites on sandbars. The bends are gentler and there are some straight sections as well. Three miles below FL 393 is a 2-mile-long section that ends in a bend to the south. The river then continues south to US 90.

Shoal River (Section A): CR 1087 to US 90

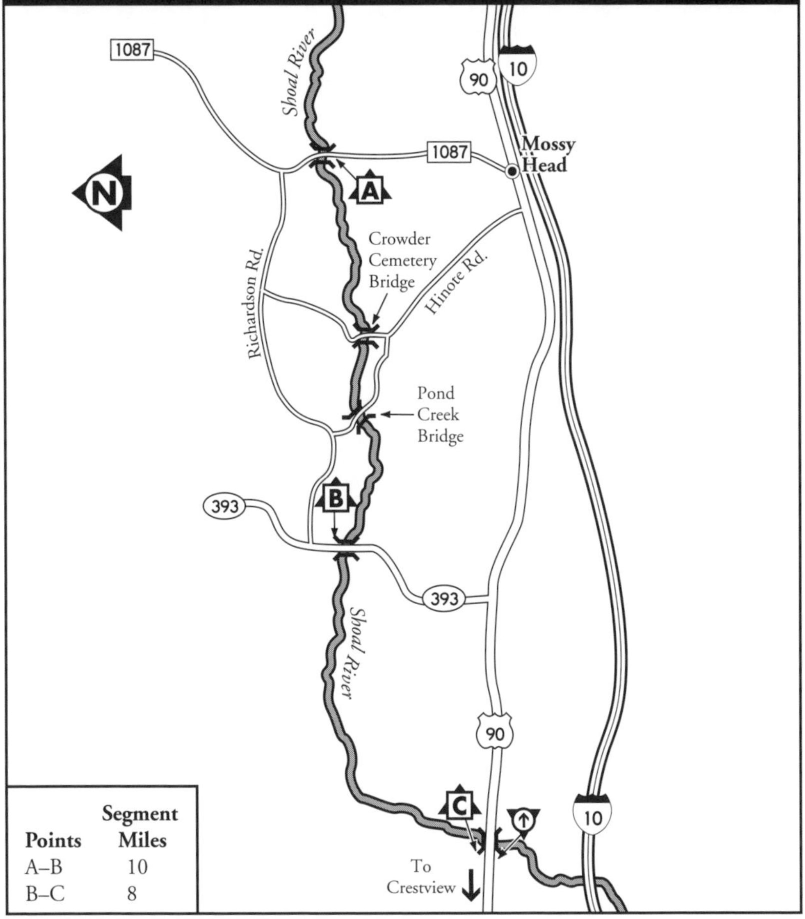

Points	Segment Miles
A–B	10
B–C	8

SHUTTLE: To reach the takeout from Crestview, take US 90 east to the bridge over Shoal River and the Ray Lynn Barnes boat launch, on the west side of the bridge. To reach the put-in continue east on US 90 to Mossy Head and CR 1087. Turn left (north) and follow CR 1087 to the bridge over the Shoal River. The access road to the water is before the bridge on the west side.

GAUGE: Visual, Web. The best way to determine that water level is in person. However, the Shoal is normally floatable year-round. To determine if the river levels are normal for any given time period the USGS gauge is Shoal River near Mossy Head, FL.

class	I
length	18
time	9
gauge	Visual, Web
level	N/A
gradient	2
scenery	B+

B

US 90 TO GIN HOLE LANDING

DESCRIPTION: Below US 90, the Shoal widens to about 100 feet with higher, heavily wooded banks. This section can be broken into two segments, from US 90 to FL 85, 10 miles, and FL 85 to Gin Hole Landing, 8 miles. There are sandbars on the insides of bends that are adequate for campsites, but most of the property on both sides is posted. Less than 3 miles downstream the river passes under I-10 with no access. Below the interstate the river begins to change. The banks lower to 1 to 4 feet high and are lined with lowland hardwoods and pine.

About 3 miles below the interstate, Titi Creek enters from the left bank. The mouth of this creek is 35 feet wide and, surprisingly, the Shoal narrows at this point to 50 to 75 feet wide and flows very swiftly for 100 yards before widening again. Sandbars are evident below Titi Creek, and small ponds begin to appear on the outside of some of the curves. Look for reeds and lily pads through here. You may also encounter small fishing boats in these quiet pools. With a number of points accessible by vehicles, the river soon begins to lose its feeling of remoteness.

Below the FL 85 access, the banks become lower again, and in some places actual swamps appear on both sides of the river. The river alternately narrows and widens until just above its confluence with the Yellow, where it becomes very narrow for nearly a mile. Campsites are scarce on this section. The best choice is on a bluff 4 miles below FL 85 on the left bank. Below the bluff private camps begin to appear.

In this area the river begins to narrow and break into runs, and in some places is completely canopied. Watch for sharp turns and obstructions in the river through here. The confluence with the Yellow River is undramatic because just above the Shoal, the Yellow has also broken into separate runs and narrows. The junction is clearly defined, however. Gin Hole Landing is about 0.5 miles downstream from the confluence of the rivers on the south bank of the property of Eglin Air Force Base. The last access point, Gin Hole Landing, is on the military reservation, however, and requires a permit for access. To obtain a permit, call (850) 882-4164.

SHUTTLE: To reach the takeout from Crestview, take FL 85 south across the Shoal River, then turn right onto Rattlesnake Bluff Road. Follow the road for about 4.5 miles and look for a

two-track sand road leading right to Gin Hole Landing, 0.3 miles to the Yellow River. There may or may not be a sign on a tree at the turn. To reach the put-in from Crestview, take US 90 east to the bridge over the Shoal River and the Ray Lynn Barnes boat launch, on the west side of the bridge.

GAUGE: Visual, Web. The best way to determine the water level is in person. However, the Shoal is normally floatable year-round. To determine if the river levels are normal for any given time period the USGS gauge is Shoal River near Mossy Head, FL.

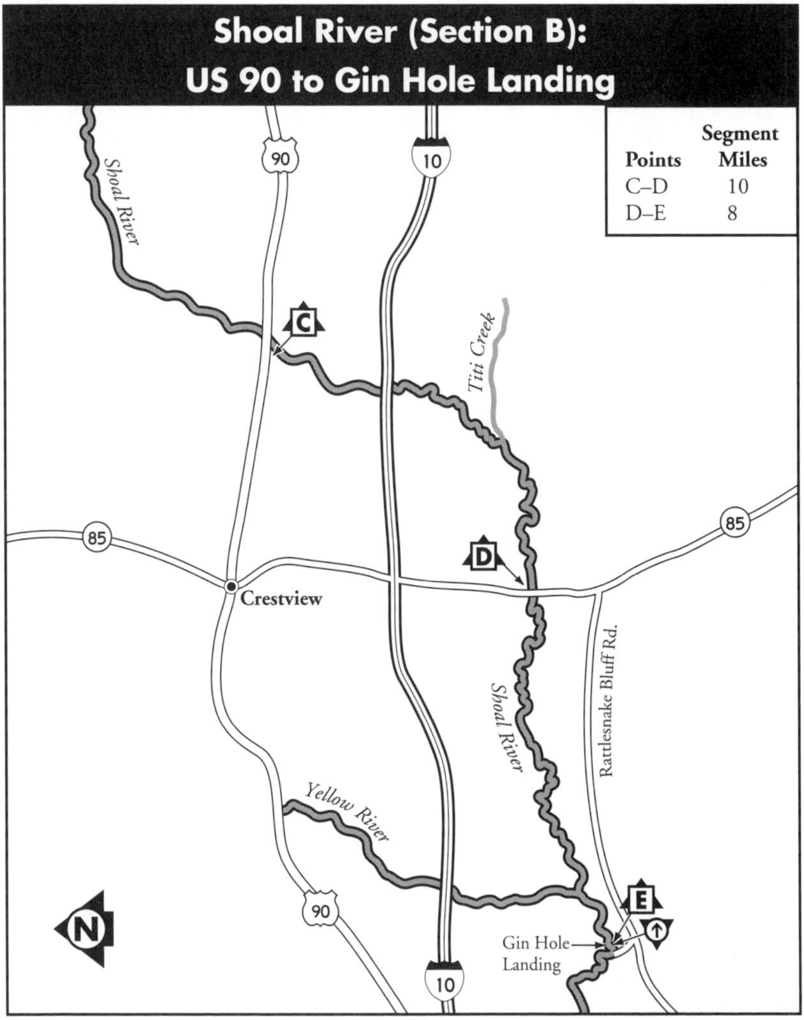

Shoal River (Section B): US 90 to Gin Hole Landing

Points	Segment Miles
C–D	10
D–E	8

Shoal River
Titi Creek
Crestview
Rattlesnake Bluff Rd.
Yellow River
Gin Hole Landing

CHOCTAWHATCHEE RIVER

The Choctawhatchee River is over 170 miles long from its headwaters in Barbour County, Alabama, to Choctawhatchee Bay near Fort Walton Beach, Florida. Of this length, there are over 100 miles of excellent canoeing, making it one of the finest touring rivers in northwest Florida. Not only is it a scenic river of high ecological significance, it is also very remote, limited in access, and offers an unusual opportunity for an extended wilderness experience.

The Choctawhatchee is a broad, shallow river that is usually yellow in color. It has an annual flooding pattern that is primarily responsible for the lack of development along its banks. The upper sections are characterized by high limestone banks, rocky shoals and drops, and sections of cascading water. After entering Florida, the river is calmer but more remote and has huge sandbars. The terrain varies from floodplain forests with upland hardwoods and pine hammocks to marshes and swampy wetlands. Wildlife is plentiful and a wide variety of animals indigenous to north Florida may be sighted along the banks.

Major tributaries of the Choctawhatchee in Alabama include Judy Creek, the East Fork of the Choctawhatchee, the Little Choctawhatchee, and the Pea River. In Florida, Wright Creek, Holmes Creek, and several springs including Blue Spring and Morrison Spring feed the river.

MAPS: Ewell, Pinkard, Daleville, Clayhatchee, Bellwood, Geneva East (Alabama), Izagora, Hobbs Crossroads, Prosperity, Caryville, Hinsons Crossroads, Ponce De Leon, Red Bay, Millers Ferry (Florida) (USGS)

A

CR 36 TO AL 92

class	I–I+
length	22
time	Varies
gauge	Web, visual
level	N/A
gradient	4
scenery	B

DESCRIPTION: At the put-in on CR 36, the West Fork Choctawhatchee River is about 35 feet wide, shallow, and has a moderate current. It soon widens to 50 feet, and at normal or slightly less than normal water levels there are a series of rocky shoals that stretch across the entire width of the stream. These shoals require some skill in maneuvering to keep from running aground. The river is a drop-and-pool waterway with the short pools having a modest current followed by a stretch of faster water over the shoals.

Judy Creek enters the river about 3.5 miles downstream. This creek is an alternate access to the Choctawhatchee at normal to high water and has several interesting drops in its 2-mile run

from CR 36 to its confluence with the river. Below Judy Creek, the river bottom becomes sandier and shallow, but there are still shoals across the river. Just above AL 27, there is a 2-foot drop over a rocky ledge that may be troublesome for the novice paddler. It should be run on the extreme left and may be portaged if necessary. It is 2.5 miles from Judy Creek to AL 27, and a total of 6 miles from CR 36 to AL 27.

The occurrence of shoals increase below the AL 27 bridge, and are frequently in sight of each other down to the confluence with the East Fork of the Choctawhatchee. The bridge from Bagwells Crossroads crosses the river about 3 miles down from the

Choctawhatchee River (Section A): CR 36 to AL 92

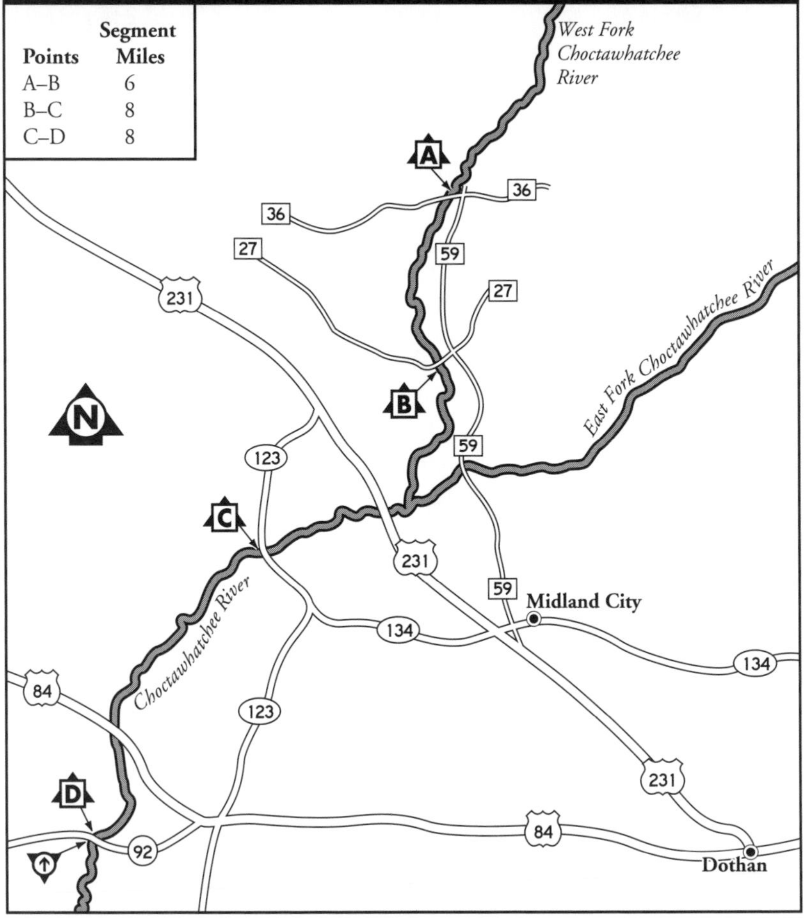

Points	Segment Miles
A–B	6
B–C	8
C–D	8

AL 27 bridge, but there is no access. It is another mile to the confluence with the East Fork. There is a strong current at that point, and the river widens to 100 feet.

The drop-and-pool characteristic ends with the confluence of the East Fork, then the river proceeds with a constant current. There are a few small shoals below this point and a few houses begin to appear. The banks are 10 to 15 feet high with an occasional sandbank where livestock come down to the water. It is 1 mile from the confluence of the East Fork to US 231. This is a two-lane bridge with no access.

Just below US 231, on the south bank, a stream has cut a deep crevice in the limestone as it enters the river. It is possible to paddle into this opening for a short distance and to look overhead at a beautiful fern fall. One mile farther downstream, a large sandbar occurs on the south bank. This bar used to be an island, the result of a change of direction in the flow of the river. It is an excellent campsite for a large party of campers. A very pretty stream that is worth a short walk to see flows into the river at the east end of this site.

About 1.5 miles farther downstream a railroad trestle crosses the river. Just downstream of the trestle is a large sandbank on the northwest side that is heavily used as an access point. It is another 1.5 miles to the AL 123 bridge and John Hutto Park, which has an excellent access point. It is a total of 8 miles from AL 27 to AL 123.

Just below the AL 123 bridge are the pilings from an old mill that can be troublesome depending on the water level. Approach with caution and watch for debris that may have been caught, creating a strainer. There is usually a clear passage on the northwest side.

The section below AL 123 is a pleasant trip with high vertical banks and a good current. Little maneuvering skill is needed after passing the site of the old mill. Because of the high banks, campsites are scarce. There are two points where modest sandbanks line the river. A small party could camp here, but they might have to share facilities with livestock from nearby pastures. It is 8 miles from AL 123 to AL 92.

SHUTTLE: To reach the lowermost takeout from Dothan, Alabama, take US 84 west to AL 92. Turn left on AL 92 and follow it west to the access on the southwest side of the bridge over the river. To reach the uppermost access from Midland City, take AL 134 west to CR 59. Turn right on CR 59, heading north to CR 36. Turn left on CR 36 to the bridge over the Choctawhatchee river.

GAUGE: Visual, Web. Checking the river in person is the most reliable method to determine the water level. However, the

Choctawhatchee is normally floatable year-round. The USGS gauge helpful in determining if the river is near average levels is Choctawhatchee near Geneva, AL.

AL 92 TO FL 2

class	I
length	29
time	Varies
gauge	Visual, Web
level	N/A
gradient	1.8
scenery	B

DESCRIPTION: This section's access points provide paddlers with routes of varied lengths. There is a nice sandbar at the AL 92 put-in that is popular with swimmers and sunbathers on warm weekends. In the next 3 miles the banks are sloping and heavily wooded. A possible campsite occurs at the point where the Little Choctawhatchee enters the river about 1.5 miles downstream from US 92. Sandbars become common until the confluence with Pates Creek, which introduces sloping, heavily wooded banks again and an end to the sandbars.

Three miles farther downstream, Claybank Creek enters from the northwest. Just up this creek, and in sight of the river, is a large sandbar that would provide camping space for several tents. About 1 mile below Claybank Creek you'll reach the bridge at AL 167. AL 167 has a poor, steep access. It is 9 miles from AL 92 to AL 167.

The banks of the river become higher at AL 167. Shortly below this access there is a high, wooded bluff on the southeast side that follows the river for about 0.25 miles. It becomes lower as the river bends to the left, revealing a large sandbar, suitable for camping, on the left bank. This is the only good campsite for the next 2 miles as the banks continue to be high down to Bellwood Bridge. There is no access to the river at Bellwood Bridge. Shortly below this bridge, the river begins a long loop to the west.

At the end of the loop is a large sandbar on the north bank with an almost vertical bank on the south side. Although there are several more sandbars in the following miles, they are very low and any rise in water level make them doubtful campsites. It is over 6 miles to the next good campsite. Interspersed with these low sandbars are vertical banks and the entrance of Bames Creek. Very large alligators have been observed in this section.

About 6 miles downstream from AL 167 the river bends to the east. There are some low pastures on the right bank that could be used for camping with permission from the owners but would probably have to be shared with livestock.

As the river turns south, the banks become very high with pastures on top. A rock bluff will be observed on the west bank and is followed 0.5 miles downstream by a boat ramp on the east

Choctawhatchee River (Section B): AL 92 to FL 2

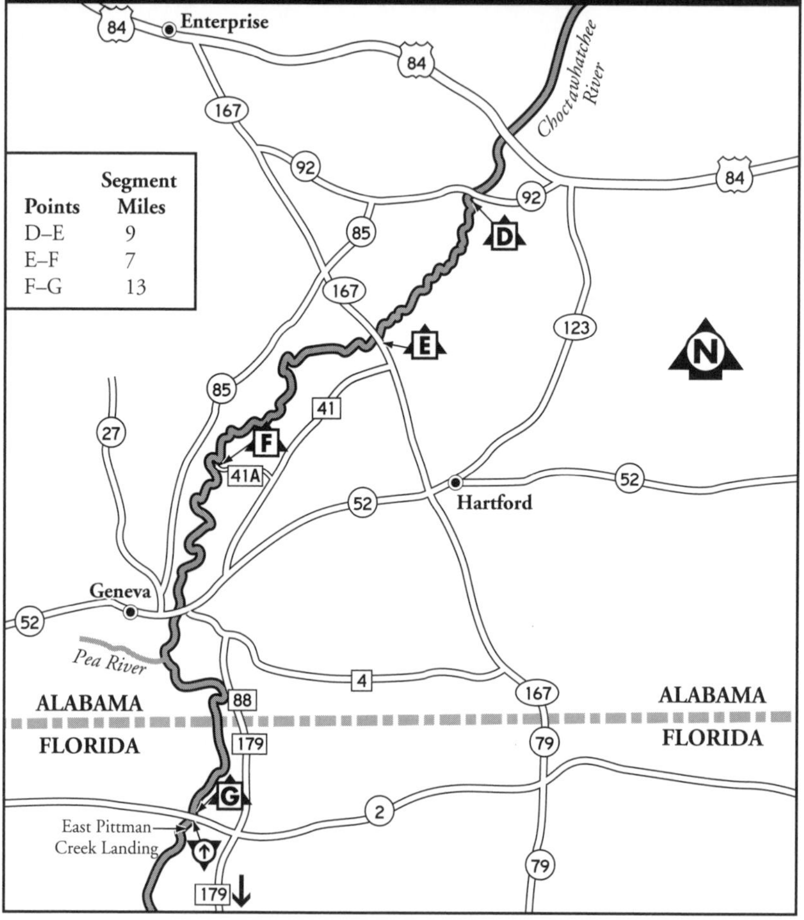

Points	Segment Miles
D–E	9
E–F	7
F–G	13

bank. The access to the ramp is from CR 41A. Shortly below this access there are several large sandbars suitable for camping. These bars have access from a road, however, and may be used for swimming and sunbathing. Downstream from these sandbars is another high, well-wooded bluff on the west bank. There is also a beaver dam on the east side with a lake behind it.

As the river bends to the east, sheer rock walls, 15 feet high, begin to appear with beautiful fern falls dripping down. This type of terrain continues almost to AL 52. One-half mile downstream from AL 52 there is an old railroad bridge that swings on the center piling. This indicates that it was probably built in the

early 1900s, when steamboats still used the river. The pilings for the bridge are made of brick, and the center piling has an unusual wooden structure built around it to protect it from floating trees during floods. There is a boat ramp at the park just above the confluence of the Pea and Choctawhatchee rivers, 0.5 miles below this bridge in the town of Geneva. It is 12 miles from AL 167 to the confluence.

The Pea River flows through south Alabama to the north of and almost parallel to the Choctawhatchee. It is a beautiful canoeing river and is excellent for canoe touring. After the confluence with the Pea, the Choctawhatchee widens to some 300 feet and remains wide over the next few miles, gradually narrowing to its customary 150-foot width. The banks continue to be high and heavily wooded, with large sandbars in the curves. It is about 5 miles from the Geneva access to the Florida state line. Somewhere in the area of the state line there is a clay bank 20 feet high on the east side with a large field on top. From this clay bank it is 3 miles to FL 2.

SHUTTLE: To reach the lowermost takeout from Exit 104 on I-10, take CR 279 north to US 90. Turn right and head east on US 90 to CR 179. Turn left on CR 179 and follow it north to Florida FL 2. Turn left and head west on FL 2 to reach East Pittman Creek boat landing on your left before the bridge over the Choctawhatchee. To reach the uppermost put-in from Hartford, Alabama, take AL 167 north to AL 85. Turn right on AL 85 and follow it to AL 92. Turn right on AL 92 and follow it to the put-in on the southwest side of the bridge over Choctawhatchee River.

GAUGE: Visual, Web. Checking the river in person is the most reliable method to determine water level. However, the Choctawhatchee is normally floatable year-round. A USGS gauge helpful in determining if the river is near average levels is Choctawhatchee at Caryville, FL.

FL 2 to Boynton Cutoff

class	I–I+
length	44
time	Varies
gauge	Visual, Web
level	N/A
gradient	1.2
scenery	B

DESCRIPTION: This section has several accesses for varying trip lengths and also makes an excellent paddle-camping trip. Downstream from FL 2 for the next 10 miles, the river is broad and shallow and has a good current as well as some of the largest sandbars found on any north Florida waterway. Sandbars of 10 to 15 acres in size are not uncommon. These sandbars are frequently covered

with tracks of the various birds and animals that inhabit this area. Of particular interest is the evidence of the beaver population. Practically driven to extinction by trappers in the early part of the century, they are obviously alive and well on the Choctawhatchee! An overnight camper on one of these large sandbars will often have the unique opportunity of seeing or hearing beavers going about their business of dragging willow branches to the water, feeding, stripping the bark of river birch, or slapping their tails on the water.

This section of the river is very remote. The few boats encountered will likely be small fishing boats, many of which do

Choctawhatchee River (Section C): FL 2 to Boynton Cutoff

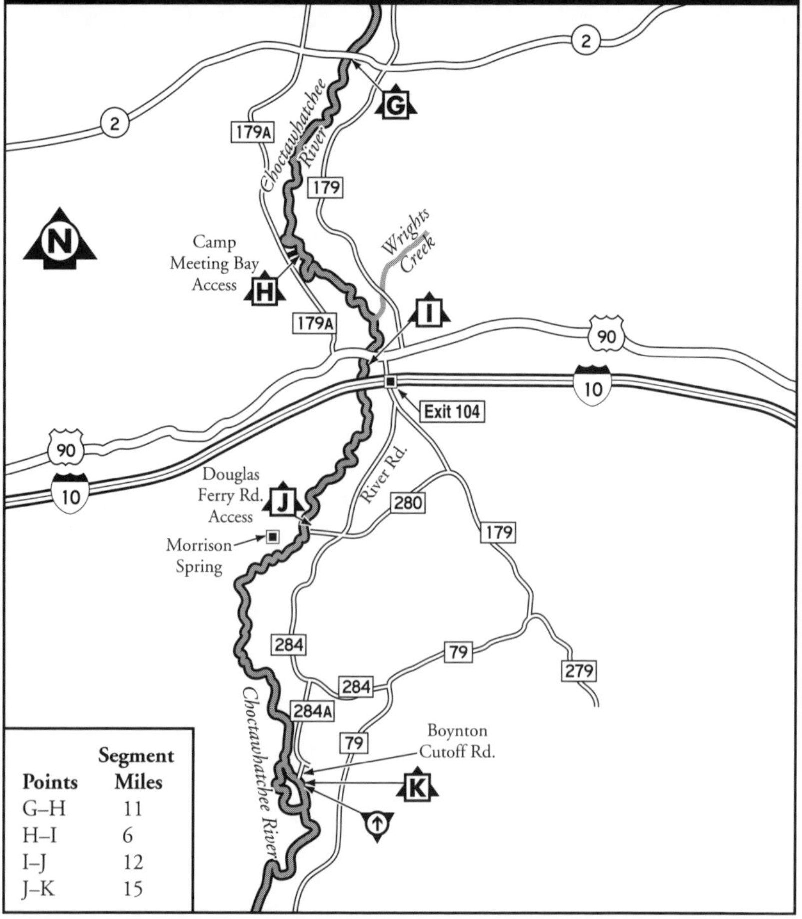

Points	Segment Miles
G–H	11
H–I	6
I–J	12
J–K	15

not carry motors but are propelled by sculling. There is a concrete landing at Curry Ferry, about 2 miles downstream from FL 2 on the east bank, and another landing on the west side at the end of a graded road opposite Dead River Lake, 3 more miles downstream. Some 5 miles below this last landing is Cork Island. This is only an island at high water, since at low water the east channel is blocked by sand. On the west bank, just opposite the island, is Blue Spring. This is the most northwest spring in Florida and is accessible only by boat. It is a deep, clear-blue hole suitable for swimming. Considering its remoteness and the swampy, inaccessible area around it, this water is probably safe for drinking if needed. Just over 1 mile below Blue Spring is Camp Meeting Bay and a concrete ramp on the west bank, 11 miles below FL 2. Camp Meeting Bay is a small community of cottages located on the top of a high, sandy bluff. Despite the height, most of the houses are built on pilings.

Three miles downstream from the Camp Meeting Bay access is the site of a former island. Annual flooding has washed away all but its northern tip, and the channel that went around it to the east now has trees growing in it. The channel to the west may also be obstructed with trees, but is navigable.

With the confluence of Wrights Creek, the river widens noticeably, the sandbars cease, and the current slows—this is less than 2 miles above US 90. At US 90, 17 miles below FL 2, the Choctawhatchee is about 100 yards wide, shallow, and has little current. This continues for 2 miles; in this section are the last of the large sandbars suitable for camping. I-10 crosses the river 1 mile below US 90. There is no access to the interstate from the river. About 1 mile below the interstate is an island whose west passage is blocked by trees. The east passage is partially obstructed with the debris caught up by old pilings. A large sand strip leads off to the east and evidently is a part of the river when the water is high. This is the last sandbar. Just below this point, the river narrows to 50 yards and the current picks up. The banks are low, but very heavily wooded. Willows and river birch often hang off the banks into the waterway and occasionally the banks are very swampy.

Five miles downstream from US 90 is a rapid at Gum Creek. The main river flows to the right—a portion flows off to the left, over a drop, through an obstructed area, and rejoins the river on the other side of a small island. The fast water can be heard as it is approached, but scouting is difficult. Even though the run is only 15 yards long, it has a standing wave and a crosscurrent, as well as the complication of downed trees. If in doubt, follow the main channel to the right.

In this area, the river begins to make wide oxbow bends that create islands. The river begins to widen again and the current slows as the landing at Douglas Ferry Road nears. Just above the landing is an island. The landing is on the east bank at the end of the island. It is 12 miles to this landing from US 90.

Beyond this landing the river continues to be wide with a good current. The banks remain heavily wooded, some 4 to 6 feet high. The run from Morrison Spring enters the river from the west about 2 miles below this access. It is 1 mile up this run to the spring, which is a 250 foot pool containing three cavities in the bottom. One of the cavities is said to be 50 feet deep, another is 100 feet deep, and a third is 300 feet deep. All three terminate in a large underground cavern of unknown dimensions. This is a popular spot for swimming and picnicking as well as for diving.

A mile below the confluence of the spring run, a large power line crosses the river, resulting in a partially cleared high area. There is also a dirt track on the west bank for about 0.5 miles below the power line. This is one of the only high, cleared areas on this section of the river. Below Morrison Spring, the river makes several large oxbow bends. Sandy Creek enters from the west side midway down one of the straighter sections. This creek is fed from Ponce de Leon Springs some 5 miles to the north. Just below Sandy Creek, there's a group of large houses on the west bank with no public access.

Less than 0.5 miles below the houses is a large island. The best run appears to be to the east, but the shortest route is west. Below the island small bayous begin to appear along with an occasional hunting and fishing camp. About 3 miles below the island the river takes a sharp turn to the south and begins a long, straight run. These long straights, broken by a few bends, will continue to just above Boynton Cutoff. The frequency of houses increases, although they tend to be set well back from the river.

At Boynton Cutoff, the main river goes west, to the right, but is narrower than the cutoff. To follow the cutoff, make a turn east. The water is always very swift in the cutoff. Just around the first bend is an old logging bridge that is usually a catchall for large logs and other debris. This bridge should be approached with caution because the water is swift and it may be difficult to find an opening. Around the next bend on the left is the takeout at the boat ramp on the east side of the river. When the Boynton Cutoff rejoins the Choctawhatchee River, the river becomes very broad and is frequented by large motorboats. It is 7 miles downstream to the bridge at FL 20.

SHUTTLE: To reach the Boynton Cutoff takeout from Exit 104 on I-10, take CR 279 south to River Road. Turn right on River Road, which becomes CR 284. Continue on CR 284 and follow it to CR 284A. Turn right on CR 284A and follow it to a right turn onto Boynton Cutoff Road, which dead-ends at the Boynton Cutoff public boat ramp, just past a few houses. To reach the FL 2 put-in from Exit 104 on I-10, take CR 279 north to US 90. Turn right and head east on US 90 to CR 179. Turn left on CR 179 and follow it north to FL 2. Turn left and head west on FL 2 to reach East Pittman Creek boat landing on the left before the bridge over the Choctawhatchee.

GAUGE: Visual, Web. Checking the river in person is the most reliable method to determine its water level. However, the Choctawhatchee is normally floatable year-round. A USGS gauge helpful in determining if the river is near average levels is Choctawhatchee at Caryville, FL.

The author wears a wide-brim hat on long paddles to tame bright sunlight and minimize face and neck burns

HOLMES CREEK

Holmes Creek begins near the Alabama–Florida line, northeast of the town of Bonifay. It is a tiny, unnavigable stream until 2 miles above Vernon, where the input from Beckton and Cypress springs enlarges it into a canoeable waterway. Except in periods of heavy rainfall, Holmes Creek tends to be clear and green. There is a wide variety of trees and the colorful reflections of many different hues of leaves and foliage in the clear water makes this a photogenic stream.

Beginning and ending in areas of high banks, the middle part of the Holmes Creek Canoe Trail runs through swamps characterized by many sloughs and bayous. Paddling into these can also provide an interesting experience. There are several small springs and creeks that feed Holmes Creek.

Trees along the banks and in the swamps include pine, a variety of oaks, magnolia, cypress, maple, sweet and black gums, and a number of others indigenous to north Florida. Alligators can be observed as well as turtles, raccoons, otters, and skunks. This stream is well known for good fishing in all seasons.

Holmes Creek has a low gradient and a lazy to almost nonexistent current. There are a few scattered houses on the higher banks, but overall the atmosphere is one of remoteness. It is a very pretty creek, easy to paddle, and offers good access. It makes an excellent one-day trip and would be pleasant for a leisurely overnight trip, even though campsites are somewhat scarce.

Although Holmes Creek flows into the Choctawhatchee River, canoeists usually prefer to takeout 6 miles above the confluence. It is another 3 miles to the Boynton Cutoff and an upstream paddle to the Boynton Cutoff access. The section of the Choctawhatchee at the Holmes Creek confluence is popular with large motorboats.

MAPS: Poplar Head, Vernon, Millers Ferry (USGS)

class	I
length	18
time	Varies
gauge	Visual
level	N/A
gradient	0.6
scenery	A+

VERNON TO MILLERS FERRY

DESCRIPTION: Over the years, paddle accesses have been opened and closed on Holmes Creek. Holmes Creek is wide at the Vernon access with high banks and some houses for the first few miles. A little over 5 miles downstream is a boat ramp with a short dock on the east bank. This is the site of Blue Spring. About 60 by 120 feet wide, and 7 to 10 feet deep, the spring emerges from a limestone cavity near the pool surface at the northeast end.

The stream alternates between high banks and swampy areas. Sloughs and backwaters become so frequent that it is difficult to distinguish between them and inflowing branches and streams. Continuing beyond the Millers Ferry Bridge means paddling all the way to the Choctawhatchee River, as the old Shell Landing is now restricted private property.

SHUTTLE: To reach the put-in from Bonifay, take FL 79 south to reach Vernon Wayside Park and a boat launch. The park is on the left just before crossing the bridge over Holmes Creek. To reach the lowermost takeout, continue south on FL 79 to CR

Holmes Creek: Vernon to Millers Ferry

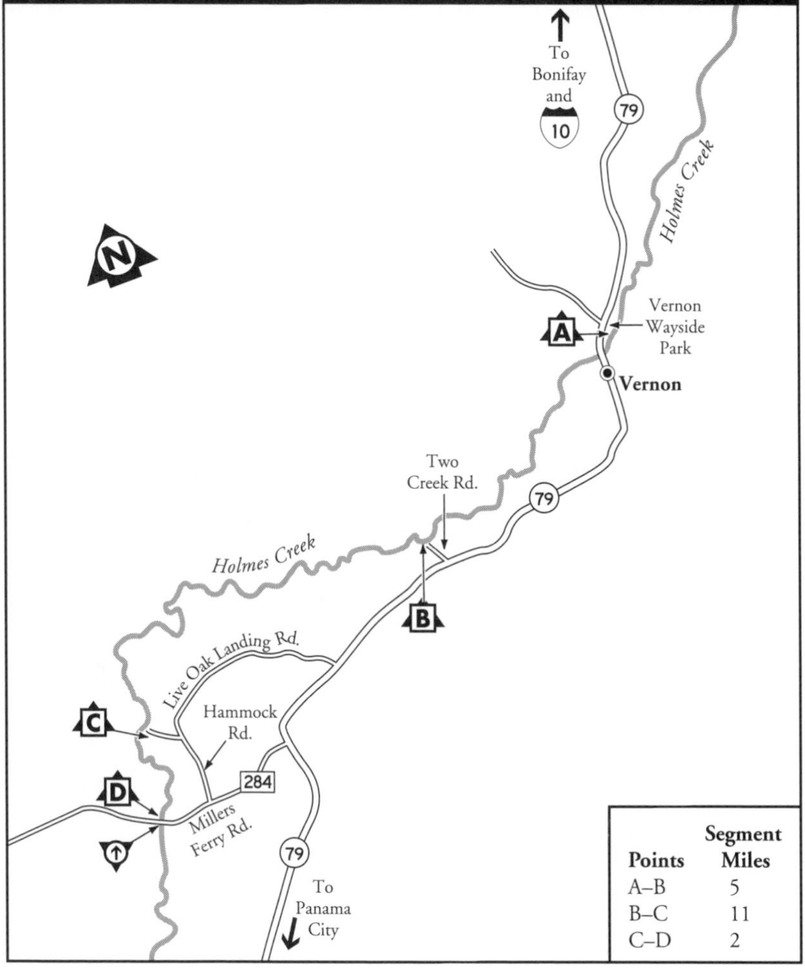

Points	Segment Miles
A–B	5
B–C	11
C–D	2

284. Turn right on CR 284 and follow it to the bridge over Holmes Creek. This private landing charges a fee for putting in or taking out your boat. Live Oak Landing is a public boat launch 2 miles upstream from CR 284. To reach it from CR 284, turn right on Hammock Road. After 2 miles, turn left onto Live Oak Landing Road and the public access there.

GAUGE: Visual. Checking the creek in person is the most reliable method to determine its water level. Holmes Creek is normally floatable year-round.

Econfina Creek is a narrow waterway

ECONFINA CREEK OF WASHINGTON AND BAY COUNTIES

Many paddlers consider Econfina Creek to be the most beautiful and challenging stream in Florida; undoubtedly, it is one of the most unique and unpredictable. The upper section of the creek drains 1,240 square miles of sandy, porous soil through a steep, narrow ravine with a gradient of than 7.9 feet per mile! The unusual composition of the soils in this area has permitted this creek to cut deep canyons some 15 feet high that result in exciting chutes of rapidly cascading water. It is the only stream in Florida that is recommended for experienced canoeists only.

On the lower section, Econfina Creek is fed by a number of outstanding springs. The Gainer Springs group consists of 3 major springs that constitute 1 of Florida's 27 first-magnitude springs. In addition, there is a bevy of other minor springs along the banks. Blue Springs, Williford Springs, Walsingham Spring, and Pitt Springs are among those that have been named. Spectacular Emerald Springs discharges from a 25-foot-tall limestone bank. This lower section is an easy run and is frequented by tubers in the summertime.

The very high banks on Econfina Creek vary from yellow sand bluffs up to 50 feet tall to beautiful limestone walls, dripping with ferns. Many plants native to the Appalachian Mountains are seen along the banks. Dogwood, redbud, masses of mountain laurel, and several varieties of wild azalea make it a garden in the spring. Oakleaf hydrangea grows in the crevices of the limestone walls and spills white flowers down the banks throughout the summer months. Trees commonly seen include beech, cedar, sweet gum, holly, magnolia, red maple, cypress, and Carolina silver bell as well as various types of pine and oak. Glimpses of wildlife are hard to catch because of the high banks, but deer, raccoon, otter, bobcat, fox, and beaver are indigenous to the area.

Luckily, these special lands have been acquired by the Northwest Florida Water Management District, and nearly the entire upper creek and much of the lower creek are bordered by public lands, keeping the setting natural. Additionally, accesses have been improved and the sand roads, while still a little ragged, are in much better shape than days gone by.

Because it is generally very shallow in the upper section, the canoeist can expect a number of pull-overs. Stobs, logs, and rock ledges are to be avoided and sharp bends need to be maneuvered. At high water, the combination of these obstructions with very fast current can be extremely hazardous. The drainage-ditch nature of this creek makes it prone to flash flooding, and it is absolutely essential to stay off the stream at high water or if thunderstorms are predicted.

Even though it is only 22 miles, paddling the entire run on Econfina Creek in a single day is not recommended. It is possible to make a comfortable one-day trip by taking out at Walsingham Bridge. Camping is a good option, whether at the primitive sites near Walsingham Bridge or along the Econfina. However, the high banks and lack of sandbars make choosing a campsite a challenge. There are a number of excellent spots high off the river in the beech woods. Beech trees have widespread branches that discourage ground cover. As a result, nice clearings, perfect for campsites, can often be found under them.

Econfina is a Muskogean Indian word that is said to mean "natural bridge." Evidently there was such a bridge on this creek near the site where FL 20 now crosses the stream. No evidence of it remains. There is another stream of the same name, but pronounced differently, about 100 miles east, between St. Marks and Perry. This Econfina Creek rhymes with "shiner"—Econfiner. (Econfina River in Taylor County rhymes with "beaner"—Econfeaner.) See Rivers of the Big Bend for more information about the Econfina River of Taylor County. Also, be aware that dogs are not allowed on Northwest Florida Water Management Land.

MAPS: Compass Lake, Cap Lake, Bennett (USGS)

class	I–II
length	10
time	Varies
gauge	Phone, visual
level	2–4
gradient	7.9!
scenery	A+

SCOTT BRIDGE TO WALSINGHAM BRIDGE

DESCRIPTION: This upper section is recommended for canoes and short sit-on-top kayaks only—sharp turns and numerous obstructions require you to get out of the boat to surmount them. The river, 15 to 20 feet wide, is generally shallow and swift at this point. Some small sandbars appear on the first few bends. Very soon, the stream begins to twist and turn with drops over submerged tree trunks and rocky ledges. The banks are from 4 to 6 feet high, canopied with trees, and in some places the stream is hardly wider than the canoe. For the next 4 miles, the creek has intermittent high-walled flumes interspersed with very short stretches of flatter, shallower water. Trees that have fallen across the creek can be very hazardous in the narrow, swift chutes that lead around blind turns.

About 4 miles above Walsingham Bridge, the banks begin to drop somewhat and the stream becomes more wide and shallow. This results in a great many obstructions in the water, such as fallen trees and large limbs, many of which must be pulled over. This is especially true in low water.

A high sandbank on the east side of the river marks the beginning of some strenuous canoeing. At low water, the next 2 miles will have numerous pull-overs. The remainder of the trip to Walsingham Bridge is spaced with some shallow spots and some sections where the water is 3 to 4 feet deep. The run from an unnamed spring flows into the creek from the east bank.

The Florida Trail (FT) runs alongside the creek this entire section, allowing the added benefit of hiking and paddling. Along the way, the FT bridges Econfina Creek twice before reaching the Walsingham Bridge. The water management district has developed a few primitive campsites for overnighters. One of these is

Econfina Creek (Sections A–B): Scott Bridge to CR 388

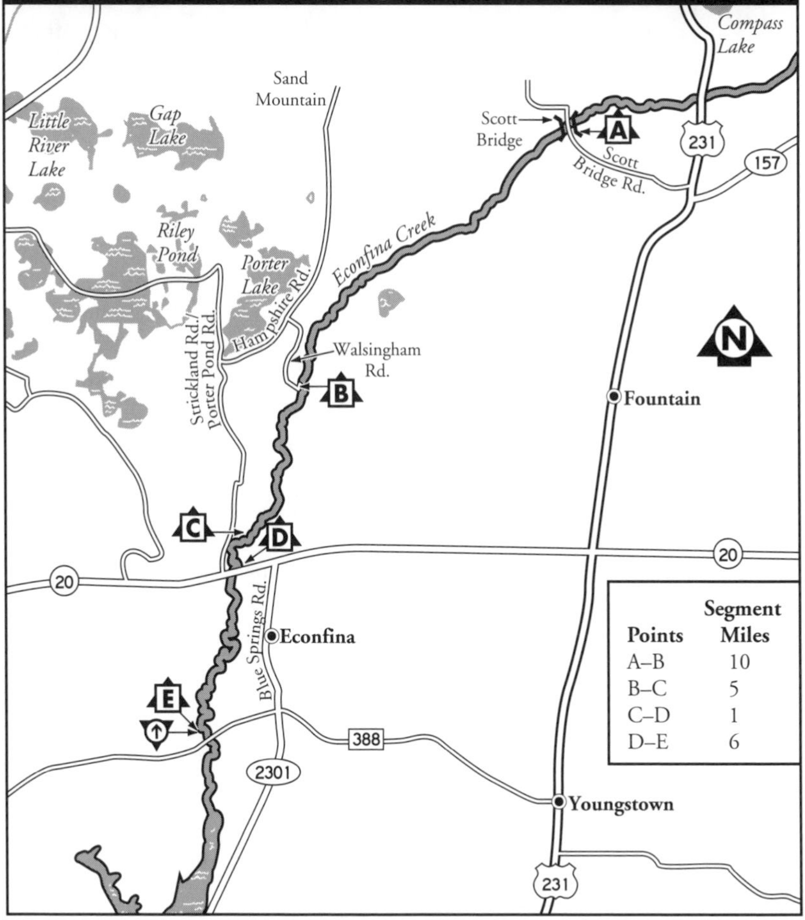

Points	Segment Miles
A–B	10
B–C	5
C–D	1
D–E	6

located by a spring boil in the middle of the river. Walsingham Bridge area has an excellent canoe launch and primitive campsites.

SHUTTLE: To reach the lowermost takeout from Panama City, take US 231 north to FL 20. Turn left on FL 20 and follow it west, bridging Econfina Creek nearby a good access, to reach Strickland Road. Turn right, north, on Strickland Road, and follow it as it becomes Porter Pond Road. Veer right at Hampshire Road and follow it to Walsingham Bridge Road. Turn right at Walsingham Bridge Road and follow it over Econfina Creek. Once across Econfina Creek, follow the gravel road to the canoe launch. To reach the Scott Bridge access, backtrack to FL 20 and head east to US 231. Turn left, north on US 231, to reach Scott Bridge Road, which is just north of CR 167. Turn left, west on Scott Bridge Road, and follow it to the bridge over Econfina Creek.

GAUGE: Phone, visual. Ideally, the Scott Bridge gauge should read 2 to 4 feet. At low water, expect more log jams. At 4 to 9 feet, be prepared for very fast water but less log jams. Stay off the river above 9 feet. Econfina Canoe Livery, at (850) 722-9032, can provide general river conditions for paddlers.

B

Walsingham Bridge to CR 388

class	I+
length	12
time	6
gauge	Phone
level	2–4
gradient	4
scenery	A

DESCRIPTION: From Walsingham Bridge to Blue Springs, the run remains scenic, although not the gorge run that the upper section is. There is a small spring, Walsingham Spring, on the west bank, about 0.25 miles below the bridge, and another spring that boils up in the river another 0.5 miles down. Mitchell Mill Creek flows in from the east bank just below the bridge. The stream is wider, the banks lower, and there are several pull-overs at normal-water level. A few houses appear on the east bank 1 mile above Blue Springs, a recreation area that is now a group campsite (by reservation only, at (850) 539-5999). It is used as an access only by those reserving the site.

Blue Springs is not visible from the river but is reached by paddling up the spring run, or by beaching at the point where the run flows into the river. Coming downstream, watch for the 10-foot-wide spring running on river left. The run enters on the east bank among some juniper stumps in the river. Paddle upstream 150 yards, and look left for the steps at the second split. There are two caves in the Blue Springs pool.

Downstream, the river banks lower and the whole setting becomes swampier. The river leaves public lands temporarily and a few houses appear. Several springs, among them Williford and Pitt, enter from the west bank. Williford is a group day-use area, and Pitt is a day-use area for everyone. Reach Econfina Canoe Livery on the west bank 2 miles below Blue Springs. It offers rentals, shuttles, and access. It is 1 mile downstream from the livery to the FL 20 access, which is on the east bank opposite Pitt Spring.

The section of river from FL 20 to CR 388 is 6 miles in length. Most of the banks, alternating between swampy and high, are private land. The creek is popular with tubers, and you may encounter a few motorboats. Even though this section can be busy, it has many springs that are attractive. The Ganier Springs group begins within 1 mile of FL 20 and emerges from both banks. Emerald Springs, the most spectacular of this group, is on the west bank and discharges from under a 25-foot limestone bank. Do not climb onto Emerald Springs or the rock bluff at these springs.

The section of Econfina Creek below the CR 388 bridge is accessible by large motorboats and is also the route for boat traffic to Deer Point Lake. It is generally not of interest to paddlers.

SHUTTLE: To reach the lowermost access from Panama City, take US 231 north to CR 388. Turn left on CR 388 and follow it to the bridge over Econfina Creek. The access is on the northwest side of the bridge. To reach the Walsingham Bridge access, backtrack to Blue Springs Road, turn left, and follow it north to FL 20. Turn left on FL 20 and follow it west, bridging Econfina Creek near a good access, to reach Strickland Road. Turn right, north, on Strickland Road and follow it as it becomes Porter Pond Road. Veer right at Hampshire Road and follow it to Walsingham Bridge Road. Turn right at Walsingham Bridge Road and follow it over Econfina Creek. Once across Econfina Creek, follow the gravel road to the canoe launch.

GAUGE: Phone. Call Econfina Canoe Livery, at (850) 722-9032, for the latest river conditions. Much of the lower river is spring-fed and floatable year-round.

CHIPOLA RIVER

The Chipola River rises in southeast Alabama and flows southward 80 miles to the Apalachicola River. In between, it goes underground, flows through a state park, and becomes part of Dead Lake. Over 50 miles of it is a canoe trail that varies from sections of swift, tree-lined, limestone creek to a broad, slow-moving stream, with occasional bluffs, cliffs, and caves. It also offers options of a hazardous log canal, a rapid, and many springs and tributaries to explore.

The Chipola becomes navigable just above the FL 162 bridge in northern Jackson County with the confluence of Cowarts Creek, Marshall Creek, and Hays Spring Run. It picks up momentum with the addition of several small streams as well as Waddells Mill Creek, and goes underground at Florida Caverns State Park. A logging canal can carry the adventurous 0.5 miles over the natural bridge to the river rise.

Although the Chipola has an aura of remoteness, it runs through heavily populated agricultural areas and except in the extreme lower section, the river is never far from fields, farms, and paved roads. The river usually varies from a smoky green to a clear emerald green depending on rainfall, runoff, and siltation. In periods of heavy rainfall it will be a muddy yellow or tan due to runoff from the red clay topsoil of the surrounding agricultural lands.

Since the terrain on the Chipola varies from high bluffs and sandy hills to lowland swamps, there is a wide variety of trees and vegetation. Almost every kind of tree indigenous to north Florida can be seen. Flowering plants include wild azalea, honeysuckle, daisies of various hues, and the spectacular cardinal flower. Alligators and turtles are the most commonly seen animals, but deer, raccoons, opossums, and turkeys can also be found.

The Chipola is noted for good fishing, with catfish, bream, bass, and even mullet frequently caught. The bird life is extremely abundant, and the lower section of the river is especially suited to birdwatching.

The Chipola is especially suited for canoe trips of several days' duration, but access points are also located at convenient intervals for day trips. However, the Chipola does not have sandbars and the lower banks tend to be swampy, therefore good campsites are not plentiful. Much of it is private property as well. Watch for areas that have obviously been used as hunting or fishing camps and do not display "No trespassing" signs.

MAPS: Cottondale East, Marianna, Oakdale, Altha West, Clarksville, Frink (USGS)

FL 162 TO FLORIDA CAVERNS STATE PARK

class	I
length	5
time	3
gauge	Phone
level	N/A
gradient	3.2
scenery	A

DESCRIPTION: This section of the river tends to be tan and shallow at normal-water levels. The banks are low and swampy for the first mile. The remains of Bellamy Bridge cross the river about 0.5 miles below the put-in. This is a historic road and the site of the bridge is a short distance west of the location of the Bellamy Plantation, a pre–Civil War farm with a colorful history.

Chipola River (Section A):
FL 162 to Florida Caverns State Park

A
167
162
162
Bellamy Bridge
Bellamy Bridge Rd.
Waddels Mill Creek
Chipola River
N
167
B
State Park Rd.
166
hazardous canal; paddling not recommended
entrance to Florida Caverns State Park
STATE PARK
166
Yancey Bridge
C
90
Marianna
90

Points	Segment Miles
A–B	5

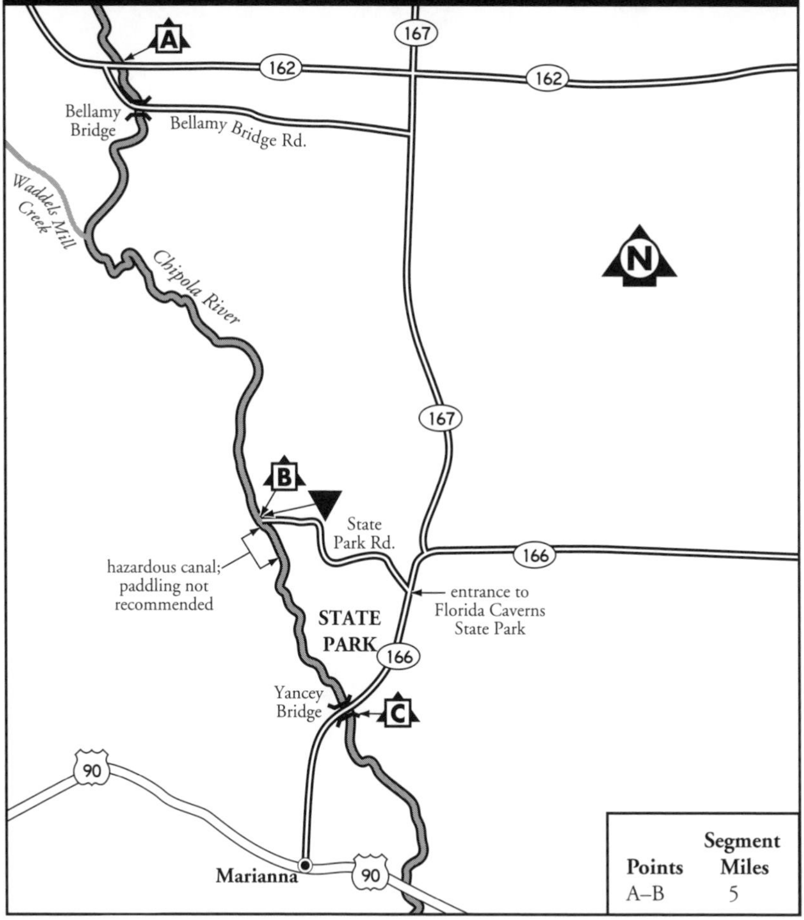

The run from Waddells Mill Creek enters the Chipola about 1.5 miles from FL 162. This millpond is formed from Rockarch Spring, a second-magnitude spring, and is a site that was frequented by the Chatot Indians. It is listed in the National Register of Historic Places. Baker Creek, a tributary of Waddells Mill Creek, is also spring fed by Daniel, Tanner, Webbville, and several unnamed springs.

After the confluence of Waddells Mill Creek, the Chipola widens considerably and becomes more like a narrow lake for about 0.5 miles. It narrows again and continues through a low, swampy area with numerous bends. The low banks in this area

Chipola River (Section B): Yancey Bridge to Peacock Bridge

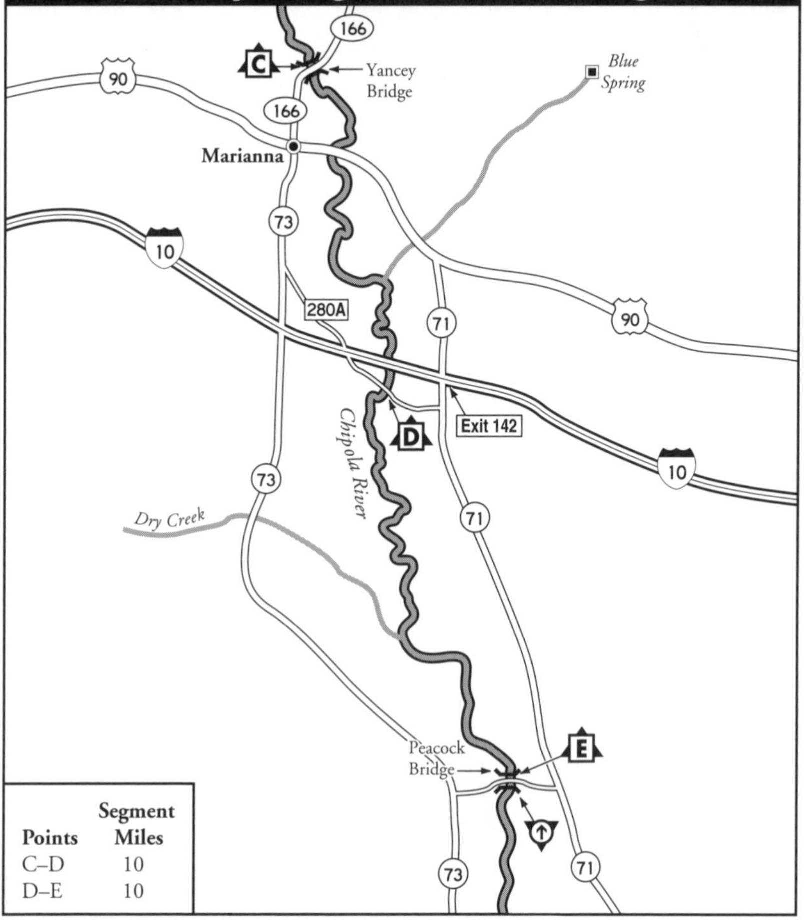

Points	Segment Miles
C–D	10
D–E	10

permit the paddler to be at eye level with the surrounding swamps and forests.

One mile above Florida Caverns State Park, Bosel Spring run enters the river from the east bank. The main spring is about 0.2 miles up the run and is a 50-foot pool with three narrow vents about 25 feet deep. The water is a clear blue, offset by bright green waterweeds. There are three other spring pools in the Bosel group, all separated by natural bridges.

A boat ramp is located at the state park where the river goes underground. A canal was dug for the purpose of floating logs down the river to river rise, where the river seeps back up from underground. This canal is 0.5 miles long, extremely narrow, and frequently choked with trees, logs, and the remains of old boats. At high water it is dangerously fast and technical; at low water there are many pull-overs. The state park service strongly recommends avoiding the canal. Smart canoeists choose to take out at the state park boat ramp and resume their trip at FL 166.

When using the state park for launching, don't forget that the gates are closed at sundown, a variable time, according to the season of the year. Be sure to check with the park ranger to find out what time the gates will be locked during your visit.

SHUTTLE: To reach the put-in from Marianna, take FL 166 north to CR 167. Veer left on CR 167 to reach CR 162. Turn left on CR 162 and follow it to the bridge over the Chipola River. Access is on the southwest side of the bridge. To reach the takeout from Marianna, take FL 166 north to the entrance to Florida Caverns State Park. There is a fee for entering the park.

GAUGE: Phone. Call Florida Caverns State Park at (850) 482-9598 for the latest stream conditions.

Yancey Bridge to Peacock Bridge

class	I
length	20
time	Varies
gauge	Phone, Web
level	N/A
gradient	1.2
scenery	B

DESCRIPTION: From Yancey Bridge it is 2-mile paddle upstream to the river rise. This is not a dramatic sight, however, as the river seems to seep back through the woods rather than rise in any one clearly defined spot. The run from Blue Hole Spring also flows into the river in this section, but having traversed almost 2 miles of swamp, it loses its clarity and is not easily identified.

Going downriver from FL 166, the banks continue to be low and swampy with some limestone in evidence. Less than 0.5 miles below the FL 166 put-in, the run from Sand Bag Springs

enters from the west bank. It is 50 yards up the run to the spring, which is located on private property, and is usually indistinguishable from the river.

The Chipola flows under US 90 2 miles down from FL 166, but there isn't good access to the river at that point. This section of the stream tends to be littered due to the proximity of the town of Marianna and heavy usage.

Just at the edge of the city limits of Marianna and about 1 mile below US 90, the Louisville and Nashville Railroad tracks cross the Chipola. The west bank is very high at this point, with a grotto carved out of the limestone that is partially the result of a natural cave and partially man-made by limestone having been removed for building purposes. A pretty little pool at the bottom of this bluff appears to be a miniature quarry as well as a spring.

The limestone wall continues along the west bank of the river for another 0.5 miles to the opening of a large cavern known locally as Alamo Cave. At low water, you can walk into the cave, which is said to penetrate deeply into the hillside. Shortly below the cave, a spring run enters from the east bank. Seventy-five yards up the run is a small, deep pool created by Dykes Spring; a couple of well-used campsites appear at this spot.

Approximately 6 miles downstream, Spring Creek, a major tributary of the Chipola, enters from the east. Fed by one first-magnitude and several second-magnitude springs, Spring Creek is the run from Merritts Mill Pond. The head spring for Merritts Mill Pond is Blue Spring. One of Florida's largest and more popular springs, the area is underlain by caves and tunnels hundreds of feet long with depths approaching 300 feet. There is a second spring 300 feet downstream and another 1,000 feet to the south. Numerous other springs are said to flow into the 4-mile-long lake that ends at a dam at US 90. Spring Creek begins just below the dam and flows about 2 miles to the Chipola River. This is an alternative put-in for a Chipola River trip that is well worth seeing. Due to the shallow water and swift current, it is difficult to paddle upstream from the Chipola into Spring Creek for any distance.

At low water, there will be several rocky shoals in the 1 mile from the mouth of Spring Creek to I-10. The access at FL 280A is less than a mile downstream from the interstate on the southwest side of the bridge. It is 10 miles from Yancey Bridge to FL 280A.

The Chipola below FL 280 offers a pleasant trip with steep, sloping banks and a number of small, rocky shoals. The river splits to run around several small islands with good runs on both sides. The current tends to be moderate to slow most of the way, but picks up on the shoals.

Dry Creek enters the Chipola about 7 miles from this access. This very long creek flows into the river from 10 miles to the west and is fed by a number of smaller creeks as well as by Spring Lake. This lake is fed by at least four springs, including Springboard, Mill Pond, Double, and Gadsen. Dry Creek is reported to be canoeable in wet weather. There are perhaps a dozen houses on this section, but they are scattered in such a manner as not to intrude on the river's seeming remoteness. It is 10 miles from FL 280A to the takeout at CR 278.

SHUTTLE: To reach the takeout from Marianna, take US 90 east to FL 71. Turn right and take FL 71 south to CR 278. Turn right on CR 278 to reach the access at Peacock Bridge. To reach the put-in from Marianna, take FL 166 north to the Yancey Bridge over the Chipola River. The boat launch is on the southwest side of the bridge.

GAUGE: Phone, Web. Call Bear Paw Adventures at (850) 482-4948 for the latest stream conditions. The Chipola is normally floatable year-round. A helpful USGS gauge to determine average river levels for any given period is Chipola River at Marianna, FL.

PEACOCK BRIDGE TO FL 71

class	I–I+
length	31
time	Varies
gauge	Phone, Web
level	N/A
gradient	1
scenery	A–

DESCRIPTION: This section can be broken into runs of 8, 10, and 13 miles, respectively. The first 8-mile run from CR 278 to FL 274 is similar to the preceding 10 miles. Sink Creek enters from the east just minutes below CR 278 and Ring Jaw Island, and shoals appear 4 miles downstream. The soft limestone bottom that is evident on most of the Chipola is especially obvious on this section. Sizable cracks in the riverbed can be seen when the water is clear and a number of oddly shaped rocks, such as Table Rock, attest to the power of the water on the soft strata.

This is one of the most popular runs on the Chipola due to the presence of Look and Tremble Rapid, a limestone shoal that crosses the river just below the FL 274 bridge. The dirt road beside the river provides easy access to the rapid, which is a popular picnic spot as well as a destination for tubers and swimmers.

At normal-water levels, the rapid has a small standing wave at the bottom and a minor hydraulic. It should be run on the east bank, or in high water through the middle. For the first 5 miles below the rapid, the banks tend to be vertical limestone 6 to 8

feet high. Tenmile Creek flows in from the west through high limestone walls and is canoeable in wet weather.

About halfway down this section, the banks become lower and gentler with only a few high bluffs. Fourmile Creek enters from the west. The current is usually helpful on this section, but slows as the river becomes deeper and broader shortly above FL 20. There are a number of houses visible from the river and several boat landings and other access points. It is an easy and pleasant float trip with rapids to lend interest. Campsites are limited due to the high banks and presence of houses and private

Chipola River (Section C): Peacock Bridge to FL 71

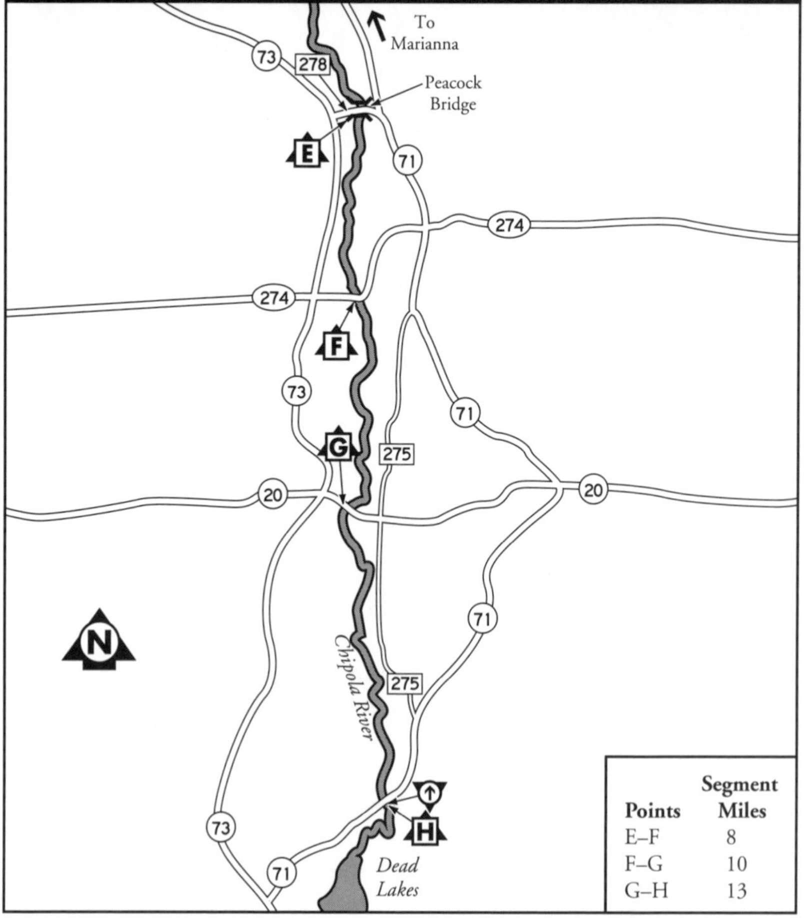

Points	Segment Miles
E–F	8
F–G	10
G–H	13

landowners. It is 10 miles from FL 274 to FL 20, and there's a good access at a wayside park.

The character of the Chipola undergoes a radical change below FL 20 as it leaves the highlands and descends into the swamps. For several miles below FL 20, the high banks and limestone bottom continue, but after the convergence of Fox Creek from the east, the banks begin to lower and the nature of the vegetation begins to change. Patches of saw grass and lily pads appear, and less is seen of oaks and pines and more of tupelo and cypress, along with some sycamore and cedar.

Juniper Creek, a sometimes canoeable stream, enters from the west 5 miles down; beyond this point the river becomes even swampier. Sloughs and bayous become more numerous and the current is slower. About 3 miles above FL 71, the river splits and flows into a thick swamp called Ward Lake. Following the current will eventually lead directly to the bridge. It is 13 miles from FL 20 to the takeout at FL 71. Don't wander too far into the swamp unless it is early in the day and you have a compass along.

Wildlife is abundant on this section and includes alligators, otters, turtles, waterbirds, and ducks (in season). Deer, raccoons, opossums, and other animals indigenous to this area are common in the woods. Fishing is said to be excellent, and catches include bass, bream, catfish, and trout. Camping would be possible in the first 2 miles, but campsites are scarce after that.

Below FL 71, the Chipola River continues through a swampy area for several miles until it runs into Dead Lake. After traversing the lake for 7 or 8 miles, it regroups and flows south through a very large swamp for another 10 miles until it flows into the Apalachicola River. It is considered unwise to travel the Dead Lake or the lower section of the river without a guide. Due to the distance, lack of access, and lack of campsites, it also is not appropriate for most canoeists.

SHUTTLE: To reach the put-in from Blountstown take FL 71 north to CR 278. Turn left on CR 278 to reach the put-in at Peacock Bridge. To reach the lowermost takeout from Blountstown, travel south on FL 71 to the private boat launch and campground on the east side of the Chipola River.

GAUGE: Phone, Web. Call Scott's Ferry General Store at (850) 674-2900 for the latest river conditions. The Chipola is normally floatable year-round. A helpful USGS gauge to determine average river levels for any given period is the Chipola River near Altha, FL.

The Central Panhandle

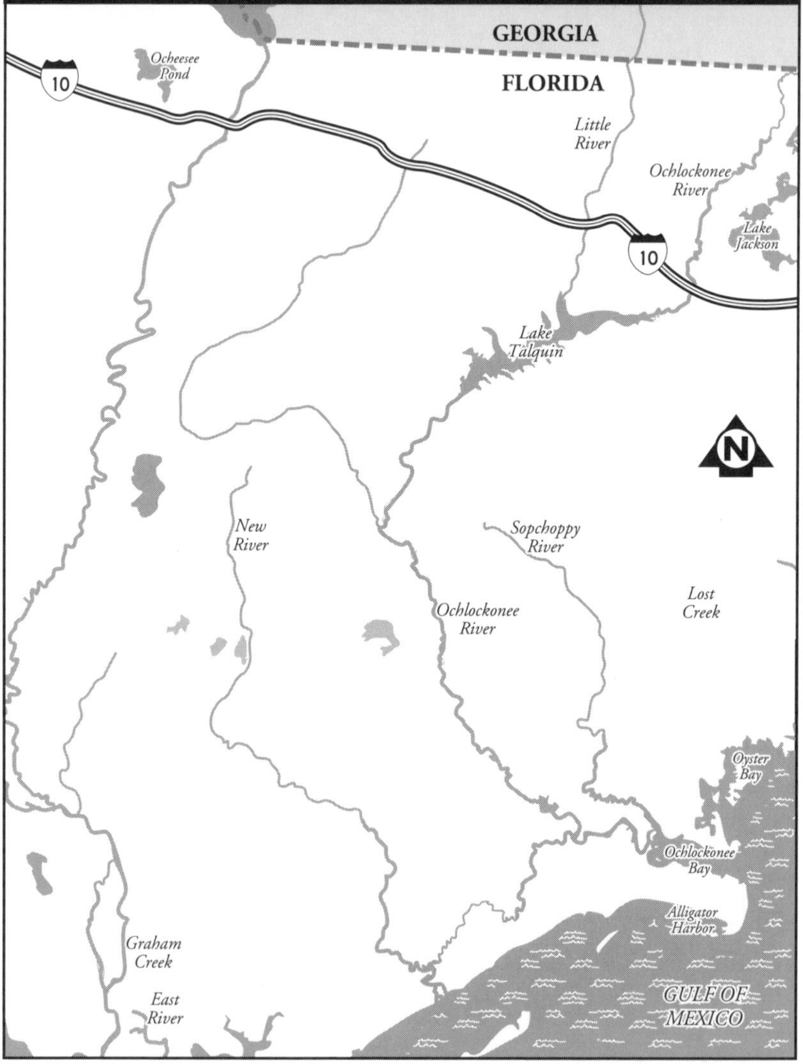

GEORGIA
FLORIDA
10
Ocheesee Pond
Little River
Ochlockonee River
Lake Jackson
10
Lake Talquin
N
New River
Sopchoppy River
Ochlockonee River
Lost Creek
Oyster Bay
Ochlockonee Bay
Alligator Harbor
Graham Creek
East River
GULF OF MEXICO

part **Two**

THE CENTRAL PANHANDLE

OCHLOCKONEE RIVER

One of north Florida's longest rivers, the Ochlockonee begins in Worth County, Georgia, and flows for nearly 150 miles to the Gulf of Mexico near Panacea, Florida. In Georgia, its major tributaries are the West Fork of the Ochlockonee and Barnetts Creek. In Florida it is fed by Telogia Creek and the Little River, but throughout its length it is also the recipient of runoff from hundreds of tiny creeks, streams, and rivulets.

Above GA 93 the stream is narrow and obstructed by deadfalls and willow trees. Below Ochlockonee River State Park it is as wide as a bay—windy, tidal, and popular with motorboats. For canoeing purposes, the sections from GA 93 to the state park, a distance of 100 miles, are preferred.

Below US 90 in Florida, the river flows for 19 miles through the man-made Lake Talquin. The lake is seldom more than 2 miles wide, but has many islands, hammocks, and finger lakes that can obscure the canoe trail. Like most lakes, it can be windy with high waves and is frequented by motorboats. There is also a dam just above FL 20 that must be portaged. Most canoeists paddle the Ochlockonee either above or below the lake.

Once it flows out of Lake Talquin, the distances between accesses lengthen. The river flows through the Apalachicola National Forest for over 50 miles with only one bridge and a very limited number of boat landings. Since the Ochlockonee is prone to extensive flooding, there are few houses or other encroachments along the banks.

Vegetation on the Ochlockonee is characterized by upland hardwoods and pine forests on the higher banks banded by a corridor of lowland trees such as cypress, black gum, birch, and willow near the water. The serpentine course of the waterway lends itself to many sandbars, and campsites are not difficult to find. The water is usually tannin-stained, except in areas where agricultural runoff may cloud it to a tannish-yellow. In fact, the word Ochlockonee comes from the Hitchiti Native American language and is said to mean "yellow river."

Upper sections of the river are owned by individuals and paper companies and care should be taken in selecting campsites. The lower

part of the Ochlockonee River flows through the Apalachicola National Forest, and there are a number of national forest recreational areas on its banks that provide good camping facilities. Most of these areas are located on the east bank off of so-called lakes that are adjacent to the river and may be difficult to find. These lakes are actually arms or backwater areas of the river. A national forest map will be invaluable to the paddler in locating these campsites. It is also wise to ask directions from fishermen about the location of specific sites.

Since most of the river is a part of various wildlife management areas, the variety of wildlife is extensive. Deer are commonly sighted, as are raccoons, turtles, and alligators. Present but less visible are black bears, wild hogs, and panthers. Endangered species found on the river are the Southern bald eagle and red-cockaded woodpecker. Fish are plentiful in the Ochlockonee and include bass, bream, and catfish.

MAPS: Apalachicola National Forest map, Cairo South, Beachton, Calvary (Georgia), Lake Jackson, Havana South, Midway, Lake Talquin, Bloxham, Ward, Smith Creek, Thousand Yard Bay, Sanborn (Florida) (USGS)

class	I
length	29
time	Varies
gauge	Visual, Web
level	N/A
gradient	1
scenery	B

GA 93 to Old Bainbridge Road

DESCRIPTION: Although adventurous canoeists sometimes put in above this point, this is generally considered the most northern section of the Ochlockonee that can be paddled with any degree of ease. Even so, it too should be avoided during periods of low water; in the summer months the overhanging branches of willow thickets can lead to an uncomfortable trip.

The stream tends to be very narrow and twisting with many obstructions such as stobs and downed trees in the waterway. Since it drains from a vast agricultural area, the water is usually a muddy brown. There are some sandbars on the insides of bends that can be used for campsites. The banks tend to be heavily forested and are usually private property. A county road crosses the river downstream, availing an access. It is 15 miles from GA 93 to FL 12.

Below FL 12 is a very remote section of river—the terrain tends to be swampy behind a corridor of banks and hardwoods. The current is generally slow and lazy, around large sweeping turns, making a long 14 miles. The water may still be yellowish in color, but is not as muddy as the upper sections because it is now draining a swampy area and is influenced by tannin-colored tributaries.

Four miles down from FL 12, the Ochlockonee flows within a mile of a large lake, Lake Iamonia, to the east. Between the river

Ochlockonee River (Section A): GA 93 to Old Bainbridge Road

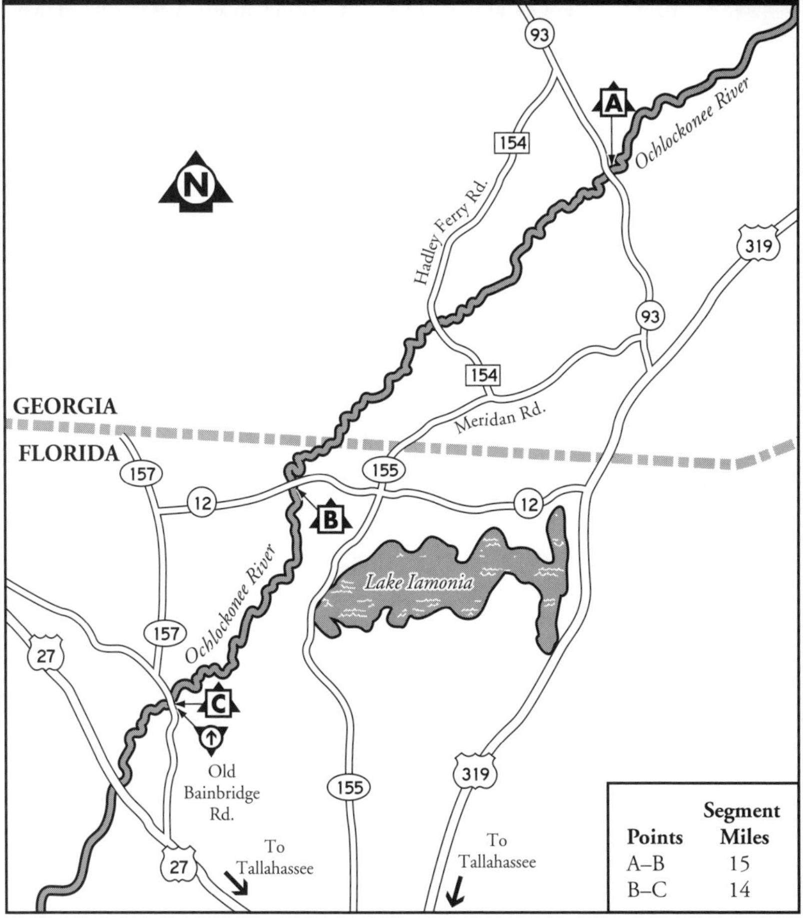

Points	Segment Miles
A–B	15
B–C	14

and the lake, there is an extensive swamp, and at its south end a number of small creeks flow in from the east bank. This is a section of river with a generous population of alligators.

The river is crooked throughout and sandbars appear frequently on the bends. There are several fishing-hunting camps, but no signs of development. As you approach the bridge at Old Bainbridge Road, fishermen in small boats may be encountered. It is 14 miles from FL 12 to Old Bainbridge Road.

SHUTTLE: To reach the put-in from Exit 196 on I-10 just north of Tallahassee, take US 27 north to Leon County 0361, Old

Bainbridge Road. Turn right on Old Bainbridge Road and follow it to a bridge over Ochlockonee River. There is a boat ramp on the northeast side of the bridge. To reach the put-in from Tallahassee, take US 319 north into Georgia and GA 93. Turn left on GA 93 and follow it to the bridge over Ochlockonee River. A boat ramp is on the northeast side of the river. To reach the take-out from Tallahassee take FL 20 west to Coe Landing Road. Turn right on Coe Landing Road and follow it to the dead end at the public boat ramp.

GAUGE: Visual, Web. The only way to determine water level is in person. However, the Ochlockonee is normally floatable year-round. To determine if the river is at average flows for any given period a helpful USGS gauge is Ochlockonee River near Thomasville, GA.

B

OLD BAINBRIDGE ROAD TO COE LANDING

class	I
length	17
time	8
gauge	Visual, Web
level	N/A
gradient	1
scenery	B

DESCRIPTION: By Old Bainbridge Road the river has become wider and less winding. However, it still has many turns and the potential for a lot of obstacles. There is some evidence of development in this section. It is 4 miles to US 27, a dual-lane highway with no good access to the river. Below US 27, the river runs very straight for 2 miles to just above the boat ramp at Tower Road. Directly above the boat ramp the river makes an oxbow around a small island; the ramp is on the east bank. It is 6 miles from Old Bainbridge Road to the Tower Road boat ramp.

Below the Tower Road boat ramp, the river begins to engage in some extreme turns again, often almost doubling back on itself. The current is very slow, and the banks begin to be low and swampy. After the first 2 miles below Tower Road, the river becomes less twisting. It flows under I-10 about 1 mile above the bridge across the Ochlockonee River. It is 5 miles from Tower Road to US 90.

Below US 90, the river becomes even wider and there is a mile-long straight stretch. Banks along this stretch tend to be high, and there are some houses on the east side for a short distance downstream. Once they are passed, the river becomes remote again. The west side of the river is owned by a private wildlife management group, and there is virtually no access. In the second mile, the river begins to wind again, and it becomes swampier as it nears Lake Talquin. Bird life is abundant in this

Ochlockonee River (Section B): Old Bainbridge Road to Coe Landing

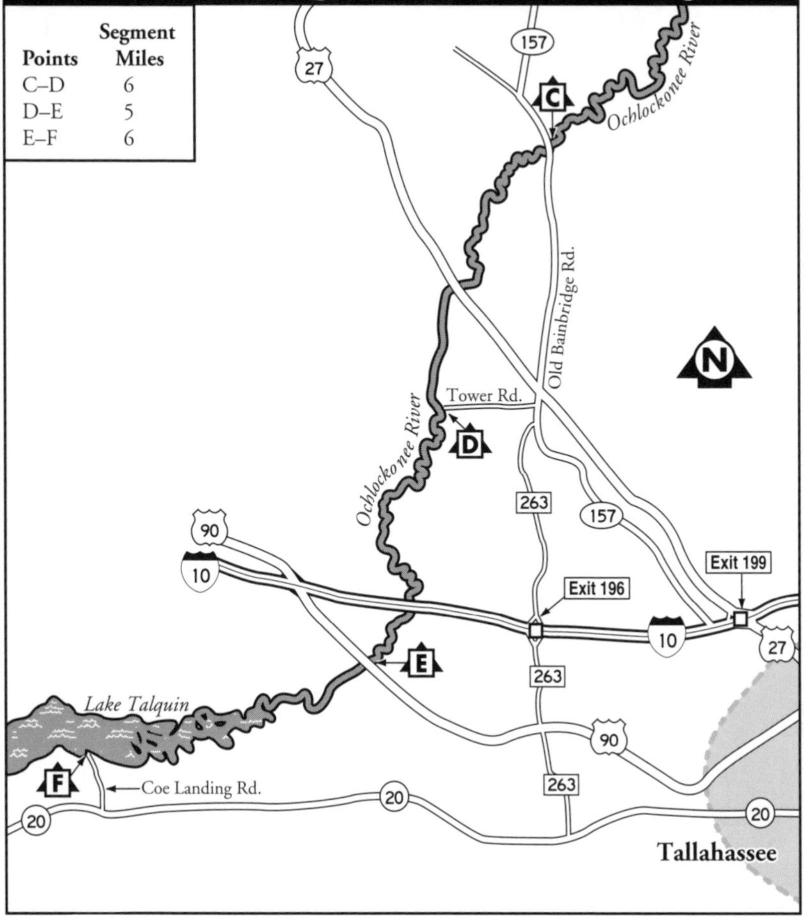

Points	Segment Miles
C–D	6
D–E	5
E–F	6

area, and there are some fine stands of pine in the highlands east of the river. By the beginning of the third mile downstream, the river widens as the lake begins. Hammocks and islands dot the waterway and by the time Coe Landing is reached, the lake is more than 0.5 miles wide. At this point, wind and waves may become a problem for the paddler. Coe Landing is located on the east bank and is easily seen from the lake. It is 6 miles from US 90 to the takeout at Coe Landing.

Lake Talquin stretches for another 13 miles to the dam at FL 20 and becomes increasingly wide. It is also frequented by large motorboats. It is a beautiful lake and a worthwhile experience for

those who enjoy lake paddling. At the end of the lake, Talquin Dam must be portaged.

SHUTTLE: To reach the put-in from Exit 199 on I-10 just north of Tallahassee, take US 27 north to Old Bainbridge Road. Turn right on Old Bainbridge Road and follow it to the bridge over the Ochlockonee River. There is a boat ramp on the northeast side of the bridge. To reach the takeout from Tallahassee, take FL 20 west to Coe Landing Road. Turn right on Coe Landing Road and follow it to a dead end with the public boat ramp (on Lake Talquin).

GAUGE: Visual, Web. The only way to determine water level is in person. However, the Ochlockonee is normally floatable year-round. To determine if the river is at average flows for any given period a helpful USGS gauge is Ochlockonee River near Concord, FL.

class	I–I+
length	46
time	Varies
gauge	Visual, Web
level	N/A
gradient	0.7
scenery	A

LAKE TALQUIN DAM TO WOOD LAKE LANDING

DESCRIPTION: The Ochlockonee is dam-controlled from this point to its terminus at Ochlockonee Bay, but water levels are usually consistent with the amount of rainfall received by the area during the previous week. The first mile below the put-in at FL 20 is a straight stretch of river 150 feet wide with a road down the east bank. There are fish camps and houses in this area; the Apalachicola National Forest boundaries begin at the end of the first bend in the river, and its remote characteristics resume. The west bank of the river is privately owned, primarily by a large paper company, and there is no access on that side for many miles. Small fishing boats are common on the lower stretches of the river, but they are seldom encountered more than 2 miles from a boat landing.

Two miles downstream from FL 20 is an access at Rock Bluff Scenic Area, which is reached from Forest Road 390. It is a high bluff on the east bank with good access to the river and a large grassy area suitable for camping.

The river alternates between long straight stretches and sharp bends. It tends to narrow in the curving sections and has a better current with sandbars on the insides of some of the bends. Three miles downstream from Rock Bluff is Stoutamire Landing, a privately owned boat launch, with some small cabins nearby. Drake Landing, also private, is 2 miles farther downstream with another high bluff on the east side of the river.

Ochlockonee River (Section C): Lake Talquin Dam to Wood Lake Landing

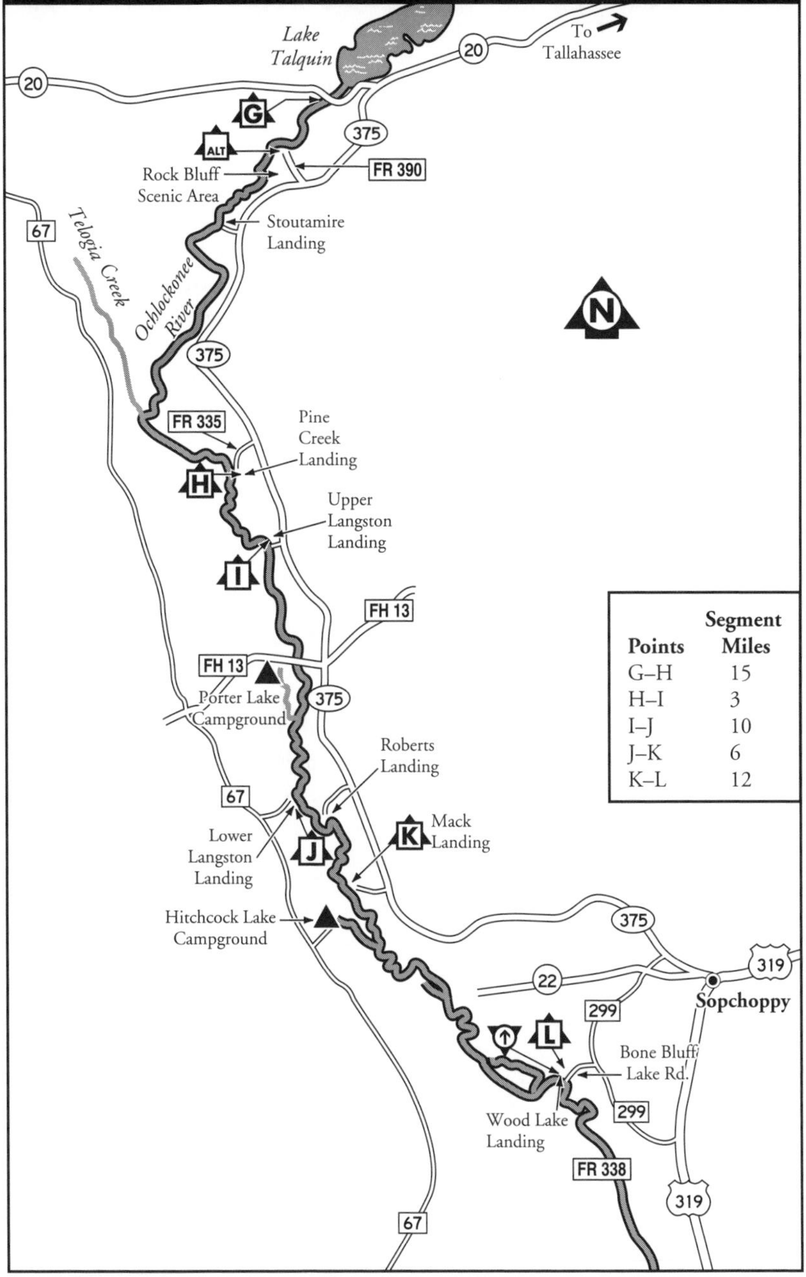

Lake Talquin
To Tallahassee
20
375
FR 390
Rock Bluff Scenic Area
Stoutamire Landing
67
Telogia Creek
Ochlockonee River
375
FR 335
Pine Creek Landing
Upper Langston Landing
FH 13
FH 13
Porter Lake Campground
375
Roberts Landing
67
Lower Langston Landing
Mack Landing
Hitchcock Lake Campground
375
22
319
Sopchoppy
299
Bone Bluff Lake Rd.
299
Wood Lake Landing
FR 338
319
67
G
ALT
H
I
J
K
L
N

Points	Segment Miles
G–H	15
H–I	3
I–J	10
J–K	6
K–L	12

Telogia Creek flows into the Ochlockonee from the west bank 12 miles from FL 20. Here is a public boat ramp, reached from FL 67 in Liberty County, and a high bank with a group of houses. From this point, it is another 3 miles to Pine Creek Landing. This is a very popular area for hunting during the season from mid-November to mid-January. Use caution in selecting a campsite, and do not take dogs or firearms on the river unless you camp on forest property and have the required licenses and permits. It is 15 miles from FL 20 to Pine Creek Landing.

The river is 150 feet wide at Pine Creek Landing with low banks on the east side and a swampy area on the west. There is a high, grassy area around the boat launch that could be used for camping. Soon after leaving Pine Creek, the river narrows again and in many spots is constricted by overhanging willow branches and downed trees. As a result, some degree of skill in maneuvering is needed. There are small sandbars scattered along the bends of the river, but they are usually covered by willow trees and river birch and are not large enough to be good campsites. This is a heavily forested section and is remote except for one house on the west bank about halfway between Pine Creek and Upper Langston Landing. Upper Langston, accessible from FL 375, is 3 miles downstream from Pine Creek on the east bank. It is privately owned; there is a fee for camping and launching.

Just before reaching Upper Langston, the river divides and becomes very narrow and swift as it flows around a small island. It is usually best to stay to the west channel. The river widens at the end of the island. From Upper Langston Landing to Forest Highway 13 is another 4 miles. This section is less remote with some houses scattered along the east bank. The bridge across the Ochlockonee at FH 13 is the first one to be encountered for 22 miles and the last one on the sections of the river covered in this guide. There is no access to the river from FH 13, which is unfortunate. Just west of this bridge, across two more bridges, is a nice campground at Porter Lake. This campground can be reached by paddling downstream from FH 13 for about 2.5 miles to the point where Porter Lake flows into the Ochlockonee and then paddling upstream to the campsite. There is no good way to identify this spot, since there are many lakes and sloughs on the west side of the river and an entire day could be spent paddling up each of them in search of the right one. These so-called lakes are actually arms or backwaters of the river. It is 13 miles from Pine Creek Landing to Lower Langston Landing.

Lower Langston Landing is located on a high, pleasant site on the west bank of the river. It is a good camping area but has no facilities. About 0.25 miles downstream from the landing, there

is a large sandbar on the east bank at the point where a small creek flows into the river. This is also a pleasant campsite and is not accessible by road. At normal- to high-water levels, these are the last campsites until Mack Landing is reached. In this section, the river continues to alternate between wide, straight sections and narrow bends. It is 6 miles from Lower Langston Landing to Mack Landing.

There is an established campground at Mack Landing with a boat launch. Unfortunately, like most of the other national forest access points, it is located off of one of the many lakes on the east side of the river that are indistinguishable from one another. When attempting to find these landings from the river, the best strategy is to ask any fishermen that you may see. Reflectors may have been nailed to trees indicating the way to Mack Landing. It can be distinguished because of the very high banks that begin to run along the east bank at this point. They are 10 to 12 feet high and look as if they have been cleared on top. They continue for 1 mile to the Roberts Landing area, where there is a privately owned boat ramp and several houses.

Although the river continues to curve for the next 3 miles, the bends are much wider and gentler than they have previously been. There is an access at Silver Lake, on the east bank, just at the end of this curving section, but it, too, is difficult to find. The paddler then enters a 2-mile-long straight section that is broad, frequented by large motorboats, and may be affected by wind and tide.

There is another mile or so of curving section and then another 3-mile stretch on an increasingly large and populated river. The banks are heavily forested in this area, with some high pinelands alternating with swamp. At high to normal water levels campsites are small and scarce. At the end of the 3-mile stretch, there is a camp on a bend on the east bank. A small, white sandbar extends to the south of it. At this point, paddlers should begin watching for the landing 1 mile downstream on the east bank of Wood Lake.

Those who wish to do so may paddle for another 10 miles to the Ochlockonee River State Park. At that point the river is the size of a small bay and is frequented by water-skiers, large powerboats, and even sailboats. It is also heavily influenced by the tide. Most canoeists prefer to end their trip at Wood Lake. It is 12 miles from Mack Landing to the takeout at Wood Lake Landing.

SHUTTLE: To reach the lowermost takeout from Sopchoppy, take FL 22 to CR 299. Turn left, south, on CR 299 to reach FR 338. Turn right on FR 338, Bone Bluff Lake Road, and follow it

to the Wood Lake Recreation Area, which has a boat landing and primitive campground. To reach the uppermost put-in from Tallahassee, travel west for 22 miles on FL 20 to the bridge across the Ochlockonee River. There is access on the west side of the river from a privately owned boat ramp. There is a fee for launching.

GAUGE: Visual, Web. The best way to determine the water level is in person. However, the Ochlockonee is normally floatable year-round. A helpful gauge to determine average river levels for this section of the river is Ochlockonee River near Bloxham, FL. This gauge is below the Lake Talquin Dam.

A distant hot sun lowering in the west

SOPCHOPPY RIVER

The Sopchoppy River drains from a large swamp south of Lake Talquin and flows for 50 miles to its confluence with the Ochlockonee at Ochlockonee Bay. Lying almost completely within the boundaries of the Apalachicola National Forest, it is an unusually remote and clean river. Sopchoppy is a Creek word said to mean long, twisted stream, an apt description of this beautiful waterway. In addition to its many twists and turns, the Sopchoppy is noted for extensive and very unique cypress formations, high limestone banks, and an overall fast current.

Highly dependent on local rainfall for its flow, the Sopchoppy can be either low stretches connecting deeper pools during dry periods or a rushing 10-foot channel after heavy rains. In either event, the sharp bends and presence of cypress knees in the water can present a challenge to the canoeist. The riverbed is primarily sand with some rock crevices; the water is a clear, but highly colored, tannic red. The high banks are occasionally broken by white sandbars suitable for picnicking or camping. Also, the Florida Trail parallels the Sopchoppy in places.

Of special interest on the Sopchoppy is the Bradwell Bay Wilderness. A virtually undisturbed scenic area, it escaped the lumbering craze of the early twentieth century and harbors a number of award-winning trees. The first 10 canoeable miles of the river flow through the wilderness. There are also 17 archeologically valuable sites along the river that are said to be the only models of aboriginal usage of the flatwoods in northwest Florida. A number of species—including the red cockaded woodpecker, Southern bald eagle, and black bear—make their homes in the area.

Vegetation is dense along the banks and includes loblolly pine forests, pine-palmetto flatwoods, cypress, titi, and other trees indigenous to the area. The steep limestone banks are covered with mosses and ferns, and in the spring wild azaleas provide a canopy of pink bloom.

MAPS: Apalachicola National Forest map, Bradwell Bay, Crawfordville West, Sopchoppy, Sanborn (USGS)

FH 13 to Sopchoppy River Park

class	I–I+
length	26
time	Varies
gauge	Phone, Web
level	N/A
gradient	1.6
scenery	A+

DESCRIPTION: Runs on the Sopchoppy River can be broken into varied segments as there are numerous accesses. The upper river begins at the most southern edge of the Grand Bay Swamp, whose runoff forms the river. It is said to be possible to canoe

Sopchoppy River: FH 13 to Sopchoppy River Park

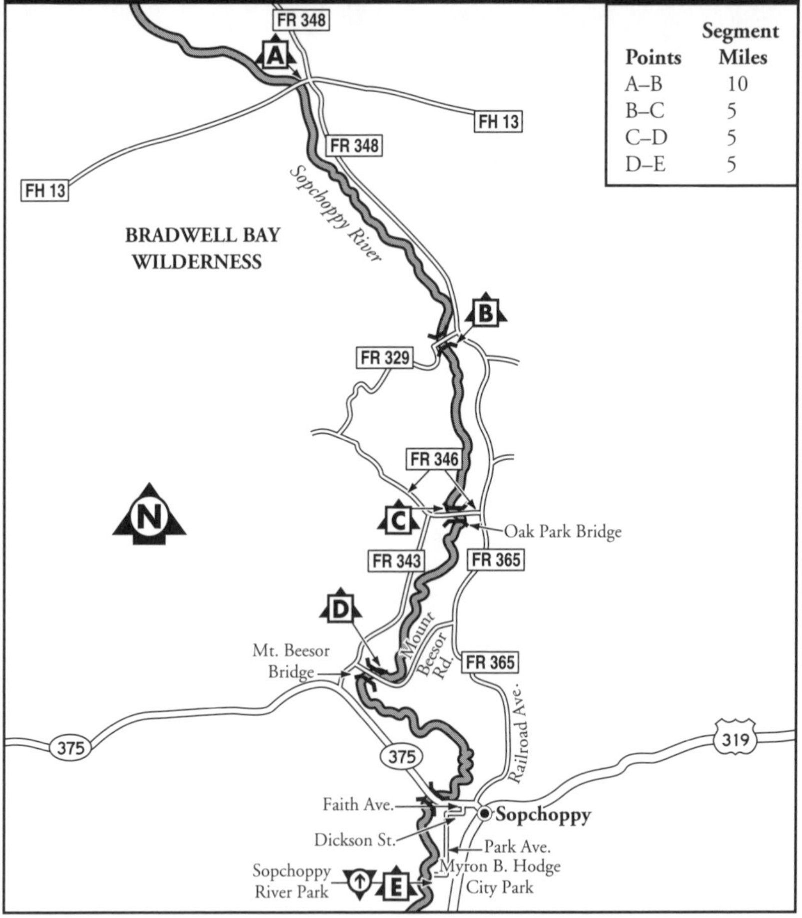

Points	Segment Miles
A–B	10
B–C	5
C–D	5
D–E	5

one bridge farther upstream, but high water and a lot of bushwhacking is required. The river is clearly defined at the Forest Highway 13 bridge, where it enters the Bradwell Bay Wilderness, but fingers off into a swampy area for about 0.5 miles downstream. Despite the swampy terrain, the current is easily detectable and will lead to a well-defined channel with banks from 1 to 3 feet high.

Very sharp twists and turns in a narrow streambed characterize this part of the river. Cypress knees and the remains of

downed trees and stumps contribute to the obstructions that must be avoided. The constant curves and swift water leave little opportunity to scout as immediate decisions are required in maneuvering. This section of the river should only be run at higher water. It is 10 miles from the FH 13 bridge to FR 329, where it leaves the wilderness.

Starting at FR 329, the Middle Sopchoppy is a very popular section of river for canoeing. It is noted for the wide diversity of beautiful and unique cypress formations. In addition to a multitude of knees of all sizes and shapes, there are long, flowing banks of cypress wood, connecting groups of knees that resemble entwined serpents, monsters, gargoyles, or whatever the active imagination can envision.

The sharp bends in the river are frequently obstructed by masses of cypress knees resulting in small rapids and falls that require fast maneuvering. There are several small sandbars in this section that are pleasant for lunching, camping, or sunbathing. It is 5 miles from the FR 329 bridge to the FR 346 bridge, Oak Park Bridge. The old Oak Park Bridge was a quaint and rustic wooden structure, which has now been replaced by a concrete bridge. Access is on the northwest side of the bridge.

From just above the Oak Park Bridge, the river begins to widen and the curves become gentler. High, limestone banks become evident, and there are several small islands that narrow the channels of the river. The vertical banks act as a watershed and in warm weather produce a cooling effect. In the winter they may be dripping with icicles. The river is deeper and easier to negotiate in this section but still requires some skill. Just before the Mount Beeser Bridge, the river leaves the national forest, and houses and other forms of encroachment appear. Small motorboats may also be seen near the end of this section. It is 5 miles from the Oak Park Bridge to the Mount Beeser Bridge.

Below the Mount Beeser Bridge, the Sopchoppy River becomes deeper, slower, and increasingly populated beyond this point. It moves from the swamps and upland hardwoods to a marshier, coastal appearance. It is 6 miles from the Mount Beeser Bridge to FL 375. However, this access is closed and paddlers should continue another mile to the Sopchoppy River Park, on the left. The park has a boat landing, picnic area, and campground. It is possible to continue to paddle on the Sopchoppy to its confluence with the Ochlockonee. It becomes increasingly broad and tidal, however, and is heavily used by motorboats.

SHUTTLE: To reach the uppermost put-in from US 319 in Sopchoppy, take Rose Street, FL 375, west just a short distance to

Railroad Avenue, FR 365. Turn right and head north on FR 365 to FR 348. Follow FR 348 to FH 13. Turn left on FH 13 and follow it a short distance to the bridge over the Sopchoppy River. Access is on the northeast side of the bridge. To reach the lowermost takeout from US 319 in Sopchoppy, take Rose Street, FL 375, west to Faith Avenue. Turn left on Faith Avenue and follow it one block to Dickson Street. Turn right on Dickson Street to reach Park Avenue. Turn left on Park Avenue and follow it to Myron B. Hodge City Park, on the right, and a boat launch.

GAUGE: Phone, Web. Call Sopchoppy Outfitters at (850) 962-2220 for the latest stream conditions. A helpful gauge to determine average river levels for this section of the river is Sopchoppy River near Sopchoppy, FL.

Zephyr lilies are a common sight in spring

LITTLE RIVER

The Little River, a tributary of the Ochlockonee, is formed a few miles above FL 12 by the convergence of the Willacoochee and Attapulgus creeks. It flows into the Ochlockonee at Lake Talquin. It is possible to put in at FL 12, but the access is poor, and the upper section of the river is characterized by many pull-overs and shallow water in all but the wettest of seasons. Further, both sides of the riverbank are owned by private hunting clubs that not only discourage its usage but make it somewhat hazardous during hunting season. This is also true of much of the lower, more runnable section, but the river is wider, deeper, and easier to maneuver, making a pleasant trip in the spring and early fall. The Little River is like a miniature version of the Ochlockonee and is a very pleasant run. Very large alligators have been sighted here, and every sandbar is a tracker's paradise.

MAPS: Quincy, Lake Talquin (USGS)

US 90 TO LAKE TALQUIN

class	I
length	9
time	5
gauge	Visual, Web
level	N/A
gradient	1.4
scenery	A

DESCRIPTION: It requires considerable skill to maneuver through the numerous obstructions on this section of the river. There is usually a pleasant current and the banks are intermittent swampy areas interspersed with some 20-foot-high bluffs. Several sandbars would make adequate campsites. I-10 crosses the river about 3 miles below US 90. It is 4 miles from US 90 to CR 268. The CR 268 access is on the southeast side of the second bridge you reach, heading west from US 90.

Below CR 268, the river widens and becomes both deeper and straighter. The sandbars disappear; the banks become high and heavily wooded. As the river nears Lake Talquin, it becomes swampier, with small bayous and sloughs off to the sides. When it flows into the lake, the water becomes shallower with many stumps showing above the water. After entering the lake, the paddler should turn left, or north, and remain on the west side. This is the upper portion of Lake Talquin; it is wide and may be windy. It is 3 miles from the confluence of Little River up the lake to High Bluff. High Bluff Recreation Area is part of Lake Talquin State Forest and has a good-quality tent campground. It is 5 miles from CR 268 to the takeout at High Bluff Landing.

SHUTTLE: To reach the put-in from Tallahassee, take US 90 west to the bridge over Little River. To reach the takeout from

Little River: US 90 to Lake Talquin

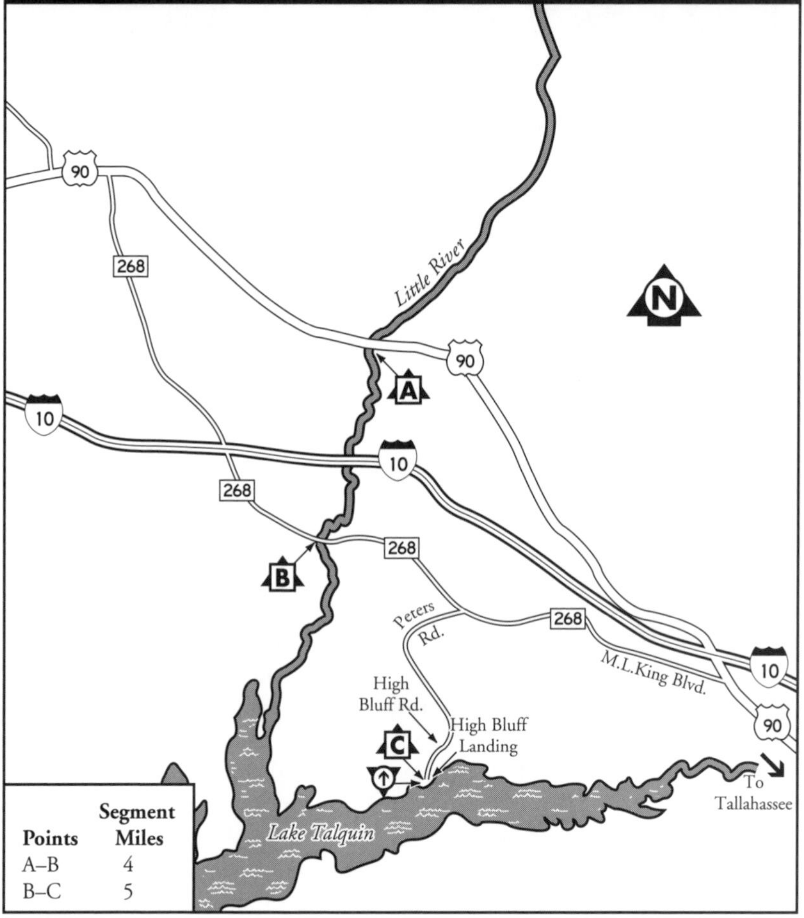

Points	Segment Miles
A–B	4
B–C	5

Tallahassee, take US 90 west to CR 268, M. L. King Jr. Boulevard. Turn left on CR 268, heading to Peters Road. Turn left on Peters Road and follow it as it turns into High Bluff Road, which dead-ends at High Bluff Landing Recreation Area, and a boat landing with a campground.

GAUGE: Visual, Web. The best way to determine water level is in person. A helpful gauge to determine average river levels for any given period is Little River near Midway, FL.

GRAHAM CREEK AND EAST RIVER

Graham Creek and East River are freshwater components of lower Apalachicola Bay estuary. These creeks are located on Florida Fish and Wildlife Conservation Lands and are managed to protect the watershed and all the life within. Known as the greater Apalachicola Wildlife and Environmental Area, these waterways meander through the vast floodplain forests in the lower Apalachicola River delta. Black bears and other wild critters call this home. Paddlers call this a new opportunity to ply their boats through many of the waterways that extend throughout this region, for the Graham Creek/East River paddle route is but one of many marked paddle paths in the Apalachicola River Wildlife and Environmental Area Paddling Trail System. Trips here can extend from hours to days. This particular trip begins on upper Graham Creek, then travels west to meet the East River. The wider East River heads southeast toward East Bay and the Gulf. Bikers take note that Fish and Wildlife have installed bike racks for locking your bike on either end of this paddle, enabling a bike shuttle.

MAPS: Apalachicola Wildlife & Environmental Area Paddle Trail System map, Beverly, Jackson River (USGS)

Graham Creek Landing to Gardner Landing

class	I
length	7.5
time	4
gauge	Visual
level	Tidal
gradient	0.2
scenery	A

DESCRIPTION: The paddle trip leaves from the landing off of CR 65. Paddlers can head upstream, under the CR 65 bridge, and a mile east to the railroad bridge. Beyond the railroad bridge, you can head left, north and up Deep Creek into Tates Hell State Forest. Most paddlers simply head west, downstream from the landing, enjoying the tupelo- and cypress-lined black water. The South Prong comes in from river right at 0.2 miles. Continue west for 2.5 miles. Here Graham Creek meets the East River. East River meanders at first, then the curves become gentler. Palms and oaks join the streamside forest mix. After 4 miles on East River, work around an island just below the confluence with Caesar Creek. Stay to the left of this island to reach Gardner Landing after 4.5 miles on East River.

SHUTTLE: To reach the put-in at Graham Creek Landing, head north on FL 65, and turn left (west), following it for 12 miles to the bridge over Graham Creek. The landing is on the southwest side of the bridge. To reach the takeout at Gardner Landing from Eastpoint, head east on US 98 to FL 65. Turn left, north, on FL

65 and follow it to Gardner Road. Turn left on Gardner Road and at the split with Butcher Pen Landing Road, head right and cross the railroad tracks to reach Gardner Landing.

GAUGE: Visual. These coastal waterways hold enough water year-round due to downstream tidal influence.

Graham Creek and East River: Graham Creek Landing to Gardner Landing

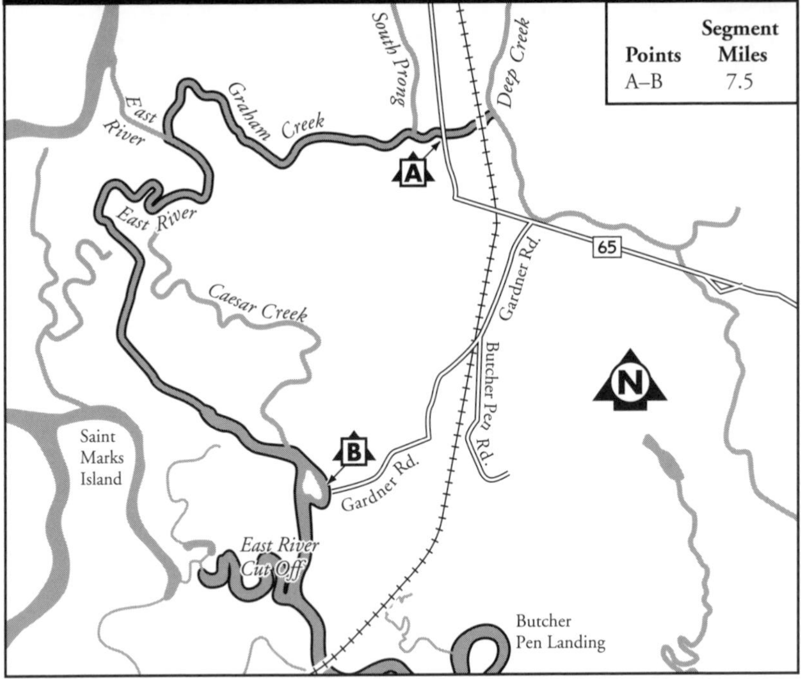

Points	Segment Miles
A–B	7.5

South Prong
Deep Creek
Graham Creek
East River
East River
Caesar Creek
65
Gardner Rd.
Butcher Pen Rd.
Gardner Rd.
Saint Marks Island
East River Cut Off
Butcher Pen Landing
A
B
N

NEW RIVER

The New River originates in the far north of the Apalachicola National Forest, draining a wide region of Liberty County bordered by the Apalachicola River on the west and the Wakulla River to the east. It can be paddled south of the FH 13 bridge, commonly known as Carr Bridge, along a corridor of the New River/Mud Swamp Wilderness. Many fallen logs and riverine obstructions make this a challenging paddle. The New River then breaks into impassable channels before becoming one main channel again in the southeast corner of the wilderness. Here it leaves the national forest and enters Franklin County and Tates Hell State Forest. By this point the river has generally sufficient flow for year-round paddling and is more open. The dark Gulf-bound waterway begins to widen and become tidally influenced before leaving the state forest and reaching Carrabelle and opening into the Gulf at Dog Island. State Forest access points along River Road, River Road West, and a bridge, ramp, and day-use area off of Gully Branch Road make trips of differing lengths very easy.

MAPS: Tates Hell State Forest map, Owens Bridge, Tates Hell Swap, Pickett Bay (USGS)

NEW RIVER EAST CAMPSITE #7 TO POPE PLACE CAMP

class	I
length	11
time	6
gauge	Visual, Web
level	N/A
gradient	0.8
scenery	A

DESCRIPTION: The river is about 30 feet wide as it enters Franklin County. The state forest has developed many access points/campsites along the upper river, which are visible as clearings from a boat. The access points/campsites have a picnic table and fire ring. Though roads parallel much of the lower New River, the complete lack of development along its banks and anywhere in the vicinity creates a wilderness aura and natural soundscape. Oaks and cedar are common on the upper river. The New tortuously twists, forming sandbars on the inside of bends while higher sand banks border the outside. Small branches feed the New. Occasionally, pine-studded bluffs reach directly to the river. Beyond the vision of a paddler, much of the state forest is pine plantation. It is 6 miles from New River East Campsite #7 to Gully Landing, with its picnic pavilion, well, and a boat ramp.

Continuing downriver, the 50-foot-wide New offers occasionally straighter sections and more river accesses, mostly on the west bank. Sand bars end and the river becomes tidally influenced. The

banks begin to lower and pines extend to the water. The river widens to 80 feet, and some grass borders the river. Pope Place access is on the right-hand (west) bank. Below Pope Place, access is difficult in the state forest due to grass banks. Once beyond the state forest, houses begin to appear and the river widens so that it opens itself to winds and becomes popular with motorboats, therefore losing its appeal to paddlers. It is 5 miles from Gully Landing to Pope Place.

New River: New River East Campsite #7 to Pope Place Camp

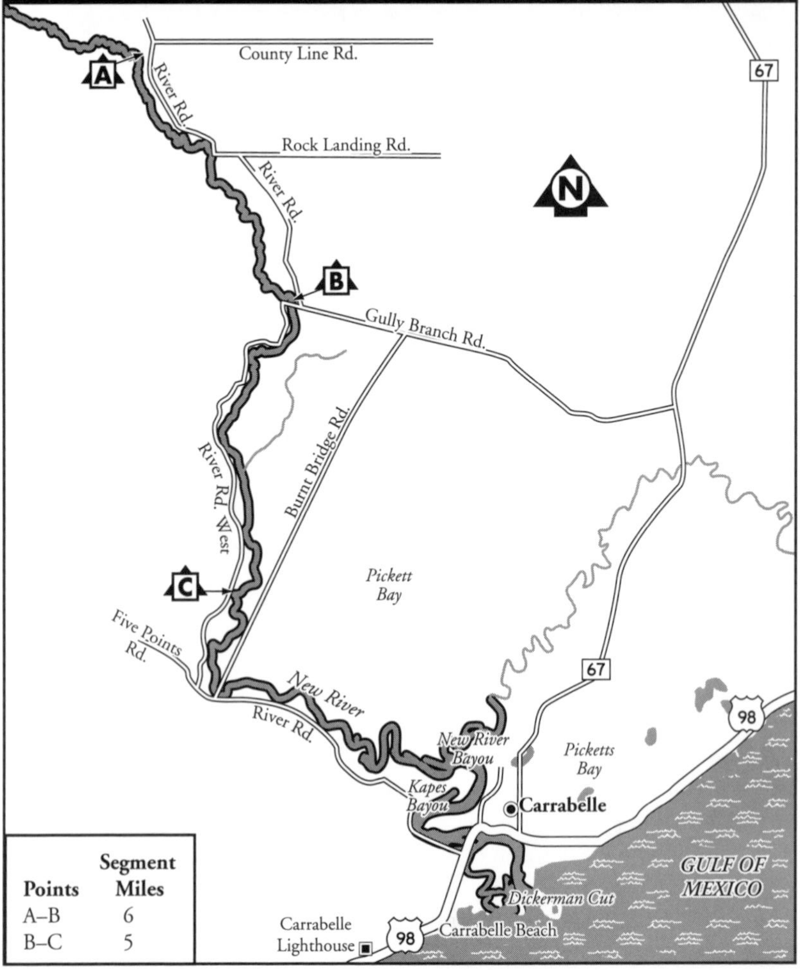

Points	Segment Miles
A–B	6
B–C	5

SHUTTLE: To reach the lowermost access from the southwest side of the US 98 bridge over the New River in Carrabelle, take River Road west, away from the Gulf, past the junction with Five Points Road. Here, veer right onto River Road West. Keep forward to reach the right turn to Pope Place Camp. To reach the uppermost access, continue north on River Road West to reach Gully Branch Road. Turn right (east) on Gully Branch Road, crossing the bridge over New River and a good access point. Turn left on River Road and follow it up to Rock Landing Road. Turn left on Rock Landing Road, then turn right on River Road to reach New River East Campsite #7. There is a landing and campsite here. New River East Campsite #7 is just south of County Line Road. High-clearance vehicles are recommended on the sandy state forest roads.

GAUGE: Phone, Web. Call Tates Hell State Forest at (850) 697-3734 for the latest river conditions. The best way to determine the water level is in person. However, the New River is normally floatable year-round. A helpful gauge to determine average river levels for the New is New River near Sumatra, FL.

A slow-flowing bend on the New River

LOST CREEK

Located entirely within the Apalachicola National Forest, Lost Creek is very similar in terrain and geography to the upper section of the Sopchoppy River, which it parallels. It drains some 10 miles through Cow Swamp and Mosquito Bay, and disappears into a sink, less than a mile below FL 368. It is smaller and more winding than the Sopchoppy. There is little development on Lost Creek, and it is a fine example of upland pine woods with a border of cypress and wetlands trees. This waterway is highly dependent on local rainfall.

MAPS: Apalachicola National Forest map, Crawfordville West (USGS)

class	I–I+
length	10
time	5.5
gauge	Visual, Web
level	N/A
gradient	2
scenery	A

FR 350 TO FL 368

DESCRIPTION: Lost Creek begins in a swampy area, but by following the current, a clearly defined riverbed will be reached. This is a narrow, twisting stream with many underwater obstructions such as cypress knees and submerged logs and stumps. Good maneuvering skills will be needed. This is a fine example of wilderness paddling. This stream should only be run during times of high local rainfall.

SHUTTLE: To reach the takeout from Crawfordville, take FL 368, Arran Road, west to the bridge over Lost Creek. Access is on the northeast side of the river. To reach the put-in, continue on FL 368 beyond the takeout and the paved road (forking to the right) becomes FR 13. FR 13 then becomes sand. Follow it to FR 350. Turn right on FR 350 and follow it to the bridge over Lost Creek. Access is on the southeast side of the bridge.

GAUGE: Visual, Web. Lost Creek can be paddled after times of abundant rainfall. A helpful gauge to determine flow rates for this creek is Lost Creek at Arran, FL.

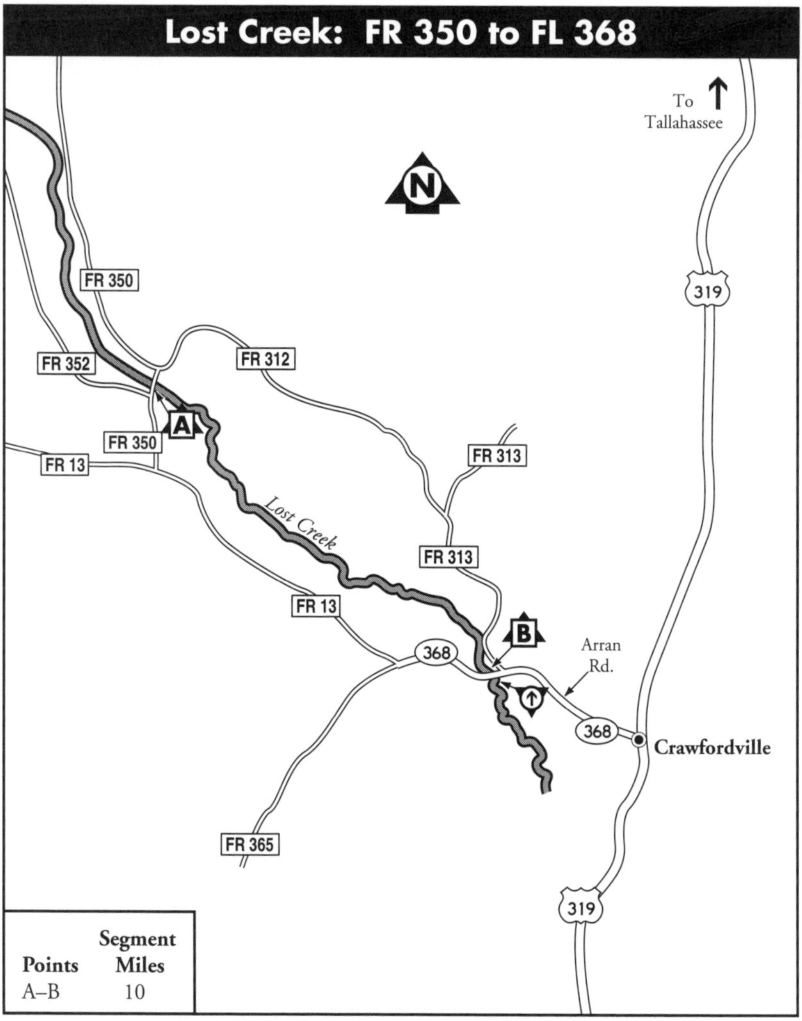

Lost Creek: FR 350 to FL 368

To Tallahassee

N

FR 350

FR 352

FR 312

A

FR 350

FR 13

FR 313

Lost Creek

FR 313

FR 13

B

368

Arran Rd.

368

Crawfordville

319

FR 365

319

Points	Segment Miles
A–B	10

The Big Bend

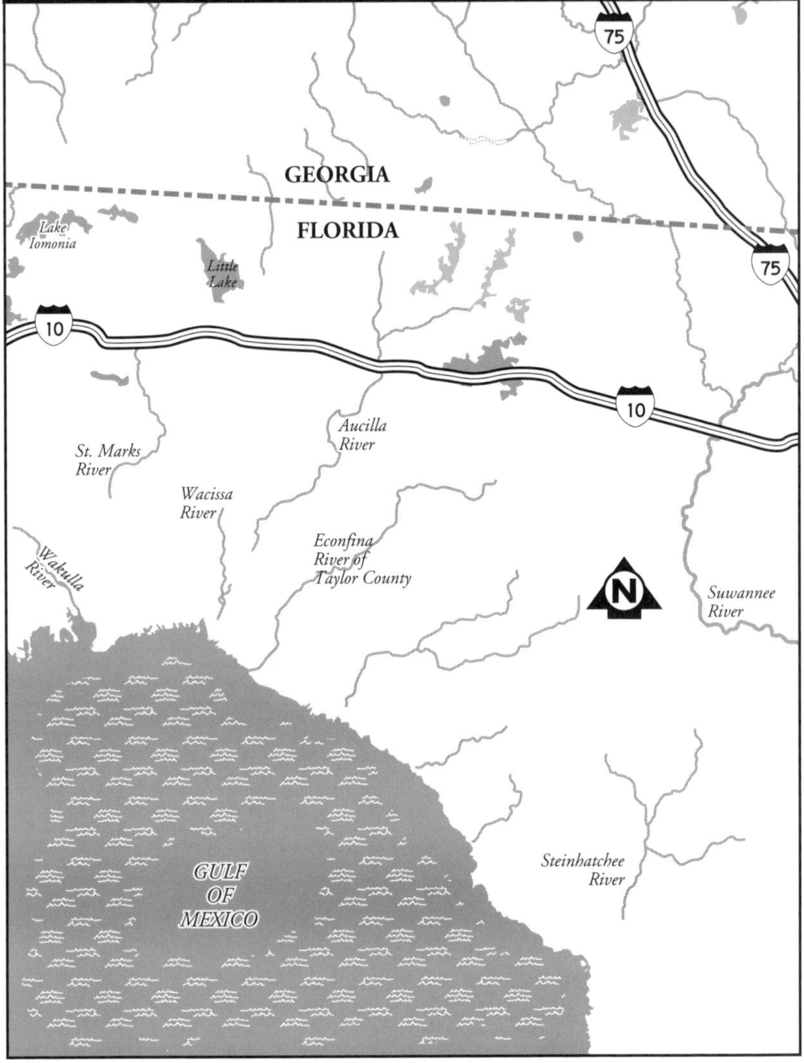

GEORGIA
FLORIDA
Lake Iomonia
Little Lake
75
10
St. Marks River
Aucilla River
Wacissa River
Wakulla River
Econfina River of Taylor County
Suwannee River
Steinhatchee River
GULF OF MEXICO
N

part **Three**

THE BIG BEND

WAKULLA RIVER

The Wakulla is a large river from its origin at Wakulla Springs. Indian Springs, Sally Ward Spring, and McBride Slough also contribute to the crystal waters of the Wakulla River. The spring is now a first-rate Florida State Park.

The primary source of the Wakulla River is Wakulla Springs. Said to be the largest spring in Florida and perhaps in the world, it is the site of a 1930s hotel and resort. The hotel is now operated by the Florida Park Service. Wildlife, especially birds and alligators, are a major attraction here. The unusual clarity of the spring water has resulted in it being chosen for a number of motion pictures over the years. Despite lengthy legal proceedings, the former owners of the resort were permitted to maintain a fence across the river just above FL 365. This fence, ironically kept in place by the state of Florida, prevents access to the first 3 miles of this navigable-to-paddle-boats stream. The old Tallahassee–St. Marks Rail Trail runs parallel to the Wakulla and provides an alternate shuttle option for hikers and bikers.

MAPS: Crawfordville East, St. Marks (USGS)

FL 365 to Wakulla River City Park

class	I
length	6
time	3
gauge	Visual
level	Spring-fed
gradient	0.2
scenery	B

DESCRIPTION: It is possible to canoe both downstream from FL 365 and return upstream, eliminating the need for a shuttle. The current is gentle, and the river is broad, clear, and very beautiful. There are several islands, but generally they can be run on either side. It is 4 miles from FL 365 to US 98. There is a public access on the southeast side of the bridge, next to an outfitter. It is 2 miles further to the takeout at Wakulla River City Park, on the east bank of the river.

SHUTTLE: To reach the put-in from Tallahassee, take FL 363 south to FL 267. Turn right on FL 267 and then quickly turn left on FL 365 and follow it to the bridge over Wakulla River. To

reach the takeout from Tallahassee, keep south on FL 363 to reach a T intersection in the village of St. Marks. Turn right on Riverside Drive and follow it to a stop sign. Turn right on Old Fort Road and come to a second stop sign. This time, keep forward on Yacht Lane to end at Wakulla River City Park and a boat ramp.

GAUGE: Visual. The Wakulla River is spring fed and remains paddleable year-round.

Wakulla River: FL 365 to Wakulla River City Park

Points	Segment Miles
A–B	4
B–C	2

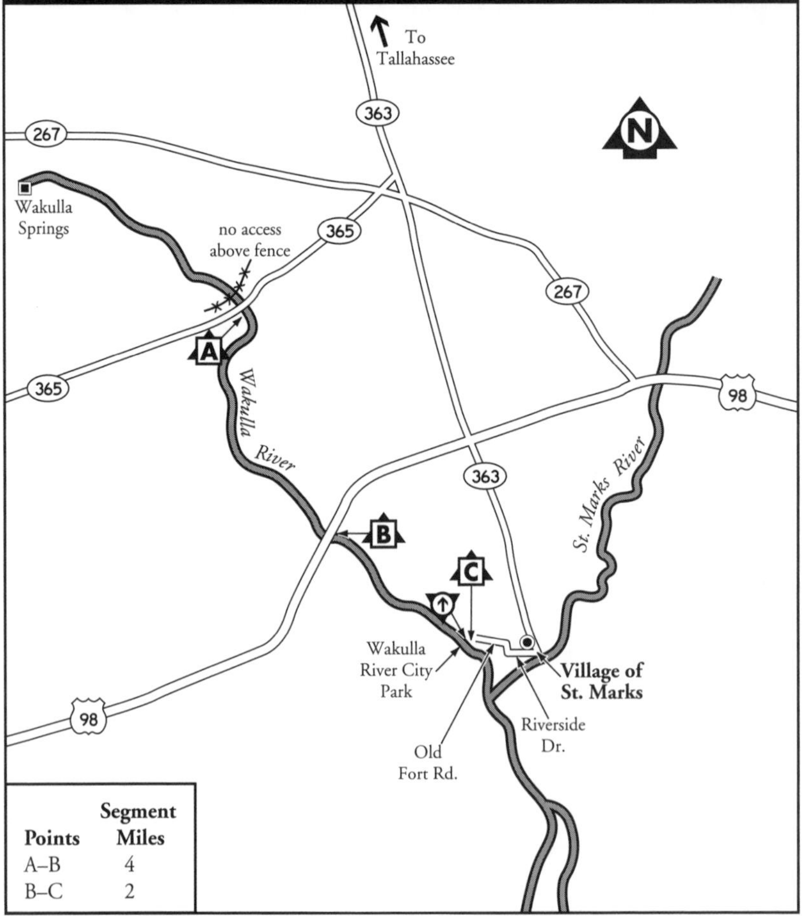

ST. MARKS RIVER

The St. Marks River flows through swampy terrain with a preponderance of cypress, magnolia, palm, and other lowland vegetation. The color of this clear, blue-green river results from its limestone bottom, and it has a variety of waterweeds above and below the surface. The current is mild, but it is possible to paddle upstream easily.

A tiny, swamp-lined stream meandering from a series of ponds north of US 90 is ambitiously named the St. Marks River, but it is not until the advent of the waters from Horn Spring that it becomes a canoeable stream. Then, just 2.5 miles later, it goes underground to form the famous Natural Bridge of historical repute. After flowing under a roadway, forming a true natural bridge, the river resumes again with St. Marks Spring and flows some 11 miles to its confluence with the Wakulla and 3 miles on to the Gulf of Mexico.

A small state park is located at the natural bridge. On this site, Confederate militia repulsed Union forces on March 6, 1865, and prevented the capture of Tallahassee, the only southern capital east of the Mississippi not taken in the Civil War.

There are several springs in the area of the Natural Bridge that are probably reoccurrences of the river. These include Natural Bridge Spring and at least four springs in the Rhodes Springs group. They rise in an area that has a dense growth of vegetation, swamp, and karst features, such as sinkholes and solution tubes. The river does not rise as a well-defined riverbed until about 0.75 miles south of FL 260 at St. Marks Springs. This area is closed to public access.

MAPS: Woodville, St. Marks (USGS)

Natural Bridge to Horn Spring

class	I
length	2.5 each way
time	3.5
gauge	Visual
level	Spring-fed
gradient	0.5
scenery	A

DESCRIPTION: Although this section of the St. Marks River is short and the access roads to Horn Spring are closed and posted, it is of paddling interest because of the deep hardwood forest, swampy terrain, and unusually large cypress trees present along the banks. A trip on this section of the St. Marks requires a paddle upstream from the Natural Bridge and a paddle back, for a trip totaling 5 miles. It is a pleasant canoeing experience in a pocket of wilderness.

Horn Spring actually consists of two springs. The larger is 75 feet in diameter and 30 feet deep. When the sediment is undisturbed, it is a clear, green color. The smaller spring, 200 feet

north, is only 30 feet in diameter. The two join to flow about 350 feet downstream into the St. Marks River.

Shortly below the influx of the spring runs, Chicken Branch enters the river from the west. Myriad unnamed seeping springs and small creeks lace the swamps beside the river. A number of very large cypress trees still stand in this area as well as magnolias, palms, and other typical lowland vegetation.

SHUTTLE: To reach the put-in/takeout from Tallahassee, take FL 363 south to Natural Bridge Road. Turn left on Natural Bridge Road and follow it to Natural Bridge Battlefield State

St. Marks River (Sections A–B): Natural Bridge to St. Marks Spring

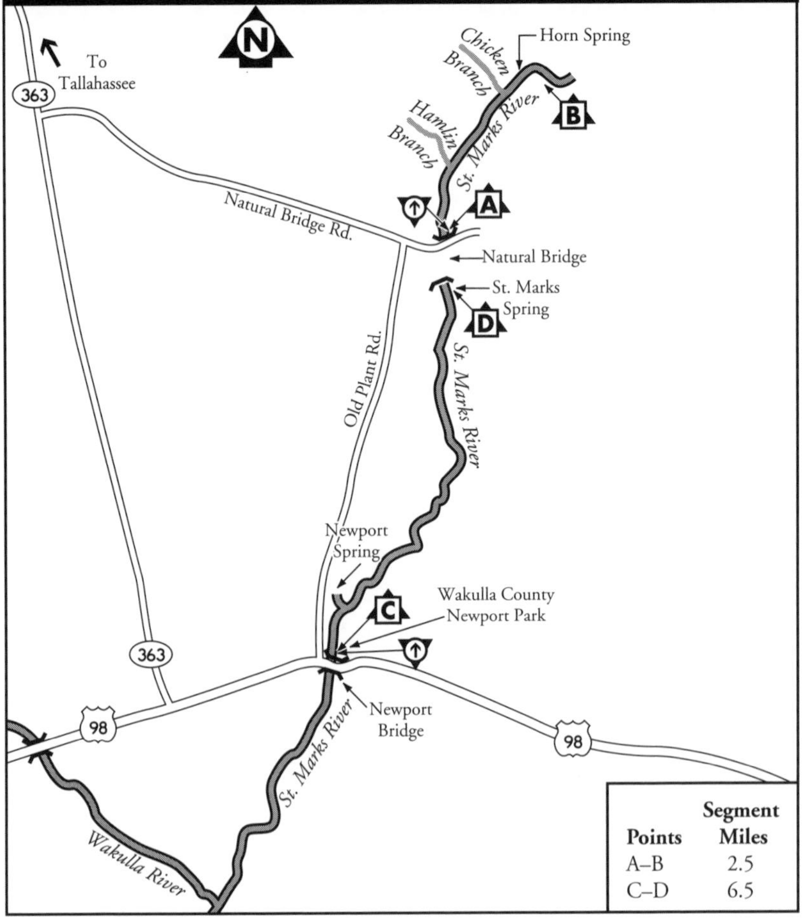

Points	Segment Miles
A–B	2.5
C–D	6.5

Historic Site. The put-in is on the left just before a bridge as the road turns to sand.

GAUGE: Visual. Horn Spring feeds this section, keeping it paddleable year-round.

NEWPORT BRIDGE TO ST. MARKS SPRING

class	I
length	6.5 each way
time	3
gauge	Visual
level	Spring-fed
gradient	1
scenery	B

DESCRIPTION: Unfortunately, the property south of Natural Bridge Park is privately owned, and there is no public access to St. Marks Spring or the rise of the St. Marks River. Therefore, to enjoy this section requires an out-and-back paddle. It is possible to paddle upstream from the Newport Bridge. However, it is a round-trip of about 13 miles.

The river from St. Marks Spring to Newport Bridge is wide and has a lively current near the headspring, but becomes narrower and slower within the first mile. It is a very clear and beautiful waterway with intermittent swamp and highland banks. About 1 mile above Newport, the run from Newport Spring, formerly called Brewer Sulphur Spring, enters from the west bank. It is characterized by its highly pungent odor of sulfur.

The confluence of the St. Marks with the Wakulla River is 5 miles below the Newport Bridge and is frequented by motorboats and is generally unappealing to paddlers.

SHUTTLE: To reach the put-in/takeout from Tallahassee, take FL 363 south to US 98. Turn left and take US 98 east to the Newport Bridge over the Wakulla River and Wakulla County Newport Park. The park and boat launch are on the east side of the river.

GAUGE: Visual. This part of the St. Marks is fed by St. Marks Spring and is paddleable year-round.

WACISSA RIVER

The Wacissa River, fed by 12 first-magnitude springs, rises broad and crystal clear. The area adjoining the river is densely forested with cypress, oak, and pine and is generally so swampy that access to most of the springs is only possible by boat. The river is very broad and flat for the first 5 miles below the headsprings, with numerous waterweeds and swampy banks. An island, about 3 miles down, is the first high ground. There is also high ground 5 miles down at Wacissa Dam, built for a narrow-gauge railroad that once crossed the river at this point. Below the dam the river narrows and runs around islands and off into swift, narrow fingers. Less than 2 miles above a recreation area, Goose Pasture, the river again broadens and continues wide past the recreation area for another 0.5 miles. This is not truly the river, however, and the water soon begins to run off into the Western Sloughs that lead into an unnavigable swamp called Hell's Half Acre.

The real Wacissa flows to the extreme west opposite Goose Pasture, and eventually into the Slave Canal. This canal was built shortly after 1831 by the Wacissa and Aucilla Navigation Company and connected the Wacissa River with the Aucilla River, thus providing a waterway to the Gulf of Mexico for the transport of cotton from the Jefferson County plantations. The canal provides a beautiful, eerie, and unusual canoeing experience on clear, shallow water through deep swamp. The two rivers join just above US 98 and the Aucilla, having just popped up again at Nutal Rise, continuing to the Gulf. Most paddlers end their trip at US 98, as limited access restricts downstream paddling.

MAPS: Wacissa, Nutall Rise (USGS)

class	I
length	9
time	4
gauge	Visual
level	Spring-fed
gradient	2
scenery	A

WACISSA SPRINGS TO GOOSE PASTURE

DESCRIPTION: Many paddlers do not go downriver on the Wacissa, but spend a pleasant day or afternoon paddling around the springs' area. The 12 named springs are scattered along the upper 2 miles of the river. Big Blue Spring, about 1 mile downriver on the east bank, is one of the most popular of the group. The pool is 120 feet in diameter and 45 feet deep over the vent. The limestone bottom is cavernous, and the spring flows from several ledges on the northwest side of the vent.

Cedar Island is 3 miles below the headspring and marks the end of the spring area. Paddlers who plan to paddle back upstream to Wacissa probably should not progress beyond this

point. There is a small cleared area on the island, good for lunch breaks and possible overnight camping for one or two tents.

The Wacissa Dam, the site of an old narrow-gauge railroad, offers a swift chute that poses no hazard for the paddler. Shortly below the dam, the Wacissa narrows and becomes interspersed with a number of low islands and hammocks, which divide the river into small channels. This area is not large, and if one chooses the wrong way, it is a simple matter to back up and start over. Just over a mile above Goose Pasture the river widens again into a long grassy area. For a mile above this grassy area the river is canopied, swift, and may have some downed trees to pull over.

Wacissa River (Sections A–B): Wacissa Springs to US 98

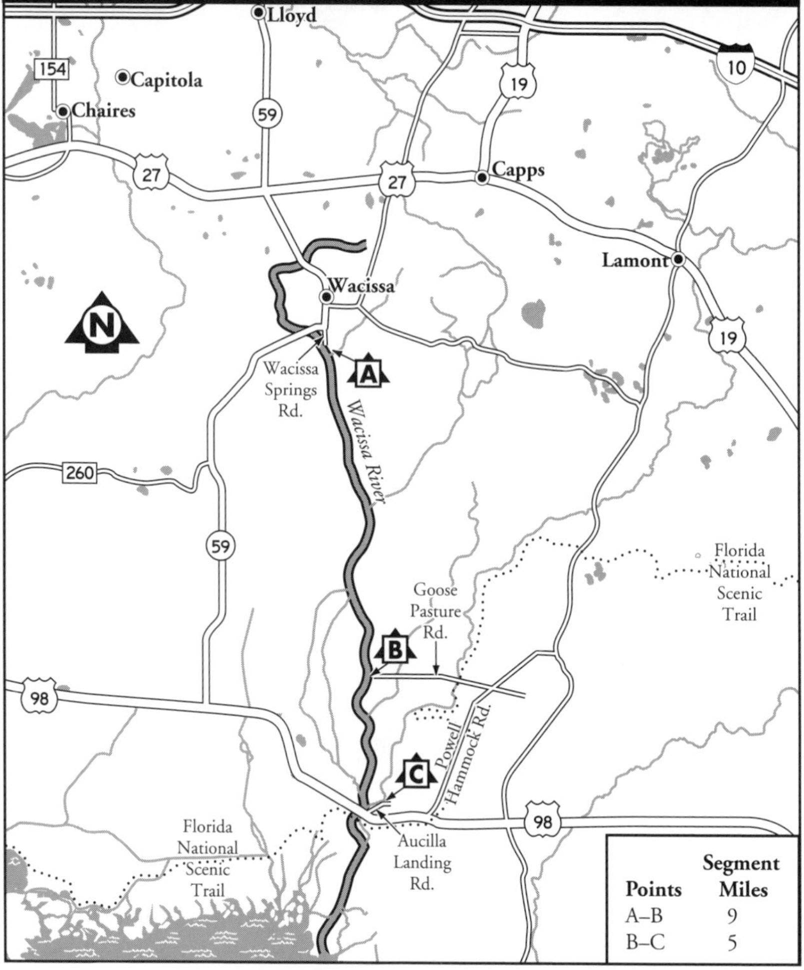

Points	Segment Miles
A–B	9
B–C	5

SHUTTLE: To reach the put-in from Newport, take US 98 east to the intersection with FL 59. Turn left, north, on FL 59, and follow it to Wacissa Springs Road. Turn right on Wacissa Springs Road and follow it until it dead-ends at a boat ramp. To reach the takeout from Newport, take US 98 east beyond the bridge over the Aucilla River. Turn left on Powell Hammock Road. Keep north on Powell Hammock Road to Goose Pasture Road (watch for signs indicating Goose Pasture Recreation Area). Turn left on Goose Pasture Road and follow it to a dead end at Goose Pasture Recreation Area.

GAUGE: Visual. The Wacissa is a spring-fed river and is floatable year-round.

B

class	I
length	4
time	2
gauge	Visual
level	Spring-fed
gradient	2
scenery	A+

GOOSE PASTURE TO AUCILLA RIVER AT US 98

DESCRIPTION: When leaving Goose Pasture, paddle to the extreme west side of the river. Follow the current through the stands of wild rice down a narrow waterway and through a swampy area for about 0.5 miles. A clearly defined channel 25 to 30 feet wide will emerge. Continue on this channel for about 1 mile. Begin watching for some very large cypress trees spaced along the left bank as the river widens. There will be a couple of small sloughs on the right side, but keep paddling and watch for some red rectangles painted on the trees on river right. Watch carefully for a small channel on the right. This is the Slave Canal. More evidence of the correct waterway will be cut logs along the waterway and occasionally visible limestone rocks lining the canal.

The Wacissa River wanders off into a large impassable swamp, Hell's Half Acre, just south of the Slave Canal. Spending the night there makes a good story but can be a frightening and uncomfortable experience.

Once in the canal, the paddler will enjoy a unique and eerie experience. This is a beautiful, clear, and shallow waterway through dense swamp. Magnificent cypress trees and other impressive hardwoods canopy the stream, and it is a rare day when you won't see alligators, turtles, and a vast variety of water birds. It is awe-inspiring to consider that human labor is responsible for what now appears to be a natural waterway. However, be prepared for overhead and underwater log obstructions.

Toward the end of the canal, the current slackens and the water deepens. Upon reaching the Aucilla, which has a much faster current at this point, paddlers should head upstream for a few hundred yards to the boat landing on the Aucilla River. The point where the two streams meet is easily recognized, as strong current flows past the Slave Canal from the east. If you reach the US 98 bridge you've gone too far.

SHUTTLE: To reach the put-in from Newport, take US 98 east to reach Powell Hammock Road. Turn left (north) on Powell Hammock Road, and head toward Goose Pasture Road (watch for signs indicating Goose Pasture Recreation Area). Turn left on Goose Pasture Road and follow it to the dead end at Goose Pasture Recreation Area. To reach the takeout from Newport, take US 98 east beyond the bridge over the Aucilla River. Turn left on Aucilla Landing Road, the first road east of the US 98 bridge, to reach a public boat ramp.

GAUGE: Visual. The Wacissa is a spring-fed river and is floatable year-round.

AUCILLA RIVER

The Aucilla begins just south of Boston, Georgia, and flows into the Gulf of Mexico south of the confluence of the St. Marks. It pops up and down with such irregularity, however, that in many places it is not a river at all but a series of lakes, marshes, and/or sinkholes. Just north of US 27, the Aucilla becomes a clearly defined river and proceeds in an orderly fashion for about 20 miles until it goes underground again. It rises some 5 miles to the south and is joined by the waters of the Wacissa, flowing through a man-made canal on to the Gulf.

The Aucilla, limestone-ringed and bedded with dark, clear, tannin water and beautiful vegetation, varies from high banks with upland hardwoods to more tropical-looking areas of cypress, palms, and palmettos. The reflections of the trees in the dark water are a treat at any season of the year. There are two relics of man-made dams on the upper section that may provide an easy whitewater experience for the novice paddler. Since the dams were built of native limestone that has now washed aside, there are no dangerous hydraulics or undercurrents. On the lower section, there are a series of rocky shoals, and at the point where the Tallahassee hills drop off the karst, a stretch of real whitewater appears. Dropping 8 to 10 feet over 30 yards of boulder-strewn river, the Big Rapid is about the best Florida has to offer to the whitewater enthusiast. A few more miles through increasingly beautiful junglelike terrain and the Aucilla goes underground. No dramatics—just a quiet pool with a few logs floating around.

Much of the river valley is now managed by the Suwannee River Water Management District, which has kept the natural setting yet improved the sand roads in the area and developed accesses. The primary accesses divide paddle trips into 2-, 13-, and 7.5-mile segments.

MAPS: Lamont, Lamont SE, Nutall Rise (USGS)

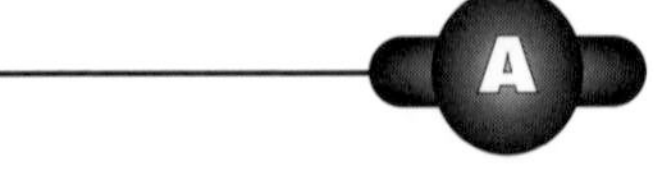

class	I
length	22.5
time	Varies
gauge	Web
level	45–51.9
gradient	1.8
scenery	A

FEDERAL ROAD #1 TO RIVER SINK

DESCRIPTION: This upper access off of Federal Road #1 is the preferred alternative to the old US 19/27 access and adds 2 miles to the paddle. The stream is small and swift here. About 1 mile below US 27 are the remains of the first of two man-made dams. These dams were constructed of native limestone and have been washed away, resulting in nice little drops or rapids. Since they were not excavated or reinforced in any way, they do not have

dangerous hydraulics or pieces of metal in them. Novice paddlers usually navigate them without difficulty, but if you're in doubt, they can easily be carried around.

This section of the river is primarily of the drop-and-pool nature, with stretches of slow water broken by rocky shoals and small drops. The high banks have typical hardwood forests; some swampy areas provide a contrast of cypress, magnolia, and titi. Camping areas are plentiful in the woods and much of the shoreline is managed by the Suwannee River Water Management District. Therefore, it is open for recreational use. It is 13 miles from the US 27 bridge to the CR 257/14 bridge.

Aucilla River: Federal Road #1 to River Sink

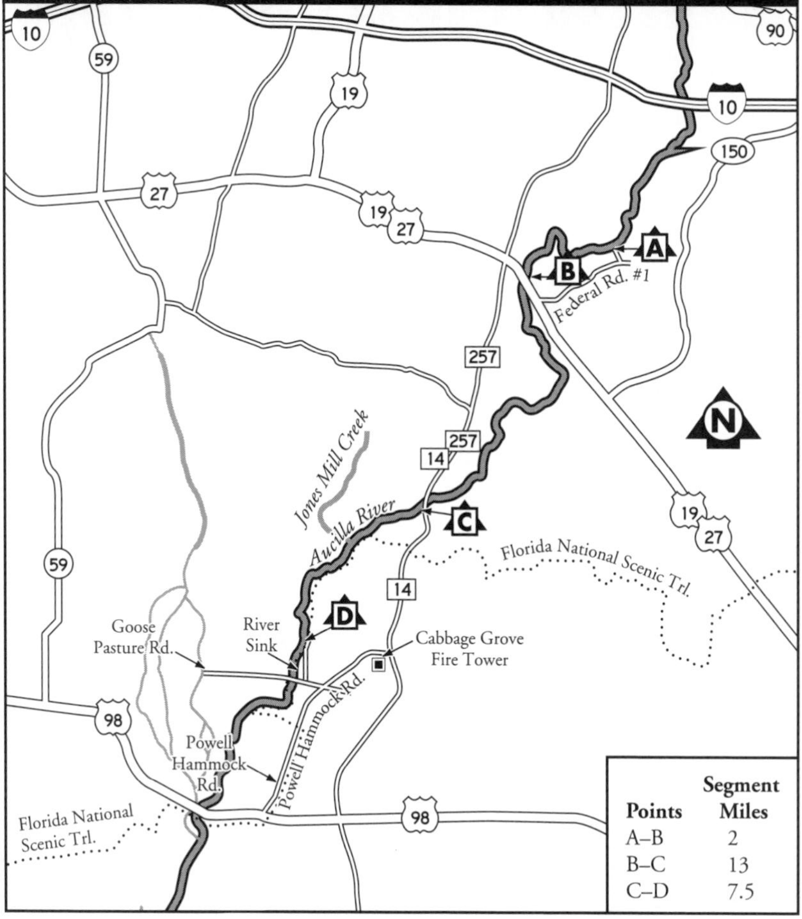

Points	Segment Miles
A–B	2
B–C	13
C–D	7.5

Below CR 257/14, there is usually a pleasant current on this section except in very low water. The banks are high and densely wooded with limestone outcroppings. Palm trees and the preponderance of resurrection fern on the banks and oak limbs provide greenery even in the midst of winter.

The first set of rapids is encountered about 2 miles downstream. It is distinguished by a small, rocky shoal followed by a sharp bend to the right. The current speeds up and a sharp turn back to the left results in a shoal of cascading water for about 40 yards. It is a fairly easy run and poses little hazard to the reasonably competent canoeist.

Jones Mill Creek entering from the west indicates that the paddler is over 3 miles downstream. The creek usually spills over a limestone ledge when it enters the river and provides a pleasant swimming hole. The banks have been cleared here and it is a nice spot for camping and picnicking. Less than a mile from Jones Mill Creek, the paddler will approach the Big Rapid. This is a boulder-strewn drop of 8 to 10 feet over a distance of about 30 yards. It is true whitewater, and should be accorded proper respect. The sound of fast water will usually be heard well in advance of the rapids, and a quiet pool at the top makes it easy to pull over for scouting. Scout from the east bank where a well-worn trail runs beside the river. At very high water it may be impossible to tell that the rapid exists. At a reasonably high level, it may be run either on the right or left. Under normal conditions, it is run only on the left, or east side, of the river. Large logs and trees have been known to get caught in the rocks at the bottom of the rapid. This makes it essential that it be scouted prior to running.

There are several interesting shoals below Big Rapid. The river continues downstream for about 3 miles before going underground. Access to this point is passable by high-clearance vehicles and is just a half-mile above the lowest access described above. The river rises again at Nutal Rise and, with the confluence of the Slave Canal from the Wacissa just above US 98, flows to the Gulf of Mexico. Access below US 98 is limited.

SHUTTLE: To reach the lowermost access from Newport, take US 98 east beyond the bridge over the lower Aucilla River. Turn left on Powell Hammock Road. Keep north on Powell Hammock Road to Goose Pasture Road (watch for signs indicating Goose Pasture Recreation Area). Turn left on Goose Pasture Road and follow it west 0.9 miles to a graded road leading right, north. Turn right at the graded road, signed "Public River Access," and follow it for 0.6 miles to the river access on the left. The actual river sink can be accessed by a rough road that spurs

off of Goose Pasture Road just west of the right turn on the graded road. The rough sink access is near a big sinkhole within sight of Goose Pasture Road. The sink access road heads north from Goose Pasture Road 120 yards to the sink. To reach the uppermost access, backtrack to Goose Pasture Road, then turn left on Powell Hammock Road to come within sight of the Cabbage Grove fire tower. Turn left at this junction and the dirt road becomes Taylor CR 14 until the crossing and access at the Aucilla, where it becomes Jefferson CR 257. Keep forward on CR 257 to reach US 19/27. Turn right on US 19/27 and cross the bridge over the Aucilla River to reach Federal Road #1. Turn left on Federal Road #1 and follow it for 2.3 miles to a left turn onto a graded road that reaches the river.

GAUGE: Web. At **www.swrmd.state.fl.us,** go to river levels, then find the Aucilla, and then find Aucilla at Lamont. The minimum runnable level is 45 feet. Flood stage is 51.9 feet.

ECONFINA RIVER OF TAYLOR COUNTY

The Econfina River of Taylor County, in the Big Bend, is not to be confused with Econfina Creek of Washington and Bay Counties. This Econfina is lesser known as a paddling destination and is certainly underused as such. Born in the swamps of Pedro Bay east of Perry, the Econfina gathers water and becomes a stream in the far east of Taylor County. Fallen trees and submerged logs generally keep it impassable to all but the most strenuous paddlers until the US 98 bridge. Here a boat ramp allows easy access the beginning of a beautiful trip through the junglelike terrain of a swamp river. Part of the river is bordered by Suwannee River Water Management District Lands, and downstream more river shore is state park land, keeping the atmosphere remote.

MAPS: Johnson Hammock, Nutall Rise, Snipe Island (USGS)

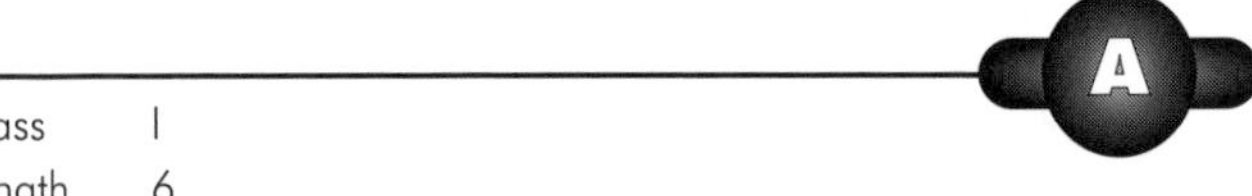

class	I
length	6
time	4
gauge	Web
level	140
gradient	2
scenery	A

US 98 TO ECONFINA RIVER STATE PARK

DESCRIPTION: This canopied black water stream flows swiftly towards the Gulf at US 98. It is 20 to 30 feet wide here. Palms and oaks hang over the stream while cypress grow tall and stately along the river and in the swamps behind the banks. Palmetto covers the floor of the high ground beneath the trees. Lily pads thrive in still waters. Expect to pull over or around downed trees along the way. The banks are often low, and water drifts off into cypress sloughs. The main channel is easily discernible, though, and sometimes small wooded islands force the stream to work around them.

Pass under a power line at 1 mile. Just downstream, look for an elevated logging tram crossing the swamp and the pilings of an old bridge on the river's edge. After many twists and turns, enter an area known as the Mill Pond. Here the current slackens and waterweeds grow along the edge of a much wider stream. These waterweeds form the river channel. High ground here and there allows you to relax out of the boat.

Just below the Mill Pond the Econfina narrows and resumes its fast-moving ways. Here are the concrete abutments of an old bridge that may be rebuilt. State park property begins over on river right. The swift water continues southwesterly and ends just beyond the Mossy Hammock Road bridge. Here the Econfina broadens a bit and houses become more common, though public

lands extend farther downstream. Tidal influences change the current's speed, but it is not long before you reach the state park boat ramp on river right.

SHUTTLE: To access the put-in from Perry, take US 98 west to the bridge over the Econfina River. A boat ramp is on the northeast side of the bridge. To reach the takeout, continue west on US 98 to CR 14. Turn left on CR 14, which dead-ends at the Econfina River State Park boat launch. A fee is required for this launch.

GAUGE: Web. The USGS gauge is Econfina River near Perry, FL. The minimum recommended runnable level is 140 cfs.

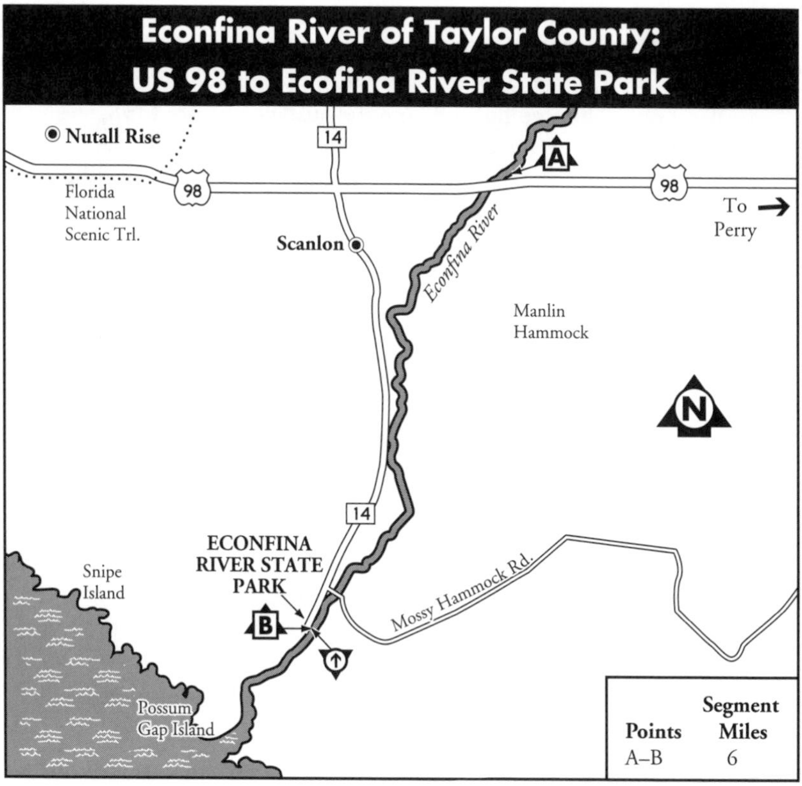

Econfina River of Taylor County: US 98 to Ecofina River State Park

Nutall Rise
14
A
98
98
Florida National Scenic Trl.
To Perry
Scanlon
Econfina River
Manlin Hammock
N
14
ECONFINA RIVER STATE PARK
Snipe Island
B
Mossy Hammock Rd.
Possum Gap Island

Points	Segment Miles
A–B	6

STEINHATCHEE RIVER

Often paddling enthusiasts will drive along and span a bridge over a waterway, and look down to see if the waterway has paddling potential. If you have traveled US 98 along the Big Bend, you have probably crossed the Steinhatchee River and wondered about its paddling potential. Add this river to your list, because it can be paddled. Furthermore it includes a "waterfall," Steinhatchee Falls, over which you can paddle. But before you throw your boat onto your vehicle, remember that the upper river, above US 98, flows into a sink and doesn't connect to the lower river. The upper river is scenic and is bordered by Suwannee River Water Management District Lands, as is much of the lower river, which becomes tidally influenced near the town of Steinhatchee.

MAPS: Clara, Jena, Steinhatchee (USGS)

A

STEINHATCHEE FALLS TO MOUTH OF STEINHATCHEE RIVER

class	I (II)
length	10
time	Varies
gauge	Phone, Web
level	Spring-fed
gradient	1.2
scenery	B–

DESCRIPTION: The Steinhatchee River is fed by Steinhatchee Springs and drains Mallory Swamp. It flows south toward the Gulf before going underground just north of US 98, near the hamlet of Tennille, and remerging 0.5 miles south. Here it stays above ground the rest of the way to the salt water. Paddlers can put in at Steinhatchee Falls or at an access a mile or so above it. That way you can run the falls or not. If you feel this limestone ledge forming a 3-foot drop is too imposing, just start below it. This ledge was used by native Indians and early settlers as a river crossing. The first segment stays in SRWMD lands and offers a natural setting on either side of the black water. As you close in on the town of Steinhatchee, houses appear on the banks and the river becomes affected by the tides, which will affect the time it takes you to make it downriver.

There are many fish camps and landings in Steinhatchee. Intrepid paddlers will make it to the mouth of the river and a boat ramp, but the trip can be shortened by using an upstream fish camp or marina of your choosing as an ending point. An outfitter offering shuttles and boat rentals is located on the river at US 98, but you must reserve your rental or shuttle at least 24 hours in advance. It is 10 miles from the falls to the river mouth.

Steinhatchee Falls

SHUTTLE: From Perry, take US 98 south to Tennille and FL 51. Turn right and head south on FL 51. Look for the left turn and sign indicating Steinhatchee Falls. Follow this road and veer right as it splits to reach the falls (the left split leads to the access above Steinhatchee Falls). To reach the takeout at the mouth of the river, return to FL 51 and head south to CR 358 and the bridge over the Steinhatchee. Turn left on CR 358 and cross the river, then make your first right onto Ed James Road to reach the takeout ramp.

GAUGE: Phone, Web. Call Steinhatchee Outpost at (352) 498-5192 for the latest river conditions. The USGS gauge helpful to determine river levels for any given time period is Steinhatchee near Cross City, FL.

Steinhatchee River: Steinhatchee Falls to Mouth of Steinhatchee River

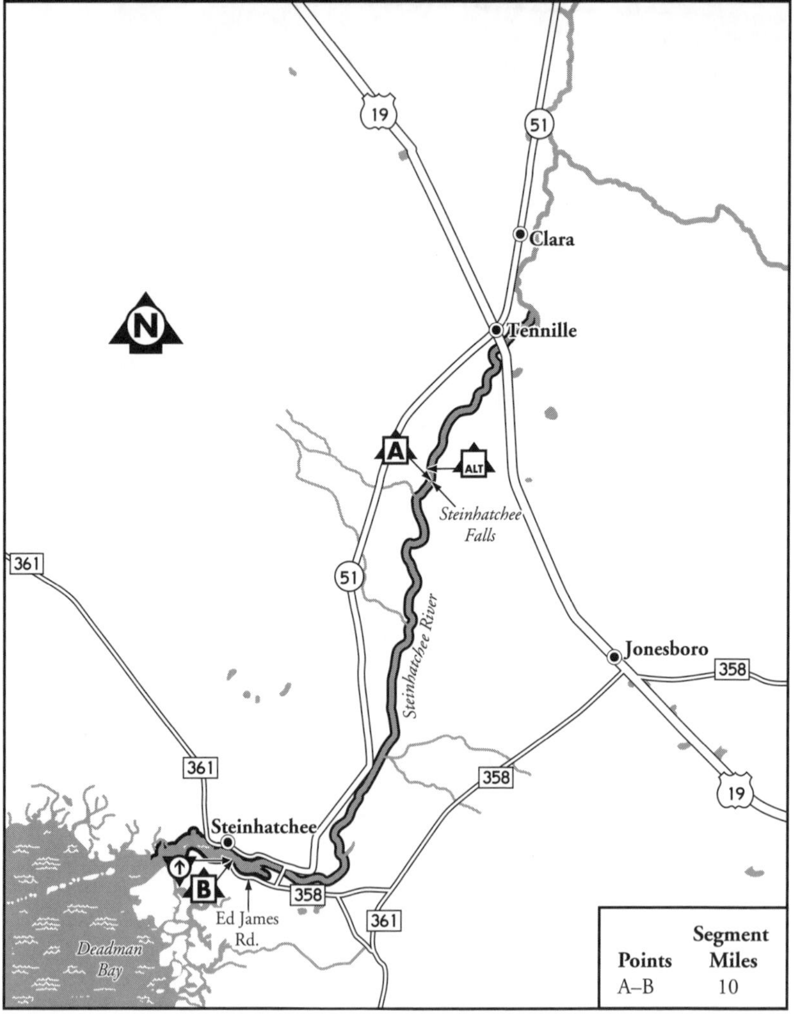

19
51
Clara
N
Tennille
A
ALT
Steinhatchee Falls
361
51
Steinhatchee River
Jonesboro
358
361
358
19
Steinhatchee
B
358
Ed James Rd.
361
Deadman Bay

Points	Segment Miles
A–B	10

A calm day on the Steinhatchee River

Once there was a legend that told of a river that went to hear a fountain sing. The song was so beautiful that the river decided to sing it to the ocean. All the way to the shores of the ocean the river sang. Soon, the mountains heard of the song that the river was singing and came from all over the land to listen. And because the song was so beautiful the mountains settled down and stayed to listen forever.

—Algonquin Indian Legend

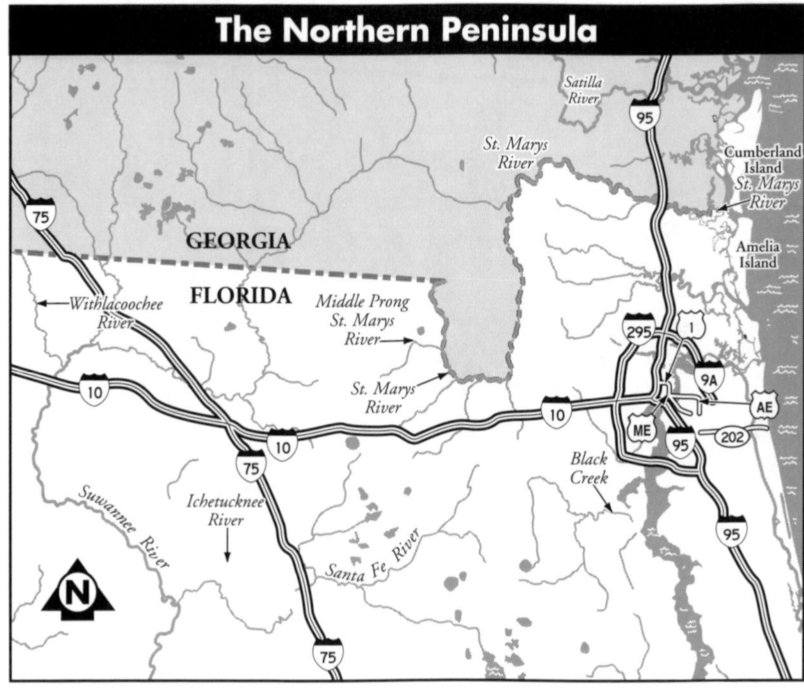

The Northern Peninsula
Satilla River
95
St. Marys River
Cumberland Island
St. Marys River
75
GEORGIA
Amelia Island
FLORIDA
Withlacoochee River
Middle Prong St. Marys River
295
1
10
St. Marys River
9A
10
AE
ME
10
95
202
75
Black Creek
Suwannee River
Ichetucknee River
95
Santa Fe River
N
75

part **Four**

The Northern Peninsula

WITHLACOOCHEE RIVER (NORTH)

There are two rivers in Florida named Withlacoochee; the southern one is said to have been named after the one in the north. The northern Withlacoochee is really a Georgia river originating northwest of Valdosta and flowing some 70 miles through the coastal plain to the Florida line. The terrain on the Withlacoochee is similar to that of the upper Suwannee, characterized by high limestone banks, clear black water, and an abundance of cypress and tupelo trees. There are also a number of small shoals in the river that serve to make the trip interesting but not dangerous. Blue Springs, a beautiful blue-green pool, empties into the Withlacoochee from the west bank just a few yards from FL 6. This spring served as a major source of fresh water for the early inhabitants of the area. Another spring, Suwanacoochee, is located on the west side of the river just above Suwannee River State Park. At one time it served as the water supply for a public swimming pool whose remains are visible beside the river.

Campsites are not common on the Withlacoochee because of the steepness of the banks and the scarcity of sandbars. Upland hardwoods such as birch, water oak, redbud, magnolia, live oak, and pines are commonly seen. In the lower areas cypress, tupelo, and other swamp trees are present. The remoteness of the river lends itself to an active bird life. The steep bank makes it difficult to sight wildlife, but the forests of this area are known to harbor black bear, raccoon, opossum, wild boar, and bobcat.

The rocky shoals are discouraging to large boats, but fishermen in smaller johnboats are often seen trying their luck at catfishing as well as angling for bream and bass.

MAPS: Clayattville GA, Pineta, Octahatchee, Ellaville FL (USGS)

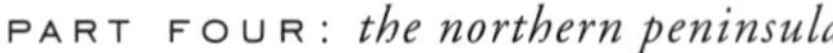

class	I–I+
length	27
time	Varies
gauge	Phone, Web
level	N/A
gradient	1.5
scenery	B

GEORGIA STATE LINE TO SUWANNEE RIVER STATE PARK

DESCRIPTION: The "With" is said to be canoeable from GA 37 to the Suwannee River during periods of good rainfall and to be easily navigable from the confluence of the Little River to the Suwannee at any time. The river is about 100 feet wide at the state line and usually has a good current. A few small shoals will be encountered. It is 5 miles from the state line to CR 150.

Sporadic houses and camps are scattered along the river banks below CR 150. Some 7 miles downriver from CR 150, there is a 10- to 12-foot opening in the high banks on the east side where water comes rushing out of the river. If followed, this stream flows for 75 to 100 yards and then disappears under a high bank. In Florida, whole rivers disappear in this manner, but it is unusual to lose just part of a river. It is 12 miles from CR 150 to FL 6.

Just below FL 6, Blue Springs flows in from the west bank. This is a very popular picnic and camping spot and will be crowded on warm weekends. The pool is 25 feet across with a single vent opening from a horizontal cavity 25 feet deep. The bottom is limestone and sand, and there is a 25-foot-high limestone bank on the south side. Blue Springs has a canoe launch. The current is milder below FL 6; the shoals become less frequent. The banks become increasingly higher and the limestone creates large white columns in fascinating shapes and forms. There are a number of unnamed springs along the banks in this section.

Just over a mile above the confluence with the Suwannee, CR 141 crosses the river, but there is no access to the water from this bridge. Suwanacoochee Spring, enclosed by a concrete wall, will be seen on the right. This spring pool is 20 feet in diameter with the water emerging from under a limestone ledge. The limestone outcrops around the pool are covered with green algae, which presents a cool and appealing spot on a warm day.

After reaching the Suwannee, the paddler must turn north and paddle upstream for a short distance to the state park boat ramp. Keep in mind that state parks close at sundown. The ranger should be informed of your trip plans and will give you the combination to the gate should you arrive late. It is 12 miles from FL 6 to the state park.

SHUTTLE: To reach the uppermost put-in from the town of Madison, travel northeast on FL 145 for about 18 miles to the bridge across the Withlacoochee. This will be just inside the

Georgia state line. A boat ramp is on the northwest side of the bridge. To reach the lowest takeout from the town of Madison, travel 17 miles east on US 90 to the bridge across the Suwannee River. Cross the river and continue to the first road to the left. This is the entrance to Suwannee River State Park.

GAUGE: Phone, Web. Call Canoe Outpost–Suwannee at (800) 428-4147 for the latest stream conditions. The USGS gauge helpful to determine flow rates for any given time period is Withlacoochee near Pinetta, FL. This gauge will be listed under gauges of the Suwannee River basin, not the Withlacoochee River south.

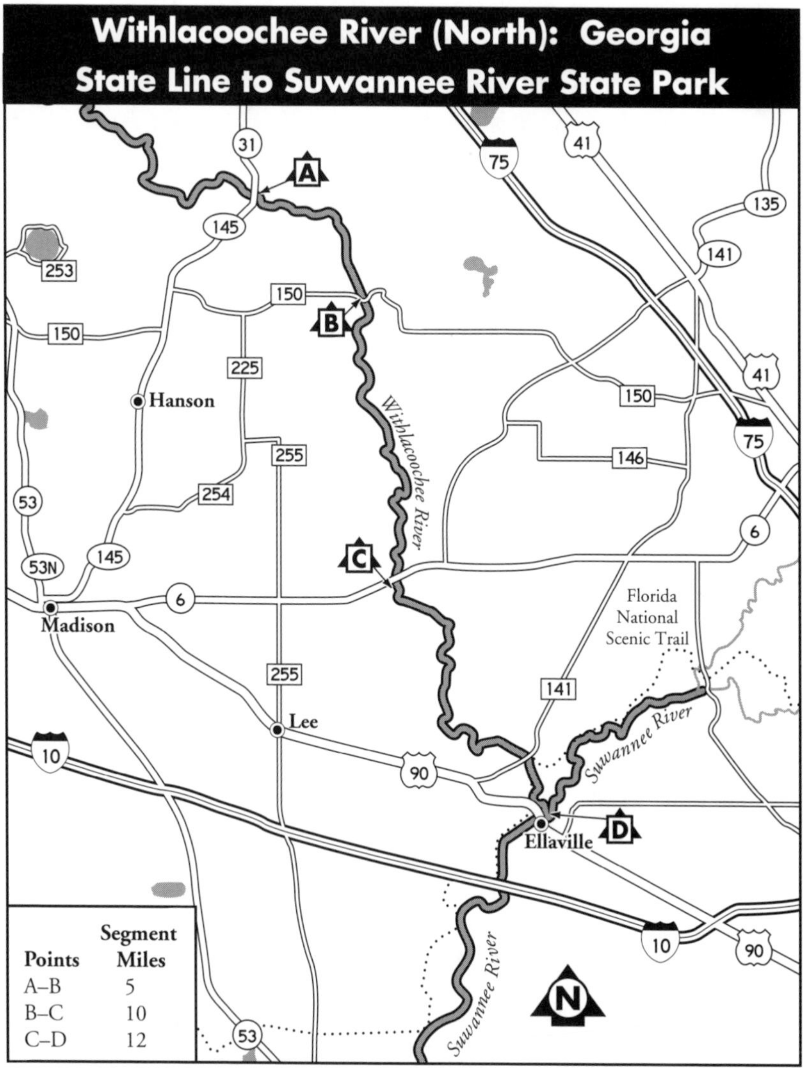

Withlacoochee River (North): Georgia State Line to Suwannee River State Park

Points	Segment Miles
A–B	5
B–C	10
C–D	12

SUWANNEE RIVER

The Suwannee River is Florida's contribution to the great rivers of the world. While it would not win any prizes for grandiose size, spectacular canyons, or mighty ports, it is one of the South's last examples of "Old Man River." The name, Suwannee, is an ancient Native American word that may have meant "echo." Spelled a variety of ways, it appears in place names throughout the southeastern United States and has come to be synonymous with Dixie and the Old South. There are paddlers who have made the Suwannee their entire canoeing career—they need no other stream and never seek one.

The Suwannee drains out of the equally famous Okefenokee Swamp. A twisting river from its beginning just above Fargo, Georgia, it loops and curves across the Florida peninsula for over 200 miles before it empties into the Gulf of Mexico. The upper stretches are characterized by sandy banks, rocky shoals, and a profusion of small waterfalls created by the entry of tiny streams. There are frequent swampy areas that provide overflow basins for flood waters. Stately cypress and gnarled tupelos often grow in the river as well as along the banks. Access is limited, and the wildlife is abundant. Only the Withlacoochee River (north), the Alapaha River, and a few creeks feed the upper reaches of the Suwannee. As a result, the current tends to be slow and lazy except around the shoal areas. At low water, it is so undisturbed by current that it resembles a long, smooth lake mirroring white limestone banks and moss-draped trees.

A few miles above White Springs, a unique geological phenomenon produces Big Shoals, the largest whitewater shoal in Florida; it can be a strenuous rapid. Immediately below Big Shoals are a couple of small springs, harbingers of the fantastic array of springs that will present themselves on the way to the Gulf. There are 22 major springs on the Suwannee and 27 on its tributary, the Santa Fe River. This accounts for the increasing size and volume of the river as it flows southward.

As in all rivers, the personality of the Suwannee undergoes a drastic change with any changes in water level. High water offers a faster current and easier paddling and makes Big Shoals a torrent of foaming, frothing turbulence. Low water is slower and more leisurely, but reveals white sandbars, gleaming castle-like limestone walls, and a treasure house of springs, caves, and grottos. In general, the Suwannee is high during the late winter and spring and becomes lower during the summer and fall. Autumn has the advantage of low water, pleasant weather, fewer bugs, and the beautiful fall colors reflected in the clear water.

Almost every tree indigenous to north Florida can be seen at some point on the Suwannee. Stands of cypress and yellow pine, gum, magnolia, maple, holly, poplar, willow, and river birch are common.

Wildlife includes deer, otters, and alligators, as well as beavers, raccoons, skunks, and armadillos.

Below Suwannee River State Park, the river broadens and becomes more accessible. This results in some motorboat traffic; the nearer the river gets to the Gulf, the larger and more powerful the boats you may encounter. However, the river passes along the Lower Suwannee National Wildlife Refuge. This public land shoreline along with the myriad tracts acquired by the Suwannee River Water Management District (SRWMD) throughout the Suwannee River Valley keeps the river wild in appearance if not in fact. The SRWMD, which covers 15 counties, has acquired 47,000 acres on the Suwannee, including 70 percent of the river frontage in the upper river basin. Furthermore, SRWMD is developing the Suwannee River Wilderness Trail, which will become a series of cabins, chickees, and campsites along the river.

Camping is allowed on SRWMD lands, but is strictly prohibited on the wildlife refuge, making campsites scarce on the lowermost river near the town of Suwannee. SRWMD has an excellent handout listing all the boat ramps and canoe launches on the Suwannee that paddlers will find very helpful.

Among other adventures on the Suwannee, I have paddled this river from top to bottom in one trip and proclaim it as the finest touring river in the state and a first-rate adventure when paddling it in its entirety. Moreover, the Suwannee River is easy, leisurely paddling for even a novice canoeist. Big Shoals can be easily scouted and portaged if necessary, and none of the other shoals are sufficiently challenging to cause a problem. Boat ramps and canoe launches are frequent along the river, allowing trips of varied lengths. Campsites are not plentiful on the Suwannee, but every year hundreds of canoe-campers manage to find a spot to pitch a tent. Start looking well before sundown and be willing to compromise; something will turn up, and once you have settled in, it will seem like home. Roads run within a few miles of the river from Fargo, Georgia, to the Gulf, and the countryside is dotted with crossroad communities and small towns. Limited supply runs can be made from the river at White Springs, Branford, and Fanning Springs and private and public campgrounds. For additional information there is an excellent Web site, ***www.canoe-suwannee.com,*** *that is dedicated to paddling the Suwannee River.*

MAPS: Suwannee River Water Management District River map, Fargo, Needmore (Georgia), Fargo SW, Benton, White Springs East, Live Oak East, Hillcoat, Fort Union, Ellaville, Falmouth, Madison SE, Dowling Park, Day, Mayo, Mayo SE, O'Brien, Branford, Hatchbend, Wannee, Fanning Springs, Manatee Springs, Vista, East Pass, Suwannee (Florida) (USGS)

class	I–I+
length	21
time	Varies
gauge	Web
level	51.6–65
gradient	0.7
scenery	A

FARGO, GEORGIA TO FL CR 6

DESCRIPTION: At Fargo, the Suwannee River has progressed 17 miles from Billy's Lake in the Okefenokee Swamp and is 60 to 70 feet wide at low water. The state of Georgia has established an interpretive center with a boat ramp at the bridge crossing in Fargo. This makes an excellent access. However, determined paddlers can start in the Okefenokee or just outside its border at a private landing off of GA 177. The banks are 2 to 5 feet high, sandy, and interspersed with large, swampy overflow areas. Campsites are scarce in high water, but some small sandbars are available when the river is low. The current is usually slow to nonexistent, so pace yourself accordingly. Cypress Creek enters from the east and Suwanoochee Creek from the west a few miles below Fargo. Enter Florida at 12 miles. The boundary is roughly marked by Tom's Creek. SRWMD lands border much of the river once you're in Florida. Woodpecker Road, a graded and fairly well-maintained throughway, runs parallel to the river on the west. There is a small shoal just above the CR 6 bridge.

SHUTTLE: To reach the uppermost put-in, head to Fargo, Georgia, located 5 miles north of the Florida–Georgia state line at the intersection of US 441 and GA 94. It is 38 miles due north of Lake City, Florida. The access is at Georgia's Suwannee River interpretive center, which has a boat ramp. To reach the takeout from Lake City, drive north on US 441 to CR 6. Turn left on CR 6 and follow it to the bridge over the Suwannee River.

GAUGE: Web. The USGS gauge is Suwannee River at White Springs, FL. It should read between 51.6 and 65 feet for the best paddling.

B

class	I–I+ (III)
length	26
time	Varies
gauge	Web
level	51.6–65
gradient	0.8
scenery	A

CR 6 TO STEPHEN FOSTER STATE PARK

DESCRIPTION: There are a few houses and trailers for the first 0.5 mile or so below CR 6, but the wilderness soon resumes. The banks have begun to be steeper since crossing the Florida state line, and this trend continues, making sandy campsites hard to spot from the water. Limestone outcroppings are more common and are frequently covered by bright green ferns, which reflect in

Suwannee River (Sections A–B): Fargo, GA to Stephen Foster State Park

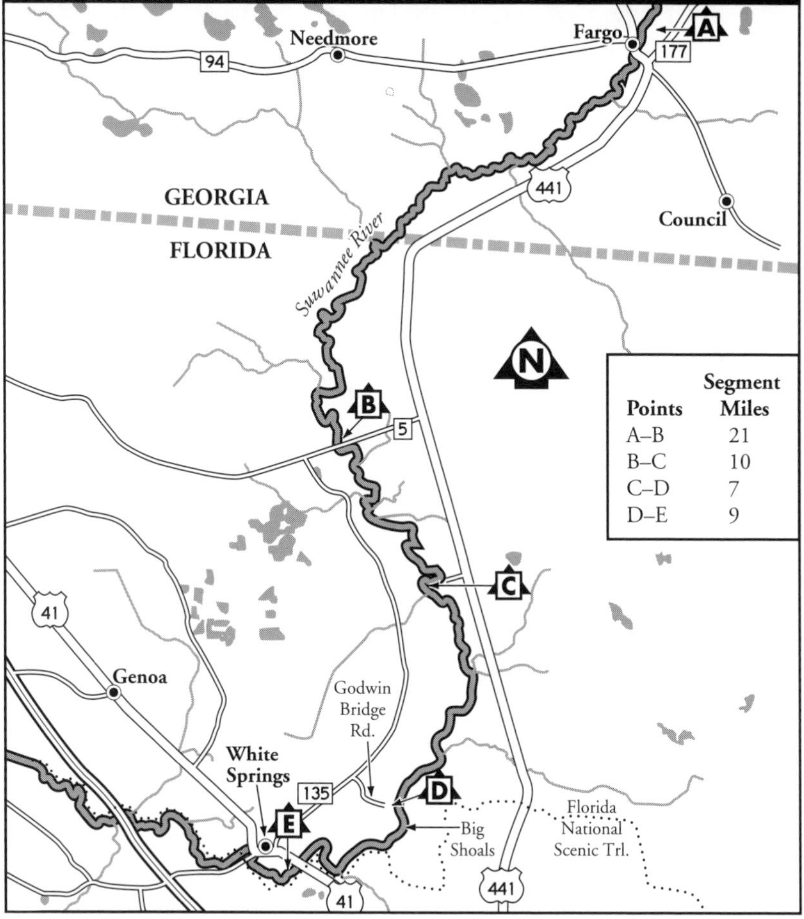

Points	Segment Miles
A–B	21
B–C	10
C–D	7
D–E	9

the still water. Tupelo and cypress growing in the water often form a line down each side of the river with hardwoods and pines growing above them on the steep banks. The effect of this natural corridor is serenely beautiful. This is an area of abundant wildlife; otters and alligators are a frequent sight for the quiet canoeist.

The waters of the upper Suwannee are extremely dark due to the tannin from the swamp. This tends to reduce the amount of fish life in this section, but bass, catfish, and bream are caught. It is 10 miles from CR 6 to Cone Bridge Road.

Below the Cone Bridge Road access, the high banks and slow water continue. The lack of access makes this one of the most

beautiful and remote sections of the river. Roaring Creek enters the river from the west just below Cone Bridge Road.

Deep Creek, a canoeable stream, flows in from the east about 3 miles above Big Shoals. Deep Creek drains 25 percent of the Osceola National Forest and is one of the two areas in the forest where creek swamps are present. It is important to several endangered species because it has extensive mature hardwood stands and very little evidence of human disturbance.

Warning signs begin to appear on trees 0.75 mile above the rapids. Big Shoals can be scouted from the left bank, and there is a clearly marked trail to follow. At very low water it may be necessary to line the canoe through on the extreme left side. At low to normal water levels it can be run against the west bank. The rapids become more aggressive with increased water levels and at high water may have standing waves 2 to 3 feet high.

The rapid consists of a double drop, with the upper drop having a curl coming in from each side so that it has to be run exactly in the middle to keep the boat dry. Thirty yards below the upper drop is another drop of 4 feet with a standing wave at the bottom. Just below the final drop is a rock, strategically located at just the point that paddlers have started congratulating themselves on having successfully run the rapids!

Big Shoals is rated a moderate to strenuous rapid depending on the volume of water flowing through it. It should always be scouted before it is run. If in doubt about your skill or the turbulence of the water, carry around. In any event it is probably wise to unload your canoe and carry all but your essentials to the bottom of the rapid. Wear your personal floatation device. There are large, sharp, limestone boulders in this rapid, and even good swimmers can bump their heads if a canoe capsizes.

Big Shoals Public Land has a canoe access, picnic area, and hiking and mountain biking trails. Those wishing to paddle Big Shoals use the old Godwin Bridge access, then head down to the US 41 bridge access. Robinson Creek enters just below Big Shoals on the east bank. Paddle into it for a very short distance to see an interesting waterfall. Like Deep Creek, it drains from the Osceola National Forest. Bell Springs, the most northern named spring on the Suwannee, is located on the east bank. It is on private property, and has been developed for use as a fish pond and swimming pool. Its drainage into the river is not identifiable as a spring run.

Downriver from the shoals, the river returns to its snail pace. Little Shoals, a series of rocky ledges, will be encountered a mile or so upstream from White Springs and serves to liven up the trip. Falling Creek enters from the east at Little Shoals. It is 14 miles from Cone Bridge Road to the US 41 bridge.

For 1 mile below US 41, the river flows around the town of White Springs. Just below FL 136 is the relic of the old springhouse for what used to be called White Sulphur Springs. Records indicate that the first springhouse was built in 1835. The Colonial Hotel and Springhouse, built in the early 1900s, served as a spa and health sanatorium until the 1960s. The spring is enclosed by the concrete foundations of the former bathhouse. Just north of the spring is the entrance to the Stephen Foster State Folk Culture Center. An annual Folk Festival is held on Memorial Day weekend. There is a museum, carillon tower, picnic tables, restrooms, and shaded walking trails, but no camping facilities. It is a little over 2 miles from the US 41 bridge down to the canoe launch at Stephen Foster State Park.

SHUTTLE: To reach the put-in from White Springs, FL, head north on CR 135 to CR 6. Turn right on CR 6 and follow it to the bridge over the Suwannee River. The lowermost takeout is just west of White Springs, off of US 41, at Stephen Foster State Park.

GAUGE: Web. The USGS gauge is Suwannee River at White Springs, FL. It should read between 51.6 and 65 feet for the best paddling.

Stephen Foster State Park to Suwannee River State Park

class	I
length	41
time	Varies
gauge	Web
level	51.6–65
gradient	0.7
scenery	A

DESCRIPTION: Varied access points make this section either a great overnight camping endeavor or several day paddles. At White Springs, the river turns and flows to the west. The Florida Trail begins to follow the north bank of the Suwannee from White Springs and will continue to do so to Suwannee River State Park. Below White Springs the high, limestone banks continue with only an occasional small sandbar. Five miles downriver and within sight of I-75, Swift Creek enters from the north. It is well named, as it rushes through a rocky canyon into the river. I-75, 8 miles downriver, offers no access to the river. It marks the beginning of an area of lower banks and beautiful sandbars.

SWRMD public lands continue on much of the river between US 41 and US 129. The high limestone walls are still present, but now the tendency is to have low banks on one side of the river and high banks on the other. At other times, vertical limestone banks on both sides will present graceful corridors that resemble the walls of castles. Caves and grottos have been worn into the rock, and the water makes hollow musical sounds as the wake of the

canoe moves along the crevices. Occasionally water can be heard dripping far up inside unseen caves inside the walls.

Within 3 miles of Suwannee Springs there is a small waterfall and a residential community in the woods on the north bank. Fishermen in small boats begin to appear and in the summertime, swimmers and sunbathers frequent the sandbars on the south bank. Despite its popularity, this section is one of the most beautiful and pristine on the entire river.

It is 18 miles from Stephen Foster State Park to Suwannee Springs and the US 129 bridge. Suwannee Springs is a town that progress has left behind. There was a post office in the town in 1834; in the early 1880s a resort hotel was built that was said to be one of the finest hostelries in the southeast. A railroad that ran to the front door of the hotel ferried guests back and forth to the town of New Branford, where they boarded a paddleboat for the journey to the Gulf. All that is left of this grandeur is the rock retaining wall that separated the springs from the Suwannee River, a few houses, and an abandoned bridge. At least six springs comprise the Suwannee Springs, four of them outside the wall that confines the main spring. In warm weather this spot is well populated with swimmers and sunbathers.

There is a railroad trestle just below US 129 and intermittent pastureland for perhaps another mile. A house on the north bank is the only sign of development until you reach the Florida Sheriffs' Boys Ranch. The north bank beyond the Boys Ranch is SWRMD land for some distance. The high limestone banks continue for several miles but begin to be less noticeable as the river straightens and the banks become sandy and heavily wooded. Sandbars are found only on the inside of sharp bends, which are now less common. Campsites are infrequent and would involve carrying gear up high banks into the woods.

Holton Creek enters the Suwannee on the north bank about 2.5 miles upstream from the junction with the Alapaha River. Its source is Holton Spring, a first-magnitude spring located 1 mile up the spring run from the Suwannee River. There is also a small spring on the south bank of the river just below the entrance of the creek. Irrigation pipes and other signs of development are evident as well. One-half mile above the confluence of the Alapaha River, another first-magnitude spring, Alapaha Rise, enters the river from the north side. This spring appears to consist of a single vent at the head of a depression about 150 feet in diameter. It is at the foot of steep, limestone walls, which persist down the 300-foot run to the river. The spring water is a very dark tannin color.

There is some controversy about the location of the actual confluence of the Alapaha River into the Suwannee. A healthy, vigorous river for over 100 miles through south Georgia, only in

Suwannee River (Sections C–E): Stephen Foster State Park to Branford

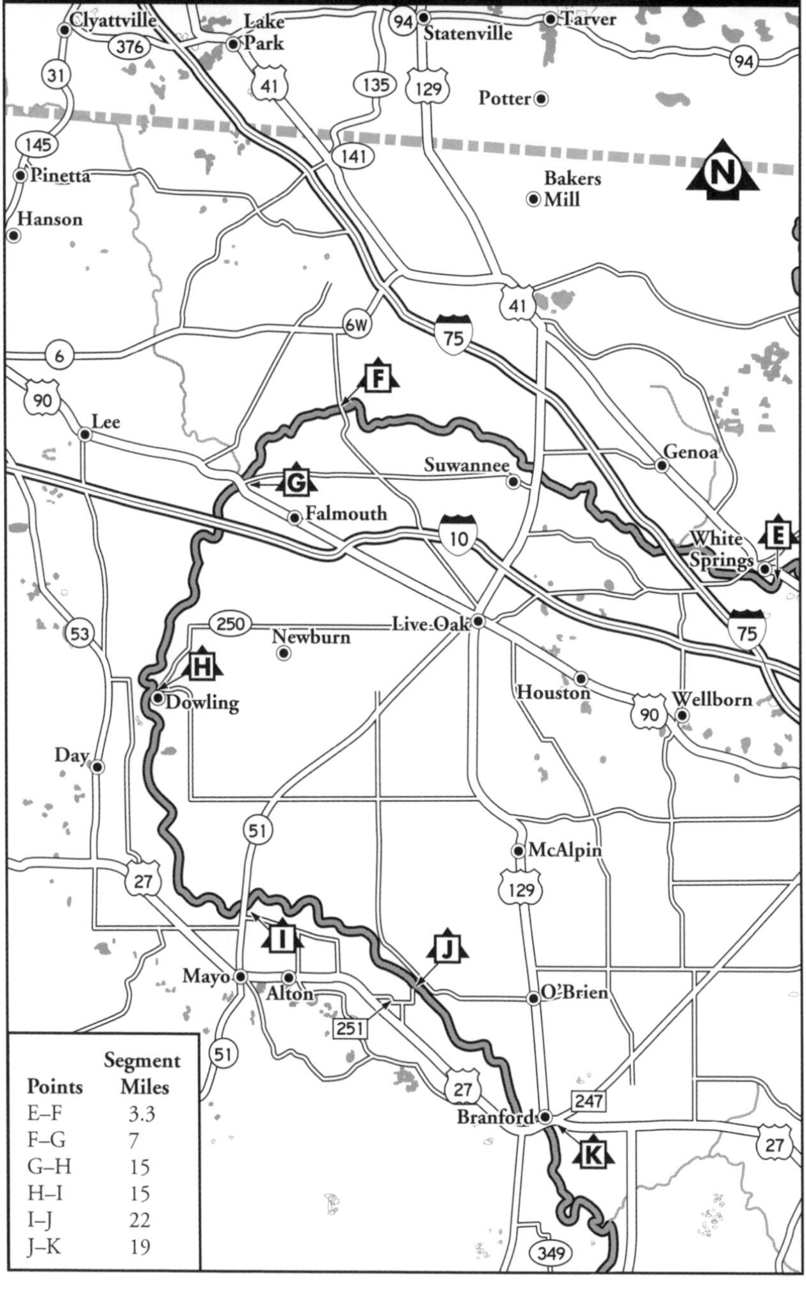

Points	Segment Miles
E–F	3.3
F–G	7
G–H	15
H–I	15
I–J	22
J–K	19

times of above-normal rainfall does it actually flow into the Suwannee. Evidently at some point between Statenville, Georgia, and south of the Florida line, the Alapaha, or some portion of it, goes underground. The result is a clearly defined riverbed leading into Florida and down to the Suwannee that is frequently either a series of potholes or is completely dry. Local people in this area believe that Alapaha Rise spring is the true resurrection of the Alapaha River.

In any event, the confluence with the riverbed of the Alapaha is 0.5 mile downstream from the spring. A Hamilton County recreation area, Gibson Park, is located here, and a boat ramp, grassy picnic site, and camping area are provided. It is 15 miles from US 129 to the Alapaha.

Below the confluence of the Alapaha, the Suwannee widens even more, and houses can be observed on both banks for the next few miles. The boundaries of the state park begin on the west side of the river less than 4 miles downstream. On the east bank, Lime Spring flows into the river. This run is also called Dry Branch or Dry Run. This is a pleasant spot for one last dip before reaching the Suwannee River State Park.

Just below this spring on the west bank is a privately owned camp store and boat ramp. Hiking trails, campsites, picnicking, water, and electricity are available in the state park. Like all Florida state parks, it closes at sundown. If you leave your car parked there, it will be protected, but be sure that you check with the ranger to get the combination to the gate in case you arrive after dark. It is 8 miles from the Alapaha to Suwannee River State Park.

SHUTTLE: To reach the lowermost takeout in this section from Live Oak, head west on US 90 to Suwannee River State Park. The uppermost put-in is just west of White Springs, Florida off US 41, at Stephen F. Foster State Park.

GAUGE: Web. The USGS gauge is Suwannee River at White Springs, FL. It should read between 51.6 and 65 feet for the best paddling.

class	I
length	30
time	Varies
gauge	Web
level	51.6–65
gradient	0.6
scenery	B

SUWANNEE RIVER STATE PARK TO FL 51

DESCRIPTION: Below the confluence with the Withlacoochee, the Suwannee widens to 150 feet before narrowing again. Occasional shoals cross the river, depending on water levels. Pass under I-10 at 3 miles. Anderson Spring, just below I-10 on the

east bank of the river, is a shallow pool about 50 feet in diameter with a 150-foot run to the Suwannee that is usually dry. Live oaks line the Suwannee's sandy banks, occasionally broken by limestone walls where nameless springs boil up. Cypress trees decline in number, and sandbars are fewer, often covered with grasses. Reach the town of Dowling Park after 14 miles.

Houses border the river, save for occasional SWRMD lands, which are marked. Reach Charles Spring at 21 miles. Here translucent, sky-blue pools are divided by a small limestone bridge. Charles Spring flows down a short run into the Suwannee River. Allen Mill Pond, at 22 miles on the west side of the river, is a 150-foot-long pond with at least three spring vents. It flows about 0.5 mile to the river. Thomas Spring is slightly over a mile south of Charles Spring on the east bank of the Suwannee.

Reach Blue Spring at 25 miles. Perry Spring, less than 2 miles north of FL 51 on the west bank, is a small spring pool with a short run emptying into the Suwannee.

SHUTTLE: To reach the put-in from Live Oak, head west on US 90 to Suwannee River State Park. To reach the takeout from Live Oak, head south on FL 51 toward Mayo. Just after the Adams Bridge over the Suwannee River, turn left into a park and boat launch, on the southeast side of the bridge.

GAUGE: Web. The USGS gauge is Suwannee River at White Springs, FL. It should read between 51.6 and 65 feet for the best paddling.

FL 51 TO BRANFORD

class	I
length	22
time	Varies
gauge	Web
level	51.6–65
gradient	0.4
scenery	A–

DESCRIPTION: The land is lower here resulting in more pressure on the underlying limestone, making the aquifer more likely to break through, creating springs. Telford Spring, 1 mile east of FL 51 on the east bank, is a small, clear pool with a run of 100 feet to the Suwannee. There are houses directly across the river. Irvine Slough is a swampy area on the east bank of the Suwannee extending from Luraville Springs, due north of Telford Spring, for about a mile downriver to the vicinity of Peacock Slough. Peacock Slough empties into the Suwannee from the east bank 1.5 miles downstream from FL 51. Bonnet Spring and Peacock Spring are its source, 1.5 miles north.

Running Springs is privately owned and fenced. An old iron bridge appears just below Running Springs. This former railroad

bridge has a large cylindrical pylon in the center. Between the pylon and the metal span are wheels. Back when the bridge was functional, these wheels would allow the entire span to pivot from its usual location crossing the river to run parallel with the watercourse, allowing paddlewheelers with tall smokestacks to pass. Cattle ranches and houses border the river here. Convict Springs, at 6 miles, has a privately owned campground nearby. The spring vent is in the northern end of a 20-by-50-foot teardrop-shaped pool that has been enclosed with a concrete wall.

Pass a few narrow wooded islands abutted by mild but perceptible shoals save a few strokes of the paddle. Mearson Spring, at 11 miles, is a 25-by-50-foot pool surrounded by high banks. It discharges about 75 feet into the Suwannee. SWRMD lands are generally on the last half of this section. Troy Spring is at 17 miles. It is a first-magnitude spring pumping 66 million gallons of water daily. Visible in its depths is the *Madison,* a Confederate supply ship that was intentionally run aground to keep it from falling into Union hands. The hull of this steamboat points toward the head of the spring. This is part of Troy Spring State Park.

Little River Springs, at 19 miles, is clear and blue. The vent is the entrance to a cave system more than 1,200 feet long and 100 feet deep. It has a short run over a sandy bottom. Branford Springs is southeast of the junction of US 27 and US 129 at the town of Branford. It is part of Ivey Memorial Park. Branford Springs is said to pump 6.8 million gallons daily.

SHUTTLE: To reach the put-in from Branford, head north on US 27 to Mayo and FL 51. Turn right on FL 51 and head north to Adams Bridge over the Suwannee River. A boat launch and park are on the southeast side of the bridge. To reach the takeout from Live Oak, drive south on US 129 to Branford and US 27. Turn right on US 27 and reach Ivey Memorial Park, on the east side of the river.

GAUGE: Web. The USGS gauge is Suwannee River at White Springs, FL. It should read between 51.6 and 65 feet for the best paddling.

F

class	I
length	42
time	Varies
gauge	Web
level	51.6–65
gradient	0.6
scenery	B

Branford to Fanning Springs

DESCRIPTION: Branford Springs is a popular cave-diving area. Below Branford Springs, pass along some SRWMD lands, where there are campsites aplenty, interspersed with houses. Limestone

banks become more sporadic below Branford. On higher ground are live oaks and pine. Low-slung humps of willow, river birch, and cypress line the river. Behind many of these humps are extensive swamps that fill when summer's thunderstorms drift over the Suwannee River valley.

Come to the confluence of the Santa Fe River at 10 miles. There was a Spanish mission here in the 1600s, near the confluence. The river widens to 200 feet below the Santa Fe, making a fairway for winds. A segment of the west bank below the confluence is SWRMD lands. Turtle Springs, at 12 miles, is a keyhole-shaped pool that makes a short run to the Suwannee. More houses appear along the river. The width of the river brings a corresponding increase in boat size. Manatees may be seen here.

Rock Bluff Springs is on the left bank. Cypress trees with huge buttresses flank the spring run. It has a large pool near the site of an old ferry crossing. Now privately owned, it pumps 27 million gallons daily. The FL 340 bridge just below Rock Bluff Springs is reached at 19.5 miles. Gornto Springs, at 21 miles, is abutted by a little county park with a boat ramp, a few campsites, and a nice dock. Below Log Landing, at 24 miles, SWRMD lands abut both sides of the river. Hart Springs, at 33 miles, is on the east side of the Suwannee. Hart Springs has a campground and camp store.

Reach the town of Old Town at 38 miles, and the start of the longest continuous populated stretch of river. The houses are all low-rises up on pilings. The banks remain populated until Fanning Springs and the US 98 bridge, the last span over the Suwannee.

SHUTTLE: To reach the put-in at Branford from Fanning Springs, take US 98 north to Old Town. Turn right on FL 349 and follow it north to US 27. Turn right on US 27 and follow it to the bridge over the Suwannee River. On the east side of the bridge is Ivey Memorial Park and a boat ramp. The takeout is at the Joe H. Anderson Sr. boat ramp, on the Dixie County side of the river, opposite Fanning Springs. From the bridge over US 98, head west, toward Perry, then turn south on 989 Street, then turn left on 155 Avenue to reach the boat ramp. There is also a canoe launch on the opposite bank at Fanning Springs State Recreation Area. If you're leaving a car overnight, consider leaving it at one of the local adjacent campgrounds for a small fee.

GAUGE: Web. The USGS gauge is Suwannee River at White Springs, FL. It should read between 51.6 and 65 feet for the best paddling.

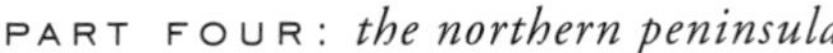

class	I
length	42
time	Varies
gauge	Web
level	51.6–65
gradient	0.6
scenery	B

G

FANNING SPRINGS TO GULF OF MEXICO

DESCRIPTION: The US 98 bridge at Fanning Springs is the lowermost bridge over the river. The town of Fanning Springs is a product of the Seminole Wars, starting out as Fort Fanning in 1836. The fort was later occupied by Confederate troops during the Civil War. From here, they successfully sank a 90-foot Union gunboat with cannon fire near the mouth of the springs. Divers can still see the gunboat. Beyond Fanning Springs, on the east bank, is Andrews Wildlife Management Area. This 4,000-acre parcel, home to the largest remaining tract of hardwood forest in the Suwannee Valley, was acquired in 1985 through the Save Our Rivers program. Four Florida State Champion trees grow here—Florida maple, persimmon, river birch, and bluff oak. Cattails and saw grass appear occasionally on the banks.

Manatee Springs State Park is reached after 9 miles. Paddlers access the park by heading directly up the gorgeous spring run alongside a boardwalk. It boils up over 80,000 gallons of clear water per minute where lots of fish, turtles, and other aquatic life thrive.

The river remains very wide from here on out. Paddlers should pick a bank to hang alongside for wind protection and better scenery. Yellow Jacket Landing, at 12 miles, is the last landing on the west bank. From here on down, the land is mostly part of the Lower Suwannee Wildlife Refuge with no camping allowed. This refuge protects most of the lower Suwannee River basin and also fronts 26 miles of the Gulf Coast, making this one of the largest undeveloped river deltas in the United States. A few houses will indicate Fowlers Bluff, on the east bank at 18 miles. Tidal influence becomes significant below Fowlers Bluff, with small tidal creeks spurring off the Suwannee. When nearing the town of Suwannee, hug the west bank. When you see houses, look for the sign to Suwannee Marina, up Demory Creek. This access is actually 4 miles above the mouth of the Suwannee River, which becomes even wider with salt marsh grasses and palm islands.

SHUTTLE: To reach the lowermost takeout from Fanning Springs, take US 98 north to the intersection with FL 349. Turn left (south), and follow Dixie CR 349 to the town of Suwannee. Turn left at SE 885 Avenue, then make a quick right on SE 228

Suwannee River (Sections F–G): Branford to Gulf of Mexico

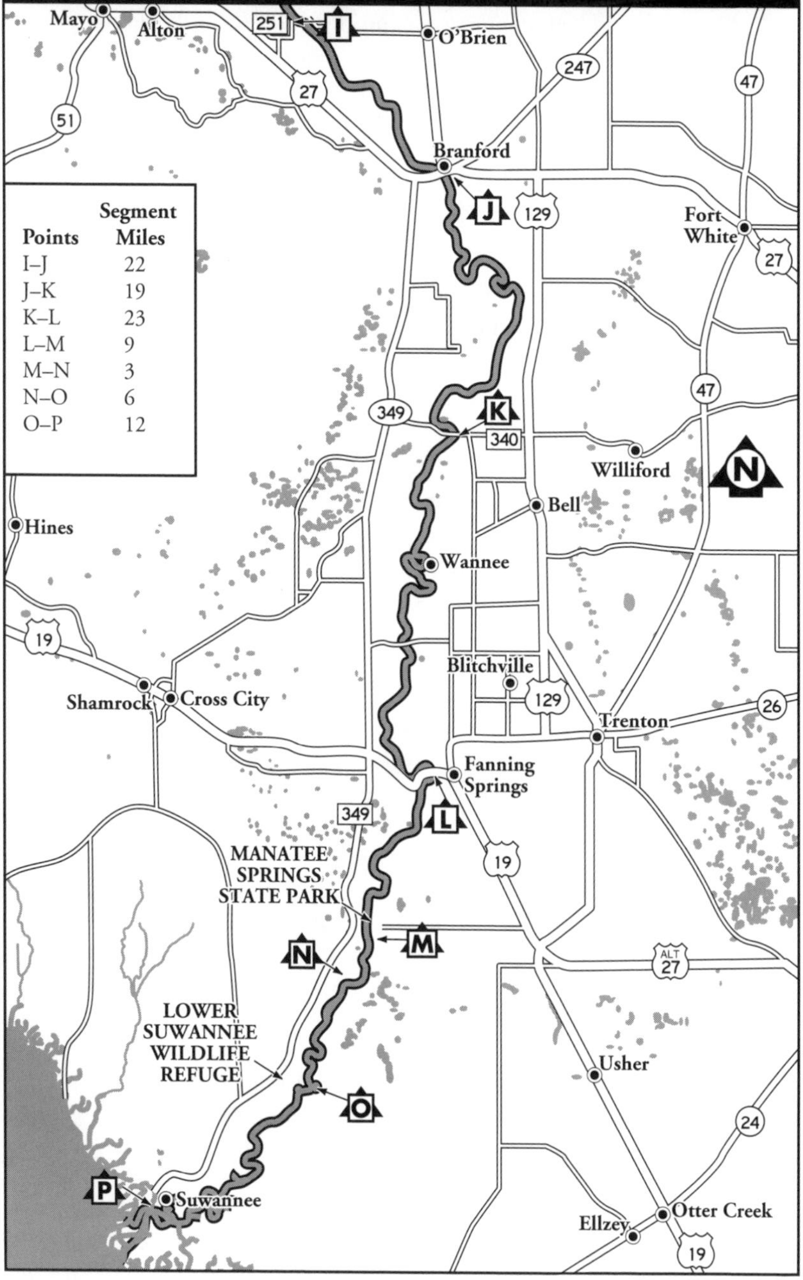

Points	Segment Miles
I–J	22
J–K	19
K–L	23
L–M	9
M–N	3
N–O	6
O–P	12

Mayo
Alton
251
I
O'Brien
247
47
27
51
Branford
J
129
Fort White
27
47
349
K
340
Williford
N
Bell
Hines
Wannee
19
Blitchville
129
Shamrock
Cross City
Trenton
26
Fanning Springs
349
L
MANATEE SPRINGS STATE PARK
19
M
N
ALT 27
LOWER SUWANNEE WILDLIFE REFUGE
Usher
O
24
P
Suwannee
Ellzey
Otter Creek
19

Street and follow it to the Suwannee Marina (**www.suwannee marinainc.150.com;** (352) 542-8159). Make sure and notify them if you wish to leave a car overnight and leave them your name and tag number. Offer to pay a parking fee when you arrive. The put-in is at the Joe H. Anderson Sr. boat ramp, on the Dixie County side of the river, opposite Fanning Springs. From the US 98 bridge in Fanning Springs, head west toward Perry, turn south on 989 Street, then turn left on 155 Avenue to reach the boat ramp. There is also a canoe launch on the opposite bank at Fanning Springs State Recreation Area. If you're leaving a car overnight, consider leaving it at one of the local, adjacent campgrounds for a small fee.

GAUGE: Web. The USGS gauge is Suwannee River at White Springs, FL. It should read between 51.6 and 65 feet for the best paddling.

SANTA FE RIVER

The Santa Fe is one of the most beautiful and unusual waterways in north Florida as well as one of considerable historical interest. It serves as the county line for Alachua County, dividing it from the neighboring counties of Bradford, Union, and Columbia. It begins in the Santa Fe lakes in the extreme northeast corner of Alachua County, flows through Santa Fe swamp, and then veers in a northwesterly direction toward O'Leno State Park where it goes underground. For its first 18 miles it is a tiny meandering stream that is not navigable. At Worthington Springs it becomes minimally canoeable for the very determined, and at FL 241, just a few miles above O'Leno State Park, it becomes a pleasant stream for even the novice paddler. At O'Leno, the river goes underground in a lazy whirlpool and follows subterranean passageways for some 3 miles to River Rise State Preserve. When the Santa Fe returns, it is as a generously sized river some 75 to 100 feet wide. This area, from O'Leno to River Rise, is owned primarily by the state of Florida, either as O'Leno State Park or as the River Rise State Preserve, and is laced with excellent hiking trails. The natural bridge provided by the Santa Fe at this point was one of the primary crossing points offered to Native Americans and early settlers. As a result, several very old roadbeds, including Bellamy Road and Wire Road, cross this area.

From the river to the confluence of the Suwannee, the Santa Fe is said to have over three dozen springs, many of them first-magnitude. The Ichetucknee River, a tributary of the Santa Fe, is a paradise of crystal-clear springs. Because of its popularity with tubers, it is better known and more highly populated. The terrain surrounding the

Santa Fe possesses almost every plant community known to the north-central Florida area. It has sandhills, swamps, flatwoods, and hardwood hammocks. The protection of the state-owned land has made a refuge for deer, turkey, otter, bobcat, and other animals indigenous to north Florida.

MAPS: Worthington Springs, Mikesville, High Springs, High Springs SW, Fort White, Hildreth (USGS)

WORTHINGTON SPRINGS TO O'LENO STATE PARK

class	I
length	11
time	7
gauge	Visual, Web
level	N/A
gradient	1
scenery	B

DESCRIPTION: At one time Worthington Springs was the site of a hotel, swimming pool, bathhouse, and recreation hall. Nothing remains of the hotel except the ruins of the concrete pool that contains the spring. The pool is located in a low wooded area on the north bank of the river just below the put-in. Today the springs area is part of the Chastain-Seay Park, which has nature trails, picnic and camping areas, and a boat launch.

Although the river is 50 to 75 feet wide at this point, clear of obstructions, and flowing at a leisurely pace, its canoeable appearance is deceiving. Shortly above CR 241, the river begins to be obstructed by willow trees that offer a challenge in maneuvering as the lazy current picks up speed. After practicing in the small willow tangles, you will be better prepared for the more technical Confusion Willow Swamp. The channel splits again and again as it enters a mile-long tangle of willow trees. This section of the Santa Fe should only be paddled in normal to high water in the winter when the branches are bare by those determined canoeists who want to paddle a river from its highest put-in point.

It is 6 miles from Worthington Springs to CR 241. Paddlers who put in at CR 241 can enjoy the upper river without the tangles of Confusion Willow Swamp. After emerging from the willow swamp above CR 241, the river becomes deep and slow and is a dark tannin color, like strongly brewed tea. The banks are steep with occasional swampy areas and rare, small sandbars on the curves. There are a few houses scattered on this section and some pastureland on the higher banks.

With the advent of Olustee Creek, the river widens to 100 feet and is deep with 10- to 15-feet-high banks. There is a road and boat ramp at this point, but it is on private property and is therefore not a public access. Olustee Creek is said to be canoeable at very high water levels. It is slightly over a mile from the confluence of Olustee Creek to I-75.

Below the interstate the river narrows again and enters O'Leno State Park. It is now about 75 feet wide with banks 4 to 6 feet high. There is a rocky shoal that provides a little interest just above the takeout at the park. There are three shoals on the river below the takeout, but you will have to paddle back up river after running them, since the river goes underground shortly below the takeout downstream from O'Leno. The park closes at sundown, so make arrangements with the ranger if you feel you may be late getting off the river.

Santa Fe River (Sections A–C): Worthington Springs to Suwannee River

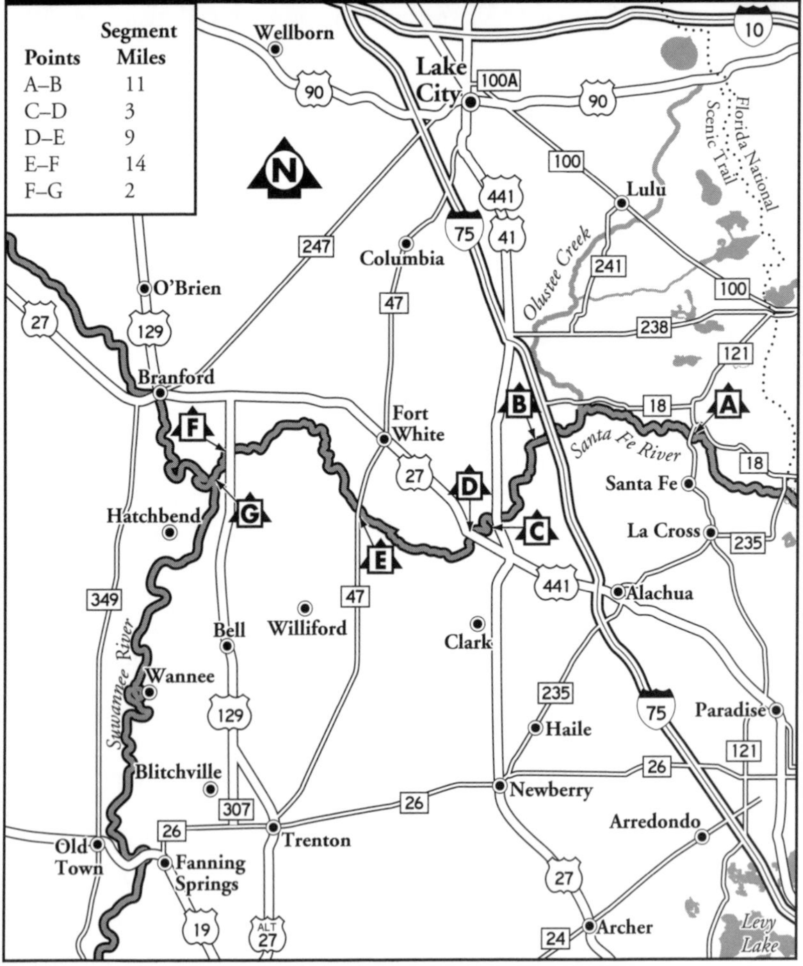

Points	Segment Miles
A–B	11
C–D	3
D–E	9
E–F	14
F–G	2

SHUTTLE: To reach the put-in from Paradise, head north on US 441 to CR 18. Turn right on CR 18 and follow it south to FL 121. Turn right, south, on FL 121 and follow it to Chastain-Seay Park, on the southwest side of the river. The park has a boat ramp under the river bridge. To reach the takeout from High Springs, take US 441 north across the Santa Fe River to O'Leno State Park and a boat launch inside the park.

GAUGE: Visual, Web. This run is recommended only in winter after heavy rains. The USGS gauge helpful in determining flow rates for any given time period is the Santa Fe River at Worthington Springs, FL.

US 441 TO RIVER RISE AND BACK

class	I
length	4
time	3.5
gauge	Phone, Web
level	Spring-fed
gradient	1.1
scenery	B

DESCRIPTION: It is only 2 miles upstream from the US 41/441 access to River Rise, and since almost all of the property on both sides of the river is owned by the state, it is a remote and beautiful trip. The current is bracing paddling upstream, but paddlers can lessen the work by ferrying back and forth with the current to remain on the inside bends and by watching behind downed trees for eddies in which to rest. Very efficient paddlers make the trip in less than 45 minutes, less experienced paddlers may choose to rest more and take an hour or two. Coming back downstream is a breeze, and the scenery is worth the effort.

At River Rise, the river suddenly reappears from underground, about 100 feet wide and flowing swiftly. Several trails meet at this point, and there is a pleasant grassy glade for picnicking. The banks around the rise are 4 to 6 feet high and heavily wooded. Paddling downstream, the banks rise 10 to 12 feet in places and are very swampy in others. Just above and within sight of the US 41/441 bridge, a spring run on the left (south) bank indicates the entrance to Darby and Hornsby springs. Darby Spring is just inside this run, and the banks around it are private property.

Hornsby Spring is almost 1 mile further northwest up this run. The main spring is a part of Camp Kulaqua, a privately owned facility that is highly developed with diving platforms, sliding boards, and retaining walls. It is probably best not to paddle into the springhead itself. The run is very beautiful, however, and there are several smaller spring boils along the way.

SHUTTLE: This out-and-back paddle has only one access point. From the town of High Springs, travel northwest on US 41/441 for about 2 miles to the bridge across the Santa Fe. There is a boat ramp on the southeast side of the river. It is reached by turning left (west) onto Boat Ramp Road just before reaching the bridge. There is also a canoe livery right at the river on the southeast side of the bridge. Canoe rental, shuttle service, and launching are available for a fee.

GAUGE: Phone, Web. Call Canoe Outpost–Santa Fe at (386) 454-2050 for the latest river conditions. From here down, the Santa Fe is normally paddleable year-round, as it is spring-fed. However, the USGS gauge helpful in determining flow rates for any given time period is Santa Fe River near Fort White, FL.

class	I
length	28
time	Varies
gauge	Phone, Web
level	N/A
gradient	1
scenery	B

High Springs to Suwannee River

DESCRIPTION: This section can be broken into varied segments. This allows paddlers to tailor their distance and desires for day or overnight trips. Accesses can be found at bridges over the river at US 27, FL 47, and US 129. The Santa Fe is wide at the US 441 access, 100 to 150 feet with banks varying from 5 to 12 feet high. The current is slow and the water is generally clear at low water levels, 5 to 15 feet deep, and without sandbars. The right-hand bank from US 441 to US 27 is part of the River Rise State Preserve. There are several shallow shoals, and at low water there is a spot where the river divides and half of it disappears into a sink near the north bank. It reappears in a boil in mid-river just above the US 27 bridge. It is 3 miles from the US 441 access to the US 27 bridge.

The section from US 27 to FL 47, 10 miles, is very popular with canoeists and divers because of the vast array of beautiful springs. The river is occasionally shallow and the occurrence of rocky shoals makes it undesirable for large motorboats. In addition, low swampy terrain makes it unsuitable for housing developments, and it is one of the loveliest spots in Florida.

There are a few houses scattered along the higher banks just below US 27, but they are soon passed. Allen Spring is located on the right bank about 1.5 miles downstream from US 27, and at low water level, a number of small, unnamed springs may also be seen. Across the river, on the left bank, 0.25 mile downstream, is Poe Spring. A large spring boil flowing from a horizontal cavern with several smaller boils nearby, this spring forms a circular

pool about 90 feet in diameter. It is connected to the river by a 175-foot run. At one time there was commercial development here, but today it is a county park. It remains a popular swimming and picnicking spot. Poe Spring marks the beginning of lowland and swampy areas along the banks that are spotted with small springs.

Lilly Spring is located less than a mile from Poe Spring on the left bank. This is the home of Ed the Hermit. Ed is friendly and welcomes visitors to his beautiful ten acres beside the grass hut in which he lives. Jonathan Spring will be on the right bank just before reaching an island in the river. At the end of the island, watch the right bank for Rum Island Spring. This is part of Rum Island Spring County Park, which has a boat launch. The Blue Spring run will be seen entering the river from the left bank. Paddle 500 feet up the run to the spring. This is a privately owned area, and canoes are not permitted to paddle over the spring vent. Nearby, in the swamp around Blue Spring, are Little Blue Spring, Johnson Spring, and Naked Spring.

It is hard to miss the Ginnie Spring run and its origin, a large oval pool that is 50 feet deep and is said to be undermined by an extensive cave system with some 1,000 feet of passages. The area from July and the Devil Springs group to below Ginnie Spring is privately owned. There is an extensive private campground, boardwalks, and facilities for scuba divers. Just downriver are July Spring on the right bank and Devil's Eye and Devil's Ear springs on the left. These springs discharge from a system of caverns and passages said to be more than 1,000 feet long and up to 95 feet deep. Devil's Eye and Devil's Ear are connected with July Spring across the river.

A mile below Ginnie Spring one encounters the first of four rocky shoals across the river. The springs have contributed a considerable current to the river, but none of the shoals are difficult to maneuver. An island just below the first shoal should be run on the southwest side. The water on this section is clear at normal to low water levels with waterweeds on the bottom and reddish-colored pebbles in the depressions in the rocks. Cypress and other lowland hardwoods are prevalent in the swampy areas. Campsites are limited both because of the posted property and the swampy terrain. But there are Suwannee River Water Management District Lands (SWRMD) on the south bank before FL 47.

From FL 47 to US 129, 13 miles, there are roads and subdivisions very near the river on the right bank, and paddlers are seldom out of sight of a house. The banks begin to be higher, climaxing with the tall narrows of Hollingsworth Bluff. There are three rocky shoals above the confluence of the Ichetucknee.

These shoals limit large motorboat traffic for the first 3 miles, but after the Ichetucknee enters the Santa Fe, the river is likely to be crowded with a great deal of motor traffic, including ski boats. There are several boat ramps along this section on the right bank.

Northbank Spring is located about 0.5 mile downstream from FL 47 on the right bank. Wilson Spring is 1.5 miles farther down, and the boat ramp at Wilson Spring Road is the last public access before the confluence of the Ichetucknee. Part of the south bank just above the Ichetucknee is SWRMD lands. After the Ichetucknee comes in, the Santa Fe widens even more, the banks lower, and the river is deeper. Despite the presence of roads and houses, this is not a heavily populated area, and there are a number of pocket swamps along the way that teem with bird life.

It is 2 more miles from US 129 to the confluence with the Suwannee. This final portion is for those who want to say that they did the whole thing. This is a wide, windy stretch of river that is crowded with every kind of motorized watercraft. There are some interesting springs, however, including the Pleasant Grove Springs on the left bank just above the confluence with the Suwannee.

SHUTTLE: To reach the put-in from the town of High Springs travel northwest on US 41/441 for about 2 miles to the bridge across the Santa Fe. There is a boat ramp on the southeast side of the river, reached by turning left (west) onto Boat Ramp Road just before reaching the bridge. There is also a canoe livery right at the river on the southeast side of the bridge. To reach the takeout from High Springs, take US 27 north to US 129. Turn left, south, on US 129 and follow it over the bridge over the Santa Fe, where there's a potential takeout at Lemmon Memorial Park. Keep traveling south on US 129 beyond the bridge and just beyond CR 138 to NW 102 Place. Turn right on NW 102 Place and follow it to NW 39 Avenue. Turn right on NW 39 Avenue and follow it to the dead end at a boat ramp on the Suwannee, a short ways below the confluence. Ellie Ray's Campground, off of US 129 and a mile above the confluence with the Suwannee, offers safer parking for a fee.

GAUGE: Phone, Web. Call Canoe Outpost–Santa Fe at (386) 454-2050 for the latest river conditions. From here down, the Santa Fe is normally paddleable year-round, as it is spring-fed. However, the USGS gauge helpful in determining flow rates for any given time period is Santa Fe River near Fort White, FL.

ICHETUCKNEE RIVER

The Ichetucknee River raises the question of how one discriminates a river from a creek, or even a spring run. From its beginning at Ichetucknee Spring, to its confluence with the Santa Fe River, it is less than 6 miles, yet it is officially designated a river. By any name, Ichetucknee is one of the most scenic waterways in north Florida. There are nine named and many unnamed springs along the first 3.5 miles of this river. They provide a leisurely current that makes paddling effortless over the crystal-clear water, white-sand bottom, and the myriad spring vents and pools.

MAPS: Hildreth (USGS)

ICHETUCKNEE SPRING TO US 27

class	I
length	3.5
time	2
gauge	Phone
level	Spring-fed
gradient	1.1
scenery	A

DESCRIPTION: The water trail begins at Ichetucknee Springs State Park and is accessible to kayaks, canoes, and tubes during the summer months. There is an entrance fee. The springs begin with the Ichetucknee or Head Spring, and in downstream order are Cedar Head, Blue Hole, Roaring, Singing, Boiling, Grassy Hole, Mill Pond, and Coffee springs. Alligator Creek and Rose Creek flow near the Ichetucknee and disappear into sinkholes north of the springs. As you paddle, you will find other springs that are unnamed.

Ichetucknee is a tuber's paradise, and access to the river is controlled by park rangers. The trail and park ends 3.5 miles south at the park's southern entrance and our takeout at US 27. The paddler who completes the remaining 2 miles below US 27 must then paddle down the Santa Fe an additional 4 miles to the next access. This can be a long and windy trip. Since no food or beverages are permitted in canoes traversing the river through the park, arrangements should be made to take on provisions when your canoe reaches US 27. From October through March or April, canoeists and kayakers usually have the river to themselves but must still observe the regulations against food and drink.

SHUTTLE: To reach the takeout from High Springs, take US 27 north to the southern entrance of Ichetucknee Springs State Park, just before the US 27 bridge over the Ichetucknee River. To reach the put-in at the northern entrance to the state park, backtrack on

US 27 to Junction Road. Turn left, north, on Junction Road, and follow it to CR 238. Turn left on CR 238 and follow it to the state park entrance, on your left.

GAUGE: Phone. Call Ichetucknee River State Park at (386) 497-2511 for the latest water conditions. However, the river is spring-fed and offers a reliable flow.

Ichetucknee River: Ichetucknee Springs to US 27

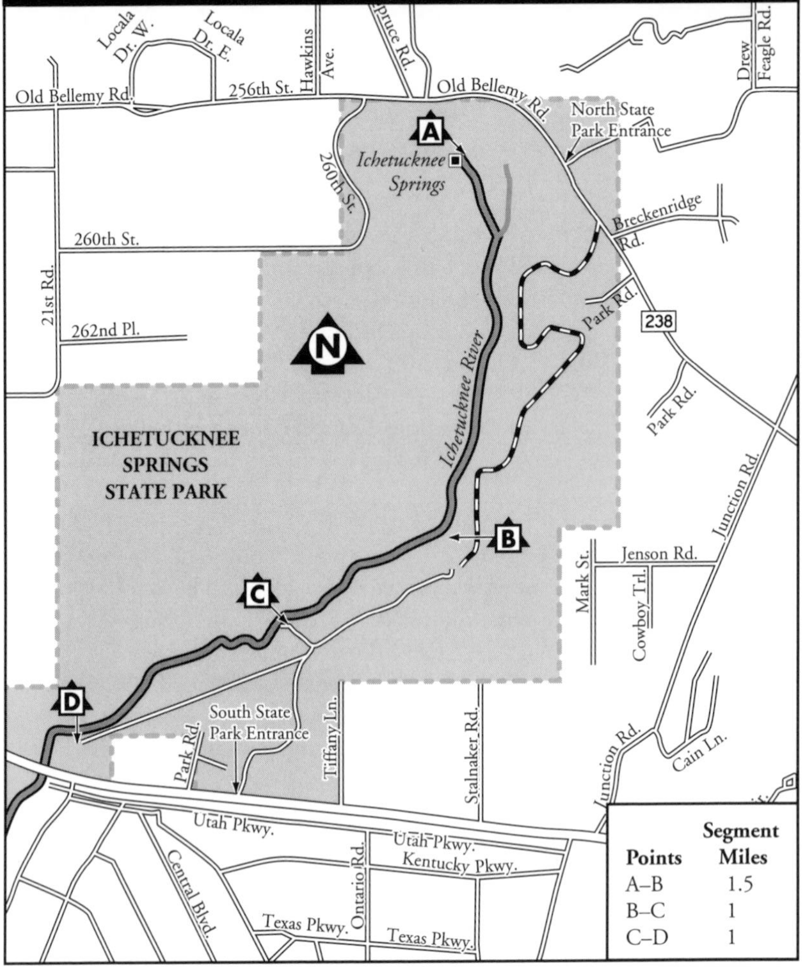

Points	Segment Miles
A–B	1.5
B–C	1
C–D	1

MIDDLE PRONG ST. MARYS RIVER

The Middle Prong is similar to the North Prong of St. Marys River, narrow and twisting with a fast current and beautiful cypress and tupelo trees, which form midstream obstacles that the paddler must negotiate. However, instead of draining Georgia's Okefenokee Swamp as the North Prong does, the Middle Prong drains Florida's Big Gum Swamp and Buckhead Swamp of the Osceola National Forest. The Middle Prong is said to provide a habitat for bear, panther, bobcat, and the red-cockaded woodpecker.

MAPS: Osceola National Forest map, Macclenny NW, Taylor (USGS)

EAST TOWER TO CR 127

class	I+
length	10
time	6
gauge	Web
level	220
gradient	3.3
scenery	A

DESCRIPTION: This section starts in a pond near the Osceola National Forest East Tower Hunt Camp. The North Prong exits from the northeast end of the pond. Although this is a very swampy area, the creek maintains a clearly defined current. There are many downed trees and other obstructions that make this a moderately strenuous trip. There are stands of willow trees above and below the CR 125 bridge, and there is access to the stream on the northwest side of the bridge. The Little River, which drains the Pinhook Swamp, flows in below the CR 125 bridge. Just a mile further down, at CR 122, there is a better access. As you progress downstream, the terrain changes from lowlands and swampy areas to higher banks and upland pine forests, which have been subject to forest fires in recent years. This section would not be canoeable in very dry weather. Paddlers can continue downstream 2 miles to the confluence with the North Prong St. Marys River, a beautiful setting. However, there is no access until 9 miles down the main St. Marys, at the FL 121 bridge.

SHUTTLE: To reach the put-in, take CR 127 north to CR 122. Turn left on CR 122 and follow it past the bridge over the North Prong to return to CR 125. Turn right on CR 125 and follow it a short distance north to CR 250 and the town of Taylor. Turn left, south, on CR 250 and follow it toward East Tower and the bridge over the Middle Prong. The access is on the southeast side

of the bridge. To reach the takeout from Exit 333 on I-10, take CR 125 north to CR 127. Turn right on CR 127 and follow it to the bridge over the Middle Prong.

GAUGE: Web. The USGS gauge is St. Marys River near Macclenny, FL. The minimum reading should be 220 cfs. Be apprised that this gauge is below the confluence of the North and Middle prongs; therefore theoretically a thunderstorm could hit one prong more than the other.

Middle Prong St. Marys River: East Tower to CR 127

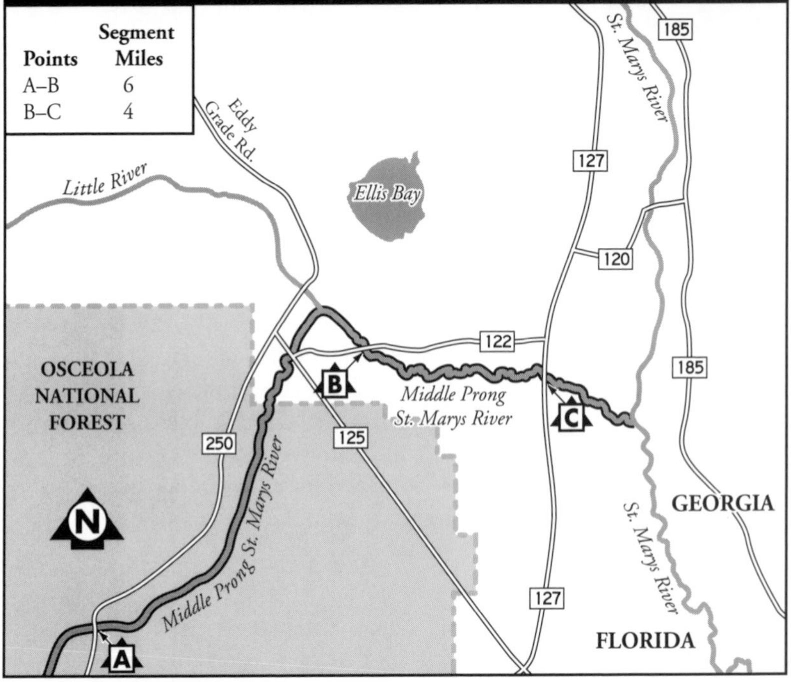

Points	Segment Miles
A–B	6
B–C	4

ST. MARYS RIVER

The St. Marys River is the border between the states of Georgia and Florida east of the Okefenokee Swamp in Georgia. The North Prong of the St. Marys flows out of the edges of the Okefenokee Swamp, while the Middle Prong begins on the east side of Buckhead Swamp in the Big Gum Swamp in the Osceola National Forest. The two streams join shortly below FL 120 in extreme north Florida to form the main St. Marys River, which flows to the Atlantic Ocean near Fernandina Beach.

Although it is over 130 miles long, it is one of Florida's lesser known waterways. For its first 40 miles, the St. Marys forms a horseshoe, flowing due south for 10 miles, then due east for 12 miles, then due north again. FL 2 crosses the St. Marys twice, defining the upper limits of the horseshoe. Above FL 2, the river continues in its northern course for some 33 miles before heading east to the Atlantic. This wide, meandering curve, combined with the many long bends in the river, can lead to directional confusion for the canoeist who is not aware of the river's orientation.

The upper reaches of the St. Marys flowing out of the Okefenokee Swamp is known as the North Prong. The North Prong is a narrow, twisting stream with a good current and beautiful cypress and tupelo trees. After the confluence with the Middle Prong, the river becomes wider and is characterized by bluffs, swamps, and snow-white sandbars. It is an excellent touring river since development along the banks is scattered and infrequent and campsites are plentiful. The best river section to tour is the 77 miles from Moniac to US 1 near

Narrow swift channels characterize the upper St. Marys River

Folkston. Many trees indigenous to north Florida are found along the St. Marys, including stands of cypress and yellow pine, gum, magnolia, maple, holly, poplar, willow, and river birch. Wildlife in this area includes deer, otter, beaver, raccoon, and alligator. The St. Marys has been considered for wild and scenic status, and concern for the river has evolved into an organization known as the St. Marys River Management Committee, which seeks to meld the interests of concerned citizens and adjoining government entities. They produce a good-quality river map. For the map and more information about the river basin, visit ***www.stmarysriver.org.***

MAPS: St. Marys River Guide, Moniac, Macclenny NW, Macclenny West, Macclenny East, Macclenny NE, St. George, Toledo, Folkston, Boulogne (USGS)

class	I–I+
length	17
time	Varies
gauge	Web
level	180
gradient	2.6
scenery	A

MONIAC TO FL 121

DESCRIPTION: This upper section of the North Prong is narrow with high banks and a good current. Cypress and tupelo trees grow in the stream resulting in obstacles that require skill in maneuvering. The river is about 15 to 20 feet wide and shaded. The water is a dark tannin color, and the white-sand bottom can be glimpsed in the shallows. Just after putting in, paddlers must navigate a troublesome section beneath a railroad bridge with old cut pilings interspersed with the current pilings. The banks rise after the first 2 miles and tend to be steep and difficult to climb. Just north of the CR 120 bridge one begins to encounter small islands in the river. Just before reaching the bridge there is a larger island with swift channels on either side. It is 5 miles from the FL 2 bridge to the CR 120 bridge. This is a difficult access that requires carrying canoes and gear for about 50 yards from the northwest side of the bridge.

This section continues with high banks, small islands, and a good current to the confluence with the Middle Prong 3 miles south. The Middle Prong enters swiftly. When the two streams meet, the river becomes much wider and shallower with gentle curves and large sandbars. The banks continue to remain high with palmetto and pine forests on top. The river continues in a southern direction for the next 8 miles. About 2 miles above FL 121, it turns to the east. There is a row of houses along the north bank 1 mile above FL 121.

St. Marys River (Sections A–C): Moniac to Scott Landing near Folkston

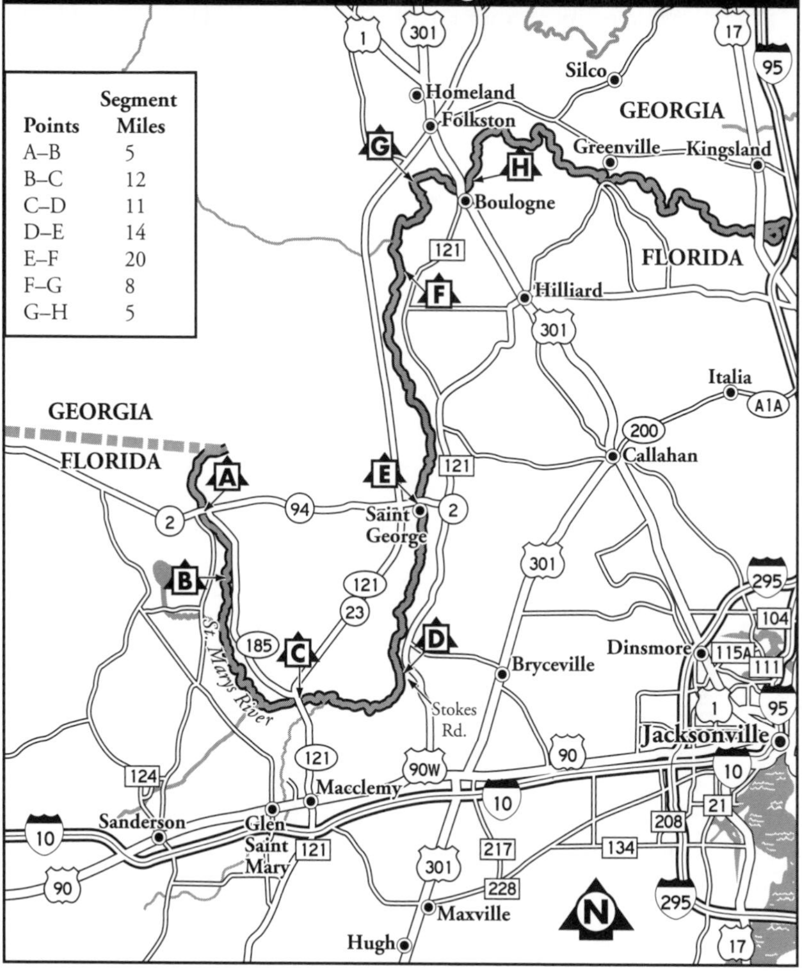

Points	Segment Miles
A–B	5
B–C	12
C–D	11
D–E	14
E–F	20
F–G	8
G–H	5

SHUTTLE: To reach the takeout from Exit 335 on I-10, take FL 121 north through Macclenny to the bridge over the St. Marys River and a canoe launch. To reach the put-in from the FL 121 bridge, continue north into Georgia and veer left onto GA 185 and follow it north to GA 94. Turn left on GA 94 and follow it a short distance to the bridge over the St. Marys. Access is on the southeast side of the bridge before the road crosses the river back into Florida.

GAUGE: Web. The USGS gauge is St. Marys River near Macclenny, FL. The minimum reading should be 180 cfs. Be apprised that this gauge is below the confluence of the North and Middle prongs, therefore theoretically a thunderstorm could hit one prong more than the other and give a bad reading for the prong you choose to paddle.

class	I
length	25
time	Varies
gauge	Phone, Web
level	160
gradient	1
scenery	B

FL 121 TO FL 2 NEAR ST. GEORGE

DESCRIPTION: The St. Marys is 50 to 75 feet wide at FL 121 with banks 15 feet high. The current is slow but helpful, and in low water downed trees may cause obstructions in the waterway. The river has many twisting turns for the first 3 miles. Here a branch of the main St. Marys leaves to meet the South Prong St. Marys, and later, downstream, the South Prong returns its stolen flow and its own rightful flow to the main river. Below the South Prong entrance, the river straightens out for 2 miles. In this straight area, the banks are high and steep. After passing the straight area, reach the old Boy Scout Camp at 6 miles, now St. Marys Cove Landing, a Baker County public park, on river right. The river begins to wind again, and there are a number of houses along the bank on the Florida side. About 2 miles below the houses, the road to Stokesville, Georgia, crosses the river. It is 11 miles from FL 121 to the Stokesville bridge.

There are several large sandbars near Stokesville Bridge, and it is a popular spot for swimming and camping. The river continues its twisting nature for another mile, then begins a 3- or 4-mile straight section. There are numerous large, high sandbanks in the twisting sections that make good campsites. This variation of twisting stream interspersed with long straight sections continues to the FL 2 bridge. There is limited access to the river for 5 miles of this section, and it is suitably remote and very beautiful. Just above the FL 2 bridge are numerous houses on the Georgia side, and the sandbanks are obviously accessible by road and popular for swimming. It is 14 miles from the Stokesville Bridge to the FL 2 bridge.

SHUTTLE: To reach the put-in from Exit 335 on I-10, take FL 121 north through Macclenny to the bridge over St. Marys River and a canoe launch. To reach the takeout from the FL 121 bridge, continue north into Georgia and veer right onto GA 23/121 and follow it north to GA 94. Turn right on GA 94 and

follow it a short distance to the bridge over St. Marys near St. George. Access is on the southwest side, in Georgia, before you cross the river.

GAUGE: Phone, Web. Call Canoe Country Outpost at (866) 845-4443 for the latest river conditions. The USGS gauge is St. Marys River near Macclenny, FL. The minimum reading should be 180 cfs.

class	I
length	33
time	Varies
gauge	Phone, Web
level	180
gradient	0.7
scenery	B

FL 2 NEAR ST. GEORGE TO SCOTT LANDING NEAR FOLKSTON

DESCRIPTION: From FL 2, the river twists and turns to the extreme with many fallen trees before straightening out. It then continues to alternate between long stretches with high banks interspersed with wide bends and sandbars. This is a very remote section with little access to the river. Campsites are scattered as the sandbars are not large, and the banks are 6 to 7 feet high. Six miles south of the Thompkins Landing access, pieces of pottery are scattered along and embedded into the banks on the Georgia side. Just north of this spot are the remains of an old bridge. It is 20 miles from the FL 2 bridge to Thompkins Landing.

Below Thompkins Landing is the final section of the St. Marys River that is considered best for canoeing. There's a concrete boat ramp at Thompkins Landing as well as a flat, grassy area and some generous sandbars that have been posted. The river continues to have 8 to 10 feet banks with alternating straight stretches and wide curves. As you progress downriver, an occasionally short stretch of swampy woods can be seen, and there are some stands of tall pines on the higher ground. Some small sloughs with lily pads and marsh grass also begin to appear.

Eight miles from Thompkins Landing, Traders Hill is reached on the Georgia side. A boat ramp, picnic tables, restrooms, and campsites are at the end of a paved road that turns off of GA 121 only a few miles south of Folkston. This is a historical spot, having once been the county seat of Charlton County, Georgia. It is the point where riverboats came up the St. Marys to deliver supplies to the area. Some of the wooden pilings from the many docks can still be seen.

The river begins to widen at Traders Hill. Though all freshwater, the river shows saltwater influence by being pushed up and down with the tides and a changing of current speed. The Seaboard Railroad trestle crosses the river just 1 mile before US

1—since this is a very active track, the sound of trains is almost constant as one approaches and leaves the trestle. Interestingly, there is a house built on the abutment of an old bridge just below the railroad trestle. Below US 1, houses appear, but it is less than a mile farther to Scott Landing public boat ramp on the Florida side. It is 5 miles from Traders Hill to Scott Landing.

Although the St. Marys continues for another 50 miles to the Atlantic Ocean from US 1, it is an increasingly wide and tidal river that is popular with very large boats. Canoeists who choose to paddle on to the Atlantic should do so with caution. That being said, there are paddlers who ply the entire river to the town of St. Marys, Georgia, and even further to Fort Clinch State Park in Florida.

SHUTTLE: To reach the takeout from Exit 28A, New Kings Road, on I-295 near Jacksonville, take US 1 north to Lake Hampton Road just before the US 1 bridge over the St. Marys. Turn right on Lake Hampton Road and follow it to Scott Landing Road. Turn left on Scott Landing Road and follow it to the ramp and St. Marys Fish Camp at the river. St. Marys Fish Camp is also where Canoe Country Outpost is located. To reach the put-in, backtrack to US 1 and cross US 1, now on CR 121. Follow CR 121 south to FL 2. Turn right, west, on FL 2 and follow it to the bridge over the St. Marys River. A boat ramp is located on the southwest, Georgia, side of the river.

GAUGE: Phone, Web. Call Canoe Country Outpost at (866) 845-4443 for the latest river conditions. The USGS gauge is St. Marys River near Macclenny, FL. The minimum reading should be 180 cfs.

A great blue heron watches over the river

BLACK CREEK

In an area dominated by the massive St. Johns River with its huge inlets and lakes, Black Creek provides nearby canoeing for those in the Jacksonville area. Flowing north into the St. Johns, Black Creek drains out of a sandy ridge of arid pine lands and scrub oak forests into a cool ravine bordered by a canopy of hardwoods and also plenty of houses. Like the many other "black" creeks, rivers, and waters in north Florida, it is named for the darkly stained tannin water that results from the acid produced by the vegetation along its banks and on the banks of the rivulets and streams that feed it.

Black Creek flows for some 20 miles from FL 16 near Penney Farms to the St. Johns. Only the first 14 miles is considered of interest to the canoeist, however, since the final 6 miles is extremely broad, tidal, and used extensively by large motorized craft.

MAPS: Black Creek Ravines map, Penney Farms, Middleburg, Middleburg SW (USGS)

FL 16 TO OLD FERRY ROAD BOAT LANDING

class	I
length	14
time	Varies
gauge	Web, visual
level	2–4
gradient	1.1
scenery	C

DESCRIPTION: Since Black Creek is very sensitive to local rainfall, it is essential to check the water gauge under the FL 16 bridge. Two to four feet is the optimal level, with water lower than 2 feet resulting in pull-overs and water above 4 feet putting paddlers in the trees. This gauge can be checked on the Web prior to attempting a trip. At the put-in, the creek is 20 feet wide with white sandbanks up to 10 feet high. Hardwoods, willows, and scrub oak are prevalent. There is a good current, and the water is a clear tea color with the white-sand bottom in evidence. The stream twists and turns with numerous logs and submerged stumps to surprise the unwary. About 1 mile downstream, a rock ledge across the creek makes an interesting rapid. Occasionally there will be a high sand bluff. Both banks of the river have posted signs making camping impossible until the conservation area below the CR 218 bridge.

For the first 3 miles the stream alternates between these high banks with curves and a corridor of hardwoods. Houses become commonplace. Finally, in the 2 miles above the CR 218 bridge, the banks become even more developed with very large motorboats tied up to private docks or housed in boat houses. In this last 2 miles the stream becomes much broader and slower and small sloughs with lily pads are seen. It is 7 miles from the FL 16 bridge

to the CR 218 bridge. There is no parking at the CR 218 bridge. However, paddlers could park their vehicles at nearby businesses after quickly loading and unloading their boats at the bridge.

Although Black Creek becomes 200 feet wide below the CR 209 bridge, it is not as populated as it would appear from the development on the creek around Middleburg. But houses are common along the creek. A half-mile before the confluence of the North Fork 3 miles downstream, paddlers reach the Black

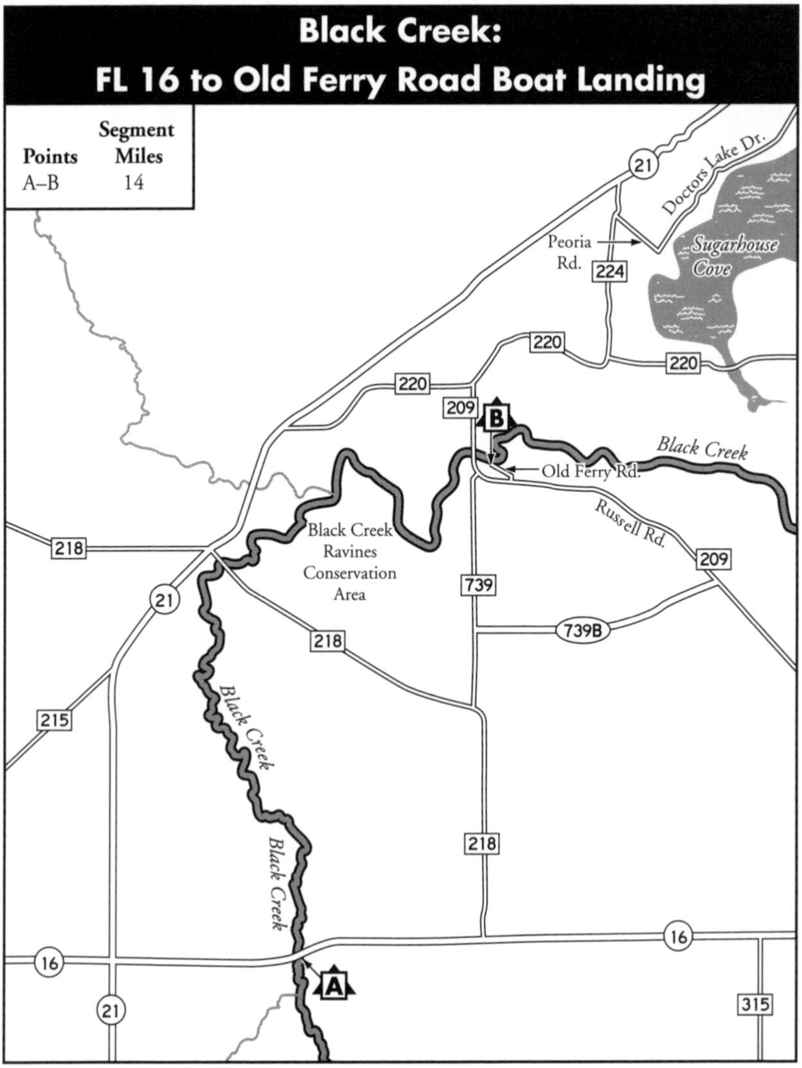

Black Creek:
FL 16 to Old Ferry Road Boat Landing

Points	Segment Miles
A–B	14

Creek Ravines Conservation Area on the south bank. This 965-acre area protects seepage slopes and steep ravines harboring a variety of flora and fauna along a 2.7-mile segment of the south shore. There is a designated primitive campsite for overnight paddlers. Hiking can be added to the mix as a trail leaves the campsite. For a camping permit, call the St. Johns Water Management District office at (386) 329-4410.

This section of Black Creek becomes very wide, affected somewhat by the tide, and can be very windy. It is also frequented by fishermen in motorboats. Beyond the conservation area intensive development begins again. At the CR 209 bridge the creek is very wide and begins to be populated with large boats. Although the remainder of the creek has some lovely spots, it is a chore for the paddler to combat wind, tide, and the wake from motorized craft to reach the St. Johns. It is 7 miles from the CR 218 bridge to the Old Ferry Road boat landing.

SHUTTLE: To reach the lowermost takeout from Exit 12 on I-295 near Jacksonville, take FL 21 south, Blanding Boulevard to College Street, CR 220. Turn left on CR 220 to CR 209. Turn right on CR 209 and cross the bridge over Black Creek, then turn left on Old Ferry Road and follow it to a public boat ramp on Black Creek. To reach the uppermost put-in from the take-out, backtrack on CR 209 and turn left, south, on CR 739 to reach CR 218. Turn left on CR 218 and follow it to FL 16. Turn right, west, on FL 16 and follow it to the bridge over Black Creek. Access is on the southeast side of the bridge.

GAUGE: Web, visual. The USGS gauge is South Fork Black Creek near Penney Farms, FL. This can be obtained on the Web. There is also a gauge at the FL 16 bridge. Both should read between 2 and 4 feet for the best paddling on Black Creek. Below 2 feet will result in many pull-overs, and above 4 feet will be overly swift and put you in the trees in the upper sections.

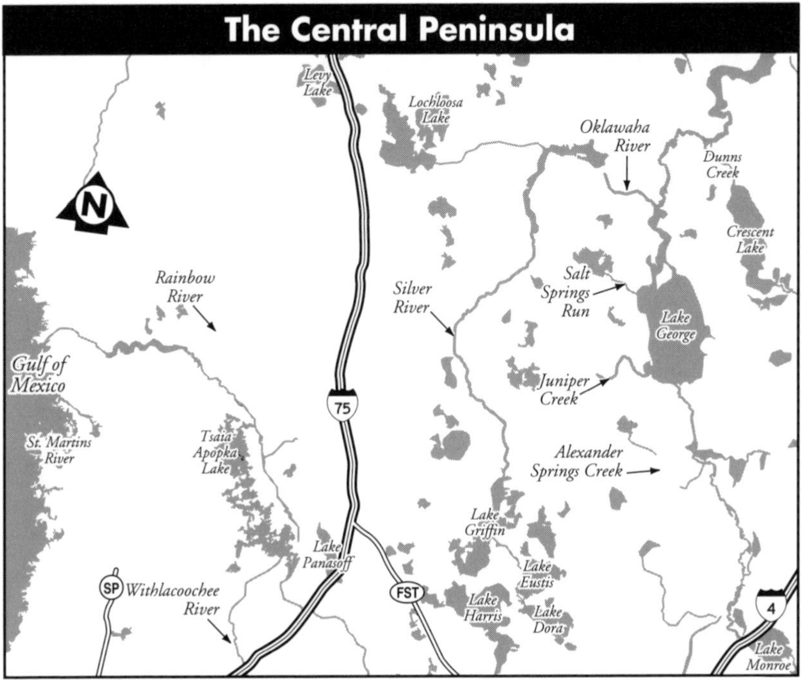
The Central Peninsula
Levy Lake
Lochloosa Lake
Oklawaha River
Dunns Creek
Crescent Lake
Salt Springs Run
Lake George
Silver River
Rainbow River
Juniper Creek
Gulf of Mexico
St. Martins River
Tsaia Apopka Lake
75
Alexander Springs Creek
Lake Griffin
Lake Panasoff
Lake Eustis
SP
Withlacoochee River
FST
Lake Harris
Lake Dora
4
Lake Monroe

part **Five**

The Central Peninsula

WITHLACOOCHEE RIVER (SOUTH)

The Withlacoochee River, south, is said to have been named after its sister river to the north, but the two rivers are separated by many miles and bear little resemblance to each other. The southern Withlacoochee, one of Florida's finest touring rivers, is over 100 miles long with 84 miles of good canoeing trail. While there is a great deal of development along some of its banks, there are also long stretches of beautiful and remote wilderness. In addition, the characteristics of the river are continually changing so that every day of paddling presents a new and different river experience.

The Withlacoochee can be found on maps in the extreme southern section of Sumter County as a tiny stream wandering through the Withlacoochee Swamp. It becomes a clearly defined waterway after leaving Green Swamp in the Richloam Wildlife Management Area of the Withlacoochee State Forest, and flows north to the Gulf of Mexico at Yankeetown.

Campsite on Withlacoochee River (South)

The diversity of the vegetation and wildlife is a reflection of the constantly changing terrain of the river. Beginning in cypress and hardwood swamp, it progresses through upland hardwood and pine forests, past cypress ponds, palmetto hammocks, and landscaped backyards. The Tsala Apopka Lake region is a miniature Everglades with an abundance of birds and reptiles, hammocks of waterweeds, and multifaceted channels. Fishing is excellent along the river. Certain sections of the river are easily accessible and are heavily populated during the warm months of the year. Other sections appear to have been abandoned to an occasional air boat and the canoeist. The river below Dunnellon enters a man-made lake, Lake Rousseau, then leaves the lake as a straight line channel, a legacy of the abandoned Cross Florida Barge Canal.

MAPS: Withlacoochee State Forest map, Lacoochee, St. Catherine, Wahoo, Nobleton, Rutland, Lake Panasoffkee NW, Stokes Ferry, Dunnellon SE, Dunnellon (USGS)

A

Lacoochee Park to Nobleton

class	I
length	25
time	Varies
gauge	Phone, Web
level	N/A
gradient	0.7
scenery	B

DESCRIPTION: For the first 2 miles, the river flows through a remote and undeveloped part of Richloam Tract of the Withlacoochee State Forest. However, the uppermost put-in is questionable for leaving your car for an extended period of time. At FL 575 there is a canoe livery which offers better parking and can shuttle you to the top.

The river is usually shallow in this area, about 30 feet wide with a moderate current. The banks of live oak, pine, and palmetto vary from 6 to 15 feet high, and there are a number of small, rocky shoals across the river. Cypress borders the stream much of the way. Below CR 575, 2 miles from Lacoochee Park, houses continually border the river until the FL 50 bridge, 12 miles downstream. Shortly below FL 50, state forest land along the left-hand bank makes camping possible, but is far from a wilderness experience. It is 2 miles from CR 575 to US 301, 2 miles from US 301 to US 98, and 6 miles from US 98 to the FL 50 bridge.

It is 7 miles from FL 50 to Silver Lake. There are a number of houses during the first mile below FL 50, but they decrease in frequency as the river enters the Croom Wildlife Management Area of the state forest. The banks began to be lower and the frequency of sandbars increases. The banks are primarily covered with highland hardwoods and pine forest, but some small swampy areas

Withlacoochee River (South) (Sections A–C): Lacoochee Park to Dunnellon

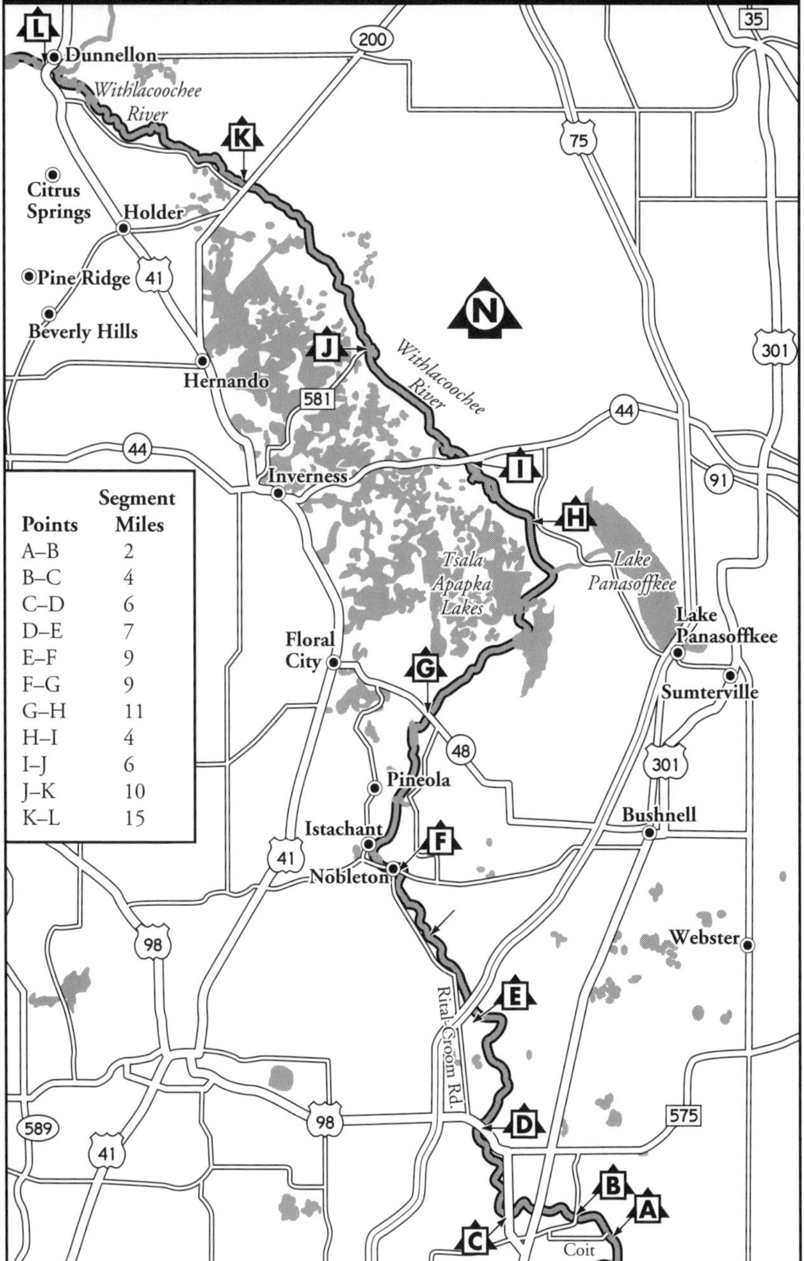

Points	Segment Miles
A–B	2
B–C	4
C–D	6
D–E	7
E–F	9
F–G	9
G–H	11
H–I	4
I–J	6
J–K	10
K–L	15

begin to occur as well. The river continues to be shallow with mild current. There are three large state forest campgrounds in the vicinity of Silver Lake, each with river access. The Little Withlacoochee enters from the east just before reaching Silver Lake, and as a result the river widens to 50 to 75 feet. Here is the first developed state forest campground, River Junction.

It is 9 miles from Silver Lake to CR 476. Silver Lake, with a campground of its own, is 0.75 miles long and 0.33 miles wide. I-75 is visible as soon as you enter the lake. The water is shallow at the dual bridges and Silver Lake campground, but deepens as the river narrows to about 40 feet wide on the other side. The banks are 3 to 4 feet high with numerous campsites under the trees. An official primitive site is located on the left-hand bank below the bridge. The color of the river darkens in this area and it's a good section for fishing. After reaching Hog Island, with a nice campground, the banks become lower and paddlers experience a swampier setting. The river splits around Hog Island. Houses become evident again just south of FL 476, especially on the right-hand bank. The water becomes shallow and choked with waterweeds, and the river widens to 150 feet.

SHUTTLE: To reach the lowermost takeout in Nobleton from Inverness, take US 41 south to Hernando CR 476. Turn left on CR 476 and follow it east to the bridge over the Withlacoochee and the canoe rental on the west side of the bridge. There is also a public park on the river, west of the canoe rental at the CR 476 bridge. To reach the uppermost put-in from Nobleton, continue east on CR 476 to US 301. Turn right on US 301 and head south to FL 50. Turn left on FL 50 and head east to CR 575. Turn right and head south on CR 575 and follow it beyond the bridge over the Withlacoochee River to Druden Street. Turn left on Druden Street and follow it to Coit Avenue. Turn left on Coit Avenue and follow it to Lacoochee Park. Just after entering Lacoochee Park, turn right at the first sand road and follow it to a high bluff bordered in concrete posts, overlooking the river.

GAUGE: Phone, Web. Call Withlacoochee River RV Park and Canoe Rental at (352) 583-4778 for river information. The USGS gauge helpful in determining flow rates for any given day is Withlacoochee River at Trilby, FL.

NOBLETON TO RUTLAND

class	I
length	24
time	Varies
gauge	Phone, Web
level	N/A
gradient	0.2
scenery	B+

DESCRIPTION: One-half mile below this access the river divides, with the left channel leading to Nobleton Park. The crossing of the old Fort King Road is on the south side of the river, just east of Nobleton Park. The fort, built in 1837, was named for Major Francis Langhorne Dade. It was an observation post and supply depot for troops stationed in the area. On 6 March 1837, the Seminole leaders, Jumper and Alligator, met with General Thomas Jessup to sign a treaty that ended one of the longest and bloodiest Native American wars in American history.

North of Nobleton the river undergoes a drastic change as it enters a series of large lakes. These lakes are shallow and clogged with waterweeds but have abundant bird life and numerous alligators. On the higher ground a few houses are scattered about, but it is a reasonably remote section. It is 9 miles from Nobleton at CR 476 to FL 48.

Below FL 48 is the section of the Withlacoochee that flows through the Tsala Apopka Lake region, a series of lakes and swamps. It is 15 miles from FL 48 to FL 44. There is seldom any current to follow; the river often wanders off among small channels, islands, and hammocks. It is one of the most beautiful and most remote part of this river. The number and variety of bird life are astonishing, and the cypress-ringed lakes and swampy hammocks provide a true wilderness experience. Campsites are scarce and road access to the river is very limited.

Just north of FL 48, the river enters Bonnet Lake, which is over a mile long. There is a private landing on the southwest side of the lake and at the northwest end. The river deepens and is 50 to 75 feet wide when it leaves the lake. A mile north of Bonnet Lake is Board Island, reputed to be the last high ground available as a campsite for many miles. Watch carefully for what looks like a small creek entering from river left to access the island.

After leaving Board Island, the river turns east and opens into a small lake with an arm reaching to the south. Shell Island is not an island surrounded by water, but a large swamp known as The Wanderings. Persons with permission to cross private property use this area for camping and fishing. After leaving this small lake, the river widens to 150 to 200 feet with a meandering channel about 30 feet wide that is not choked by weeds. Another mile of paddling reveals a larger lake with an arm to the south where Jumper Creek

enters the river. This creek is canoeable but originates in swamp and has no access. This is part of the Withlacoochee State Forest. Past Jumper Creek, the stream turns north, and one should stay on the east side of the three small islands in the river. Soon a pasture appears on the west side that continues for over 1 mile, and there are occasional canals and rough tracks that indicate that houses may be nearby although they are not visible from the river.

Soon another large, shallow lake begins, and Outlet River comes in from the east from Lake Panasoffkee. The channel is less clear as the river is overgrown with waterweeds. Going west, the lake narrows and some houses are visible, set well back from the water line. There is a small lock still at the Carlson area, 11 miles below FL 48. There's a public boat ramp off of CR 470 that allows entry both above and below the small lock. There are a number of houses and a small community at this site. The shallow lake continues for another 2.5 miles. This is one of the shallowest sections of the entire river, and during very dry weather it may be necessary to walk the canoe in some areas. The FL 44 access is via a short canal on the southeast bank of the river.

SHUTTLE: To reach the uppermost put-in in Nobleton from Inverness, take US 41 south to Hernando CR 476. Turn left on CR 476 and follow it east to the bridge over the Withlacoochee and a canoe rental on the west side of the bridge. There is also a public park on the river, west of the canoe rental at the CR 476 bridge. To reach the lowermost takeout from Inverness, take FL 44 east to the bridge over the Withlacoochee River. A public boat ramp is located on the southeast side of the bridge and the river is accessed via a short canal.

GAUGE: Phone, Web. Call Nobleton Canoe and Boat Rental for river information at (352) 796-4343. The USGS gauge helpful in determining flow rates for any given day is Withlacoochee River at Nobleton, FL.

C

Rutland to Dunnellon

class	I
length	31
time	Varies
gauge	Phone, Web
level	N/A
gradient	0.8
scenery	B

DESCRIPTION: North of FL 44 the river becomes deeper and is 150 to 200 feet wide and lined with hardwood swamps. The river will occasionally narrow to 100 feet and there will be short stretches of high ground, but there is little current. Scattered homesites as well as small communities of riverside homes are evident all along this section, and campsites are few. There is a

public access at the boat ramp off of CR 581 with boat rentals and a store. It is 6 miles from FL 44 to CR 581. Immediately north of CR 581, on the east bank, is the entrance to the Gum Slough. This slough flows into the Withlacoochee from Gum Springs, about 5 miles to the northwest. Gum Springs are a group of at least seven individual springs.

The confluence of Gum Slough adds a little current to the river and it continues at about 100 feet wide for another mile. It then begins to divide around hardwood islands that are low and swampy. The canoeist can stay on the west side of these islands and enjoy a beautiful and remote hardwood swamp filled with wading birds, osprey, and alligators, as well as very tall pond cypress trees.

As the swampy area decreases, houses begin to appear on the west side of the river and are scattered along at irregular intervals until FL 200 is sighted. FL 200 has an access. It is 10 river miles from CR 581 to FL 200. There are very few campsites in the first 16-mile section since the terrain that is not swampy tends to be posted private property. It is possible to find an occasional spot for one or two tents, but one should watch carefully, take advantage of a site when one is spotted, and not plan to camp a large group.

The modest current continues north of FL 200, and the banks are from 4 to 10 feet high, with houses scattered along the way. There are numerous campsites along this section, but they are obviously accessible by road and can be littered. The river is 75 to 100 feet wide and twists through gentle curves and high banks for about 5 miles before opening into a large swamp again. This wide swampy area, with waterweeds and fingers of water reaching into cypress stands, is very beautiful and should be relished as one enters the final miles of the canoe trail.

At the northeast end of the swamp, small hills appear and the houses begin again. The crystalline Rainbow River enters from the north just 1 mile before reaching Dunnellon and the takeout. It is 15 miles from FL 200 to Dunnellon.

SHUTTLE: To reach the uppermost put-in from Dunnellon, take US 41 south to FL 44. Turn left on FL 44, east to the bridge over the Withlacoochee River. A public boat ramp is located on the southeast side of the bridge, and the river is accessed via a short canal. The takeout in Dunnellon is located at the boat ramp at City Hall, just north of the US 41 bridge over the Withlacoochee River.

GAUGE: Phone, Web. Call Nobleton Canoe and Boat Rental for river information at (352) 796-4343. The USGS gauge helpful in determining flow rates for any given day is Withlacoochee River near Holder, FL.

RAINBOW RIVER

The Rainbow River is a short tributary of the Withlacoochee River, near the town of Dunnellon. It has historically been a tourist attraction and has been heavily developed. Houses line much of the river bank between Rainbow Springs and the Rainbow River's confluence with the Withlacoochee. The state of Florida now runs the springs as a state park. Downstream, Marion County runs a park where paddlers can launch their boats and enjoy the unspoiled ultra-clear waters where fish, turtles, and other underwater life are easily visible in both the depths and shallows of the river.

This run can be quite busy on weekends with tubers, canoers, kayakers, and motorboaters all vying for a spot on the water.

MAPS: Dunnellon (USGS)

class	I
length	3.6
time	2
gauge	Visual, Web
level	N/A
gradient	0.4
scenery	B

K. P. Hole Park to CR 484

DESCRIPTION: Paddlers who want to get on the water but don't feel like paddling should make this easy run from K. P. Hole Park to CR 484. If you feel like getting a workout, you can paddle upstream from K. P. Hole to the state park, then drift back down past K. P. Hole and on down to the takeout. The water and aquatic life here is fascinating. A snorkel is in order for those inclined. Swaying grasses and boulders contrast with sandy sections of the river bottom. Some parts of the river are surprisingly deep. The wild underwater nature of the run contrasts mightily with the house-lined banks. Bird life is abundant despite the development. Some sections of the river have wooded banks of moss-draped cypress, providing relief from the house parade, especially beyond the 2-mile mark. A ban on alcohol and disposable food containers is strictly enforced on the river. Tubes and canoes are available for rent at K. P. Hole Park.

SHUTTLE: To reach the put-in, head north on US 41 to 99th Place. Turn right on 99th Place and cross the railroad tracks. Just after the railroad tracks, turn left on SW 190 Avenue and follow it a short distance to K. P. Hole Park, on your right. To reach the takeout from the intersection of US 41 and CR 484, Pennsylvania Avenue in Dunnellon, head east on CR 484 to the bridge over the Rainbow River and a canoe/kayak/tube exit on the southeast side of the bridge.

GAUGE: Visual, Web. The Rainbow River is spring-fed and is runnable year-round. However, the USGS gauge helpful to determine flow rates for any given day is Rainbow Springs near Dunnellon, FL.

Rainbow River: K.P. Hole Park to CR 484

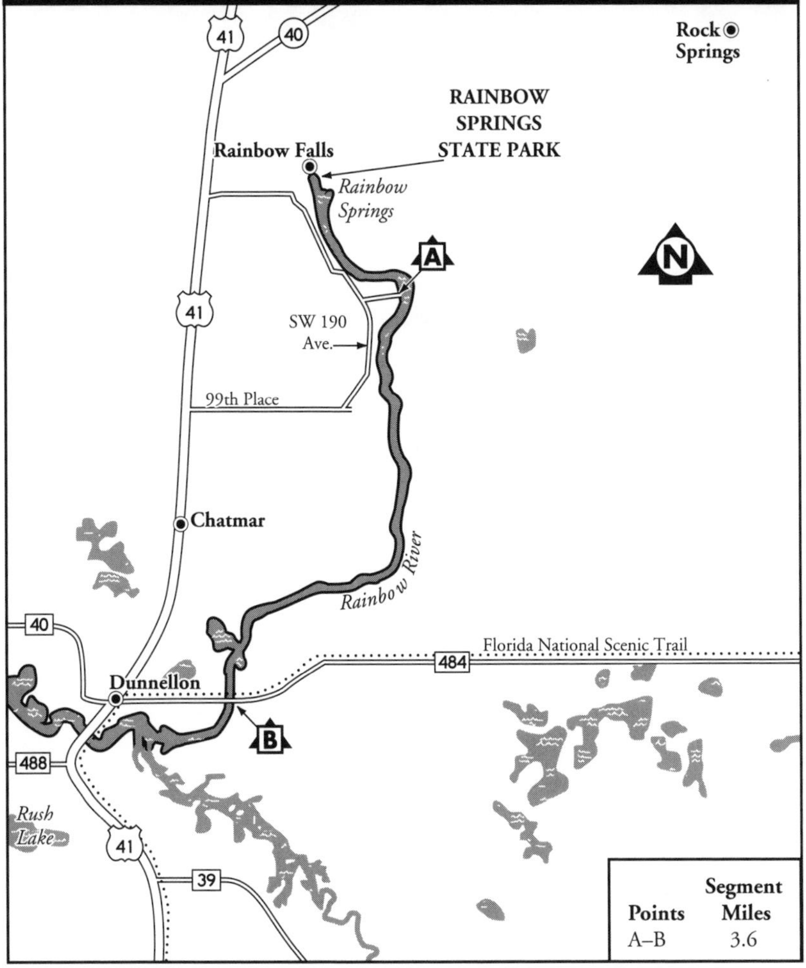

41
40
Rock Springs
RAINBOW SPRINGS STATE PARK
Rainbow Falls
Rainbow Springs
A
N
41
SW 190 Ave.
99th Place
Chatmar
Rainbow River
40
Florida National Scenic Trail
484
Dunnellon
B
488
Rush Lake
41
39

Points	Segment Miles
A–B	3.6

SILVER RIVER

Silver Spring, which feeds Silver River, has long been a central Florida tourist attraction. Located east of Ocala, much of the beautiful Silver River corridor below the springs is now part of Silver Springs State Park. River access has been improved with the establishment of Silver River State Park. Now you can follow the current downstream to the Silver River's confluence with the Ocklawaha, rather than beating your way upstream from the Ocklawaha all the way to the head spring.

MAPS: Silver River State Park map, Ocala East, Lynne (USGS)

A

class	I
length	5
time	Varies
gauge	Phone, Web
level	Spring-fed
gradient	1
scenery	A

SILVER RIVER STATE PARK TO RAY WAYSIDE ACCESS

DESCRIPTION: The Silver River was where the first glass-bottomed boats were used. And they are still in use today, to see

Silver River: Silver River State Park to Ray Wayside Access

Points	Segment Miles
A–B	3

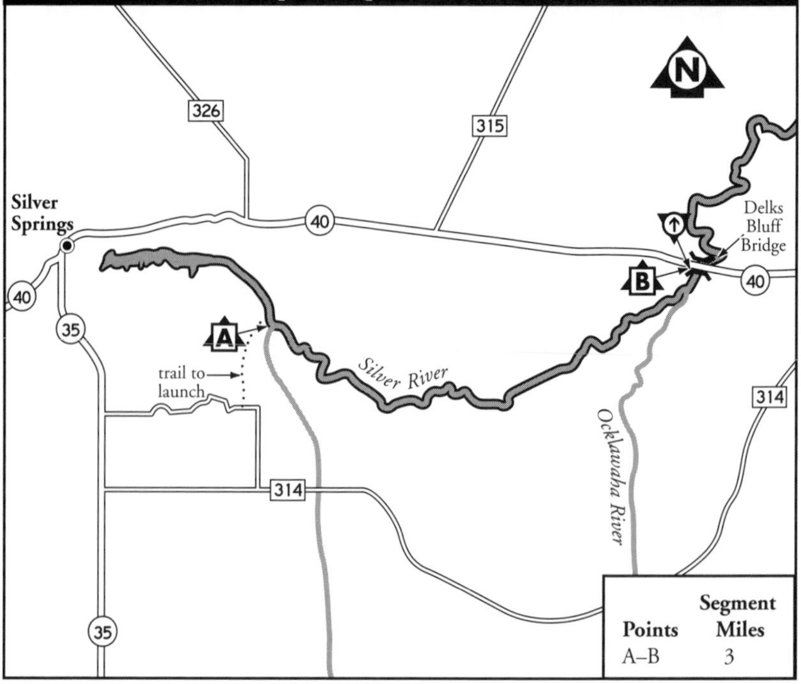

the array of aquatic life below the water's surface. I can still remember touring Silver Springs as a kid, looking down on another world below. Nowadays, canoers and kayakers can launch from the state park, heading either upstream to the springs, or downstream to the Ocklawaha River. However to reach the park canoe and kayak launch, you must tote your boat 0.7 miles to the Silver River. Once on the river, you can enjoy spring water measured at 550 million gallons of water flowing per day. It is 2 miles up to the springhead from the launch. You must stay in your boat while on Silver Springs attraction property. It is 3 miles downstream to the Ocklawaha River through junglelike banks with waterweeds bordering the steady current. The takeout is downstream on the west bank of the Ocklawaha River.

SHUTTLE: From Ocala, take FL 40 east to Ray Wayside, on the right before bridging the Ocklawaha River. To reach the put-in, backtrack west on FL 40 to FL 35. Turn left, south, on FL 35 to reach the Silver River State Park entrance, on your left.

GAUGE: Phone, Web. Call Silver River State Park at (352) 236-7148 for the latest river conditions. The USGS gauge helpful in determining flow rates for any given day is Silver River near Ocala, FL.

OCKLAWAHA RIVER

The Ocklawaha River has been the center of one of the most prolonged environmental controversies in Florida. Slated to be the primary vehicle for the Florida Cross State Canal, it has been extensively channelized and developed. The canal project has been abandoned for good, and some sections of the river remain in their original wilderness state. Ironically, condemnation of the river's borderlands has now resulted in protected banks on the Ocklawaha and a protected corridor of the Cross Florida Greenway.

Some sections of the river have been rendered less than desirable for paddling. The stretch of river from Moss Bluff to CR 314 was channelized to allow muck farming. The original channel is being restored after the area was acquired by the St. Johns River Water Management District. Downstream, Rodman Dam, part of the ill-fated canal, alters the river, but is a decent lake paddle for those inclined.

That being said, the recommended sections are among the best in the state. Wildlife management areas border most of the river, making for a wild setting and overnight camping opportunities. The Ocklawaha is said to be a very old river geologically, and as a result has created a mile-wide valley. It has a sand bottom and its waters tend to be very clear with occasional areas where the tannin from the swamps colors the water in a darker hue. The lower areas have deciduous trees such as tupelo, gums, red maple, sweet bay, and some outstanding examples of the bald cypress. When the terrain is higher, upland hardwoods such as oak, magnolia, and beech predominate.

Alligator-eye view of kayaker on Ocklawaha River

Animal and bird life are abundant with the usual raccoons, skunks, and armadillos present, as well as deer, foxes, and otters. Fishing is said to be excellent, with catfish, red-breasted bream, shellcrackers, and speckled perch being most sought after.

MAPS: Ocala National Forest map, Lynne, Fort McCoy (USGS)

FL 40 TO FL 316

class	I
length	19
time	Varies
gauge	Phone, Web
level	N/A
gradient	1.4
scenery	A

DESCRIPTION: This run can be broken into two segments, from FL 40 to Gores Landing and Gores Landing to Eureka West. The put-in starts on a canal that leads to the lowermost part of the Silver River, then shortly meets up with the Ocklawaha, and then the river begins winding through hardwood forests and swamp. Occasionally there will be bluffs up to 15 feet high on the east bank, and these often contain rope swings and evidence of being established campsites. About 4 miles north on this section, small streams began to enter and the river flows through a very heavily wooded area with junglelike terrain. Spring and fall are good times to see this swamp hardwood forest of cypress and gum color out. The river current is moderate. Lilies border the inside of river bends where the current slackens.

The wildlife management areas on both banks keep the river wild in appearance. There is a public campground with a boat ramp at Gores Landing, 10 miles downstream from FL 40. Also in this section are Dead River and Cedar Creek, where short side trips may be made.

North of the confluence with Eaton Creek there is a very high bluff along the east bank with some houses on top. From this point to Eureka West is only 2 miles. A boat landing is reached on the east bank before going under the CR 316 bridge. Just beyond the bridge, paddlers will pass an old circular concrete bridge abutment. This is a remnant of the days when steamboats plied the Ocklawaha. Their high smokestacks couldn't pass under bridges of that time, so the bridges were built so they could pivot and allow passage of the steamboats. The Eureka West boat landing, part of the Cross Florida Greenway recreation areas, is just beyond the abutment on river left.

Ambitious paddlers could continue beyond Eureka West into Rodman Reservoir. Below CR 316, the river enters the area that has been flooded by the Rodman Dam. Many canoeists enjoy this section because of the wide variation of bird life that can be

Ocklawaha River: FL 40 to FL 316

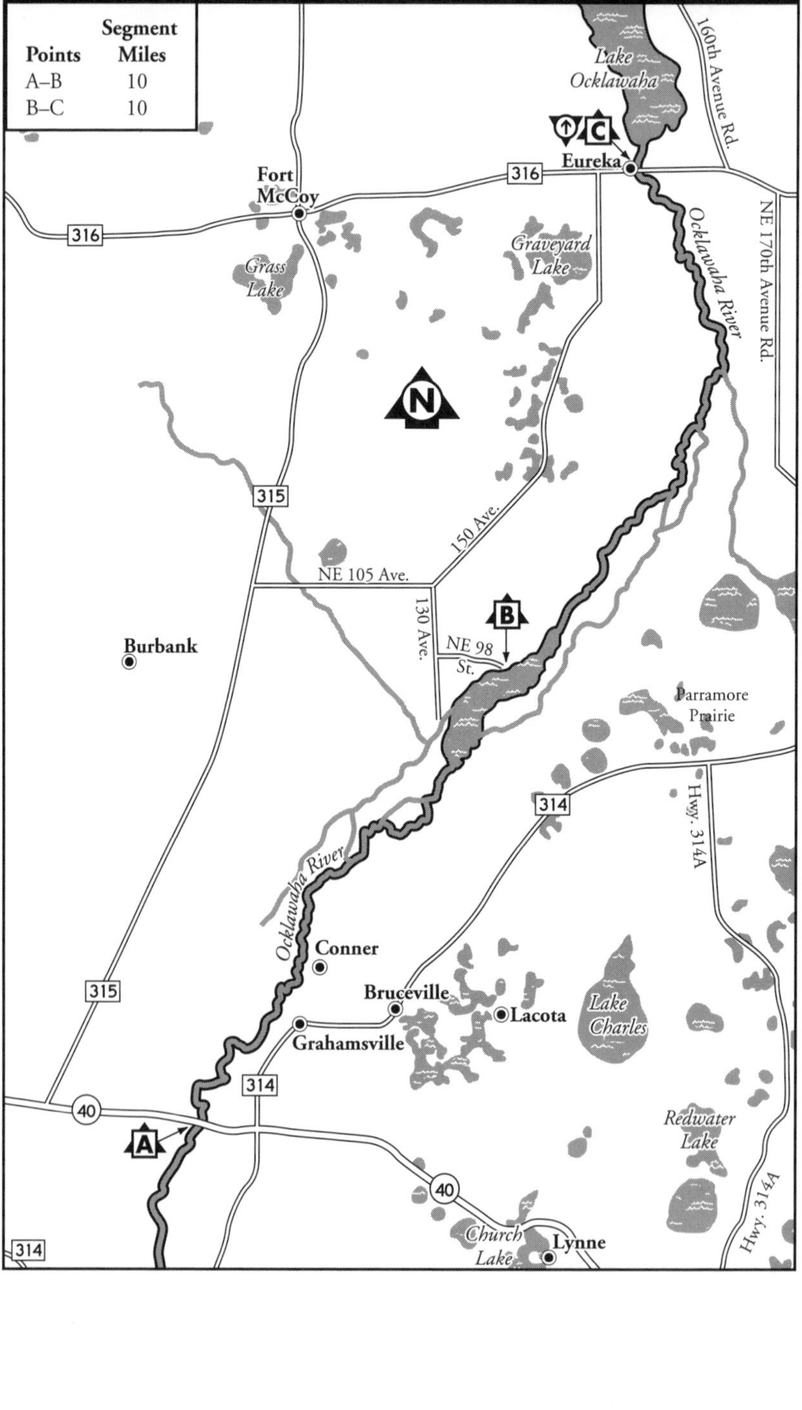

Points	Segment Miles
A–B	10
B–C	10

Lake Ocklawaha
160th Avenue Rd.
C
Eureka
316
Fort McCoy
316
NE 170th Avenue Rd.
Ocklawaha River
Grass Lake
Graveyard Lake
N
315
150 Ave.
NE 105 Ave.
130 Ave.
B
NE 98 St.
Burbank
Parramore Prairie
314
Hwy. 314A
Ocklawaha River
Conner
315
Bruceville
Lacota
Lake Charles
Grahamsville
314
40
A
Redwater Lake
40
Hwy. 314A
314
Church Lake
Lynne

observed. It is lake canoeing, however, and can be windy. For the paddler who chooses this section, there is an access 8 miles north at Cypress Bayou. It is also possible to paddle an additional 10 miles to Orange Springs and on to Rodman Dam. Below Rodman Dam, there are an additional 5 miles to the ramp at FL 19. The old river channel comes in on the right, below the dam run. Then, the river breaks into numerous channels. Stay right at the first split beyond the old river channel. From here it is 4 more miles to meet the St. Johns River. The river splits many times here, so be aware and generally stay with the southernmost channels. The last big bluff is near an old Native American mound. It was once a river stopping point for the old steamboats. The forest service has erected an interpretive display here.

Additionally, paddlers can put in 3 miles above FL 40 at CR 314. The river is about 50 feet wide and beautiful hardwood forests begin, leaving the unattractive channelized river behind. The spring-fed Silver River enters from the west shortly before FL 40. It is possible to paddle up Silver River for 5 miles to the spring, but the current is very swift, there tends to be heavy motorboat traffic, and the concessionaires do not permit traffic in the spring area.

SHUTTLE: To reach the uppermost put-in from Ocala, take FL 40 east to Ray Wayside Park, on the west side of the bridge over the Ocklawaha. To reach Gores Landing from Ocala, take FL 40 east to CR 315. Turn left on CR 315 to NE 105 Avenue. Turn right on NE 105 and follow it to 130 Avenue. Turn right on 130 Avenue and follow it to NE 98 Avenue. Turn left on NE 98 and follow it to end at Gores Landing. There is a launch fee here at this park with a resident on site. To reach the lowermost takeout from Ocala, take FL 40 west to CR 315. Turn right on CR 315 and follow it north to CR 316. Turn right on CR 316 and follow it east to 152 CT Road. Turn left on 152 CT Road to reach Eureka West Boat ramp.

GAUGE: Phone, Web. Call Ocklawaha Canoe Outpost at (352) 236-4606 for the latest river conditions. The USGS gauge helpful in determining flow rates for any given day is Ocklawaha R at Moss Bluff, FL.

ALEXANDER SPRINGS AND ALEXANDER SPRINGS CREEK

Alexander Springs runs amidst the Ocala National Forest. This is a very popular recreation area. Alexander Springs is a first-magnitude spring with a flow of 76 million gallons daily. The springhead is in a large pool about 200 feet in diameter that is a popular swimming area. Beyond the springhead, the creek runs down a wide channel bordered by palm, maple, pine, and live oak draped in Spanish moss. Water lilies, cattails, and other vegetation thrives atop the water, channeling the stream flow. Paddlers will choose their route among braided channels created by the watery vegetation. Downstream, islands create channels of their own. There is an entrance fee at Alexander Springs. If you want to avoid the fee, you can start at CR 445, but you will miss the uppermost part of the run. Be aware that Alexander Springs Recreation Area also has a good-quality campground.

MAPS: Ocala National Forest map, Alexander Springs (USGS)

class	I
length	7
time	3
gauge	Visual
level	Spring-fed
gradient	0.7
scenery	A

ALEXANDER SPRINGS TO FR 552

DESCRIPTION: The run begins just below the roped-off swim area at the 72 °F springhead. The clear water is immediately evident. Look for wildlife above and below the surface. For the first 5 miles, the stream is wide but broken into channels created by watery vegetation at the surface. Underwater vegetation sways in the current of the crystalline spring run.

Downstream, a few houses are located along Ellis Landing, on the south bank. The stream becomes narrower and more winding and is frequently divided by hammocks of palms and other vegetation. It becomes a broad, slow-moving stream again before entering the St. Johns River. It is best for the canoeist not to paddle on to the St. Johns since it is several miles up the river to a landing. The concessionaire at Alexander Springs Recreation Area rents canoes. They offer shuttle service for private boats. Paddlers will pass the concessionaire's landing on the right-hand bank. It is a half-mile further to the national forest boat ramp on the left-hand bank.

Beach camping at its finest

Alexander Springs and Alexander Springs Creek: Alexander Springs to FR 552

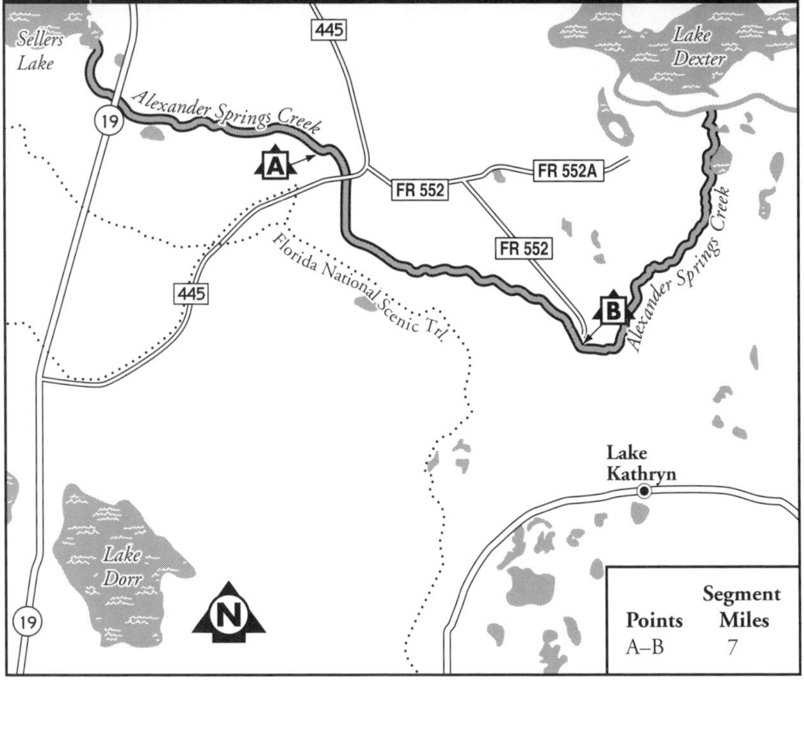

Points	Segment Miles
A–B	7

Lone kayaker on Alexander Springs Creek

SHUTTLE: To reach the put-in from Ocala, travel east on FL 40 to FL 19. Turn right (south) on FL 19 and follow it to CR 445. Turn left on CR 445 and continue for about 4 miles to the entrance to Alexander Springs Recreation Area. To reach the takeout from Alexander Springs, continue east on CR 445, passing the bridge over Alexander Springs Creek. Turn right on FR 552 and follow it, veering right again at 3 miles, away from FR 552A. FR 552 dead-ends at a landing on lower Alexander Springs Creek. FR 552 can be soupy after prolonged rains.

GAUGE: Visual. This spring averages over 70 million gallons per day and should always be runnable.

JUNIPER SPRINGS AND JUNIPER CREEK

Juniper Springs may be one of the clearest streams in Florida. The springhead is enclosed in a rock-and-concrete wall that provides a large swimming pool. The water flows out of the pool through a flume that powers a waterwheel once used for generating electricity. The put-in is a short distance below the waterwheel. Juniper Creek starts very narrow below rich canopied woodland. It then enters the gorgeous Juniper Prairie Wilderness, through which it flows until just above the FL 19 bridge. Paddlers will use all their skills navigating the sharp turns, cypress stumps, and overhanging palms and other trees. Kayaks in excess of 14 feet are not recommended. After rains, the crystalline waters can become stained, and the resulting higher water can make the run even more challenging. Be apprised that this run can be very busy on nice weekends and inexperienced paddlers can turn the run into "bumper boats." Go during the week if possible.

MAPS: Ocala National Forest map, Juniper Springs (USGS)

JUNIPER SPRINGS TO FL 19

class	I+
length	7
time	4
gauge	Visual
level	Spring-fed
gradient	3.7
scenery	A+

DESCRIPTION: Your adventure starts when you carry your boat through beautiful palm-topped woods on a paved trail to Juniper Creek. Most of the stream is very narrow and constricted with palm trees, cypress trees, live oaks, and dense vegetation. Be prepared to duck under and work around numerous overhanging trees. The water is so clear that its depths are deceptive. Fern Hammock Springs adds to the flow. A sign indicates your entry into Juniper Prairie Wilderness. The national forest has provided a resting spot within the Juniper Prairie Wilderness called Halfway Landing. It is about halfway through the run. This is not an access point, but simply a place to picnic and relax. There is no public access to Juniper Creek from the launching area to FL 19.

After Halfway Landing, the stream occasionally broadens into large grassy areas and divides around hammocks of palms and grass. Alligators are frequently seen in this area. Sweetwater Springs comes in from the left-hand bank, but is not open to the public. Old bridge pilings running across the stream indicate you are close to FL 19. The open area continues to FL 19 where the access is on the southeast side of the bridge. The stream continues for another 3 miles to Lake George, but there is no access for several miles, and the lake is a large body of water subject to high winds and waves.

Canoes can be rented at the Juniper Springs Recreation Area concession stand. Shuttle service from FL 19 is included in the price of rental. Private canoes can arrange for a shuttle as well on a space available basis.

SHUTTLE: To reach the put-in from Ocala, drive east on FL 40 to Juniper Springs Recreation Area, on your left. To reach the takeout, continue east on FL 40 to FL 19. Turn left, north, on FL 19 and follow it to reach Juniper Wayside. The parking area and takeout is on the southeast side of the bridge.

GAUGE: Visual. Juniper Creek is spring-fed and has a near constant flow.

Crystalline waters flow forth from Juniper Springs

Juniper Springs and Juniper Creek: Juniper Springs to FL 19

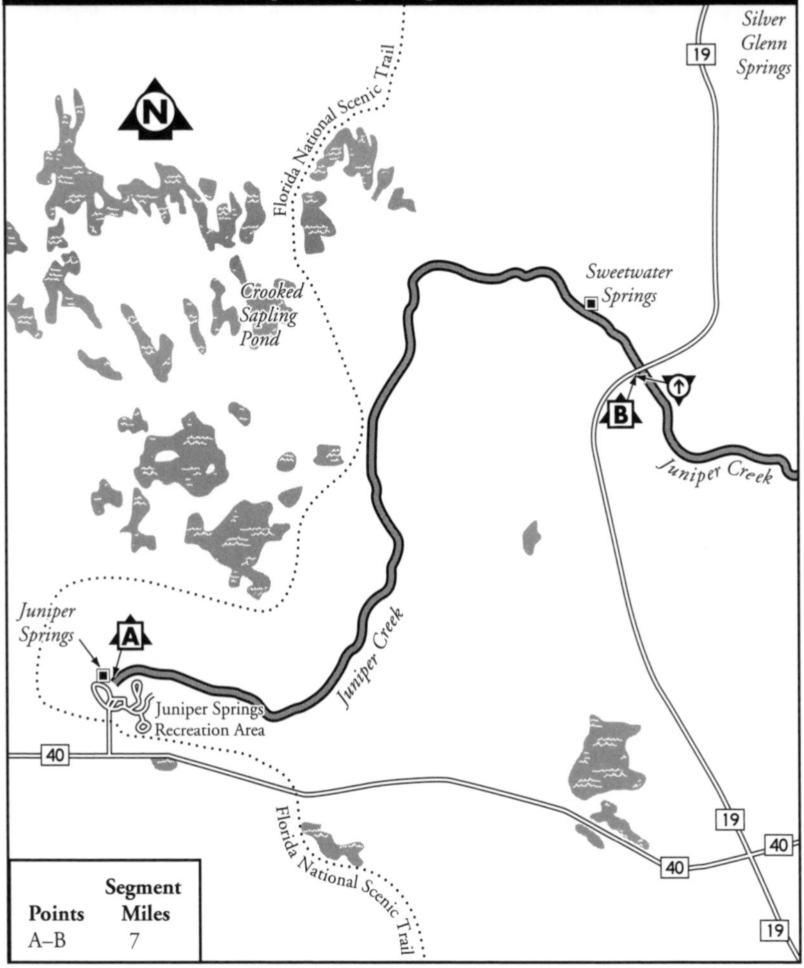

Points	Segment Miles
A–B	7

SALT SPRINGS AND SALT SPRINGS RUN

Salt Springs, so named for the minerals in its waters, pours forth over 60 million gallons of water per day. A vast recreation area has been developed around these springs, including a campground, swimming area, day-use area, and marina downstream from the springs. Despite the overwhelming presence of humans on its upper stretches, once downstream the setting becomes wild. Salt Springs Run is known for its wildlife. However, this scenery comes with a price as the 4-mile trip ends at Lake George, where there is no takeout, forcing paddlers to paddle upstream against the current. Paddlers can scout part of their run via the Salt Springs Trail, which leads to the south bank of the run below the springs.

MAPS: Ocala National Forest map, Salt Springs (USGS)

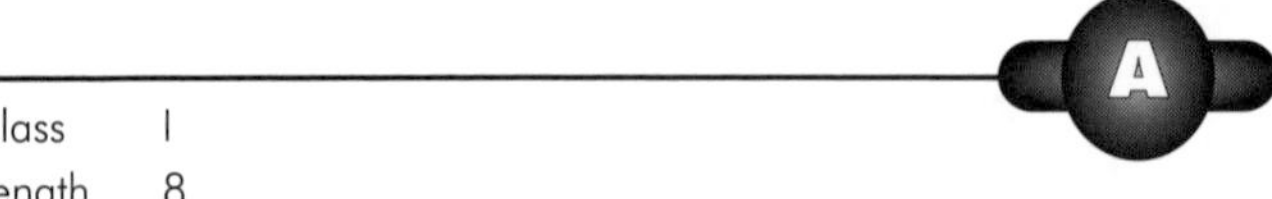

class	I
length	8
time	5.5
gauge	Visual
level	Spring-fed
gradient	1.0
scenery	B+

SALT SPRINGS TO LAKE GEORGE AND BACK

DESCRIPTION: This run starts at the Salt Springs marina. You can paddle upstream a short distance to the springs. Fish are normally seen finning around the spring boils. From the springs, the clear, wide channel of Salt Springs Run heads east for Lake George. Marsh borders the river. There is high ground on river left near the site of the Indian Mounds. Once at Lake George, 4 miles below Salt Springs, paddlers can relax at Salt Springs Bar and look over one of Florida's most picturesque lakes. If you want to explore the lake, Salt Springs Cove, to the left of Lake George after you leave Salt Springs Run, it is one of the most gorgeous shorelines in the state.

With the bountiful wildlife and historical value of this run, paddlers continue to hope that the forest service will one day install a ramp at the lower end of the run, eliminating the out-and-back nature of the run as it currently exists.

SHUTTLE: To reach the Salt Springs Marina from the community of Salt Springs, head south on FL 19 below the split with CR 314. The marina entrance road is on the east side of the road.

GAUGE: Visual. Salt Springs Runs is a spring-fed waterway and is floatable year-round.

Salt Springs and Salt Springs Run: Salt Springs to Lake George and Back

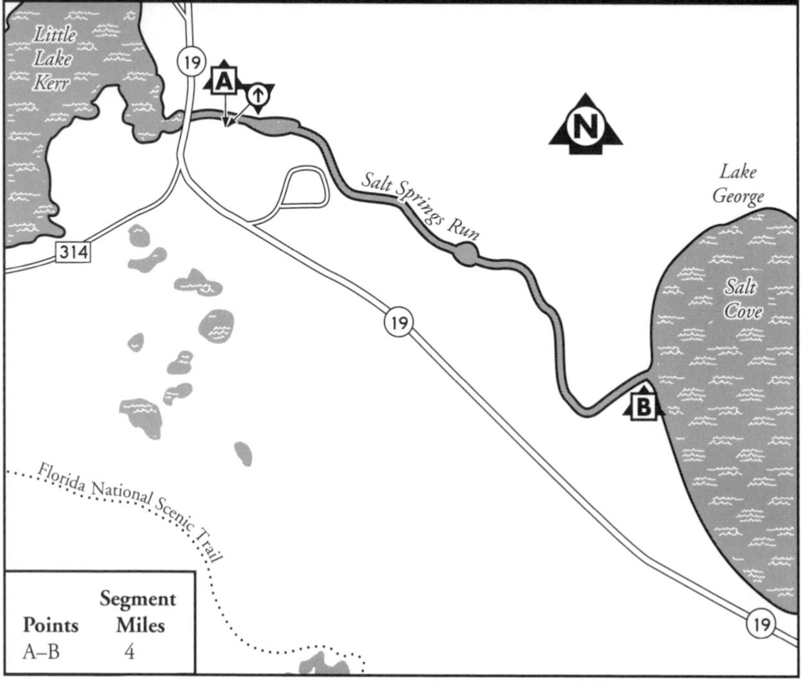

Little Lake Kerr

19

A

N

Salt Springs Run

Lake George

Salt Cove

314

19

B

Florida National Scenic Trail

19

Points	Segment Miles
A–B	4

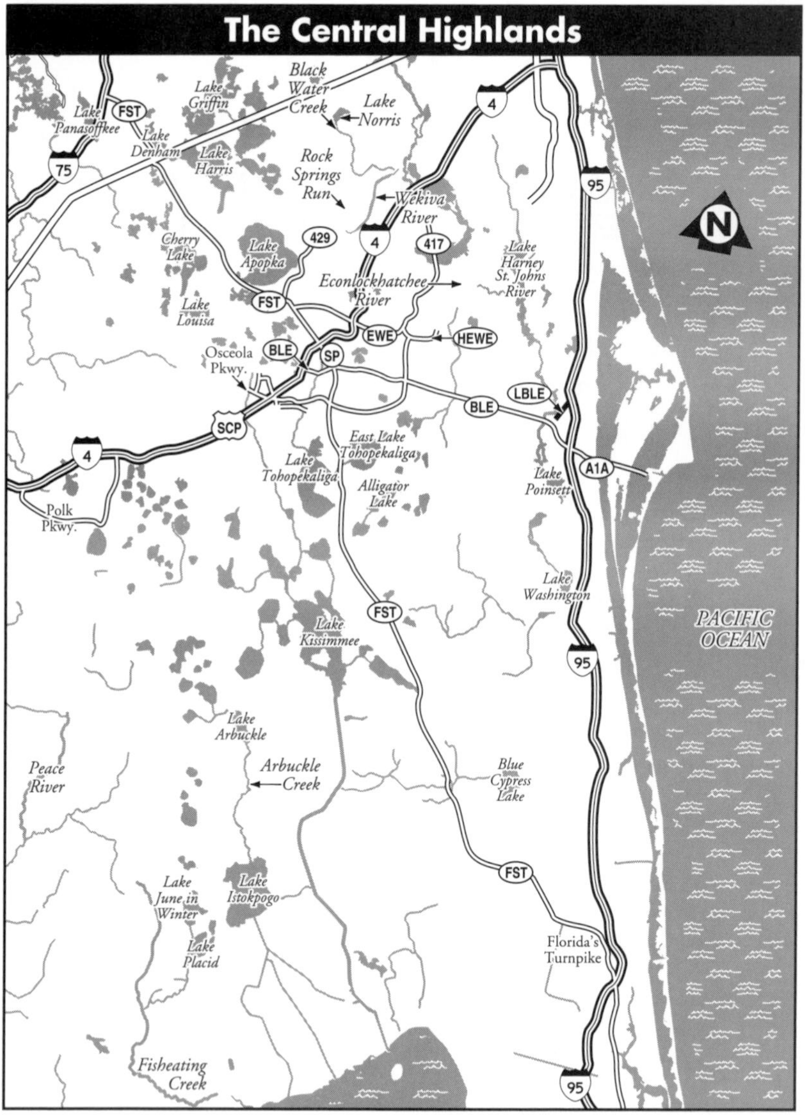

The Central Highlands

Lake Panasoffkee
FST
Lake Denham
75
Lake Griffin
Black Water Creek
Lake Norris
Lake Harris
Rock Springs Run
Wekiva River
4
95
Cherry Lake
Lake Apopka
429
417
Lake Harney
St. Johns River
Econlockhatchee River
FST
Lake Louisa
EWE
HEWE
Osceola Pkwy.
BLE
SP
LBLE
BLE
SCP
East Lake Tohopekaliga
Lake Tohopekaliga
Alligator Lake
A1A
Lake Poinsett
Polk Pkwy.
Lake Washington
FST
Lake Kissimmee
PACIFIC OCEAN
Lake Arbuckle
Arbuckle Creek
Peace River
Blue Cypress Lake
FST
Lake June in Winter
Lake Istokpogo
Lake Placid
Florida's Turnpike
Fisheating Creek
N

part **Six**

THE CENTRAL HIGHLANDS

WEKIVA RIVER AND ROCK SPRINGS RUN

The Wekiva River in Orange County begins at Wekiwa Springs State Park and flows north for 15 miles to the St. Johns River. Rock Springs is located 7 miles to the northwest, near Apopka, and flows southeast into the Wekiva River about 0.5 miles below Wekiva Springs. Both of these streams are very popular, located in a large metropolitan area and likely to be crowded during the warm months and on weekends. They are beautiful crystalline waterways, however, and have maintained a surprising degree of remoteness and freedom from encroachment considering their location. The lower portion of the Wekiva River is not recommended—as one nears the St. Johns River, the Wekiva becomes very broad and developed. To avoid paddling into a potentially windy and unpleasant experience on the St. Johns, most paddlers prefer to take out about a mile below the FL 46 bridge at a state-owned canoe launch.

The terrain on both Wekiva River and Rock Springs Run is a fine example of semitropical Florida wetlands and swamp. Cabbage palm, cypress, and other lowland trees abound, as well as other hardwoods that frequently canopy the waterway. It is truly an oasis among ever-expanding greater Orlando.

MAPS: Sorrento, Sanford SW, Forest City (USGS)

KINGS LANDING TO WEKIVA MARINA

class	I
length	8
time	4
gauge	Visual
level	Spring-fed
gradient	1.2
scenery	A

DESCRIPTION: After paddling down a small canal from King's Landing to the Rock Springs Run, paddlers enter a deep channel between lily pads and water reeds. The waterway itself is 30 to 40 feet wide but the navigable channel is only 10 to 15 feet across. Bring your short kayak or a canoe to negotiate the twists and turns on Rock Springs Run. Also, try to avoid summer weekends or you will be negotiating between other paddlers and tubers.

The first 4 miles of this paddle trail are among the most beautiful examples of lowland hardwoods and clear, green water of any stream in Florida. Tall trees with slender trunks form a complete canopy over the river in many places. Following this section, the river widens to 50 feet and then up to 100 feet in sections. It is shallower, and white sand can be glimpsed between the waterweeds on the bottom. Some 3 miles further downstream, the river narrows again to 20 to 30 feet and becomes deeper. The sandy bottom is still in evidence and the canopy of hardwoods resumes.

Wekiva River and Rock Springs Run (Sections A–B): Kings Landing to Canoe Launch below SR 46

Points	Segment Miles
A–B	8
B–C	11

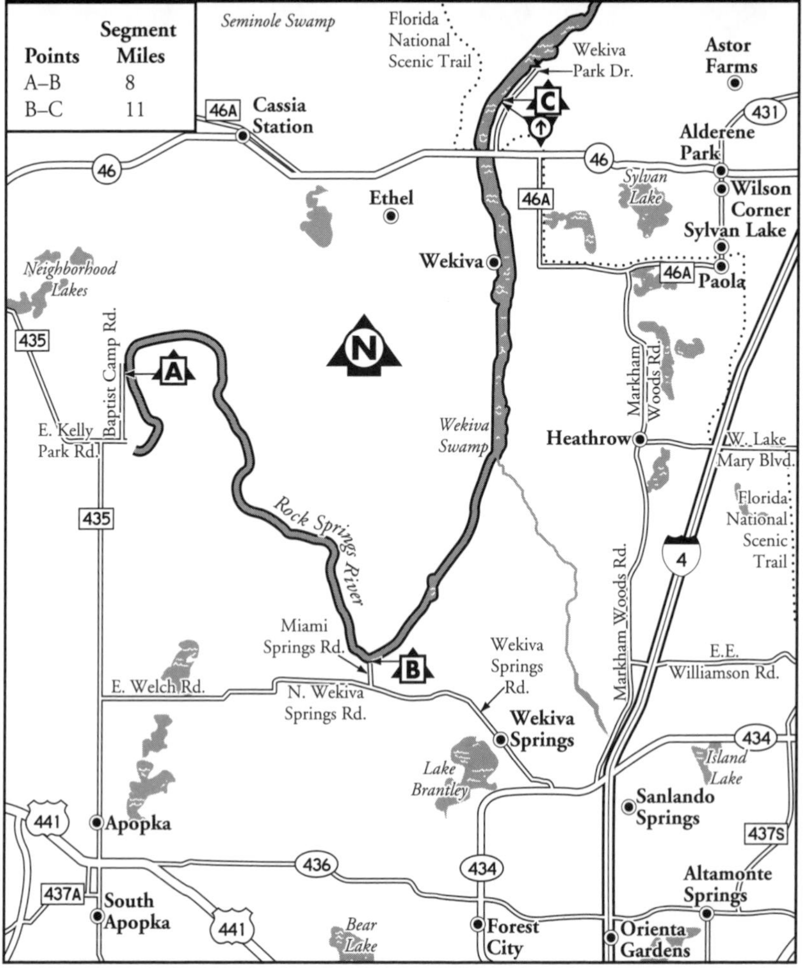

At the confluence of the Wekiva River, canoeists may turn right and paddle up to the entrance to Wekiva Spring. This is the location of Wekiva Springs State Park, which has camping and canoe launching facilities. There is considerable current in the Wekiva River, but it is only 0.5 miles to the spring and is well worth the effort.

Shortly below the confluence of the Wekiva River with the Rock Springs Run is the Wekiva Marina. This is a privately owned public access facility with canoe rentals, a restaurant, store, and dock.

SHUTTLE: To reach the takeout from Apopka, drive north on FL 435 to Welch Road. Turn right on Welch Road and follow it to Wekiva Springs Road to reach Miami Springs Road. Turn left on Miami Springs Road to reach Wekiva Marina. To reach the put-in, backtrack to FL 435, then turn right, north, on FL 435, to Kelly Park Road. Turn right on Kelly Park Road; continue for 0.125 miles and turn left on Baptist Camp Road. Continue north for less than a mile to King's Landing. There is a small fee for launching.

GAUGE: Visual. Rock Springs Run is spring-fed and runnable year-round.

Wekiva Marina to Canoe Launch Below SR 46

class	I
length	11
time	6
gauge	Visual, web
level	Spring-fed
gradient	0.9
scenery	B

DESCRIPTION: After leaving the marina, the river turns north. It varies from 50 to 150 feet wide, dividing around islands. The Little Wekiva River enters from the right 3 miles downstream. A railroad trestle appears another 5 miles downstream.

The river widens dramatically just below the trestle to over 300 feet and resembles a small lake of grass and reeds. In this area, a canal on the left bank leads to a tourist attraction called Wekiva Falls. This facility has canoe rentals, camping, and a small river-boat that tours up the Wekiva for a mile or so. It offers takeout service for a fee. This shallow, grassy area continues to FL 46.

A free takeout on state-owned property is on the right-hand bank about a mile below FL 46 and is the best place to end your run on the Wekiva, unless you plan to paddle down to and across the St. Johns River at Debary (off High Banks Road in Volusia County).

SHUTTLE: To reach the put-in from Exit 94 on I-4, take FL 434 west to Wekiva Springs Road. Turn right on Wekiva Springs Road and follow it to a stop light at Miami Springs Road/Hunt Club Road. Turn right on Miami Springs Road to reach Wekiva Marina. To reach the takeout, backtrack to I-4 and turn left, north, on Markham Woods Road to reach Markham/Longwood Road. Turn left on Markham/Longwood Road and follow it to FL 46. Turn left on FL 46 and follow it just a short distance to Wekiva Park Drive. Turn right on Wekiva Park Drive and follow it about a mile to a state-owned canoe launch, on the left.

GAUGE: Visual, Web. Wekiva River is spring-fed and runnable year-round. The USGS gauge helpful in determining flow rates for any given day is Wekiva River near Sanford, FL.

Calm Florida streams are great for kids

BLACKWATER CREEK AND LAKE NORRIS

Blackwater Creek—tight and hauntingly beautiful as it snakes through an ancient, maybe prehistoric, cypress swamp—is thought by many locals to be the "impassable waterway." Born on the waters of Lake Norris, it stretches for over 20 miles, eventually emerging onto the Wekiva River just upstream from the St. Johns River. Many hardy souls have tried to traverse the entire waterway and have met with difficulties—extreme difficulties. The middle section is mined with dead snags hiding in tea-stained low water, and nature has barricaded the lower reaches with countless deadfalls. Past the confluence with Seminole Creek and Sulphur Run, the waterway totally disappears into a myriad of tiny fingers, none large enough to support a canoe, and doesn't reform until just prior to the Wekiva.

Impassable? Sure! But not to be missed. Most folks paddle upstream on the Blackwater to Lake Norris. Intrepid paddlers will try the 4 miles downstream from Lake Norris Road to the CR 44A bridge. Below that you are on your own. Just stick to the upper stretch of Blackwater, never wandering more than a few miles from Lake Norris. The channel is deeper and there are fewer obstructions to contend with, except in low-water conditions. The silence of the cypress forest is sometimes hypnotizing, and the mood may only be broken by the passing of an animal resident.

Lake Norris is the jewel of the trip. It is now part of the St. Johns River Water Management District Lands. The 2,352-acre preserve protects an extensive hardwood swamp forest on the west bank. There are purportedly upward of 100 osprey nests on the lake. The cypress woodlands extend into the lake, creating a 150-foot-wide buffer in many places—an intriguing area to explore—that plays host to wildlife aplenty. The adventuresome boater can spend hours investigating the lake shore, weaving a canoe through the maze of cypress. And, except for one Boy Scout camp and a few rustic homesites, the surrounding area is a de facto wilderness sanctuary.

MAPS: Paisley, Pine Lakes (USGS)

Blackwater Creek Bridge to Lake Norris and Return

class	I
length	2–7
time	Varies
gauge	Visual, Web
level	N/A
gradient	0.5
scenery	A

DESCRIPTION: From the bridge, turn left and paddle upstream toward Lake Norris. At moderate to high water conditions, you will encounter very few obstructions, while at lower water you must negotiate some deadfalls and bottom snags. There is a very slight current and the meandering streambed

creates a lively, challenging slalom course. Watch for two sets of ancient wood pilings crossing the creek. They were set years ago for bridge construction. The first is about 0.5 miles from the put-in, and the second spans the mouth of the stream that meets Lake Norris at 1 mile.

Lake Norris is a large body of water, and wind conditions can kick up sizable waves, so it's best to paddle around the periphery of the lake. Besides, that's where the gnarled cypress forest grows out of the water, so the scenery is much more tantalizing. For the

Blackwater Creek and Lake Norris (Sections A–B): Blackwater Creek Bridge to CR 44A

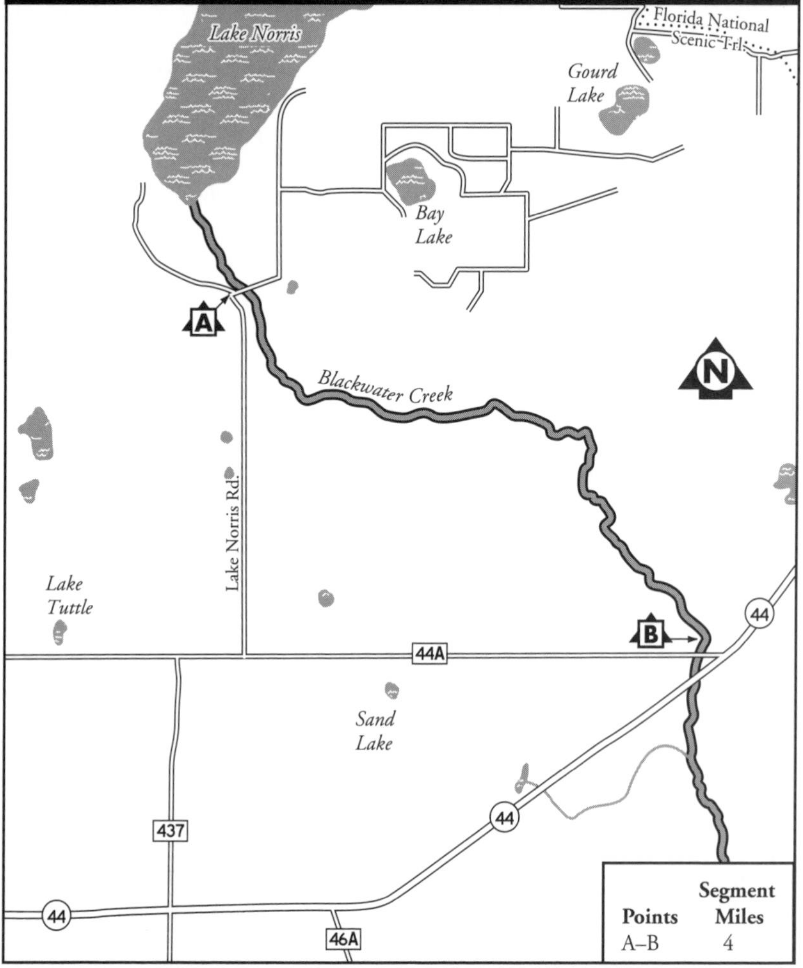

Lake Norris
Florida National Scenic Trl
Gourd Lake
Bay Lake
A
Blackwater Creek
N
Lake Norris Rd.
Lake Tuttle
44
B
44A
Sand Lake
437
44
44
46A

Points	Segment Miles
A–B	4

best trip into this forest, paddle along the west side of the lake. Turn around at your discretion or paddle the entire lakeshore. Then return to the put-in via Blackwater Creek.

SHUTTLE: From Eustis take FL 44, Orange Avenue, to CR 437. Turn left and drive north for 2 miles to the intersection with CR 44A. Turn right and travel east to Lake Norris Road. Turn left on Lake Norris Road to the bridge over Blackwater Creek. Access is down a dirt ramp on the northwest approach to the bridge.

GAUGE: Visual, Web. What you see at the put-in is what you get. The USGS gauge helpful in determining flow rates for any given day is Blackwater Creek near Cassia, FL.

LAKE NORRIS ROAD TO CR 44A

class	I
length	4
time	4–6
gauge	Visual, Web
level	N/A
gradient	0.5
scenery	A

DESCRIPTION: Beautiful? You bet! Difficult? Absolutely! Fun? That depends on your tolerance for carry-overs and your skills at boat handling around difficult deadfalls and other obstructions.

From the put-in, turn right and paddle under the bridge. At low water levels, you will encounter obstructions almost immediately. At higher levels, the first mile or so provides almost clear passage. Beware, though, the situation only gets worse as you proceed downstream. Even under the best of conditions, this trip will consume several hours. But, for the adventurous paddler who tackles it, the experience of the enclosed swamp and the solitude that comes with it may well be worth the effort.

SHUTTLE: To reach the takeout from Eustis, take FL 44, Orange Avenue, to CR 437. Turn left and drive north for 2 miles to the intersection with CR 44A. Turn right on CR 44A and follow it to the bridge over Blackwater Creek. To reach the put-in, backtrack on CR 44A and travel west to Lake Norris Road. Turn right on Lake Norris Road to the bridge over Blackwater Creek.

GAUGE: Visual, Web. What you see at the put-in is what you get. The USGS gauge helpful in determining flow rates for any given day is Blackwater Creek near Cassia, FL.

ECONLOCKHATCHEE RIVER

The Econlockhatchee River, known to locals as the Econ, is a jewel in the midst of fast-developing eastern Orange and Seminole counties. This beautiful stream has mostly escaped the rampant growth that has consumed many of the area's natural attributes. The upper river challenges your paddling skills as it winds through the dim light of a mysterious cypress forest. Not far below the CR 419 bridge, the river reacquires a wild aura as it passes through the Little Big Econ State Forest. Things are slow and easy on the lower river as the Econ enters the open expanse of the St. Johns valley. Those with a bent for the supernatural may be interested in the glowing Oviedo Lights. Many people claim to have seen them at night above the water while standing on the CR 419 bridge. This strange luminescent phenomenon has long been part of the local lore of the Econ.

MAPS: Oviedo SW, Oviedo, Geneva (USGS)

class	I
length	15
time	7
gauge	Phone, Web
level	N/A
gradient	1
scenery	A

FL 50 TO CR 419

DESCRIPTION: This section of the Econ will bring paddling skill to the fore as sharp turns, cypress knees, deadfalls, and moderately swift current present a challenge. Check on stream conditions before attempting this trip. During low water the number of carry-overs becomes intolerable, and the river can be dangerous after major rainstorms. The towering cypresses keep the stream in perpetual shade, which makes this stretch attractive for summer paddling. The beauty of the cypress forest and wild nature of the streamside setting provide a memorable trip.

Fifteen miles can be an excessive run on such a twisty stream. However, a private outfitter has a takeout 9 miles below FL 50, if the river gets to be a bit much. It is 6 more miles to the CR 419 bridge. Watch for submerged concrete obstacles under the CR 420 bridge 2 miles into the run. Three power lines will be encountered beyond the bridge. The Econ's banks are not very accessible during the early going, but sandy banks appear beyond the 6-mile point. A major milestone occurs at the confluence with the Little Econlockhatchee River. From this point, it is just a short distance to the bridge at CR 419.

SHUTTLE: To reach the put-in from Orlando, drive east on FL 50 to just before the bridge on the northwest side and a private canoe livery, Hidden River Park, that charges a small launch fee. To reach the takeout, continue east on FL 50 to Chuluota Road.

Econlockhatchee River (Sections A–B): FL 50 to FL 46

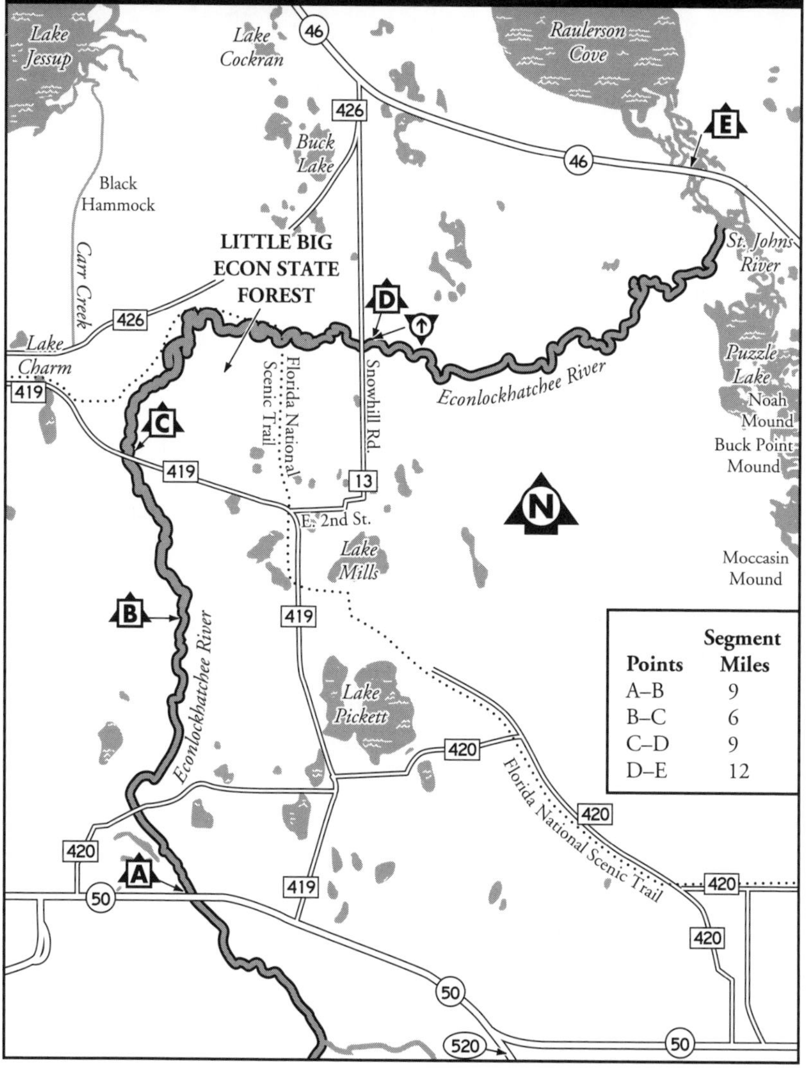

Points	Segment Miles
A–B	9
B–C	6
C–D	9
D–E	12

Turn left on Chuluota Road, which becomes CR 419 in Seminole County. Keep north on CR 419 until Willingham Road, just before the CR 419 bridge on the right.

GAUGE: Phone, Web. Call Hidden River Park, located at the put-in for river conditions. Their number is (407) 568-5346. The Econ is normally paddleable year-round. The USGS gauge helpful in determining flow rates for any given day is Econlockhatchee River near Oviedo, FL.

class	I
length	21
time	Varies
gauge	Phone, Web
level	N/A
gradient	0.6
scenery	B+

CR 419 TO FL 46

DESCRIPTION: This run can be broken into two portions and is also suitable for camping since much of the sand-bottomed river travels through the Little Big Econ State Forest, ending at the Snowhill Road bridge. There are designated camping locales along the river in the forest. It is 9 miles from CR 419 to Snowhill Road bridge.

The character of this section of the Econ is markedly different from the previous section. However, the state forest setting maintains a wild aura. The cypress trees give way to hardwoods on high, sandy banks. The river bottom stays sandy. Fallen trees still pose occasional obstacles. Seasonal wildflowers add color and interest. Cedars are abundant in places. After the first 2 miles the Econ widens, the current eases a bit, and deadfalls cease to be a problem. However, before reaching an abandoned railroad trestle spanning the river 2 miles from Snowhill Road, the river narrows and twists again. The trestle now supports a footbridge that is part of the Florida Trail System.

The paddling is easy below the Snowhill Road bridge. The river is moderately wide, the current slow, and deadfalls are not a problem. The riverbanks are high, sandy, and shaded by oaks during the first 9 miles. The banks become lower as the 9-mile point is passed; and the oaks are replaced first by cabbage palms, and then by grassy prairie as the St. Johns valley is entered.

The Econ merges into the St. Johns River above the FL 46 bridge. Turn north and paddle toward the FL 46 bridge, visible in the distance. The St. Johns is wide at this point and can be rough on windy days, so stick to the left bank. There is considerable powerboat and airboat traffic on the St. Johns, so use caution.

SHUTTLE: To reach the put-in from Oviedo, take CR 419 east to the bridge over the Econlockhatchee River. Turn left just past the bridge onto Willingham Road and reach a canoe launch that

requires a carry to the river. To reach the lowermost takeout from Oviedo, take CR 426 east to FL 46. Turn right on FL 46 and follow it to C. S. Lee Park, on the northwest side of the bridge over the St. Johns River.

GAUGE: Phone, Web. Call Hidden River Park at (407) 568-5346, located at the put-in, for river conditions. The Econ is normally paddleable year-round. The USGS gauge helpful in determining flow rates for any given day is Econlockhatchee River near Oviedo, FL.

Gentle Arbuckle Creek

ARBUCKLE CREEK

Located near Sebring in south central Florida, Arbuckle Creek flows for 23 miles from Lake Arbuckle to Lake Istokpoga, stretching through cypress strands, open grass prairies, ranch land, and an occasional oak hammock. Originally the creek was known to the Native Americans as Weokufka, or "muddy water," although later it was apparently named Arbuckle after a family of local settlers. Lake Istokpoga (Native for "dangerous waters"), at 27,692 acres, is one of the five largest lakes in the state, and in early spring it is drawn down, causing low water levels in Arbuckle Creek.

For the first 10 miles, the creek runs along the western border of Avon Park Bombing Range. A portion of this range is a wildlife management area and becomes very active with hunters during the winter hunting season. Fishing is very productive in the creek with fine concentrations of bass, bluegill, and shellcracker; wild turkey are frequently seen along the banks. The paddler will likely encounter some boaters and fishermen along the waterway and, in general, will find them quite friendly.

MAPS: Lake Arbuckle, Lake Arbuckle NE, Lake Arbuckle SE, Lorida (USGS)

A

LAKE ARBUCKLE TO ARBUCKLE CREEK ROAD

class	I
length	12
time	6
gauge	Phone, Web
level	N/A
gradient	0.3
scenery	B+

DESCRIPTION: This first 2 miles constitute the most scenic section along the entire creek. It snakes through a dense cypress swamp and is lined with tall trees shading a large percentage of the waterway. The channel is only about 30 feet wide, and the current is swift, as indicated by the bottom vegetation bending to follow the flow. Numerous overhangs, deadfalls, and submerged logs obstruct the creek, requiring careful maneuvering to negotiate. Wildlife is abundant and it is not uncommon to see turtles, barred owls, and red-tailed hawks.

The boat ramp is on the south shore of Lake Arbuckle. After launching, the paddler should border the shore to the east and then pass under the CR 64 bridge and enter the creek. The pilings from an old railroad trestle will be encountered 2.1 miles from the put-in. After 0.2 miles, the paddler will pass a short dredged canal on river right that leads to a boat ramp on Arbuckle Road. Before attempting this section of the creek, you should check with local boaters or fish camps concerning any obstructions to through traffic. A wide lake-like area in the creek,

about 1 mile upstream of the takeout at Arbuckle Creek Road, is prone to severe hyacinth jams and could force you into a long, difficult portage through a cypress swamp on the east or along a heavily overgrown dike on the west.

Beyond the boat ramp canal off Arbuckle Road, the right shoreline opens up into ranch land while a dense cypress swamp remains on the other shore. About 1.4 miles later, the creek narrows and the swamp emerges again on the western bank. This terrain continues until about 4 miles into the trip, at which point Morgan Hole Creek enters on the left side, and the surrounding

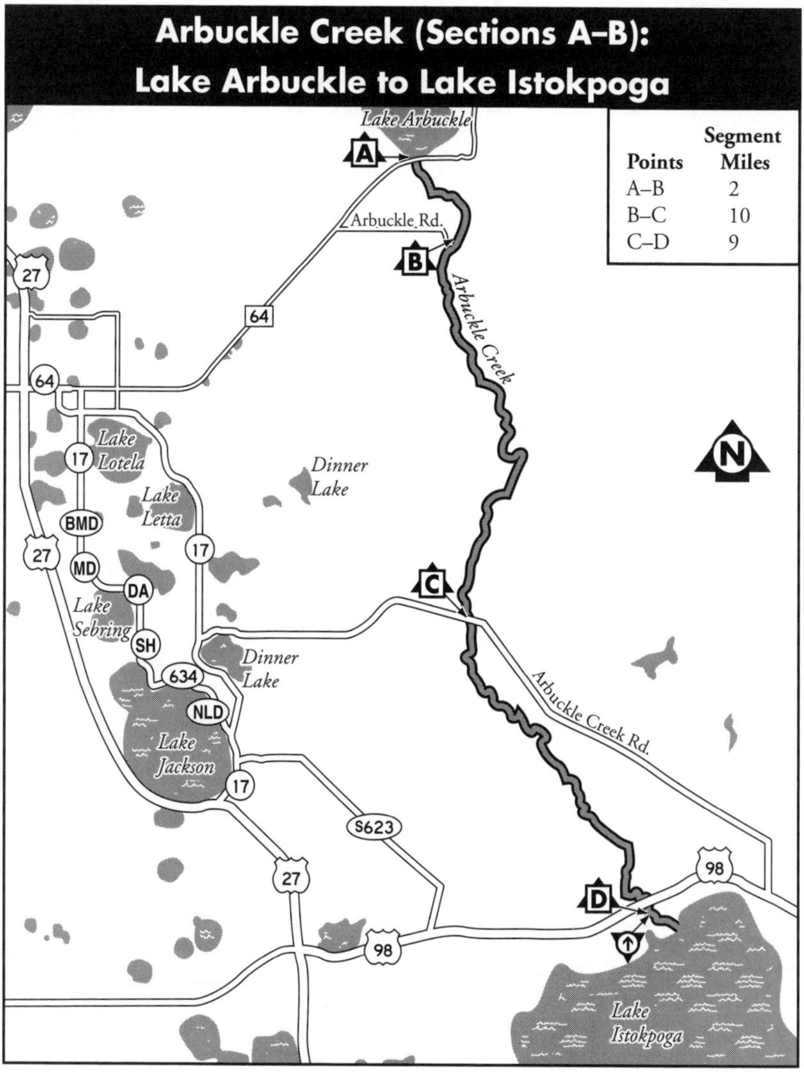

Arbuckle Creek (Sections A–B): Lake Arbuckle to Lake Istokpoga

Points	Segment Miles
A–B	2
B–C	10
C–D	9

vegetation opens up. Marsh grass on the east and a high dike on the west line the creek.

Eight miles from the put-in, the creek separates into two channels. The one to the right follows the dike past a rancher's culvert and pumping station, while the left passage flows through a cypress stand. Both lead into the wide, lake-like area described earlier. The Arbuckle Creek Road bridge is about a mile downstream of this point. The takeout is at a ramp on the right, immediately upstream of the bridge.

SHUTTLE: To reach the put-in from the town of Avon Park, drive east on CR 64 to the south end of Lake Arbuckle. A fish camp is on the left (north) side of the road just west of the bridge over Arbuckle Creek. Access is down a concrete ramp. To reach the takeout from Avon Park, proceed south on FL 17 and continue to follow it as it zigzags for 6.8 miles past Lakes Lotela and Letta to the intersection with CR 17A, Arbuckle Creek Road. Turn left on Arbuckle Creek Road to the bridge over Arbuckle Creek. The boat ramp is on the northwest bridge approach.

GAUGE: Phone, Web. Call William's Fish Camp at (863) 453-6229 for the latest creek conditions. Arbuckle Creek is normally paddleable year-round. The USGS gauge helpful in determining flow rates for any given day is Arbuckle Creek near De Soto City, FL.

B

class	I
length	9
time	4
gauge	Phone, Web, visual
level	N/A
gradient	1.3
scenery	B

ARBUCKLE CREEK ROAD TO LAKE ISTOKPOGA

DESCRIPTION: For the first 4.5 miles of this section, the creek traverses open ranch land. Although there are numerous pockets of cypress and oak, they are too widely scattered to provide shade. The next 1.5 miles pass through a dense oak forest with an abundance of small areas for good campsites, including an excellent spot 100 yards north of the railroad bridge, 5.5 miles from the put-in. The site is on the east shoreline and overlooks a small rapid formed by a series of limestone rocks and a drop in the creek bed. The rapids should be run over two small standing waves just to the left of an islet on the right side of the channel. At low water, exposed rocks in mid-creek and a limestone ledge along the left make it very difficult to negotiate this area.

One-half mile past the rapids, the main creek channel enters a man-made canal. Tall spoil banks are partially vegetated, interrupted only by cuts where the original creekbed, now overgrown

with aquatic plants, meanders across the canal. About 1 mile from the takeout, the canal begins to follow the original channel as it snakes gently past a cypress swamp on the left. Immediately after the creek passes under the US 98 bridge, you will encounter a fish camp on the right. The takeout is up a concrete boat ramp into the camp, where there will be a nominal ramp-users' charge.

SHUTTLE: The takeout is reached from Avon Park by taking US 27 south to US 98. Turn left on US 98 and travel east to the bridge over Arbuckle Creek. A fish camp with a boat ramp is located on the southwest approach to the bridge.

To reach the put-in from the takeout, continue on US 98 east to a graded lane, Arbuckle Creek Road. Turn left on Arbuckle Creek Road and travel north for 1.2 miles, then stay left, northwest (still on Arbuckle Creek Road), to a bridge over Arbuckle Creek. A boat ramp is located on the northwest side of the bridge.

GAUGE: Phone, Web, visual. Call William's Fish Camp at (863) 453-6229 for the latest creek conditions. Arbuckle Creek is normally paddleable year-round. The USGS gauge helpful in determining flow rates for any given day is Arbuckle Creek near De Soto City, FL.

PEACE RIVER

The Green Swamp, northeast of Tampa, is the headwaters for four of the finest rivers in the state: the Ocklawaha, Withlacoochee, Hillsborough, and Peace. The Peace River flows for approximately 133 miles from Lake Hancock near Bartow in Polk County to Charlotte Harbor near Punta Gorda. The river basin encompasses 2,400 square miles of primarily agricultural and ranch land, and numerous creeks and streams empty their contents into the river along its entire length. The Peace is considered to be 1 of the 13 major coastal rivers in Florida, which means it has an average discharge at its mouth of 1,000 cfs or more. As might be expected, almost 70 percent of the annual flow in the river (on average) occurs from June through October, after the onset of the wet summer weather. Despite the high nutrient levels caused by the discharge from phosphate mines and agriculture, the river retains a fair water quality and indeed supports a fine population of fish.

The Peace River is steeped in a rich natural and cultural history. In 1842, by virtue of an agreement between General Worth and the infamous Native American chief Billy Bowlegs, the Peace was established as the boundary between Native territory to the east and land for the white man to the west. During the Seminole Wars, numerous battles occurred along the banks of the Peace. At the confluence of the Peace and Payne Creek, south of Bowling Green, the Seminoles attacked a trading post at the start of the Third Seminole War, and one of the last battles of that war was fought near Fort Meade.

The Peace River can be paddled for almost 62 miles from Fort Meade to Arcadia. Below Arcadia the Peace becomes wide and is frequented by motorboats and personal watercraft, losing its appeal to paddlers.

Narrow, deep channels with high banks alternate with broad sections and quiet pools as the river passes through dense woodlands. Sand bluffs give way to shoreline flats, thickly carpeted with grasses and enclosed by the surrounding woods, making ideal campsites. The nearby forest abounds with deer and other wildlife, and the observant paddler will see numerous bird species, including herons, egrets, and kingfishers.

MAPS: Homeland, Bowling Green, Wauchula, Zolfo Springs, Gardner, Limestone, Nocatee (USGS)

Author Johnny Molloy plies the Peace River

class	I
length	22
time	Varies
gauge	Phone, Web
level	N/A
gradient	1.2
scenery	B

FORT MEADE TO ZOLFO SPRINGS

DESCRIPTION: The upper Peace flows out of Lake Hancock in central Polk County before becoming canoeable above Fort Meade, the official start of the river as a Florida Canoe Trail. Here the river is around 25 feet wide and meanders south. Many access points allow for trips of varied distances. From Fort Meade, the river enters Hardee County and reaches Paynes Creek State Historic Site after 12 miles. Little Charlie Creek enters the river 4 miles farther, just below the CR 664A bridge. Gentle riffles sliding over a rock bottom occasionally speed up the moderate current. Below Wauchula, the Fazzini Wilderness Environmental Education Center occupies part of the east bank.

SHUTTLE: To reach the takeout from Fort Meade, head south on US 17 to the bridge over the Peace River just before reaching Zolfo Springs. Turn right just south of the bridge into Pioneer Park and a public boat launch. To reach the put-in from Fort Meade, head east on US 98 to the boat launch at Fort Meade Recreational Park, on your right, after the bridge over the Peace River.

GAUGE: Phone, Web. Call Canoe Outpost at (863) 494-1215 for the latest river conditions. Peace River is normally paddleable year-round. The USGS gauge helpful in determining flow rates for any given day is Peace River at Fort Meade, FL.

class	I
length	23
time	Varies
gauge	Phone, Web
level	N/A
gradient	1.1
scenery	A

ZOLFO SPRINGS TO GARDNER

DESCRIPTION: Although this section can be paddled in a single day, that would do it an injustice—it is ideal for camping. Despite the large number of groups using this river on busy weekends, which occurs during spring and fall, fine campsites are so numerous that you can be virtually certain of finding one. A word of warning, though, for all paddlers: The majority of the land along this section is private property, owned by the Ben Hill Griffin Peace River Ranch, and they have a policy against campers using the eastern shore of the river. This policy will be made strikingly clear by the countless "No Trespassing" signs stationed along the left bank. The western shore, except for a few posted areas, is open for camping.

The launch area at Pioneer Park is down a concrete ramp. Below the ramp on the river, a V-formation of rocks creates a small shoal. Half a mile from the put-in, the river will pass beneath the FL 64 bridge, the last such structure you'll encounter until a steel-trussed wooden bridge at 13 miles. Tall bluffs support a forest of palm, oak, and cypress draped with Spanish moss. Small clear streams flow noisily into the river at intervals.

In the cool, dry winter season—also the prime time for canoe camping—the river will run nominally low. This will expose numerous sandbars and create shallow pools. In addition, deadfalls and normally submerged logs will surface. Although minor obstacles for the canoeist and kayaker, these features prove to be major obstructions for powerboaters and may restrict their access to this section of the Peace, a blessing for all paddlers.

Several bigger side streams intersect the river along this section. Troublesome, Hickory, Oak, and Limestone creeks enter from the west, and Charlie Creek, the largest contributor, comes in from the east. Limestone Creek is a very descriptive name. It flows into the Peace about 16 miles from Pioneer Park, and its presence is announced far in advance by the appearance of limestone rock formations along the banks. The banks of Limestone Creek are also lined with rock and, at low water, the undercutting due to erosion is clearly visible. Charlie Creek, also called Charlie

Peace River (Sections A–C): Fort Meade to Arcadia

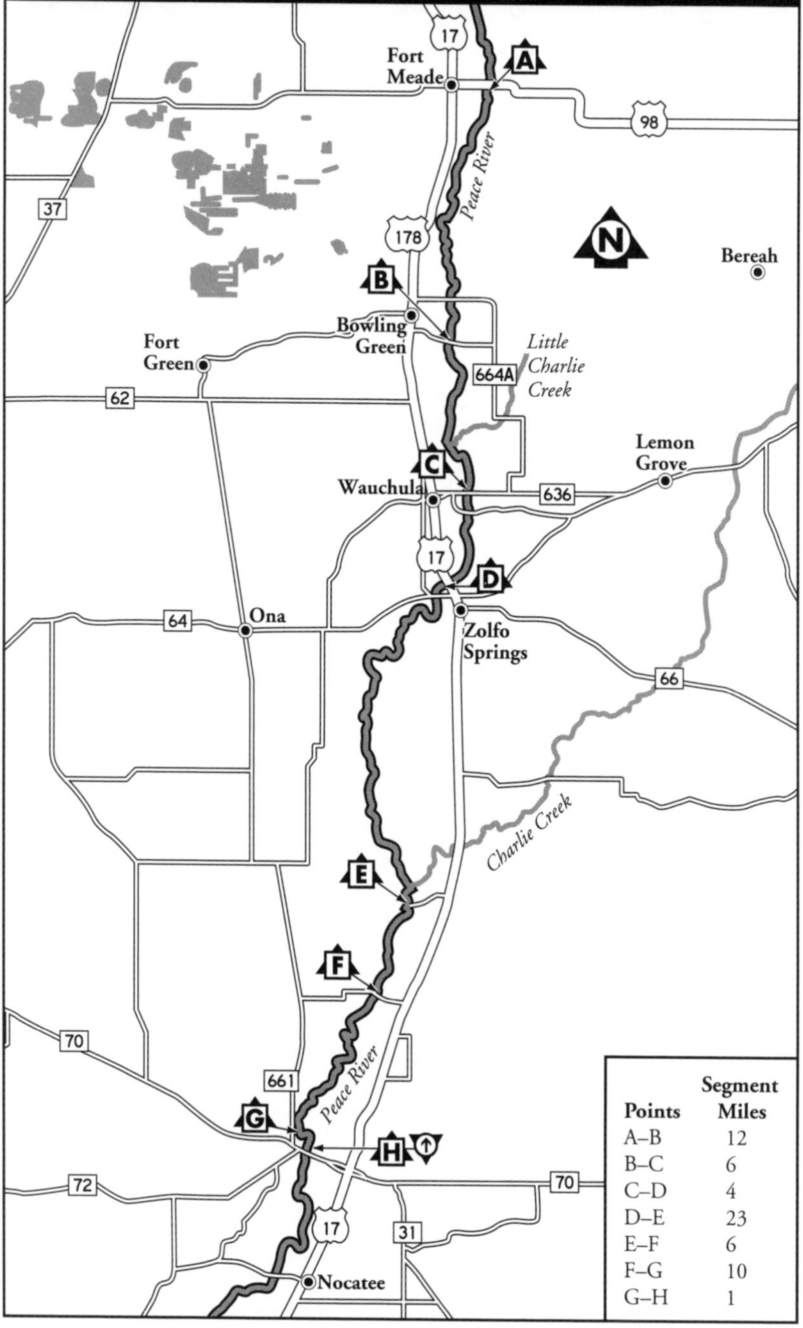

Fort Meade
Peace River
Bereah
Bowling Green
Fort Green
Little Charlie Creek
Lemon Grove
Wauchula
Ona
Zolfo Springs
Charlie Creek
Nocatee
17 98 37 178 664A 62 636 64 66 70 661 72 31

Points	Segment Miles
A–B	12
B–C	6
C–D	4
D–E	23
E–F	6
F–G	10
G–H	1

Apopka Creek, is a corruption of a Native American name which literally translates as "trout-eating place." This is a popular area for hunting fossils, most notably shark's teeth. This significant feeder stream, just above Gardner, adds considerable flow to the Peace.

SHUTTLE: The takeout is reached from Zolfo Springs by traveling south on US 17 for 10.2 miles past FL 64 to the town of Gardner. Turn right (west) onto River Road, identified by a small sign for a public boat ramp. Continue on this road for 1.5 miles until it dead-ends at the boat ramp. There is ample parking in the area. The put-in is at Pioneer Park, just north of Zolfo Springs, on the west side of US 17, just south of the bridge over the Peace.

GAUGE: Phone, Web. Call Canoe Outpost at (863) 494-1215 for the latest river conditions. Peace River is normally paddleable year-round. The USGS gauge helpful in determining flow rates for any given day is Peace River at Zolfo Springs, FL.

class	I
length	17
time	Varies
gauge	Phone, Web
level	N/A
gradient	0.6
scenery	B

Gardner to Arcadia

DESCRIPTION: With the addition of Charlie Creek, the river widens to 80 or more feet. The river, however, is less winding. The few bends do create larger sandbars. The current moderates, but fallen trees are common in the river. The banks remain high, with occasional low swampy areas, where willows are abundant. Both sides of the creek are posted with very little places to camp, other than at Brownville boat ramp, with a fine campground, and Oak Hill, owned by Canoe Outpost. Brownville boat ramp is reached after 6 miles and is on the east bank.

Houses become common for a while after Brownville. The most popular day trip on the Peace extends from Brownsville boat ramp to Arcadia, a distance of 11 miles. After Walker Branch enters the river from the west, bends resume for a couple of miles, then the river straightens again. The river passes under a wooden railroad trestle a mile above Arcadia. The Canoe Outpost access is on the right, shortly beyond the trestle.

SHUTTLE: The takeout is at American Legion Park, just west of Arcadia, on the northwest side of the FL 70 bridge over the Peace. The put-in is reached from Arcadia by traveling north on US 17 to River Road in Gardner. Look for a sign indicating Peace River Public Boat Ramp. Turn left (west) onto River Road and follow it for 1.5 miles until it dead-ends at the boat ramp. There is ample parking in the area.

GAUGE: Phone, Web. Call Canoe Outpost at (863) 494-1215 for the latest river conditions. Peace River is normally paddleable year-round. The USGS gauge helpful in determining flow rates for any given day is Peace River at Arcadia, FL.

FISHEATING CREEK

Fisheating Creek is undoubtedly one of the prettiest streams in Florida. Tea-colored water journeys swiftly through thick cypress swamps and beside hardwood hammocks only to open into small lakes where wildlife abounds. This area, especially the upper creek, is in an area little disturbed by humans. Now managed by the state of Florida, Fisheating Creek had been in the hands of ranchers who left the river as it was, and no development occurred. The high water mark of the streamshed is now the boundary of a wildlife management area. Wildlife does abound here—turkeys, deer, hogs, alligators aplenty, and more birds than I can identify. Special rules apply to the upper watershed as you have to pass through private land to reach the put-ins; therefore, only the state-sanctioned concessionaire operating the waterside campground and livery near Palmdale is allowed to take paddlers upstream. You must contact the outfitter to reach the upper Fisheating Creek access, upstream of US 27. You can paddle upstream directly from US 27, but it is a tough paddle practically speaking, due to swift currents. Downstream from US 27, paddlers can put in and head down, or put in at the public ramp on FL 78 near Lake Okeechobee and head upstream. It pays to contact the concessionaire before attempting a trip here.

Originating in Highlands County from a swamp near Hen Scratch, Fisheating Creek flows south down a channel before resuming its original banks and becoming paddleable near the town of Venus. It is here that the wildlife management area and attendant restrictions

Fisheating Creek offers swift channels between cypress trees

ensue. Starting at Ingrams Crossing the river makes a tortuous yet beautiful course for US 27, in a Florida reminiscent of a century ago. Below US 27, the creek continues for another 20 miles. However, in the past, waterweeds have blocked boat progression in places. Hopefully the weeds will be cleared, allowing a trip all the way to the "Big O" from upper Fisheating Creek. Furthermore, drawdowns on Okeechobee and the annual dry season occasionally render the creek too shallow in winter. Spring and fall are popular times to paddle. Longer kayaks may have trouble negotiating sections of the river.

MAPS: Fisheating Creek Canoe trail map, La Belle NW, Palmdale, Lakeport (USGS)

INGRAMS CROSSING TO PALMDALE

class	I
length	16.5
time	Varies
gauge	Web
level	1.5 kayaks, 2.5 canoes
gradient	1
scenery	A+

DESCRIPTION: This section, simply one of the most scenic in the state, can be halved for a day trip of 8 miles. The full 16.5 miles is best done as an overnight trip. The entire segment passes through the Fisheating Creek Wildlife Management Area and lives up to its name. The paddle itself begins at Ingrams Crossing. Here the southbound creek is 30 to 40 feet wide and is bordered by cypress and live oak hammocks. Air plants and Spanish moss fight for space on the streamside trees. The creek soon narrows and reveals its winding nature. The serpentine stream opens into lakes, where the current slackens and the scenery varies. Campsites are more abundant up here.

The creek turns east at Sand Lake, a shallow body of water bordered by marsh. Below the lake begins miles of traveling through glorious cypress swamp, which is often only 10 feet wide or smaller. The current speeds up in these swamps, keeping paddlers on their toes. In other places Fisheating Creek widens and narrows at a whim.

After 8 miles the creek enters the Burnt Bridge area. This is the starting point for the wonderful day trip leading down to Palmdale and US 27. The pattern of lakes and narrow streams continues. Lemon Lake is the largest body of water down here. Sandbars become more frequent as Fisheating Creek nears US 27. The takeout is located at Picnic Lake.

SHUTTLE: The shuttle on this upper section must be handled by the concessionaire on US 27. Therefore, you must take US 27 to Fisheating Creek Campground in Palmdale, then get a shuttle upstream.

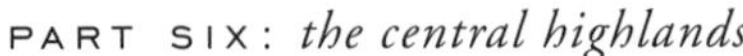

GAUGE: Web. The USGS gauge is Fisheating Creek at Palmdale, FL. The minimum recommended runnable level is 2.5 for canoes and 1.5 for kayaks.

class	I
length	21
time	Varies
gauge	Web
level	1.5 kayaks, 2.5 canoes
gradient	0.8
scenery	A

PALMDALE TO OKEECHOBEE

DESCRIPTION: This section is wild and beautiful as well but more open. Fisheating Creek continues east under US 27, twisting and winding its way toward Lake Okeechobee. The cypress swamps continue east of Palmdale, alternating with a series of lakes. Rock Lake is reached after 5 miles; Spring Board Hole Lake comes next. Darby Hole Lake is the last in the series of lakes. At 8 miles, the stream enters Cowbone Marsh, an open area that has been choked by weeds in the past and is impassable in that state. Hopefully this will be cleared in the future. Check on the status before attempting a trip through here. Paddlers often start on FL 78 near Okeechobee and paddle upstream to the blocked point, or downstream from US 27 and return. Cowbone Marsh continues for 3 miles and then comes to one last lake area, known as Double Lakes. The last 8 miles are stream paddling, often through open ranch lands broken by occasional oak hammocks.

SHUTTLE: To reach the put-in from Clewiston, take US 27 north to Palmdale. The state-sanctioned concessionaire is on the west side of the road, north of the bridge over Fisheating Creek. To reach the takeout from Clewiston, take US 27 north to Moore Haven, then take FL 78 north to the boat ramp at Fisheating Creek.

GAUGE: Web. The USGS gauge is Fisheating Creek at Palmdale, FL. The minimum recommended runnable level is 2.5 for canoes and 1.5 for kayaks.

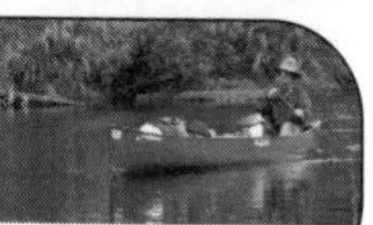

Fisheating Creek (Sections A–B): Ingrams Crossing to Okeechobee

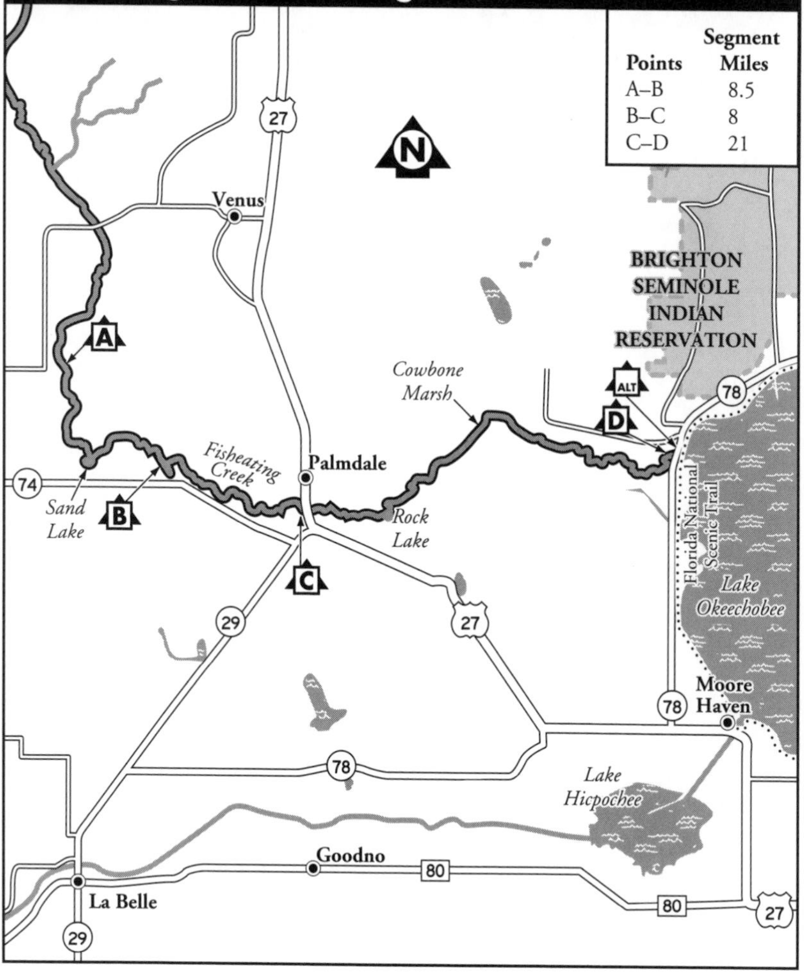
Points Segment Miles
A–B 8.5
B–C 8
C–D 21
N
27
Venus
A
BRIGHTON SEMINOLE INDIAN RESERVATION
Cowbone Marsh
ALT
D
78
74
Sand Lake
B
Fisheating Creek
Palmdale
Rock Lake
C
Florida National Scenic Trail
Lake Okeechobee
29
27
Moore Haven
78
78
Lake Hicpochee
Goodno
80
80
La Belle
29
27

The Atlantic Coast

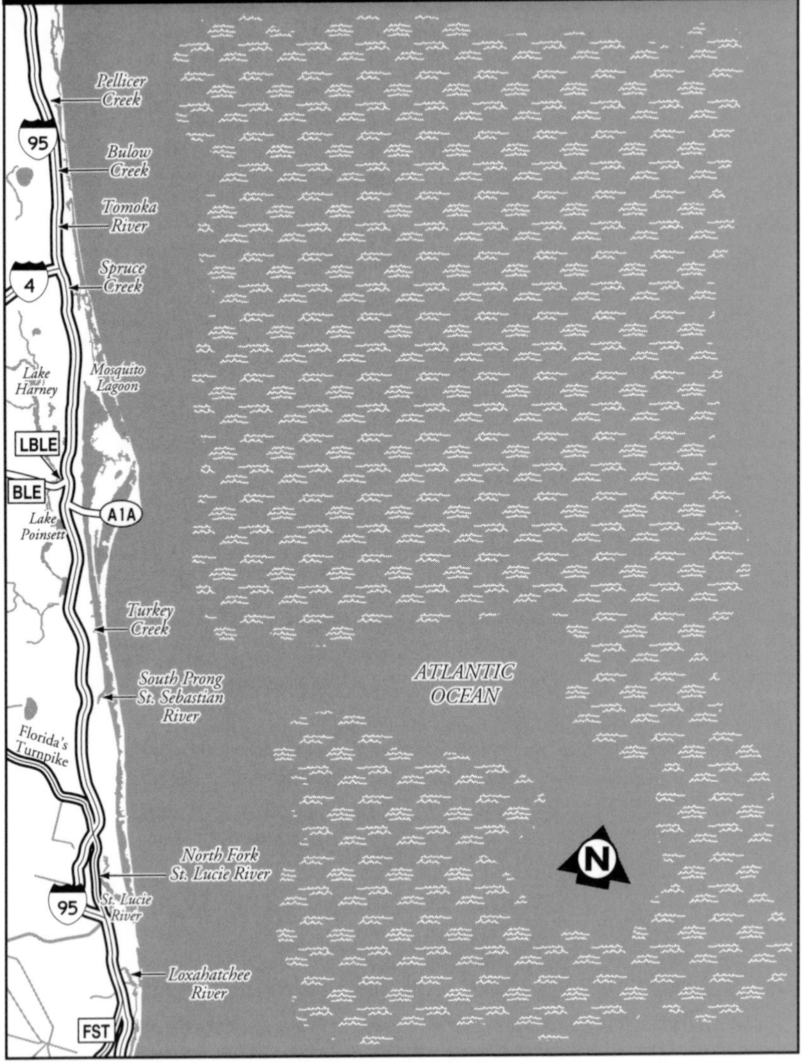

Pellicer Creek
95
Bulow Creek
Tomoka River
Spruce Creek
4
Lake Harney
Mosquito Lagoon
LBLE
BLE
A1A
Lake Poinsett
Turkey Creek
South Prong St. Sebastian River
ATLANTIC OCEAN
Florida's Turnpike
North Fork St. Lucie River
N
95
St. Lucie River
Loxahatchee River
FST

part Seven

THE ATLANTIC COAST

PELLICER CREEK

The powers that be in Florida realized ahead of the curve what a treasure they have in Pellicer Creek. Before the lands along this coastal waterway could be developed, the St. Johns River Water Management District bought them, and now 8 miles of shoreline on the south bank from the upper river section down to the creek mouth at the Matanzas River are preserved. Much of the north bank east of I-95 was already part of Faver–Dykes State Park. The newer lands were once part of Princess Estate, a lodge built of coquina blocks. The paddling here covers the transition from fresh water to tidal stream. If you paddle the lower creek, consider the tides and the wind, which can push unabated across the open marsh flats.

MAPS: Faver–Dykes State Park map, Dinner Island NE (USGS)

CRACKER CREEK TO PRINCESS PLACE PRESERVE

class	I
length	6
time	2.5
gauge	Visual
level	Tidal
gradient	Tidal
scenery	A

DESCRIPTION: Bring your camera on this photogenic waterway. Paddlers can start their trip on Cracker Creek, off of CR 204, and ply this lovely creek, draped in hardwoods hanging over the water, for a short distance before entering Pellicer Creek. If the winds are howling you can head upstream on Pellicer Creek. Downstream on Pellicer Creek, you'll pass under the US 1 bridge, which has less favorable shuttle parking than CR 204. Below the US 1 bridge, the right bank houses the Florida Agricultural Museum. After passing under the noisy I-95 bridge, the lands become protected on both banks. The right bank is part of the 3,900-acre Princess Place Preserve, with trails and a boat ramp of its own, should you decide to continue east 1.5 miles beyond the Faver–Dykes boat ramp. Marsh grass is present, and tidal influence is felt on the lower creek. Often one bank will have pines, palms, and cedars while the other side will be marsh

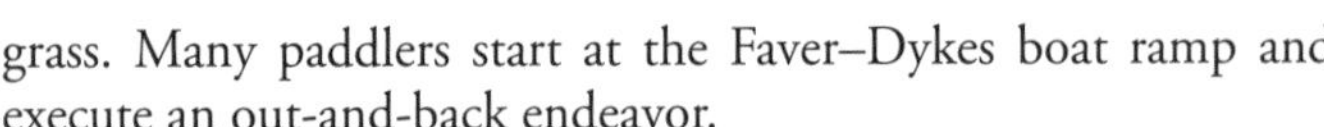

grass. Many paddlers start at the Faver–Dykes boat ramp and execute an out-and-back endeavor.

SHUTTLE: To reach the Princess Place Preserve takeout from Exit 298 on I-95, head south on US 1 to Old Kings Road. Turn left on Old Kinds Road, passing back under the interstate, and watch for the left turn into Princess Place Preserve. Once inside the preserve, follow the signs to the boat ramp. To reach the upper access, return to US 1 north, then turn left on CR 204. Head west just a short distance on CR 204 to reach the bridge over Cracker Creek.

GAUGE: Visual. This tidal creek is floatable year-round.

Pellicer Creek: Cracker Creek to Princess Place Preserve

Points	Segment Miles
A–B	4
B–C	1.5

Cracker Creek
Pellicer Creek
Pellicer Creek
Hemming Point
Florida Agricultural Museum
Old Kings Rd.
1
95
204
A
B
C
N

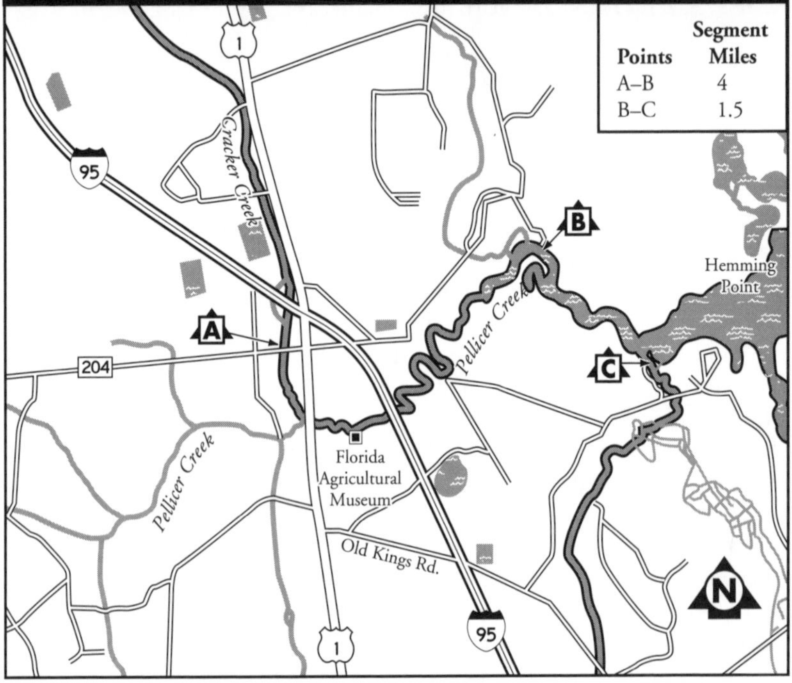

BULOW CREEK

Bulow Creek is a trip back into Florida history as well as an opportunity to explore a coastal marsh. The put-in is near Ormond Beach at the Bulow Plantation State Historic Site. This site is a relic of the early 1800s when a number of sugar plantations dotted the Florida Atlantic coast. These plantations were burned and abandoned during the Second Seminole War. Paddlers should take the opportunity to visit the old sugar mill and other ruins. There are also nature trails that are worth exploring. Bulow Plantation and the adjacent Bulow Creek State Park form a substantial portion of the west bank of upper Bulow Creek. The park is noteworthy for its rich stand of hardwood hammock.

Bulow Creek originates in Graham Swamp, approximately 3.5 miles upstream from Bulow Plantation. The creek is an easy 13-mile day trip starting out at the plantation, going upstream to the origin, and then paddling down to the terminus at the Intracoastal Waterway at High Bridge Park. There is an alternate takeout on Walter Boardman Lane that reduces the trip length to 10.5 miles. If you don't want to paddle upstream or backtrack, the trip from the plantation put-in to the takeout at High Bridge Park is 5.5 miles.

MAPS: Flagler Beach East, Flagler Beach West (USGS)

Bulow Plantation to High Bridge Park

class	I
length	5.5
time	3
gauge	Visual
level	Tidal
gradient	Tidal
scenery	B–

DESCRIPTION: Bulow Creek flows lazily in a general north to south direction. Bulow Plantation is located at the transition between the cabbage palm hammock that lines upper Bulow Creek and the grassy coastal marsh of lower Bulow Creek. Paddling upstream from the plantation, the grassy marsh is gradually succeeded by a narrower stream with margins overhung with palms and swamp hardwoods. A fair number of osprey nests can be seen along this stretch of Bulow Creek, making paddling especially rewarding during spring when the ospreys are building nests and feeding their young.

At 3.5 miles upstream from the plantation, the snags and deadfalls of Graham Swamp make further progress difficult, and most paddlers will head back downstream. Going south from Bulow Plantation, the creek flows through a broad, grassy coastal marsh. A stream enters from the right at 0.8 miles, as does a canal

at 1.5 miles. You reach a large grassy island at 1.8 miles with the main channel going to the right. The alternate takeout on Walter Boardman Lane is located at 3.5 miles. Another mile of paddling and a channel branches off to the right. This is the natural Bulow channel. The straight-ahead channel is a man-made shortcut to the Intracoastal Waterway. The natural channel meanders almost 2 miles to reach the Waterway, whereas the man-made channel is less than 1.5 miles to the same point. Paddlers taking the natural channel should turn right where the stream again intersects the man-made channel at 0.2 miles from the takeout.

Bulow Creek:
Bulow Plantation to High Bridge Park

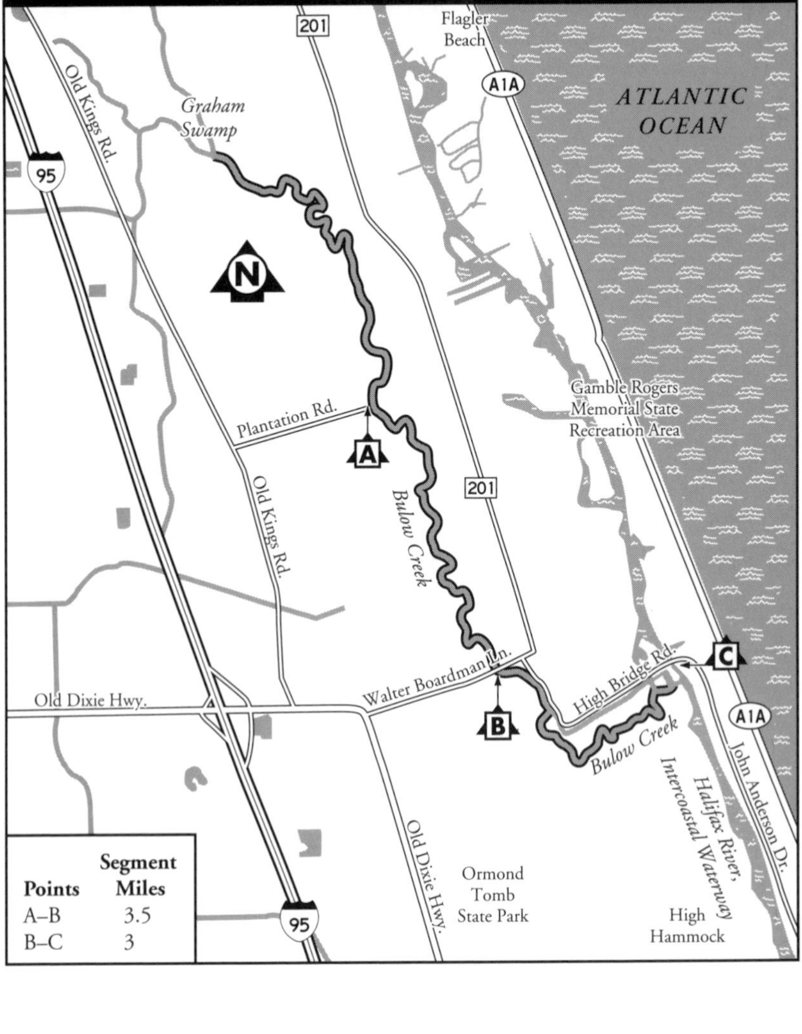

201
Flagler Beach
A1A
ATLANTIC OCEAN
Old Kings Rd.
Graham Swamp
95
Plantation Rd.
A
Old Kings Rd.
Bulow Creek
201
Gamble Rogers Memorial State Recreation Area
Walter Boardman Ln.
Old Dixie Hwy.
B
High Bridge Rd.
C
A1A
Bulow Creek
Intercoastal Waterway
Halifax River,
John Anderson Dr.
Old Dixie Hwy.
Ormond Tomb State Park
High Hammock
95

Points	Segment Miles
A–B	3.5
B–C	3

Looking out over Bulow Creek

SHUTTLE: To reach the lowermost access from Exit 278 on I-95, take Old Dixie Highway east, noting Old Kings Road as you pass by. Keep forward, then turn left on Walter Boardman Lane, crossing Bulow Creek at an access, before reaching High Bridge Road. Turn right on High Bridge Road, crossing the bridge over the Halifax River to reach High Bridge Park on your right. There is a boat ramp on the southeast side of the bridge. To reach the uppermost access, backtrack to Dixie Highway, then turn right, north, on Old Kings Road. Look for the sign to Bulow Plantation Ruins State Park. Turn right on rough Plantation Road and follow it to enter the state park and reach the boat launch. There is a fee for entering the park.

GAUGE: Visual. Bulow Creek is a tidal stream that can be paddled year-round.

TOMOKA RIVER

The north-flowing Tomoka River drains a narrow coastal region between the Halifax River lagoon and the St. Johns River valley. The Tomoka provides a diverse paddling experience. The upper river is narrow and flows between tall cypresses; in contrast, the lower river is broad and flows through the open expanses of a coastal marsh. A substantial portion of the lower Tomoka lies within Tomoka State Park. The Timucuan native Indian town at the site of the park prompted early Spanish explorers to name the stream Rio de Timucas (River of the Timucuans). Later settlers corrupted "Timucas" to "Tomoka."

It's a good thing that the state park is there, guaranteeing sure-fire access. Since Ormond Beach/Daytona has grown, the upper river accesses are not easy to get onto or off of. The bridges and land under them are public property. However, there is no roadside parking, and paddlers have to be speedy launchers. Put your boat in or get it off the river quick. The upside of all the development is that once you have put in your boat, you can simply park at a nearby business or shopping center lot and walk a short distance back to the river. These launchings on FL 40 and US 1 will contrast greatly with a launch at the state park, where paddlers are welcome and boats are for rent if you don't have your own. Furthermore, Strickland Creek and Thompson Creek, branches of the Tomoka River, are within the state park and provide excellent paddling opportunities of their own.

MAPS: Tomoka State Park map, Daytona Beach, Ormond Beach (USGS)

Brian Babb paddles a sit-on-top kayak on the Tomoka River

FL 40 TO TOMOKA STATE PARK BOAT LAUNCH

class	I
length	8
time	Varies
gauge	Visual
level	Tidal
gradient	Tidal
scenery	C

DESCRIPTION: Most paddlers will start and end their trips at Tomoka State Park. However, from the FL 40 bridge, it is possible to paddle upstream for 1.5 miles to Priest Branch and beyond, but fallen trees will likely become problematic beyond here. Heading north, downstream, from the FL 40 bridge, the paddler passes a series of canals into a residential subdivision. Grover Branch enters on the left as the Tomoka makes a turn to the northeast and passes under I-95. The river now becomes broad, and the banks are lined predominantly with tall palm trees. A large number of these palms have toppled into the water, and many are submerged only a few inches below the surface. Self-propelled craft easily clear most of these trees, but powerboats must stay farther out in the channel—a welcome benefit for paddlers. Numerous osprey nests are located along the Tomoka, and these birds may be seen performing their household chores. A little over a mile downstream, the Tomoka divides to pass around a long, skinny island nearly a mile in length. Ahead are the East Coast Railway bridge and the US 1 bridge. It is 4 miles from the FL 40 bridge to the US 1 bridge.

Stream flow ceases below the US 1 bridge, and the river is tidally influenced. Considerable residential development is apparent on the left bank, but the right bank is all part of Tomoka State Park. Then the riverbanks become mostly marsh. However the natural character of the marsh has been altered by a large number of mosquito-control canals cut back into the marsh. Paddlers will first pass Thompson Creek, then Strickland Creek, on river right before coming to the North Beach Street Bridge. Parts of the right bank are beautifully forested with palm, cedar, and pine. Reach the park boat ramp on river right a half-mile below the Beach Street Bridge. It is 4 miles from US 1 to the Tomoka State Park boat ramp. Paddlers can continue north beyond the landing into the wide-open Tomoka Basin and the Halifax River.

SHUTTLE: To reach the uppermost access from Exit 268 on I-95, take FL 40 west to the bridge over the Tomoka River. To reach the lowermost access from Exit 268 on I-95, take FL 40 east to Beach Street in the town of Ormond Beach. Turn left on Beach Street and follow it to Tomoka State Park and a boat launch. There is a fee to enter the state park.

GAUGE: Visual. The Tomoka is primarily a tidally influenced river and can be paddled year-round.

Tomoka River: FL 40 to Tomoka State Park Boat Launch

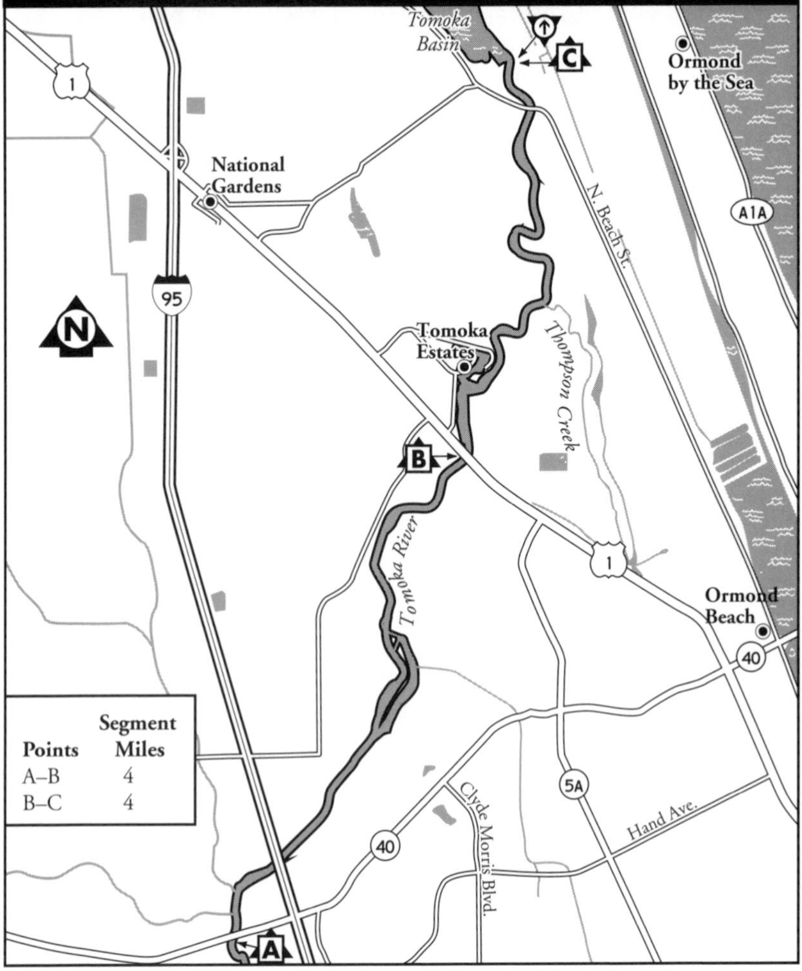

Points	Segment Miles
A–B	4
B–C	4

SPRUCE CREEK

As with many waterways on the Atlantic Coast, Spruce Creek has been a desirable target for people who want to live on the water. The attendant development around such residential areas has followed. The old upper access on Spruce Creek, off of Airport Road, has been cut off, and more of the creek is lined with houses. The good news is that a lower portion of Spruce Creek is now part of the Volusia County park system, Spruce Creek Park. The canoe launch at Spruce Creek Park is here to stay, but this means all paddling adventures on Spruce Creek are now there-and-back affairs. Paddlers should note that the canoe launch is not usable at low tide; however, paddlers in an estuarine waterway such as this should always plan their excursions around the tides.

MAPS: New Smyrna Beach, Samsula (USGS)

SPRUCE CREEK PARK TO I-95

class	I
length	5
time	Varies
gauge	Visual
level	Tidal
gradient	Tidal
scenery	C

DESCRIPTION: The paddle leaves Spruce Creek Park in a canal through marsh grass. Keep along the north shore of Strickland Bay to enter Spruce Creek. Paddlers in fragile boats should avoid the razor-sharp shells in the bay. Pass under the Florida East Coast Railroad bridge after 1 mile and enter Spruce Creek. Ahead is a very pronounced horseshoe bend. A narrow channel to the right offers a shortcut that eliminates over 0.5 miles of the trip. Those taking the long way around the bend will pass the imposing bluffs for which Spruce Creek is known. The creek continues to wind its way generally northwest until reaching the I-95 bridge. It is possible to paddle farther upstream but heavy development between I-95 and Airport Road and above makes it less desirable. Your best overall bet in this area is to explore the waters of the adjacent 2,500-acre Spruce Creek Preserve near Spruce Creek Park. Here you can follow Spruce Creek as it transitions from saltwater marsh to freshwater marsh to hardwood swamp stream. Spruce Creek is a designated Outstanding Florida Water.

SHUTTLE: To reach Spruce Creek Park from Exit 256 on I-95, take FL 421, Dunlawton Road, east to Nova Road, SR 5A. Turn right on Nova Road, SR 5A, and follow it to US 1. Turn right, south, on US 1, and follow it to Spruce Creek Park, on your right.

GAUGE: Visual. Spruce Creek is heavily influenced by the tides. Paddlers should avoid the Spruce Creek Park canoe launch at low tide and plan their paddle around the tidal fluctuation.

Spruce Creek: Spruce Creek Park to I-95

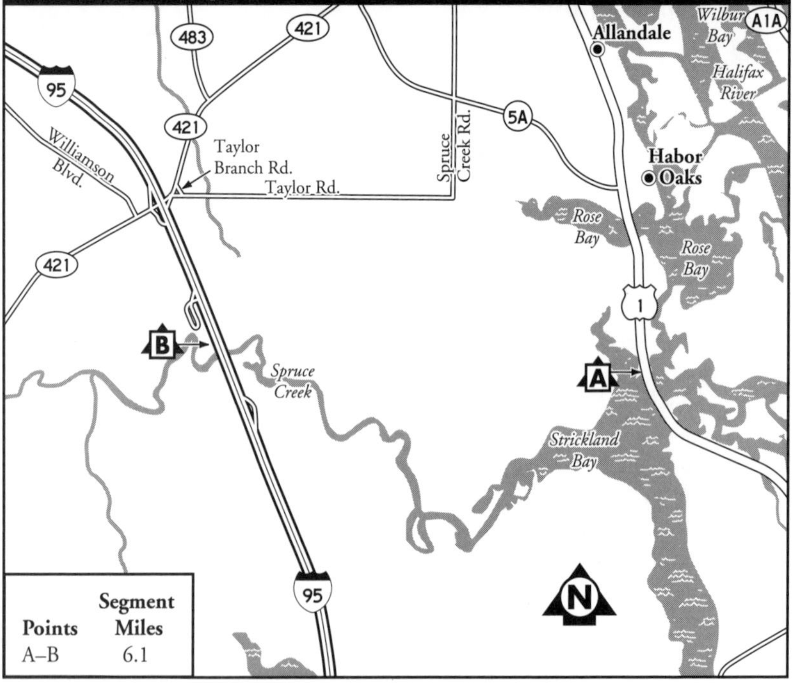

Points	Segment Miles
A–B	6.1

TURKEY CREEK

Turkey Creek provides a pleasant half-day of canoeing that includes an opportunity to explore a nature sanctuary run by the Audubon Society. Lower Turkey Creek flows through a hardwood swamp which puts on a fall display of reds, yellows, and oranges, but is bordered by houses on its outermost edges. The upper portion of the creek winds through the hardwood hammocks and high, sandy bluffs of Turkey Creek Sanctuary and is worth every stroke to get there. A canoe landing at the sanctuary provides access to a network of interpretive nature trails. Be apprised that this out-and-back paddle can get busy on weekends.

MAPS: Melbourne East (USGS)

GOODE PARK TO TURKEY CREEK SANCTUARY

class	I
length	4
time	2
gauge	Visual
level	Tidal
gradient	Tidal
scenery	B

DESCRIPTION: The trip upstream commences in the estuarine mouth of Turkey Creek at the Indian River lagoon and proceeds through a broad region of braided channels that can be confusing. The outermost channels are bordered by houses. Hopefully the best way will be signed on your trip. Waterfowl are plentiful, and manatees are occasionally seen.

The main drainage of Turkey Creek trends southwest and passes under Port Malabar Boulevard 1.25 miles from Goode

Paddling inside Turkey Creek Sanctuary

Park. This is where the paddling gets really good. Enter Turkey Creek Sanctuary and the character of the stream changes dramatically, leaving the residential development behind. The channel narrows, and the current quickens as the stream flows through a dimly lit rich forest of palms and live oaks broken by sand bluffs where pines grow. Paddlers should be alert for numerous deadfalls where turtles are often seen. Reach the sanctuary canoe landing at 1.75 miles. Here paddlers can park their boats and explore the boardwalks of the sanctuary. Paddlers can continue 0.25 miles above the landing to a water control structure and the end of the paddle.

SHUTTLE: To reach the beginning of this out-and-back paddle from Exit 173 on I-95, take FL 514 east to US 1 in Malabar. Turn left on US 1 and follow it north to Port Malabar Boulevard. Turn left on Port Malabar Boulevard and follow it to Bianca Road. Turn right on Bianca Road and follow it to a dead end and a boat ramp at Goode Park.

GAUGE: Visual. Turkey Creek is tidally influenced and is paddleable year-round.

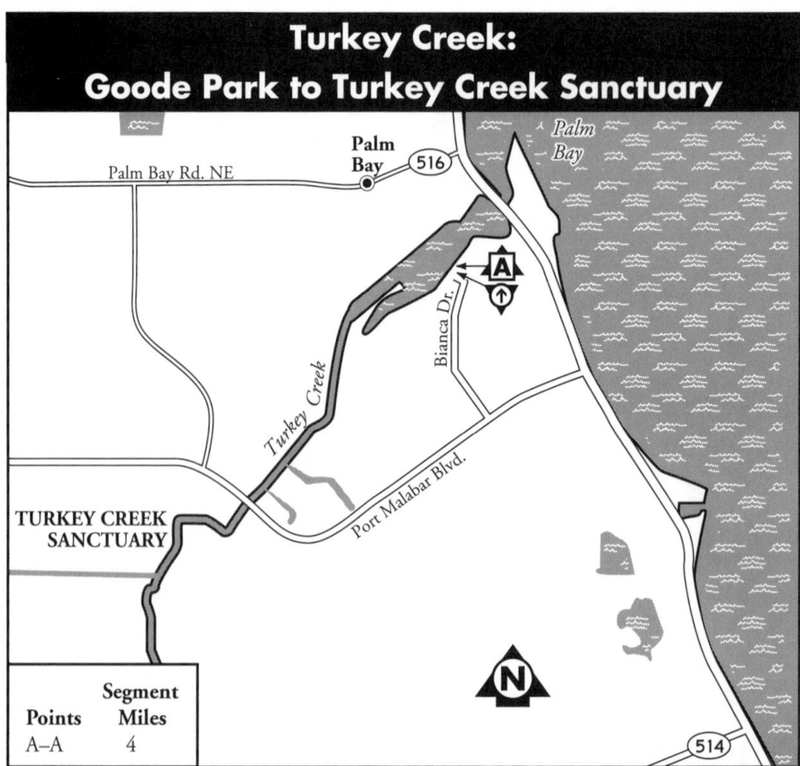

SOUTH PRONG OF THE ST. SEBASTIAN RIVER

The St. Sebastian River, also simply called Sebastian Creek, is a three-prong system. The North Prong and South Prong share a common mouth into the Indian River lagoon with a man-made flood-control canal. The South Prong meanders north behind the coastal ridge that separates it from the Indian River. Sluggish stream flow and a wide channel on the lower river provide an easy day of paddling after winding through the narrower upper section. Large oaks hang out from steep but accessible banks overlooking ultra-clear tan waters. Donald McDonald Park makes an excellent paddling base and alternate take-out point.

MAPS: Fellsmere, Sebastian (USGS)

CR 512 TO DALE WIMBROW PARK

class	I
length	4.5
time	2.5
gauge	Visual, Web
level	N/A
gradient	Partly tidal
scenery	B

DESCRIPTION: The South Prong starts out narrow, 20 feet or so, and sections of the channel have tree cover. Other sections are open and shrouded by vines. Paddlers should be alert to submerged deadfalls during the first 1.5 miles—especially while negotiating the switchbacks in the moderate current. There is some residential development downstream. The South Prong opens up below the 2-mile point. The meanders become tortuous, and in some places the stream nearly doubles back on itself. Banks are mostly low with occasional sand bluffs. Cabbage palms, ferns, and oaks lean out to provide roosts for anhingas and herons. Gators and turtles also call this stream home. The South Prong has numerous dead-end false channels and sloughs awaiting the unwary paddler.

Downstream the west bank becomes part of the St. Sebastian River State Buffer Preserve, where the banks remain wild. The preserve has a boat landing and campsite near the old John Carleton homesite. To camp here you must make reservations (call (321) 953-5004). The preserve also has hiking trails aplenty so you can double your fun. The South Prong, now devoid of current, has widened to near 200 feet as it nears Dale Wimbrow Park, 0.8 miles below the preserve boat landing. The channel into the Dale Wimbrow boat ramp soon appears on the right. Campers at Donald McDonald Park can continue 0.5 miles downstream to a slough on river right and use the campground landing.

Calm waters of the South Prong St. Sebastian River

SHUTTLE: To reach the takeout from Exit 156 on I-95, take Indian River CR 512, Fellsmere Road, east to Roseland Avenue. Turn left on Roseland Avenue and follow it to Dale Wimbrow County Park, on your left. To reach the put-in, backtrack to CR 512 and return west to its intersection with CR 510. Turn right, north, on Watervliet Street (Watervliet Street is just across from the junction with CR 510), and follow it just a short distance to Canoe Launch Cove Road and a small park and launch just for hand-propelled craft.

GAUGE: Visual, Web. The South Prong of the St. Sebastian River is a tidally influenced stream that can be paddled year-round. The USGS gauge helpful in determining flow rates for any given period is South Prong St. Sebastian River near Sebastian, FL.

South Prong of the St. Sebastian River: CR 512 to Dale Winbrow Park

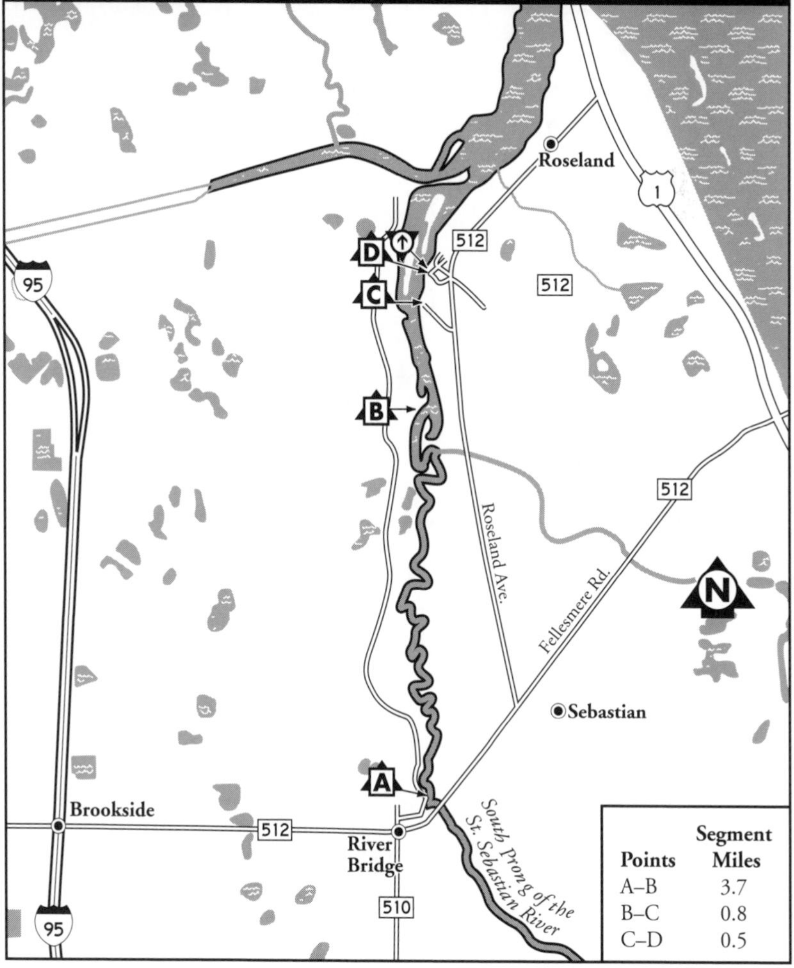

Roseland

1

512

512

D

C

95

B

512

Roseland Ave.

Fellesmere Rd.

N

Sebastian

A

Brookside

512

River Bridge

510

South Prong of the St. Sebastian River

95

Points	Segment Miles
A–B	3.7
B–C	0.8
C–D	0.5

NORTH FORK OF THE ST. LUCIE RIVER

The North Fork and South Fork of the St. Lucie River join to form an extensive drainage system that enters the Atlantic Ocean at the coastal city of Stuart. The South Fork has been channelized into the St. Lucie Canal, which connects Lake Okeechobee with the Intracoastal Waterway. Fortunately, the North Fork has been designated an Aquatic Preserve, a move that has protected the river and its immediate environs from the burgeoning development that is consuming land in this part of Florida. The upper North Fork flows between banks overhung with large oaks, palms, and maples with an understory of ferns. Numerous side streams enter the St. Lucie at regular intervals. However, topographic maps reveal these "side streams" to be remnants of oxbows that were short-circuited many years ago. The river below Prima Vista Boulevard is not attractive to paddlers due to the extensive powerboat traffic.

MAPS: St. Lucie (USGS)

A

class	I
length	4
time	2
gauge	Visual
level	Tidal
gradient	Tidal
scenery	B

RIVER PARK MARINA TO WHITE CITY PARK

DESCRIPTION: The St. Lucie flows south from White City Park through a corridor of high banks with some houses but is mostly bordered by the richly wooded aquatic preserve. The main channel averages 80 to 100 feet wide, so deadfalls are not a problem, but obstacles will be encountered on some of the old oxbows.

A set of power lines crosses the river 1.5 miles downstream. Paddlers with plenty of time on their hands will want to explore some of the oxbows. Most of these oxbows return to the main channel, but a few are dead ends. At 3 miles, the river passes through a wide spot that has the appearance of a small lake. Channel markers indicate the way on the lower river. Begin to look for mangroves here and expect tidal influences to increase. An intersection of five channels with a small island in the center indicates that Prima Vista Boulevard is just 0.1 mile away. After passing under Prima Vista Boulevard, paddlers must circle around a large peninsula to the right to reach the River Park Marina boat ramp.

SHUTTLE: To reach the takeout from Exit 126 on I-95, take CR 712, Midway Road, east to US 1. Turn right on US 1, heading south to Prima Vista Boulevard. Turn right and head west on Prima Vista Boulevard, and then turn left into River Park

Marina, just after the bridge over the St. Lucie River. There is a boat ramp and canoe rental here. To reach the put-in, backtrack to CR 712, Midway Road, and return west toward I-95 until you pass over the North Fork of the St. Lucie River and White City Park, which has a boat launch.

GAUGE: Visual. The North Fork St. Lucie River is tidally influenced and paddleable year-round.

North Fork of the St. Lucie River: River Park Marina to White City Park

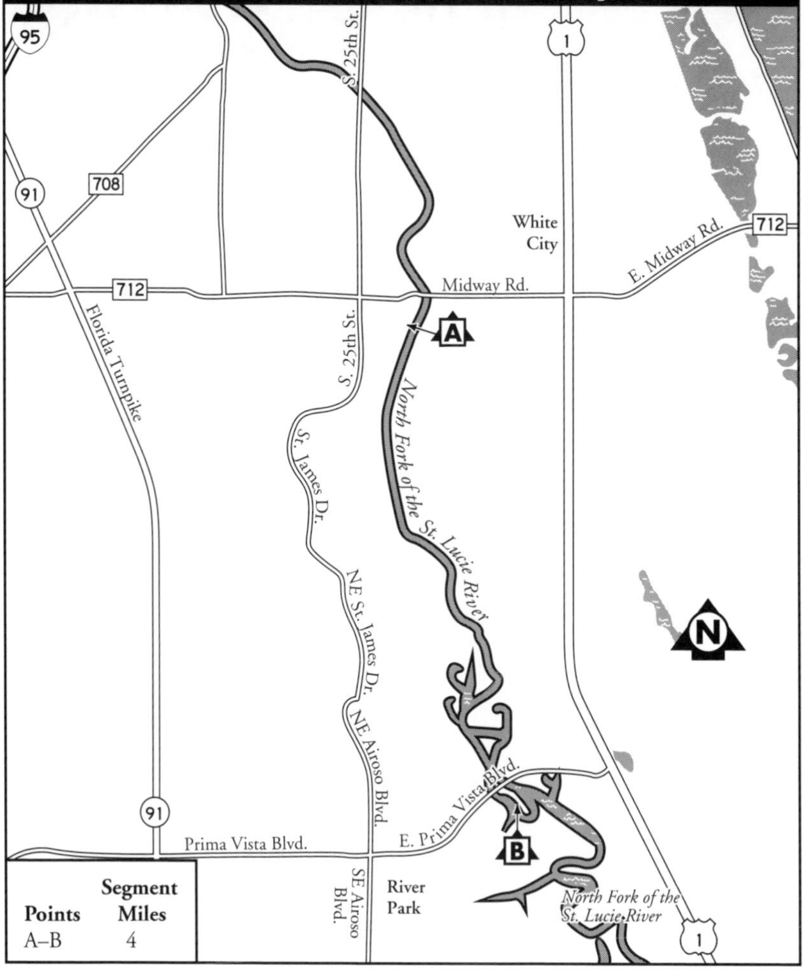

Points	Segment Miles
A–B	4

The current on the St. Lucie River can be nonexistent in places

LOXAHATCHEE RIVER

The Loxahatchee is the only stream in Florida to be designated a National Wild and Scenic River, and just a few minutes on the stream will convince you that this designation is richly deserved. The upper river is a delight to kayakers and canoeists as it zigzags through a stunningly beautiful cypress swamp. Shortly after entering Jonathan Dickinson State Park, the Loxahatchee changes abruptly as it takes on the sedate character of an estuarine mangrove swamp. It is customary for paddlers to take a lunch break at the Trapper Nelson Interpretive Site. Trapper Nelson, "the wild man of the Loxahatchee," was a locally famous eccentric who developed a unique homestead years ago along the Loxahatchee. Canoe docks, picnic facilities, and drinking water are available at Trapper Nelson's. Park rangers give daily presentations on the wildlife, vegetation, and lore of the Trapper Nelson site. Loxahatchee translates from Native American as "Turtle River." During low water, common in winter, paddlers will have to pull their boats and longer kayaks will have difficulty maneuvering the sharp bends and fallen trees of the upper Loxahatchee.

Jonathan Dickinson State Park rents boats for there-and-back trips on the river, and a private outfitter rents boats at the put-in.

MAPS: Rood (USGS)

RIVER BEND PARK TO JONATHAN DICKINSON STATE PARK

class	I
length	6.5
time	2–4
gauge	Phone
level	N/A
gradient	2
scenery	A+

DESCRIPTION: Soon after leaving River Bend Park, moderately fast water will sweep the paddler into a cypress forest. Adept maneuvering is required to dodge cypress knees and negotiate the sharp turns. Ahead, a carry-over ramp traverses an old dam. Dappled sunlight filters through the canopy of tall cypresses that line the Loxahatchee. Strangler figs entwine many of the cypresses, and pond apple trees are seen. Since this section of river has no true banks (unless the water is low), there are few opportunities to go ashore before you reach Trapper Nelson's.

A Native American mound lies back from the east bank at 1.2 miles. A low concrete dam at 1.3 miles provides a carry-over ramp. This dam has a drop of about 2 feet, and during normal water conditions most people paddle straight over the top. Florida's Turnpike and I-95 bridges are encountered at 1.5 miles.

Trapper Nelson's dock is a welcome sight at the halfway point and provides a spot to stop for lunch. Soon after leaving Trapper Nelson's, there is an abrupt transition from cypress forest to

mangrove swamp. The Loxahatchee broadens, and the current becomes imperceptible as the river comes under tidal influence. High wind sometimes presents a challenge on this stretch. Cypress Creek enters from the left at 3.3 miles, as does Kitching Creek at 3.6 miles. Before reaching the state park boat ramp, the river passes the park canoe rental area. Do not take out here; rather, continue to the park public boat ramp, visible up a short channel to the left.

Loxahatchee River: River Bend Park to Jonathan Dickinson State Park

JONATHAN DICKINSON STATE PARK
B
ALT
Trapper Nelson's Dock, boat access only.
Cypress Creek
Loxahatchee River
Tequesta
N
Loxahatchee Wild and Scenic River
95
Limestone Creek
Southwest Fork Loxahatchee River
706
Indiantown Rd.
A
809
91
1

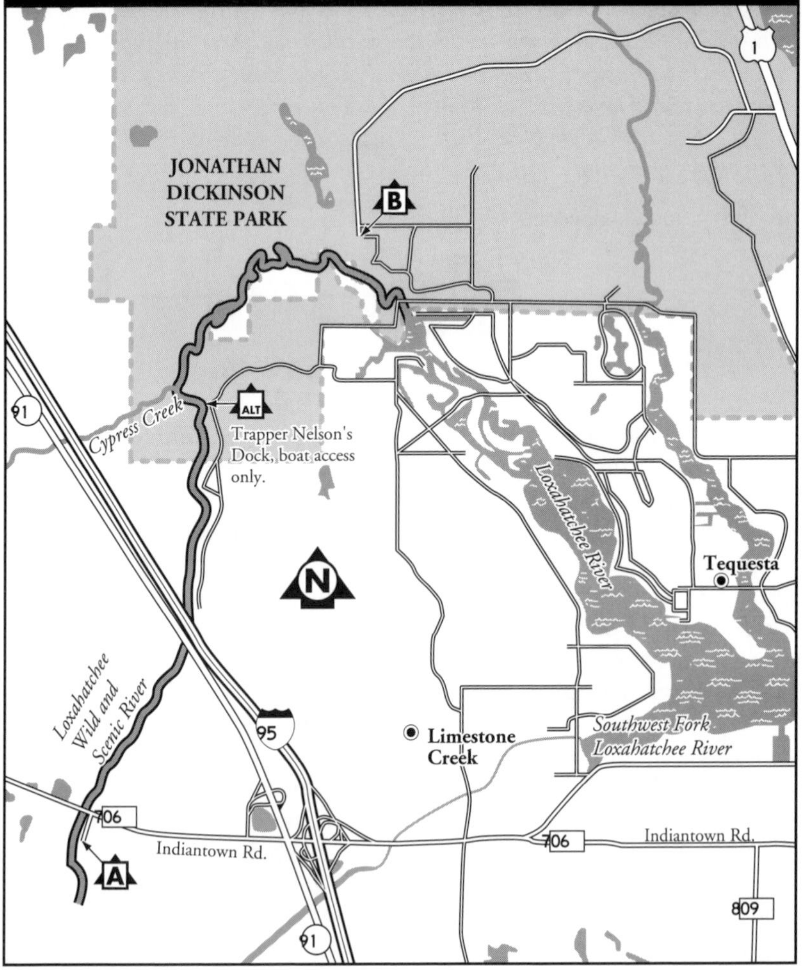

Trapper Nelson's Place on the Loxahatchee River

SHUTTLE: To reach the takeout from Exit 87A on I-95, take FL 706, Indiantown Road, east to US 1. Turn left on US 1 north and follow it to Jonathan Dickinson State Park, on your left (the park charges an entrance fee). Follow the signs to the park boat ramp. To reach the put-in, backtrack to I-95, continuing west on Indiantown Road 1 mile to River Bend Park. Use the main park entrance, not the east or west entrance. Parking is in front of the outfitters, and you'll have to carry your boat from the parking area to the river. Be aware that on Tuesday and Wednesday, the River Bend gates close at 3:30 p.m. Park outside the gates during this time.

GAUGE: Phone. Call Jonathan Dickinson State Park at (772) 546-2771 for the latest river conditions.

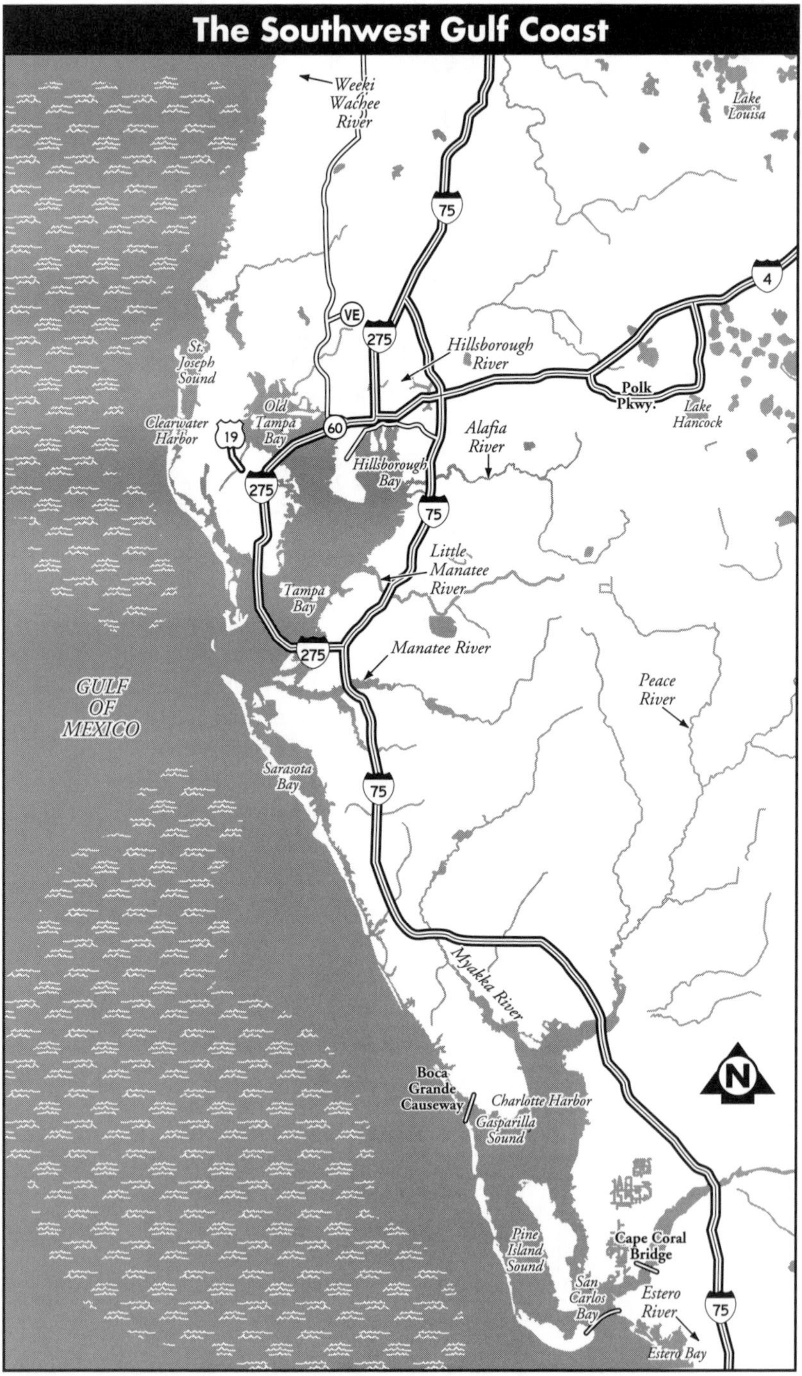

The Southwest Gulf Coast

Weeki Wachee River
Lake Louisa
75
4
VE
275
Hillsborough River
St. Joseph Sound
Polk Pkwy.
Lake Hancock
Old Tampa Bay
Clearwater Harbor
19
60
Alafia River
Hillsborough Bay
275
75
Little Manatee River
Tampa Bay
275
Manatee River
Peace River
GULF OF MEXICO
Sarasota Bay
75
Myakka River
Boca Grande Causeway
Charlotte Harbor
Gasparilla Sound
Pine Island Sound
Cape Coral Bridge
San Carlos Bay
Estero River
75
Estero Bay
N

part **Eight**

THE SOUTHWEST GULF COAST

WEEKI WACHEE RIVER

Florida has approximately 320 springs, which discharge an estimated total of 8 billion gallons a day. Seventy-seven of these are first-magnitude springs (discharging 64.6 million gallons per day or more), greater than any other state in the nation. Of these, many have been left natural and incorporated into state parks or major recreation areas, while others, such as Weeki Wachee, were once developed commercially. Weeki Wachee Springs has now been purchased by the state of Florida, and its longtime status as an attraction complete with mermaids and waterslides is up in the air. The natural aspects of the spring will be protected, especially with the purchase of adjacent river lands by the Southwest Florida Water Management District. However, many riverside houses have been built up and others have been here for some time.

Weeki Wachee Springs is located west of Brooksville and north of Tampa. It is the source of a river of the same name, which flows for about 8 miles through coastal swamp, until it empties into the Gulf

The clear waters of the Weeki Wachee are fun to paddle

of Mexico near the small town of Bayport. Bayport was once a major trade center and the Weeki Wachee River was used as a transportation route for barges hauling goods to nearby Brooksville. This ended, though, when the railroad was built through Brooksville.

The name Weeki Wachee comes from the Creek language and literally means "little spring" (Wekiwa chee). Contrary to its Native American name, it is a major spring and does create a very swift current in the upper 6 miles of the river. Downstream of Rogers Park, the river broadens and slows as it begins to meander through a coastal tidal marsh. As the river approaches the Gulf of Mexico, the current flow becomes dominated by tidal action and the influence of the spring discharge diminishes.

A good run with little tidal influence extends from the livery at Weeki Wachee Springs to Rogers Park, 6 miles downstream. Although several miles of this river are highly developed, especially the last two before Rogers Park, the upper river retains a wild character and is quite a beautiful place to paddle. However, its high concentration of powerboat traffic on the weekends—especially in summer—makes me recommend it for weekday paddling only. If you must go on a weekend, do so in the early morning.

MAPS: Bayport (USGS)

A

class	I
length	8
time	4
gauge	Visual, Web
level	N/A
gradient	2.5
scenery	B

WEEKI WACHEE SPRING TO THE GULF OF MEXICO

DESCRIPTION: The first section of the run is the best. The river is about 40 feet wide at the put-in and soon narrows to less than 20 feet. Both banks of the river are undeveloped and the spring flows crystalline and colorful since few motorboats make it up this far. Wildlife is easily spotted below and above the water surface. Paddlers will have to keep their eyes downstream, too, as the river flows surprisingly swiftly, with sharp bends and curves. Water oaks and some palm trees are intermingled with the cypress in the adjacent woodland swamp that canopies the river. Other areas are open with grassy shoreline.

The first sign of civilization is a private campground at 2 miles, on river right. After 3 miles, the right bank is part of the Chassowitzka Wildlife Management Area. Two developed beach/picnic areas make convenient points for paddlers to stop.

Development increases downstream and if the motorboats are running, the river will cloud somewhat. Houses occupy one bank or another. Canals spurring off the Weeki Wachee will sometimes

cause paddlers to stop briefly, but the proper course is either signed or very evident.

Reach Rogers Park and a canoe launch after 6 miles. This park also has a swim area, restrooms, and boat launch. Below FL 595, you will travel through more dense development, past continuous sea walls and countless boat docks. After leaving the residential area, the river passes channel markers and side streams. Large tidal marsh grass borders the Weeki Wachee. The channel is about 200 yards wide here. The fishing is excellent here, and manatees are frequently seen. The Mud River comes in from the north 0.75 miles below the residential area, originating at Mud River Spring, and makes a very nice trip in its own right. The numerous side creeks and bays are interesting to explore in this lower tidal zone if you haven't had enough paddling yet.

SHUTTLE: To reach the lowermost access from the intersection of US 19 and FL 50 (Cortez Boulevard), west of Brooksville, travel west on FL 50 until the road dead-ends at a small park and

Weeki Wachee River:
Weeki Wachee Spring to the Gulf of Mexico

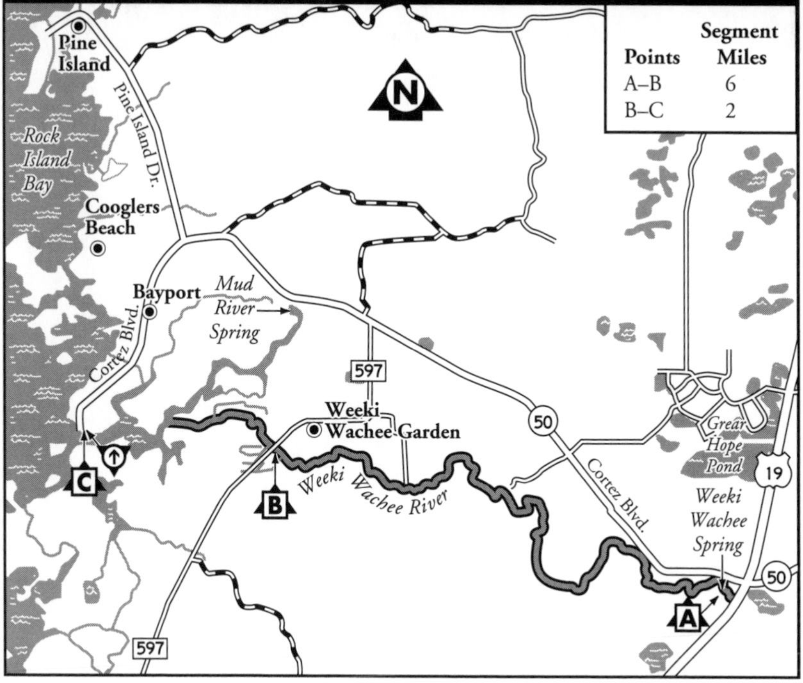

Points	Segment Miles
A–B	6
B–C	2

Pine Island
Pine Island Dr.
Rock Island Bay
Cooglers Beach
Bayport
Mud River Spring
Cortez Blvd.
597
Weeki Wachee Garden
Weeki Wachee River
50
Cortez Blvd.
Grear Hope Pond
19
Weeki Wachee Spring
50
597

Enjoying a group paddle on the Weeki Wachee

the Gulf. There is a fishing pier on the south side and a boat launch up a short canal just before reaching the pier. To reach the uppermost access from the intersection of US 19 and FL 50, drive to the parking area at the Weeki Wachee Springs attraction and look for the road leading into the private livery.

GAUGE: Visual, Web. The Weeki Wachee River is spring-fed and runnable year-round. However, the USGS gauge to help determine flow rates for any given time period is Weeki Wachee River near Weeki Wachee Springs, FL.

HILLSBOROUGH RIVER

The Hillsborough is a long and diverse river, flowing for nearly 54 miles from the Green Swamp north of Lakeland to Hillsborough Bay in Tampa. It is a river rich with history. Thousands of years ago, the Timucuan and Calusa tribes inhabited the surrounding land, and remnants of their burial mounds can still be found not far from the river. The Seminoles, a mixture of northern Creeks and the surviving Calusas, later emerged along the Hillsborough. As American pioneers hungered for Florida land, they came in contact with these tribes, and the Seminole Wars were inevitably ignited. Fort Alabama, now called Fort Foster, was built along the river and remains as a reminder of that bloody conflict. The river was originally named Lochcha-popha-chiska ("river where one crosses to eat acorns") by the Seminoles, an obvious reference to their love of the large oak trees that line the shores. The British named it after the earl of Hillsborough, a colonial secretary in the 1700s.

The river is fed by 690 square miles of natural drainage, most of which results from five main tributaries, including Flint and Blackwater creeks. During the wet summer season, rain runoff swells the river, while during the dry winter and spring months, the water level is low and maintained primarily by baseflow from Crystal Springs near the Green Swamp headwaters.

As the Hillsborough proceeds southwest toward Tampa Bay, it traverses a variety of terrain, predominantly a mixture of cypress and hardwood forests, much of which is protected by 16,000-acre Wilderness Park, part of Southwest Florida Water Management District Lands and managed by Hillsborough County. A series of riverside parks, part of the greater Wilderness Park, provide boat launching and relaxation locations. The well-known Seventeen Runs area is a mixed hardwood swamp, which contains southern red cedar, cabbage palmetto, and cypress. Although the underlying surface in the area is sand and clay, numerous limestone formations in the upper river create frequent mild rapids. About 10 miles downstream of the Green Swamp, the river enters another protected area, Hillsborough River State Park, one of the oldest and largest parks in the state. Virtually all the riverfront from the Green Swamp headwaters to the I-75 overpass is protected by these preserves. The paddling is still pleasant until reaching Fowler Avenue, when greater Tampa overwhelms the river and it becomes a watery avenue between riverside homes.

MAPS: Zephyrhills, Wesley Chapel, Thonotosassa (USGS)

class	I–II
length	6
time	3
gauge	Visual, Web
level	N/A
gradient	1.9
scenery	A

CRYSTAL SPRINGS TO HILLSBOROUGH RIVER STATE PARK

DESCRIPTION: Do not use the bridge over the Hillsborough as an access. There is no legal parking near the bridge over the Hillsborough. Adjacent Crystal Springs Park is a private park but offers boat launching for a fee with much better and legal parking. Enter the Hillsborough and enjoy those 40 million gallons per day of spring water. For the next several miles, the river water is sparklingly clear and flows swiftly through a thick forest of oak, cypress, and palm. The river has a sand bottom with numerous limestone formations and, in many places, the water racing over the limestone creates small whitewater rapids. Occasionally, the paddler will also encounter deadfalls or other major obstructions, which must be carried over.

Blackwater Creek enters the Hillsborough about 3.7 miles from the put-in. Three-quarters of a mile later, the river passes under a wooden bridge and Fort Foster appears on the left. At this point, US 301 spans the river at what is called Burnt Bridge.

About 1 mile past the bridge, you will encounter the State Park Rapids, a 150-yard stretch of river with three Class II drops separated by smooth water. Each drop is accented by a cluster of limestone rocks and standing waves. The first and third drops are best paddled on the left; the safest route for the second drop is along the right. The rapids can also be portaged along a footpath on the left. Within 0.5 miles of the rapids, you will pass a wooden bridge and then the state park's canoe concession. The public takeout is around the next left turn in the river, on the left, up a shallow dirt slope.

SHUTTLE: To reach the put-in from Exit 265 on I-75, take FL 582 east to US 301. Turn left on US 301 north, passing the state park and following it across the Hillsborough River before entering Pasco County to reach Chancey Road. Turn right on Chancey Road and follow it a short distance to Crystal Springs Road. Turn right on Crystal Springs and follow it to Crystal Springs Park, on your right. To reach the takeout, backtrack to US 301 and head south to Hillsborough River State Park and their boat launch. Both the put-in and takeout are fee launches.

GAUGE: Phone, Web. Call Canoe Escape at (813) 986-2067 for the latest river conditions. The Hillsborough River normally is paddleable year-round. The USGS gauge to use to determine

flow rates for any given time period is Hillsborough River below Crystal Springs near Zephyrhills, FL.

HILLSBOROUGH RIVER STATE PARK TO SARGEANT PARK

class	I–I+
length	6.5
time	4
gauge	Phone, Web
level	N/A
gradient	1.2
scenery	A

DESCRIPTION: This section of the Hillsborough contains the well-known Seventeen Runs, an area of cypress swamp where the river branches into numerous swift, shallow creeks. The entrance to the Runs is about 3 miles downstream of the put-in. Prior to that point, the river channel is broad and the current slow as it traverses a forest thick with oak, cypress, pine, and cedar. The water is darkly stained by the tannin seeping from the surrounding land, and it obscures the occasional limestone rock embedded in the sand bottom.

Just before the beginning of Seventeen Runs, pass Dead River Park on the left shore. This park offers river access but is only open Friday through Sunday. Paddlers can leave a car at Dead River Park, extending their weekend-only run by 3 miles from Crystal Springs.

Kayaks are not advised to tackle Seventeen Runs, due to too much getting in and out of the boat to pull over logs and such. Over the next several miles, you will encounter numerous deadfalls, and carry-overs are a near certainty, depending on the water level. The river continues to separate into multiple branches, most being impassable due to shallow bottoms, or what appears to be an endless series of major obstructions. Good luck choosing the right channel. For the most part, the terrain in this area is thick with tree roots, leaf litter, deadfall, and some poison ivy. Very few places are clear enough for going ashore. In the last mile of this section, the river gradually broadens and the current slows.

The end of the section is marked by the appearance of a wooden boardwalk from Sargeant Park. At this point, Flint Creek enters from the left and the Hillsborough continues on to the right. The takeout is reached by paddling straight ahead past the boardwalk and into a narrow canal leading into Sargeant Park.

SHUTTLE: To reach the takeout from Exit 265 on I-75, take FL 582 east to US 301. Turn left on US 301 north and follow it to Sargeant Park , on your left. To reach the put-in, continue north on US 301 and head to Hillsborough River State Park and their boat launch. Both the put-in and takeout are fee launches.

Hillsborough River (Sections A–D): Crystal Springs to Rotary Park

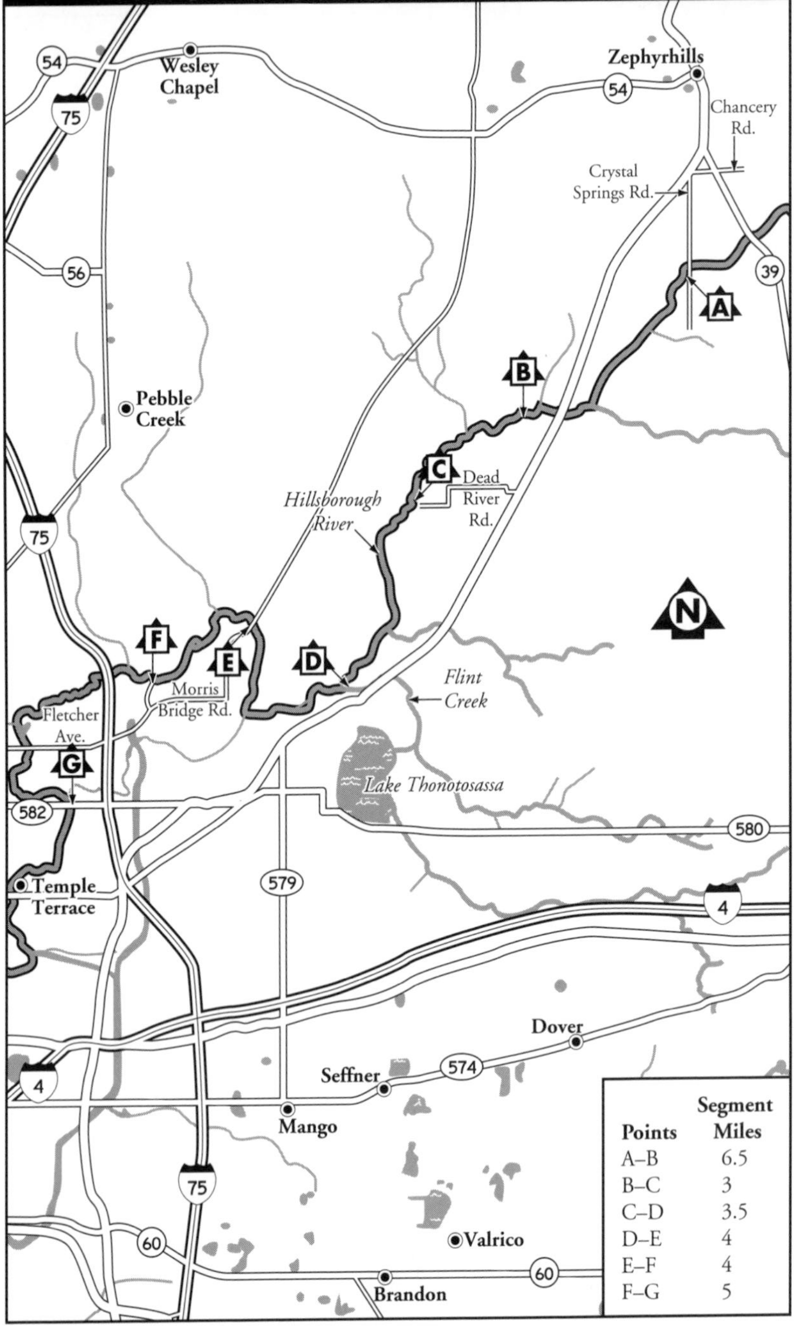

Points	Segment Miles
A–B	6.5
B–C	3
C–D	3.5
D–E	4
E–F	4
F–G	5

GAUGE: Phone, Web. Call Canoe Escape at (813) 986-2067 for the latest river conditions. The Hillsborough River is normally paddleable year-round. The USGS gauge helpful in determining flow rates for any given time period is Hillsborough River at Morris Bridge near Thonotosassa, FL.

SARGEANT PARK TO TROUT CREEK PARK

class	I
length	8
time	4
gauge	Phone, Web
level	N/A
gradient	1
scenery	A

DESCRIPTION: Access at this point is down a gentle slope into a small basin. From here, proceed north down a short, narrow canal, and past a boardwalk on the right. The canal ends at the confluence of Flint Creek and the Hillsborough River. At this point, the paddler should turn left and proceed downstream. For the next several miles, the journey is quite pleasant. An occasional deadfall will be encountered, and although these may require a carry-over, they may also block powerboats from using this section of river. The channel is broad and the water slow-moving as it passes through a protected tropical landscape of cypresses, oaks, and palms. At any given time, hundreds of white ibis might inhabit this area and treat you to a special show as they swoop through the trees en masse, filling the air with the sporadic sound of drumming wing beats.

At about 2 miles, the river turns north and continues in that general direction to Morris Bridge Park. As the sunlight filters through the dense forest foliage, it creates a patchwork of bright green hues contrasted with deep shadows. After 4 miles, the river passes beneath Morris Bridge. A boat launch is at the county park on the left, just past the bridge.

The tea-colored river meanders southwest from Morris Bridge, still in the protection of greater Wilderness Park, part of which is a nature classroom run by the county school department. The canopied river keeps its sense of isolation amid many twists and turns. Trout Creek Park boat launch is on river left.

SHUTTLE: To reach the takeout from Exit 266 on I-75, take Morris Bridge Road east to Trout Creek Park. Turn left into the park and follow it to the boat launch. To reach the put-in, return to I-75 and head south to Exit 265. Head east on FL 582 and follow it to US 301. Turn left on US 301 north and follow it to Sargeant Park, on your left.

GAUGE: Phone, Web. Call Canoe Escape at (813) 986-2067 for the latest river conditions. The Hillsborough River is normally

paddleable year-round. The USGS gauge helpful in determining flow rates for any given time period is Hillsborough River at Morris Bridge near Thonotosassa, FL.

class	I
length	5
time	2
gauge	Phone, Web
level	N/A
gradient	0.6
scenery	B–C

TROUT CREEK PARK TO ROTARY PARK

DESCRIPTION: The Hillsborough River begins to open below Trout Creek Park, though still retaining its wild aura until the I-75 overpass. The river continues to meander below I-75 and turns south at Lettuce Lake. Below Lettuce Lake, houses begin to appear along the banks with regularity. Pass under the Fletcher Avenue Bridge at 3 miles. Temple Terrace lies along the Hillsborough. The river jogs to the east before reaching Rotary Park, on busy Fowler Avenue. Below here houses line the river, and it loses any feel of remoteness and will be a disappointment after the tranquility of the upper river.

SHUTTLE: To reach the takeout from Exit 265 on I-75, take FL 582 west to Rotary Park, on the right before bridging the Hillsborough River. Turn left into the park and follow it to the boat launch. To reach the put-in, return to I-75 and head north to Exit 266. Head east on Morris Bridge Road and follow it to a left turn into Trout Creek Park, on your left.

GAUGE: Phone, Web. Call Canoe Escape at (813) 986-2067 for the latest river conditions. The Hillsborough River is normally paddleable year-round. The USGS gauge helpful in determining flow rates for any given time period is Hillsborough River at Morris Bridge near Thonotosassa, FL.

ALAFIA RIVER

The Alafia River (pronounced AL-uh-FYE) extends for about 45 miles from meager beginnings near the town of Mulberry until it widens into a substantial waterway and empties into Hillsborough Bay near Riverview. The north prong flows east to west through the gently rolling hills of the Polk uplands and the flatwood forests of the Gulf coastal lowlands. During periods of unusually heavy rainfall the Alafia River basin sustains very high water flow rates, although its average discharge rate is not high enough to rank it as a major Florida coastal river. In its upper reaches, the river passes through cattle land and near phosphate mines; though these contribute to high nutrient concentrations and low dissolved oxygen levels, the Alafia retains a fair water quality.

The section of the Alafia covered in this guide extends for 26 miles from the Keysville Bridge in east Hillsborough County to the Alafia boat ramp in a residential area of the town of Riverview. The section above Keysville Bridge is not included because it is shallow, narrow, and not readily accessible and has numerous obstructions. Below the Alafia boat ramp, the river widens substantially and, although it can be paddled, it is not recommended because of a large volume of powerboat traffic. Between these points, the Alafia is moderately swift and, at numerous places, small formations of riverbed limestone have created short whitewater rapids. It meanders through beautiful oak canopies and past areas heavily vegetated with cypress trees, cabbage palms, and palmettos. Although wildlife is not abundant on this river, the observant paddler may see numerous bird species, opossums, raccoons, cattle, and, possibly, an alligator relaxing on the riverside.

The river passes through two county parks—Alderman's Ford and Lithia Springs. Lithia Springs has swimming, restrooms, shower facilities, and a developed camping area. Alderman's Ford has restrooms, a very nice nature walk along boardwalks and dirt trails, and a primitive camping area.

Located within 35 miles of the greater Tampa area, the Alafia is a popular river. Be apprised that certain sections of it can be quite crowded on weekends, especially during the summer. However, on weekdays it is quiet and you may have the whole river to yourself.

MAPS: Nichols, Keysville, Lithia, Dover, Riverview, Brandon (USGS)

class	I–I+
length	7
time	3
gauge	Phone, visual, Web
level	Below red marker
gradient	2.1
scenery	C

KEYSVILLE BRIDGE TO ALDERMAN'S FORD COUNTY PARK

DESCRIPTION: The first 6 miles of this run are on the North Prong of the Alafia. For the first few miles, the river meanders through heavily vegetated landscape. In this section, the Alafia flows past nearby strip mines and cattleland, but these are not readily observable since the banks are high on both sides. Eventually the right bank reaches a height of 30 to 40 feet, giving the river landscape a mountain-like quality. Two-and-a-half miles downstream from the put-in point, the river flows beneath a railroad trestle, turns to the right, and carries over a 30-yard stretch of very mild rapids. The Alafia enters the Alderman's Ford County Park boundary 1.5 miles later. In this area, cypress trees are abundant and the sides of the river are heavily vegetated.

About 1.5 miles past the boundary of Alderman's Ford, the river narrows to 10 or 15 feet, and the south prong enters from the left. Approximately 0.5 miles later, the river flows beneath a footbridge, widens again, and passes under CR 39. Just before another footbridge crosses the river, a channel flows in sharply from the left. This channel leads to the take-out point, a nice wooden dock located 100 yards upstream on the right.

This section of the Alafia is quite secluded—you will likely not see another person until Alderman's Ford. However there are signs of civilization, and the beautiful scenery does not occur until the last couple of miles of the run. The primitive parking near the Keysville Bridge contrasts mightily with the well-developed Alderman's Ford area.

SHUTTLE: To reach the takeout from Exit 254 on I-75, take US 301 south to Bloomingdale Avenue. Turn left and head east on Bloomingdale Avenue. Follow Bloomingdale Avenue to Lithia–Pinecrest Road, CR 640. Turn right and head southeast on Lithia–Pinecrest Road and follow it to CR 39, passing the bridge over the Alafia River. Turn left on CR 39 and follow it to Thompson Road. Turn left on Thompson Road and follow it to Alderman's Ford Park, on the right. To reach the put-in, backtrack to CR 39, and turn left, north, on CR 39, passing the bridge over the Alafia River and continuing north to Keysville Road. Turn right on Keysville Road and follow it to the bridge over the Alafia River. A rough access is on the southeast side of the bridge.

GAUGE: Phone, visual, Web. Call Alafia River Canoe Rentals at (813) 689-8645 for the latest river conditions. Also, at the Alderman's Ford Launch there's a pole at the launch. If the river level is at the red mark on the pole, do not undertake the trip unless you are a proficient paddler. The USGS gauge helpful in determining flow rates for any given time period is North Prong Alafia River at Keysville, FL.

Alafia River (Sections A–C): Keysville Bridge to Alafia Boat Ramp

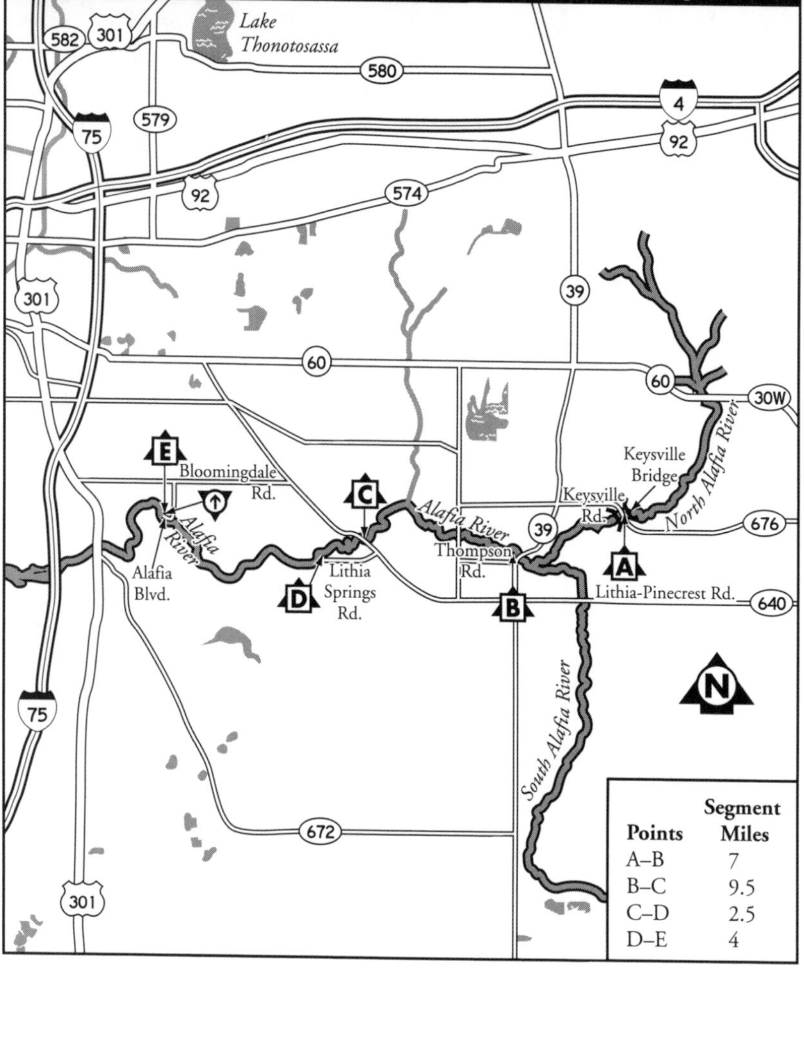

Points	Segment Miles
A–B	7
B–C	9.5
C–D	2.5
D–E	4

B

class	I–I+
length	11.5
time	6
gauge	Phone, visual, Web
level	N/A
gradient	1.5
scenery	B

ALDERMAN'S FORD PARK TO LITHIA SPRINGS PARK

DESCRIPTION: While the section of the Alafia from Keysville Bridge to Alderman's Ford is generally secluded, this section of river tends to be quite crowded. On weekends it is a very popular area. However, on weekdays it is quiet and you may be alone on the river. The popularity of this section is also evident in the moderate amount of trash littering the river and its banks. This offsets the otherwise scenic beauty of the landscape.

The Alderman's Ford canoe-launch area is on a side channel off the main river. Proceed to the left from the wooden dock, and about 100 yards downstream make a gradual left turn onto the Alafia. At this point, the river passes beneath a footbridge, part of the county park boardwalk system. In the next quarter-mile, the river turns from due north to west to east and then begins a general westerly direction of flow.

This section of the Alafia meanders through beautiful oak and cypress woodlands. The banks are occasionally 4 to 5 feet high. In most places, though, the shoreline is shallow and sandy. There is private property along the river, so be sure to respect the property rights of others. Between Alderman's Ford and Lithia Springs, there are at least six sets of mild whitewater rapids. At low-water levels, some of these become impassable because of exposed rocks and require a portage or carry-over. The first of these occurs approximately 1.5 miles downstream from Alderman's Ford, and the rest are spaced at irregular intervals.

At 5.5 miles, the river flows past a gouged-out area of forest. There is a sloped bank of white sand and a rickety-looking brick structure on each side. These are the remnants of an old railroad trestle that was disassembled years ago; it is not a safe place to stop for picnicking or camping. Most potential campsites are below the old railroad trestle and before CR 640. At 9.5 miles, the Alafia passes beneath CR 640. One-quarter mile farther downstream, on the right, are the docks for Alafia Canoe Rental. It offers a good access point for a fee. The takeout at Lithia Springs County Park is 2 miles past the CR 640 bridge. At this point, the river is flowing southwest and turning to the northwest.

SHUTTLE: To reach the takeout from Exit 254 on I-75, take US 301 south to Bloomingdale Avenue. Turn left and then head east on Bloomingdale Avenue. Follow Bloomingdale Avenue to Lithia–Pinecrest Road, CR 640. Turn right and head southeast

The author takes a break

on Lithia–Pinecrest Road and follow it beyond the bridge over the Alafia River. Ahead, turn right on Lithia Springs Road to reach Lithia Springs Park and a fee canoe launch. To reach the put-in, return to Lithia–Pinecrest Road and turn right, southeast, and follow it to CR 39. Turn left on CR 39 and follow it to Thompson Road. Turn left on Thompson Road and follow it to Alderman's Ford Park, on the right.

GAUGE: Phone, visual, Web. Call Alafia River Canoe Rentals at (813) 689-8645 for the latest river conditions. Also, at the Alderman's Ford Launch there's a red pole at the launch. If the river level is at the red mark on the pole, do not undertake the trip unless you are a proficient paddler. The USGS gauge helpful in determining flow rates for any given time period is Alafia River at Lithia, FL.

LITHIA SPRINGS PARK TO ALAFIA BOAT RAMP

class	I–I+
length	7.5
time	3
gauge	Phone, Web
level	N/A
gradient	0.7
scenery	B

DESCRIPTION: The first 3 miles of this section contain some of the most scenic landscapes on the entire Alafia. Huge oaks line high banks and the tree canopy shades up to 75 percent of the river area. The shore is heavily vegetated with palmettos and numerous varieties of ferns and vines. The current is moderately swift, and creates several sets of whitewater rapids as it flows over

limestone rock formations. There are countless overhanging trees and branches that can snag the unwary paddler, especially when negotiating a tight turn.

From the put-in, you will pass beneath a large overhead pipe and swings around the county park on the left. At 0.4 miles, the Lithia Springs basin, which is the park swimming area, empties into the Alafia. The tannin-stained water is mixed with silt and dirt, and when it meets the crystal-clear discharge from the spring it creates a very noticeable contrast line.

Just past Lithia Springs, Little Fishhawk Creek enters the river from the south, and 1 mile later Fishhawk Creek enters, also from the south. Except at low-water level, both can be paddled, although Little Fishhawk Creek is extremely narrow. Four miles downstream of the put-in, the Alafia passes beneath Bell Shoals Bridge (no access) and, from this point on, the shoreline becomes highly developed. The river broadens and becomes quite sluggish. For the next 3.5 miles to the takeout, you will likely encounter much powerboat traffic. The takeout is on the right (east) side of the river at a concrete boat ramp lined with high retaining walls.

SHUTTLE: To reach the takeout from Exit 254 on I-75, take US 301 south to Bloomingdale Avenue. Turn left and head east on Bloomingdale Avenue. Follow Bloomingdale Avenue to Kings Road. Turn right, south, on Kings Road and follow it to Alafia Boulevard. Veer right on Alafia Boulevard and follow it to the Alafia boat ramp, on your left. To reach the put-in, return to Bloomingdale Avenue and head east to Lithia–Pinecrest Road, CR 640. Turn right and head southeast on Lithia–Pinecrest Road and follow it to Lithia Springs Road, after the bridge over the Alafia River. Turn right on Lithia Springs Road to reach Lithia Springs County Park and a fee canoe launch.

GAUGE: Phone, Web. Call Alafia River Canoe Rentals at (813) 689-8645 for the latest river conditions. The USGS gauge helpful in determining flow rates for any given time period is Alafia River at Lithia, FL.

LITTLE MANATEE RIVER

For about 40 miles, the Little Manatee stretches across southern Hillsborough County from its origin as a tightly twisting creek near Fort Lonesome and Wimauma, until it broadens and empties into Tampa Bay near Ruskin. The Little Manatee River is now a mostly protected watershed, thanks to the state of Florida and Hillsborough County. Little Manatee River State Park has been in place for some time now, and now the state and county have purchased additional parcels. This protection is partly due to Little Manatee River's designation as an Outstanding Florida Water. Now, in ever-expanding coastal Florida, this river will remain an enchanting place to wet your boat. If you paddle the Little Manatee River in the dry winter months, you will encounter a shallow, narrow waterway enclosed by steep banks, heavily vegetated with oaks, pines, willows, and an occasional cedar. High above, the trees form a thick canopy that shades most of the river and, below, numerous small beaches will invite you to stop and enjoy a refreshing swim.

If you paddle this river in the wet summer season, though, its character will be remarkably different. High water will cover a large number of the swimming beaches and, during periods of recent heavy rainfall, the swift current will race you through the branches of the overhead tree canopy. During times of especially high precipitation, it is best to avoid the section of the river upstream (east) of US 301 and remain in the downstream area, where the riverbed broadens and is not subject to rapid water-level fluctuations.

Distance-wise, the paddling options on this river are numerous, with five good access points stretched out along its 16.5-mile distance. Below US 301, the river can be paddled as an out-and-back if you don't want to use the outfitter conveniently located at 301, or simply don't have two cars for a shuttle. The busier period on this river is March through August.

MAPS: Wimauma, Ruskin (USGS)

LITTLE MANATEE RIVER NATURE PRESERVE TO CAMP BAYOU NATURE PRESERVE

class	I
length	17
time	Varies
gauge	Phone, Web
level	N/A
gradient	1.5
scenery	B

DESCRIPTION: The uppermost section is the wildest section of the river, part of the Little Manatee River Nature Preserve, and is the most difficult to paddle at high water. The narrow channel causes rapid water-level fluctuations after heavy rainfall, and the

gradient of the riverbed produces a swift current, which can propel the paddler through snags and overhanging tree branches. This section is also the site of a drop in the riverbed which, though unnoticeable at high water, creates a small waterfall at low water during the dry season. The remainder of these first 3.5 miles snakes through tall wooded banks and past a few small, sandy beaches until it flows beneath the bridge and a potential put-in/takeout at CR 579.

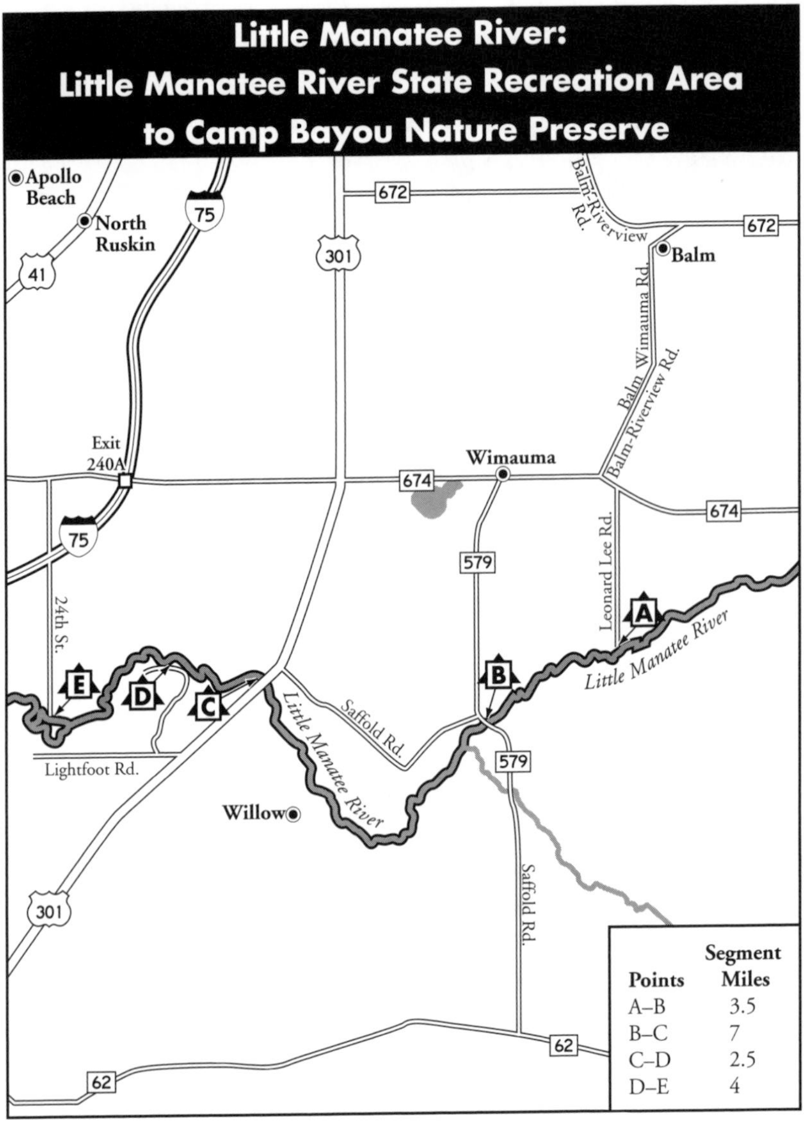

Little Manatee River: Little Manatee River State Recreation Area to Camp Bayou Nature Preserve

Points	Segment Miles
A–B	3.5
B–C	7
C–D	2.5
D–E	4

The first 3.5 miles below CR 579 are much like the previous section. The narrow river snakes its way through tall wooded banks, and the swift current can race to high-water levels when rainfall has been heavy. Oaks and willows line the shore and create an overhead canopy that occasionally opens up as the river widens.

The observable riverside is totally undeveloped except for two major structures. The first, a water intake gate for a local Florida Power Corporation plant, is located just past 6 miles. It appears quite suddenly through the trees and disappears just as quickly as the river turns sharply to the north and back into the surrounding woods. Less than 2 miles from here is an old, long abandoned railroad trestle. This massive brick structure with overhead steel support was built in 1913 and was used by the famous Orange Blossom Special. At low water, sandy beaches are exposed nearby, providing lovely places to stop for a rest. Below the trestle, the river broadens gradually and the tree canopy gives way to more open areas. There are fewer deadfalls and obstructions to negotiate, and the channel does not wind as much as it does upstream. Reach US 301 and an adjacent outfitter at 10.5 miles.

The first 3 miles below US 301 are quite pleasant as the river meanders gently through a pretty, wooded area which includes the Little Manatee State Recreation Area on the south shore. The first mile has numerous overhangs and obstructions, which must be carefully negotiated, but it clears up beyond that. Past 3 miles, the river broadens to about 150 feet and becomes shallow and slow. Enter "civilization" before ending the trip. The takeout is located on the north shore, up an asphalt street ramp that appears to dead-end in the river.

SHUTTLE: To reach the lowermost access from Exit 240A on I-75, take FL 674 west to 24th Street. Turn left on 24th Street and follow it to the dead-end at Camp Bayou Nature Preserve and the Little Manatee River. To reach the uppermost access from Exit 240A on I-75, take FL 674 east to Leonard Lee Road. Turn right on Leonard Lee Road and follow it south to the bridge over the Little Manatee River.

GAUGE: Phone, Web. Call Canoe Outpost at (813) 634-2228 for the latest river conditions. The USGS gauge helpful in determining flow rates for any given time period is South Fork Little Manatee River near Wimauma, FL.

MANATEE RIVER

The Manatee River flows into the Gulf of Mexico and Tampa Bay west of the city of Bradenton after extending for nearly 40 miles through central Manatee County. It is supplied principally from 150 square miles of watershed, and along its entire length countless creeks drain their contents into it. The river traverses the Gulf Coastal lowlands, and the surrounding area is marked by pine flatwoods, sandhills, and hammock communities.

Historically, the land was used for cattle-grazing, farming, and harvesting timber, and many of the local coniferous trees were also used for turpentine production. Later, east of what is now the city of Bradenton, numerous small communities were quickly developed and almost as quickly disappeared. Rye was at the eastern end of a commercial boat traffic route that originated in Bradenton. Today the area is growing much like all southwest Florida, but the river banks are still largely natural, especially near Rye Wilderness Park and the adjacent Boy Scout camp.

In the 1960s, a dam was constructed on the river and Lake Manatee was formed. This 2,400-acre reservoir provides potable water for Sarasota and Manatee counties and is also part of the Lake Manatee State Recreation Area, which offers boating, swimming, and camping. The dam gates are opened at irregular intervals to release overflow into the river, especially after heavy rains. In the narrow river channel near the dam, the discharge from the lake can raise the water level several feet in an hour. The opening of the gates is announced well in advance by a series of siren blasts from the dam structure.

MAPS: Parrish, Rye, Verna (USGS)

class	I
length	7
time	Varies
gauge	Phone
level	Tidal
gradient	1.1
scenery	B

RYE WILDERNESS PARK TO FORT HAMER

DESCRIPTION: The lower you are on this river, the more tidally influenced it becomes. Because of this, many paddlers go one way and return to the same access point. Use the tides to your advantage! The Lake Manatee Dam can be reached most easily by paddling upstream from Rye Wilderness Park. The dam is 3 miles upstream of Rye Wilderness Park. If the dam gates have been opened, the current will be swift, especially near the dam. In spite of these conditions, round-trips, even from Fort Hamer, are possible and done as much or more than one-way trips. Call Ray's Canoes or the dam phone number for the latest information if you think a water release is likely.

March through early summer is the busy season on the Manatee. There are two side streams on the lower river worth taking for short trips. Mill Creek enters the Manatee from the south a mile east of Fort Hamer, and Gamble Creek enters from the north just downstream from there. Gamble Creek meanders for several miles through tall grasses typical of coastal marshes and is composed of numerous mazelike braided channels. The river widens considerably below the confluence with Mill Creek. Powerboat traffic increases in the last section to Fort Hamer, making this part of the paddle less desirable. Below Fort Hamer the river braids into wide channels before becoming so wide as to make winds and power boats a factor.

East of Ray's Canoe Hideaway, the riverbed begins to narrow and bluffs gradually appear on the sides. Some of these are bare sand bluffs that drop into pleasant beaches ideal for rest stops. One of these is located on the south shoreline near the Flying Eagle Boy Scout Camp, just upstream of a double switchback in the river. There are several others between the Rye Wilderness Park and the dam.

Manatee River: Rye Wilderness Park to Fort Hamer

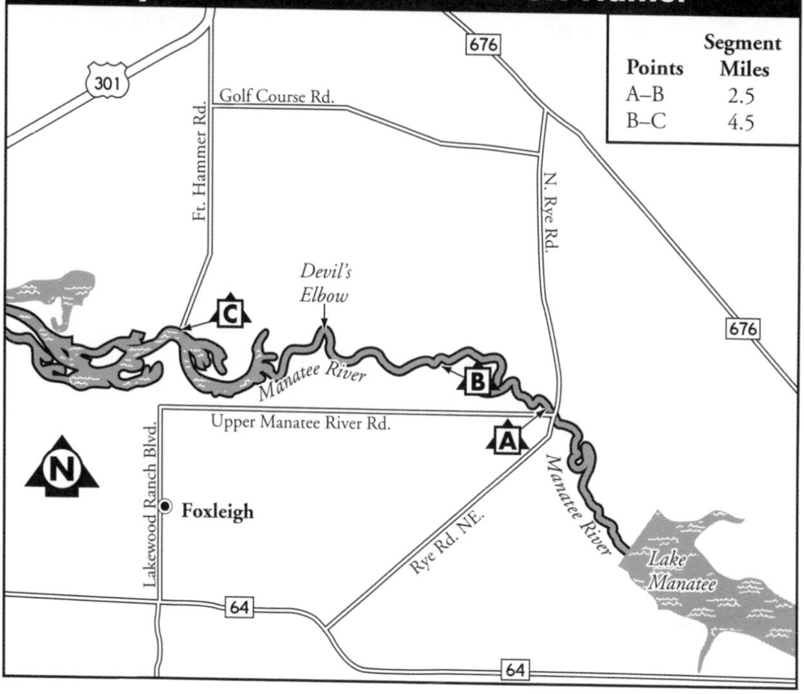

Points	Segment Miles
A–B	2.5
B–C	4.5

The scenic Myakka River

East of the Rye Road bridge, the bluffs are higher, with tall sand pines growing on them. Only an occasional building or trailer can be seen through the thick vegetation to mar the fine scenery in this area. If the dam gates are open, the roar of the rushing water can be heard at least a mile away. As the dam is approached, you might encounter patches of discolored foam. This is formed as the water bubbles over the spillway at the foot of the dam. Due to swift current and possible obstructions, you should not approach the dam too closely.

SHUTTLE: To reach the takeout from Exit 224 on I-75, take US 301 north toward Parrish. As US 301 veers left (north), make an acute right turn onto Fort Hamer Road. Follow Fort Hamer Road south to dead-end at a boat ramp on the Manatee River. To reach the uppermost put-in, backtrack on Fort Hamer Road, then turn right, east, on Golf Course Road and follow it to Rye Road. Turn right, south, on Rye Road and follow it to Rye Wilderness Park and a canoe/skiff launch on the southwest side of the bridge over the Manatee River.

GAUGE: Phone. Call Ray's Canoe Hideaway for latest river conditions at (941) 747-3909. You can also call the Lake Manatee Dam office at (941) 746-3020 for dam release information.

MYAKKA RIVER

One of Florida's designated state scenic rivers, the Myakka originates in east central Manatee County, in cattle country. From there it winds southwesterly, enters Sarasota County, and becomes a central feature of Myakka River State Park, a 58-square-mile park. While in the park it merges with Clay Gully and opens into Upper Myakka Lake, a beautiful expanse of water known for its alligators. Upper Myakka Lake is the beginning for paddlers, and the river is generally paddleable year-round from this point. Upper Myakka Lake empties into a river channel bordered by open grasses and some hardwood hammocks. The river then passes below FL 72 and becomes much less traveled by boaters as it enters the state park wilderness preserve. Entrance into the preserve is limited to 30 people per day, and a permit is required. The Myakka flows riverine for another 1.5 miles before opening into Lower Myakka Lake, which narrows and then opens again into the Deep Hole, which has been certified to be at least 142 feet deep.

Below Deep Hole, the river resumes its riverine characteristics and leaves Myakka River State Park. It then makes a winding, southerly course for Charlotte Harbor, where it empties into the Gulf. The section below the park is little paddled, due to a long run of 16 miles combined with a long shuttle. The river down here is quite scenic, and part of the riverbank is protected by the Carlton Tract, land owned by Sarasota County. After passing below the I-75 overpass, the Myakka reaches Snook Haven and a good place to take out. Below this point, the river quickly widens and becomes the domain of the powerboat set.

MAPS: Myakka River State Park map, Myakka City, Old Myakka, Myakka River (USGS)

UPPER MYAKKA LAKE TO STATE PARK SOUTH ENTRANCE

class	I
length	3
time	2
gauge	Phone, Web
level	N/A
gradient	0.3
scenery	A

DESCRIPTION: This section is often paddled as an out-and-back. The boat ramp is at the south end of Upper Myakka Lake, so paddlers have the option of extending their trip from the south end of Upper Myakka Lake to the north end of the lake, then paddling down to the river channel, winding among the grasses before coming to a Park Drive bridge over the river. This bridge is a popular alligator-viewing spot, and onlookers will be atop the bridge gator-spotting. Below the bridge you may glimpse an old

palm cabin built by the Civilian Conservation Corps back in the 1930s. There is a small picnic area nearby. Paddlers may want to take out just downstream of here, at the south picnic and parking area. This parking area is inside the park and offers better parking than the side of FL 72, which offers no parking. However, it requires a 50-yard carry from the water to the parking area. Be apprised that much of this paddle is on open water and is extremely subject to winds, especially during winter, which is also when many tourists are on the river.

SHUTTLE: To reach the takeout from Exit 205 on I-75, take FL 72 east to Myakka River State Park. Enter the park and head up the park road to a picnic area shortly on the right. To reach the put-in, continue north past the entrance station on Park Drive, bridging the Myakka, and turn left into the concession area. The boat ramp is past the Myakka Outpost Store on the edge of the lake. Canoes and kayaks are for rent here.

GAUGE: Phone, Web. Call Myakka River State Park at (941) 361-6511 for the latest river conditions. The USGS gauge to help determine flow rates for any given time period is Myakka River at Myakka City, FL.

B

class	I
length	16
time	9
gauge	Phone, Web
level	N/A
gradient	0.5
scenery	A

Myakka River State Park to Snookhaven

DESCRIPTION: Overnight trips are possible on this section, but it is somewhat complicated. First you have to call Sarasota County Parks and Recreation at (941) 861-9830 to get a permit. You can start inside the state park, but you can't leave a car there overnight. And you must arrange to leave a car at the takeout as well. This is why many people choose to make a long day of it and paddle the entire 16 miles. When planning this endeavor, make sure to add the time for a long shuttle into your day.

The river twists and turns before opening into Lower Myakka Lake. Most paddlers enjoy the river and Lower Myakka Lake, and then backtrack upstream, forgoing the 16-mile downstream trek. Below Lower Myakka Lake the river narrows and is bordered by high sandy banks, grown up with laurel oaks, live oaks, and palms. Expect occasional blow-downs to stretch across the river, but boats can generally pass. The limestone river bottom creates occasional shoals, especially when the river pinches in. The current is generally mild to nonexistent, except where the river narrows. Paddlers will have to portage around a dam on the river

Myakka River (Sections A–B): Upper Myakka Lake to Snookhaven

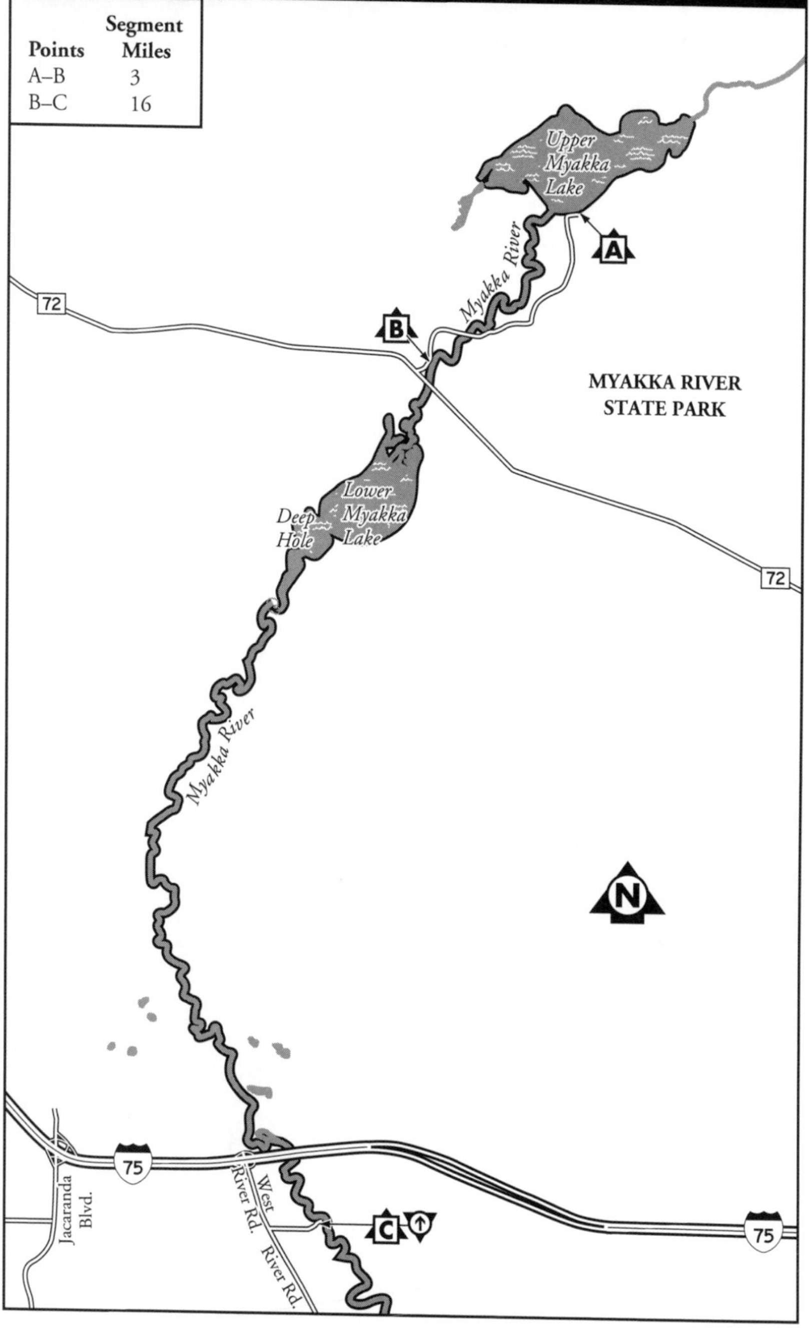

Points	Segment Miles
A–B	3
B–C	16

below the wilderness area. Portage on river left, in the Carlton Tract, as river right is posted. Be very careful around posted land down here, as some landowners will exercise their rights. After passing under the I-75 bridge, motorboats will become more common. The Snookhaven boat ramp is closed on Sundays.

SHUTTLE: To reach the takeout from Exit 191 on I-75, take River Road south to Venice Road. Turn left on Venice Road and follow it to Snookhaven Restaurant. They have a boat launch for a fee. To reach the put-in from Exit 205 on I-75, take FL 72 east to Myakka River State Park. Enter the park and head up the park road to a picnic area shortly on the right.

GAUGE: Phone, Web. Call Myakka River State Park at (941) 361-6511 for the latest river conditions. The USGS gauge to help determine flow rates for any given time period is Myakka River near Sarasota, FL.

Palm tree leans over the Myakka River at Myakka River State Park

J. N. "DING" DARLING NATIONAL WILDLIFE REFUGE (COMMODORE CREEK CANOE TRAIL)

Sanibel and Captiva islands, located in the Gulf of Mexico across San Carlos Bay from Fort Myers, are reached via the busy Sanibel Causeway. Believe it or not, at one time these barrier islands were relatively undeveloped, providing a quiet refuge for those seeking solitude or a shell-hunting excursion along the well-known beaches. Development finally came to the islands, however, and rustic terrain has given way to condominiums, hotels, and apartments. Thankfully, the community insisted that the changes be made in step with nature: thus, the island visitor may still experience a somewhat natural setting. Better still, a large section of the islands was designated as the J. N. "Ding" Darling National Wildlife Refuge and protected from future encroachment.

Vegetated with mangrove and saw grass, the refuge is home for a variety of animals, including ospreys, moorhens, brown pelicans, and alligators. Winter migration brings an abundance of northern visitors, such as blue-winged teals, pintails, mergansers, and Yankees, to name a few. Paddling offers an excellent way to tour the refuge and observe the wildlife, along one of the two established canoe trails. The two trails are Commodore Creek and Buck Key. Unfortunately, the Buck Key Canoe Trail was destroyed by the hurricanes of 2004, and at press time the refuge was unsure of the trail's future.

MAPS: Nautical chart 11427, Sanibel (USGS)

COMMODORE CREEK

class	I
length	2.5
time	Varies
gauge	Visual
level	Tidal
gradient	Tidal
scenery	B

DESCRIPTION: The Commodore Creek Trail is located at the southeast corner of Tarpon Bay. This marked trail snakes through tidal mud flats and stands of red mangrove. It offers excellent views of wading birds and small marine animals scurrying along the seabed. The trailhead is reached by paddling 0.75 miles west of the Tarpon Bay Marina along the south shore of the bay.

SHUTTLE: From Exit 131 on I-75, take Daniels Parkway west to Ben C. Pratt/Six Mile Cypress Parkway, CR 865. Turn left on CR 865 and follow it to Summerlin Road, CR 869. Turn left on CR 869 and follow it to Sanibel Island. CR 869 becomes CR

J.N. "Ding" Darling National Wildlife Refuge (Commodore Creek Canoe Trail)

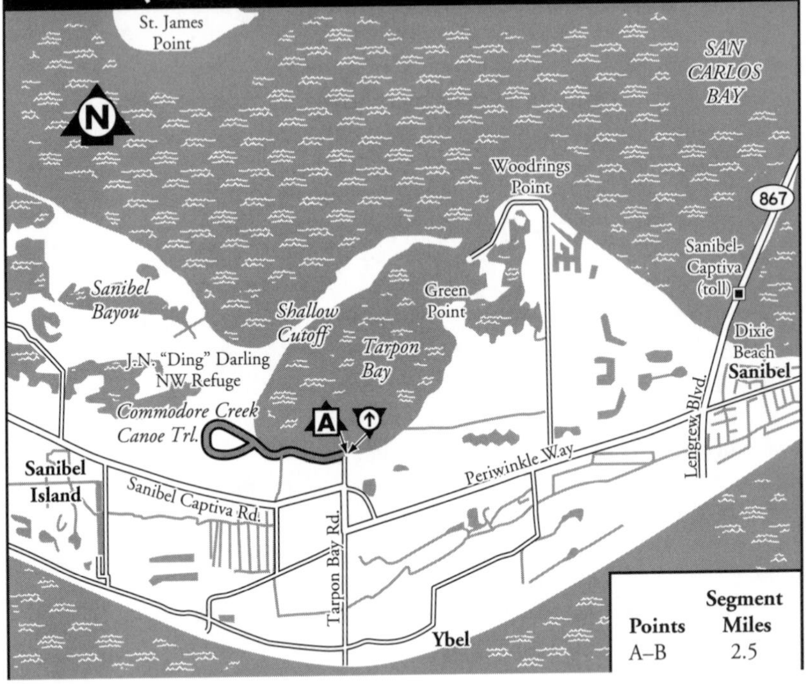

Points	Segment Miles
A–B	2.5

867. Once on the island turn right on Periwinkle Way and follow it to Palm Ridge Road. Turn right on Palm Ridge Road and follow it to Tarpon Bay Road. Turn right on Tarpon Bay Road, and it leads to Tarpon Bay Marina and a pay launch leading into Tarpon Bay.

GAUGE: Visual. Try to catch the trail on a rising or high falling tide.

ESTERO RIVER

Located in a once quiet area now being overwhelmed by Fort Myers to the north and Naples to the south lies the community of Estero. Bounded on the west by Estero Bay and on the east by the Corkscrew Swamp, Estero was established in 1894 by a religious visionary from Chicago, Dr. Cyrus Reed Teed. Dr. Teed was the founder of a religion that advocated communal living, communal ownership of property, and celibacy. He called this new religion Koreshanity, which is derived from Koresh, the Hebrew word for Cyrus. Among this religion's most unique beliefs was the theory that the Earth was a hollow sphere. Life existed on the inner surface and overlooked the sun, stars, and universe in the center. In 1896, Dr. Teed even conducted an experiment with a simple device, known as a rectilineator, which proved to him that the Earth's surface was indeed concave, a central feature of his theory.

The bulk of the Koreshan settlement was built on the Estero River, about 5 miles upstream from Estero Bay. Although the movement declined after Teed's death in 1908, many of the buildings remain intact and are preserved as part of Koreshan State Historic Area. This park, which extends for a mile along the Estero River, has a beautifully wooded camping area, nature trails, a concrete boat ramp, and, of course, the historic Koreshan settlement.

Estero is a Spanish word meaning "estuary" and was first applied long ago by explorers as they sailed into the bay. Estero Bay is an ecologically rich area in which red mangrove and turtle grass provide a continuous food supply for the large fish population. This productive area has been qualified as a State Aquatic Preserve, and much of the land within 2 miles south of the Estero River and extending through the park is state-owned and protected.

The section of the Estero River covered in this guide extends for 5 miles from the point where it passes beneath US 41 until it flows into Estero Bay. Along this course the character of the river changes dramatically, beginning as a narrow waterway channeled by limestone and shaded by large oaks, and eventually broadening as it flows through the Spartina grass and mangrove of the tidal marsh. The flow of the river is affected by the tides, so paddlers may want to check local tide tables while planning a trip, though it is not necessary. Because of extensive powerboat traffic on weekends, the ideal time to paddle this river is during the week. However, it is definitely worth a trip into Estero Bay to visit Mound Key State Archeological Preserve. Mound Key was the site of Calos, capital city of the fierce Calusa tribe, who ruled South Florida. A walking trail and interpretive information on the island caps a fine paddle on the Estero River.

MAPS: Koreshan State Historic Area map, Estero (USGS)

class	I
length	5.5
time	Varies
gauge	Visual
level	Tidal
gradient	Tidal
scenery	B+

US 41 to Mound Key

DESCRIPTION: This is an out-and-back paddle, 5.5 miles each way. From the launch point, paddle to the west under the US 41 bridge. Along the first mile, the south shore is in the state park, and for the first 0.25 miles several buildings of the historic Koreshan settlement can be seen through the woods on the left. Although the north shore is developed with several trailer parks, their associated docks, and boat slips, the scenery is still quite nice. Large oaks draped with Spanish moss and bromeliads shade most of the river area, and the lush shore vegetation is highlighted with an occasional wild hibiscus. Layers of limestone, stained green in irregular patterns by fungi and dripping wet from the damp mosses that cling to it, protrude from the riverbanks. It is not uncommon to see an alligator resting on a submerged log or outcropping, its body partially obscured by the dark, tannin-stained water. The state park boat ramp is concrete and has stone retaining walls. It is on the south side of the river and very easy to find. This is a good beginning point if you want to shave a mile off your trip.

Beyond the state park boat ramp, proceed to the left (west) toward Estero Bay. Within 2 miles of the put-in, the river passes a large trailer park and another residential area, both on river right. The channel is about 60 yards wide here, and the south shore is lined with tall Australian pine trees. At 2.5 miles, Halfway Creek enters from the south. This lovely little waterway meanders through a brackish marsh and, in places, separates into multiple channels that weave their way through mangrove and turtle grass. All the vegetation looks alike, so it's easy to become confused; but with a compass and knowledge of the current direction at the mouth of the creek, you can eventually find the main channel.

Mangrove is the predominant vegetation from Halfway Creek to Estero Bay, although there is also a lot of Spartina grass and, on the high ground, some Australian and sand pines. A quarter mile past Halfway Creek, a long narrow bay protrudes to the south-southeast; at its mouth lies the wreckage of a sunken boat. The wheel house is always visible and, at low tide, the bow can be seen angling out of the water. For safety reasons, the hulk should not be approached too closely. The dark, tannin-stained water obscures the view, making it difficult to see pieces of hull wreckage that may obstruct the paddler.

From this point on, the river meanders gently to Estero Bay past a number of small bays and side streams, which are interesting areas to explore in their own right. At 3.6 miles, a channel enters the river from the northeast. This side creek winds its way through a thick mangrove forest, and the observant paddler is likely to see herons and egrets perched in the roots, or an osprey soaring overhead. Just past 4 miles, the river enters Estero Bay and the influence of the tides becomes quite pronounced. Caution should be exercised in this area, for moderate chop, enough to swamp a canoe, can develop quickly in the bay. Kayakers with covered

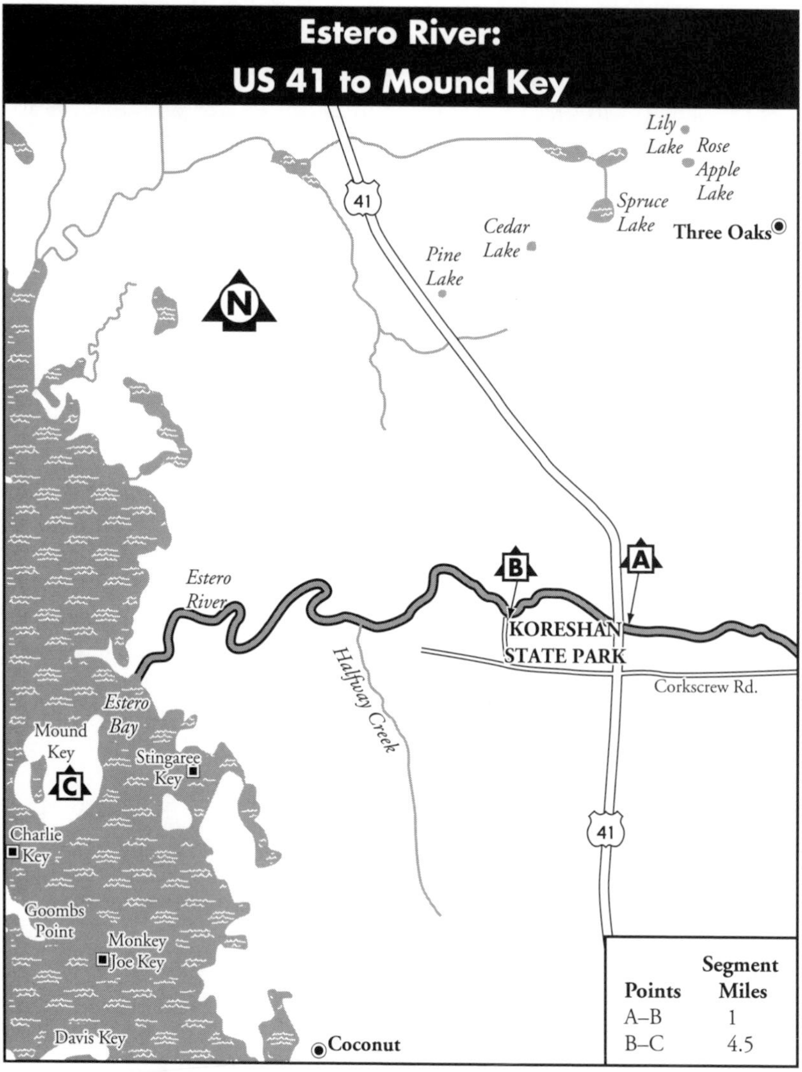

Estero River: US 41 to Mound Key

Lily Lake
Rose Apple Lake
Spruce Lake
Three Oaks
41
Cedar Lake
Pine Lake
N
Estero River
B
A
KORESHAN STATE PARK
Halfway Creek
Corkscrew Rd.
Estero Bay
Mound Key
C
Stingaree Key
41
Charlie Key
Goombs Point
Monkey Joe Key
Davis Key
Coconut

Points	Segment Miles
A–B	1
B–C	4.5

hatches will have no problems. Oyster beds, with their sharp, damaging shells, are located near some of the mangrove thickets.

Horseshoe crabs can be seen in the water and scurrying along the sand on mangrove islands. Mullet may surprise you as they jump out of the water next to your boat and continue along in a series of airborne arcs. Occasionally paddlers may notice the ghostly form of a stingray passing underneath. Paddlers should then aim for Mound Key. It is the biggest island in the center of the bay. The island's walking trail connects the north and south landings. Stretch your legs and explore the mounds of the island and water courts dug by the Calusa.

SHUTTLE: From Exit 123 on I-75, travel west on Corkscrew Road, CR 853, for 2 miles to US 41, or Tamiami Trail. Turn right (north) and proceed for 0.25 miles to the bridge over the Estero River. Estero River Outfitters is located on the northeast side of the bridge. There is ample parking, and boats may be launched from a small wooden dock for a nominal fee.

GAUGE: Visual. Try to time your out-and-back with the tides.

Paddlers admire the lush vegetation from mid-river

The movement of a canoe is like a reed in the wind. Silence is part of it, and the sounds of lapping water, bird songs, and wind in the trees. It is part of the medium through which it floats, the sky, the water, and the shores. A man is part of his canoe and therefore part of all it knows. The instant he dips his paddle, he flows as it flows, the canoe yielding to his slightest touch and responsive to his every whim and thought. . . .

—Sigurd F. Olson

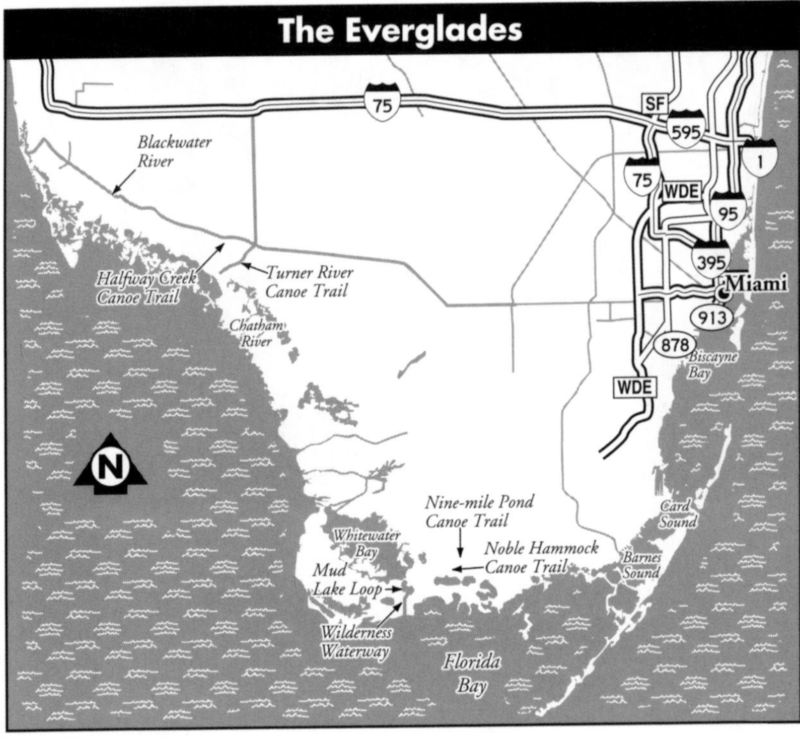
The Everglades
75
SF
595
1
75
WDE
95
395
Miami
913
878
WDE
Blackwater River
Halfway Creek Canoe Trail
Turner River Canoe Trail
Chatham River
Biscayne Bay
Card Sound
Barnes Sound
Nine-mile Pond Canoe Trail
Noble Hammock Canoe Trail
Whitewater Bay
Mud Lake Loop
Wilderness Waterway
Florida Bay
N

part **Nine**

THE EVERGLADES

BLACKWATER RIVER AT COLLIER-SEMINOLE STATE PARK

The Blackwater River is part of a 13.5-mile canoe circuit that winds through Collier-Seminole State Park wilderness preserve. This preserve is at the western extreme of the Everglades and features a prime example of the mangrove forest that forms the outer rim of south Florida. The canoe circuit includes tidal creeks and bays as well as the Blackwater River. A diverse community of wildlife, including roseate spoonbills and manatees, inhabits the preserve. The tides add another dimension to paddling in the preserve. Current in the creeks becomes moderately swift during tidal change, and even the Blackwater River reverses flow on the incoming tide.

MAPS: Collier-Seminole State Park paddle map, Nautical Chart #11430 Lostmans River to Wiggins Pass, Royal Palm Hammock (USGS)

COLLIER-SEMINOLE STATE PARK LOOP

class	I
length	13.5
time	6
gauge	Visual
level	Tidal
gradient	Tidal
scenery	A

DESCRIPTION: There are special requirements for canoeing at Collier–Seminole. All paddlers must file a float plan at the entrance station. This requirement is dictated by the high potential for getting lost among the myriad mangrove islands. The rangers will brief all paddlers on the tide situation and stress the necessity for a compass and map (a nautical chart is recommended). All paddlers doing the entire loop must travel counterclockwise through Mud Bay to Palm Bay and then up the Blackwater River. Be prepared to start your trip early in the morning, as you must return to the ranger station by a specific time, unless you are staying at the Grocery Place backcountry campsite, which also requires a permit.

The trip commences at the Collier-Seminole boat ramp. The first 0.5 miles is on a wide man-made channel to the Blackwater

River. The upper river is narrow and winds through a mangrove forest. The red mangrove with its characteristic prop roots forms the first echelon of mangrove. The black mangrove, with its hundreds of pencil-like pneumatophore roots sticking out of the muck, is back on higher ground. The trail leaves the Blackwater River at 1.8 miles, where a sign directs paddlers to turn right into a tidal creek. This narrow creek almost forms a tunnel through the mangrove. A small bay marks the 2-mile point, and Mud Bay is close at hand.

Those arriving at Mud Bay at low tide will soon discover the source of its name, as there are areas where canoes must be pulled

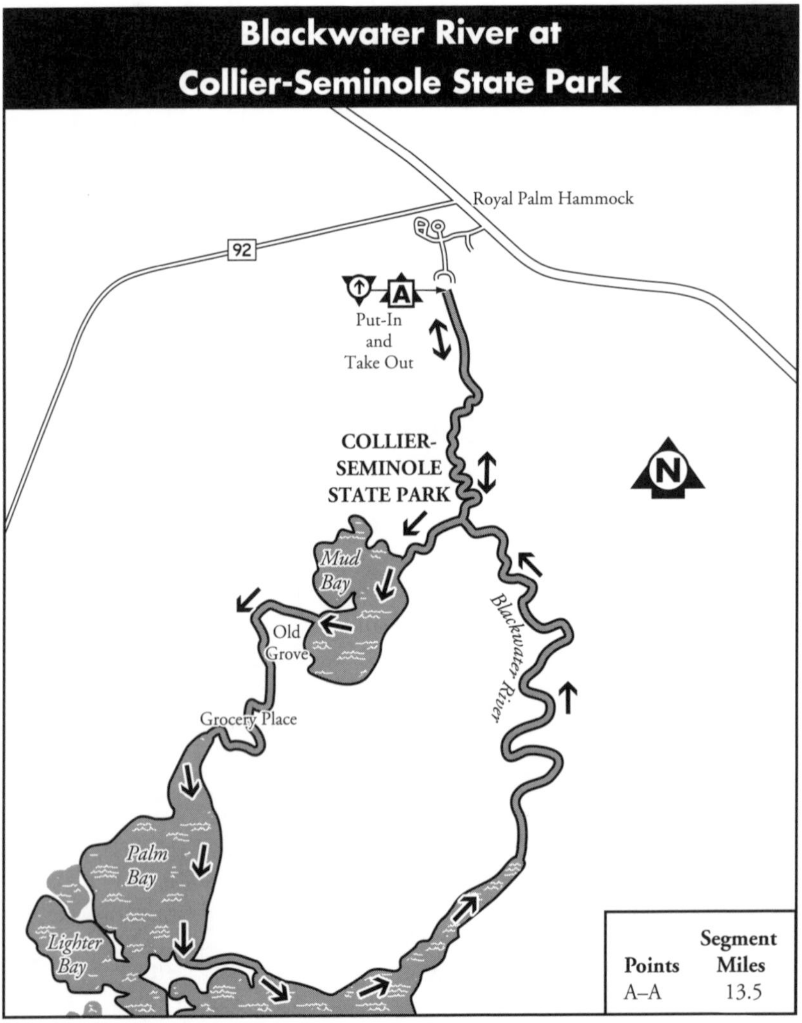

Blackwater River at Collier-Seminole State Park

Royal Palm Hammock
92
Put-In and Take Out
COLLIER-SEMINOLE STATE PARK
N
Mud Bay
Old Grove
Blackwater River
Grocery Place
Palm Bay
Lighter Bay

Points	Segment Miles
A–A	13.5

over mud bars. Bear to the left toward the large island upon entering the bay. Keep to the left side of the island and head into Royal Palm Hammock Creek. West Palm Run comes in on the right as Royal Palm Hammock Creek turns to the south. The Old Grove, one of only two spots of high ground on this trip, is passed on the left at 3.5 miles.

Grocery Place, the other high point and designated camping area, is on the right at the mouth of a stream at 4.5 miles. Early settlers arranged for supply boats to cache provisions on this spot, thus the origin of the name. Royal Palm Hammock Creek enters the open expanse of Palm Bay downstream of Grocery Place. Paddlers should stick to the left bank from this point until reentering Blackwater River.

You will enter the Ten Thousand Islands region at 6 miles, and it is very easy to get lost here among the numerous look-alike mangrove islands. For this reason it is essential to keep the mainland to the immediate left of the canoe. Another mile of paddling and you will enter Blackwater Bay. Continue bearing left and go into the mouth of the Blackwater River. Channel markers are spaced at intervals going up the river. A branch of Gill Rattle Creek is passed on the right at 7.5 miles, as is another side stream at 10 miles.

SHUTTLE: Collier-Seminole State Park is located off of US 41 south of Naples.

GAUGE: Visual. This paddle is tidally influenced. Try to time your trip with the tides.

EVERGLADES NATIONAL PARK AND THE WILDERNESS WATERWAY

Mention the Everglades and water comes to mind. After all, it is known as the River of Grass. The Everglades is actually a mosaic of numerous ecosystems, from sawgrass plains to pinelands to tropical hardwood hammocks to coastal prairies to sandy islands in the Gulf of Mexico. Paddlers will find themselves plying the brackish, mangrove-bordered waters and the coastal areas along the Gulf.

Simply put, Everglades National Park is one of the best paddling destinations in America, featuring the most extensive warm-water paddling area in the United States. Outings can range from two hours to two weeks. Settings range from the ultra-narrow Hells Bay Canoe Trail to miles-wide Florida Bay and even more open Gulf of Mexico. Fifty-two designated backcountry sites scattered among the islands, beaches, rivers, and bays of the Everglades allow for years of paddling trips without repeating yourself. Day paddlers have several excellent designated routes that will give a good taste of what watery adventures the Glades have to offer.

MAPS: Everglades National Park map, NOAA chart #11430, 11432, 11433, Waterproof Chart #39, 41

class	I
length	99
time	Varies
gauge	Visual
level	Tidal
gradient	Tidal
scenery	A+

FLAMINGO TO EVERGLADES CITY

DESCRIPTION: There are hundreds of potential routes and describing them would take a book all by itself. As the author of *A Paddler's Guide to Everglades National Park,* I know that exploring both the "inside" and the "outside" of the Everglades paddling area will enhance your appreciation of this unique ecosystem. The "inside" is the area of rivers, creeks, and bays between the freshwater river of grass, and the "outside" is the waters of the Gulf of Mexico that are pocked by mangrove islands, coastline, and beaches. The outside is better suited for sea kayaks, with so much open water subject to unpredictable winds.

The Wilderness Waterway is a 99-mile marked path maintained by the park service. It starts in Flamingo and leads to Everglades City. But most paddlers travel north to south, to avoid facing strong north winds that occasionally penetrate the Glades. From Flamingo, paddlers follow the Coast Guard markers to #48, just north of Whitewater Bay, and then follow rectangular brown signs erected by the park service. These signs are numbered, increasing toward Everglades City, and have an arrow

pointing on one side or the other. However, this arrow *does not always* point you in the right direction. So double-check your chart and don't blindly follow the arrows of the Wilderness Waterway. Though the Wilderness Waterway is the most well-known paddle trail in the park, it is far from the best or most interesting travel route in the park.

You must plan an overnight trip to the Everglades. To access official park information call (305) 242-7700 and ask for a **www.nps.gov/ever.** With the trip planner you can sketch out a trip, but that is all you can do from home. Wilderness permits, required for all overnight camping, are available only in person at

Everglades National Park and the Wilderness Waterway: Flamingo to Everglades City

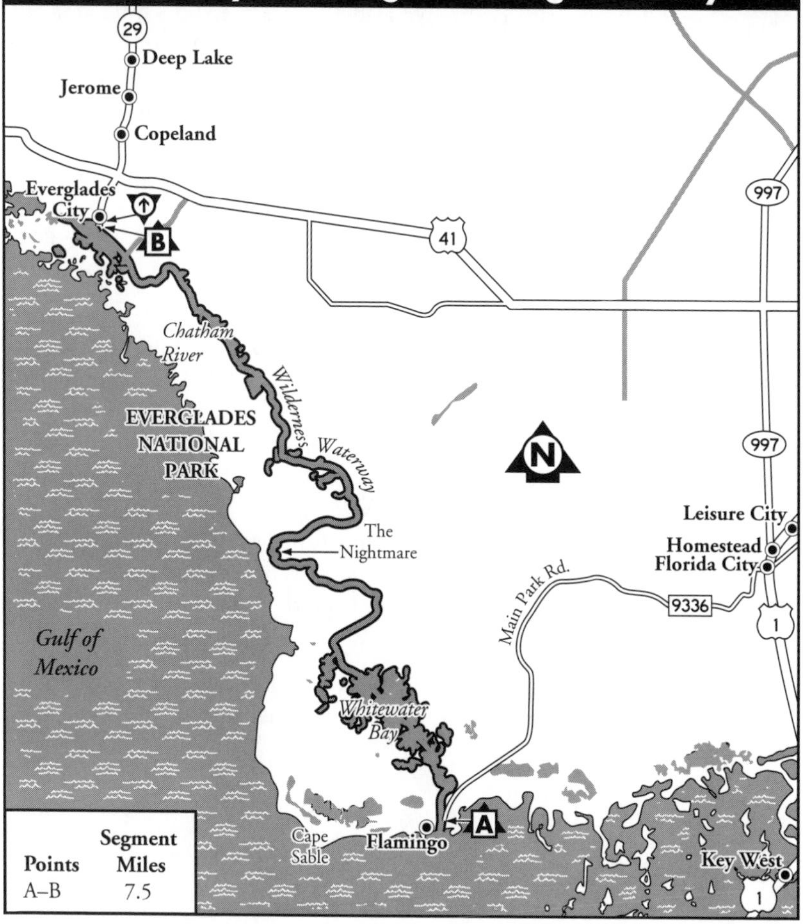

Points	Segment Miles
A–B	7.5

Flamingo and Gulf Coast ranger stations and may be obtained in person up to 24 hours in advance of a trip.

Head to the permit desk at Flamingo or Gulf Coast ranger stations and make a backcountry trip request with park staff. Have alternate routes planned once you're at the permit desk; this way, if campsites are already reserved, you'll have an alternate route ready. Once your permit is issued and park regulations are explained to you, you must pay a permit fee.

Be aware of heavy-use periods. The general paddling season in Everglades National Park runs from November through April. Insects, thunderstorms, and occasional hurricanes conspire to keep the Everglades backcountry nearly deserted May through October. When the first north breezes cool and clear the air, reducing insects, paddlers turn their eye southward for the Everglades. A few campsites begin to fill on weekends, but the crowds really come around Christmas. The period between Christmas and New Year's is the Everglades' busiest. Expect full campsites and plan alternative trips. After this, weekends can be busy, yet you can nearly always get into the general vicinity of where you want to go. Plan your trip during the week for the most solitude. The next big crowds come around President's Day weekend in February. The last big hits come during mid-March, when college students flock to the Everglades for overnight trips. Again, get to the ranger stations early and you should be able to get a hold of some campsites. As the weather warms up in April, visitation tapers off, dying by the end of the month.

SHUTTLE: To reach Flamingo from Miami, take the Florida Turnpike south to its end and then take US 1 in Florida City. Keep south on US 1 to reach FL 9336 and signs for Everglades National Park. Stay with FL 9336 and follow it 38 miles (on Main Park Road) beyond the park entrance to Flamingo. To reach the north end of the Wilderness Waterway in Everglades City, return to Florida City and turn left, north, on FL 997 to US 41, Tamiami Trail. Turn left, west, on US 41 to reach CR 29. Turn left on CR 29 and follow it south 3 miles to Everglades City and the Everglades National Park Gulf Coast ranger station.

GAUGE: Visual. The Wilderness Waterway and the paddling area of Everglades National Park are tidally affected.

HALFWAY CREEK CANOE TRAIL

This route is a microcosm of south Florida in many ways. It reveals human hands on the landscape and offers a good view of the beauty left under park protection. First, paddle down a man-made canal, definitely a part of modern south Florida. Come to an attractive habitat of saw grass, cattails, and trees islands. Then enter a strange and wonderful mangrove tunnel that turns into a brackish stream beneath a taller shady forest. Leave the park boundary, pass by houses, then go under the bridge of an artificial causeway to emerge in the wide-open, busy Chokoloskee Bay, ending your paddle at Gulf Coast Ranger Station. Consider paying for a shuttle from an outfitter to make this a one-way day paddle. This creek is not on the waterproof charts, but the route is marked most of the way, and the Big Cypress National Preserve Visitor Center produces a decent map of this trail. The Big Cypress Preserve has also marked a loop off of Halfway Creek, making a shuttle unnecessary.

MAPS: Halfway Creek Canoe Trail map, Big Cypress National Preserve map, Everglades National Park map, Ochopee, Chokoloskee, Everglades City (USGS)

TAMIAMI TRAIL TO GULF COAST RANGER STATION

class	I
length	7.5
time	4
gauge	Visual, phone
level	Tidal
gradient	Tidal
scenery	A

DESCRIPTION: Start your trip on the Tamiami Trail, US 41. Put into the canal and being paddling southwesterly. Note the limestone banks here. The water is crystal clear and bordered by saw grass, cattails, and occasional mangroves. Other freshwater plants adorn the higher dry land of the south bank. Soon pass the markers of an airboat trail crossing the canal. Leave the 40-foot-wide canal and come to the first lake at mile 1. Keep southwest. Numerous palms grace the shore.

Pass marker #1 toward the end of the lake, which meanders, and keep west past marker #2. A beautiful variety of south Florida vegetation is all around. This offers some of the most scenic paddling in this entire guidebook. Paddlers headed toward the Gulf will be looking at the green side of these markers. Paddlers heading away from the Gulf will be seeing the red side of these same markers.

The trail alternates between small lakes and narrower creeks, keeping a generally southwesterly direction. Stay with the markers. Past marker #6, arms of trees crowd the slender creek until the trees eventually form a tunnel that continues for a good distance.

Keep a reasonable pace, not going too fast among the twists and turns of the tunnel. The water here is plenty deep, but at times you'll have to duck your head under vegetation. Watch for a bit of land on creek right where you can get out and take a break.

Farther down the tunnel, Halfway Creek takes on a murky, pungent aspect. More fallen trees and brush lie in the water. The canopy rises as you proceed downstream. Tidal influence increases. Come to a major split in the creek at 5.5 miles. To your left, east, a creek leads toward Turner Lake and Left Hand Turner

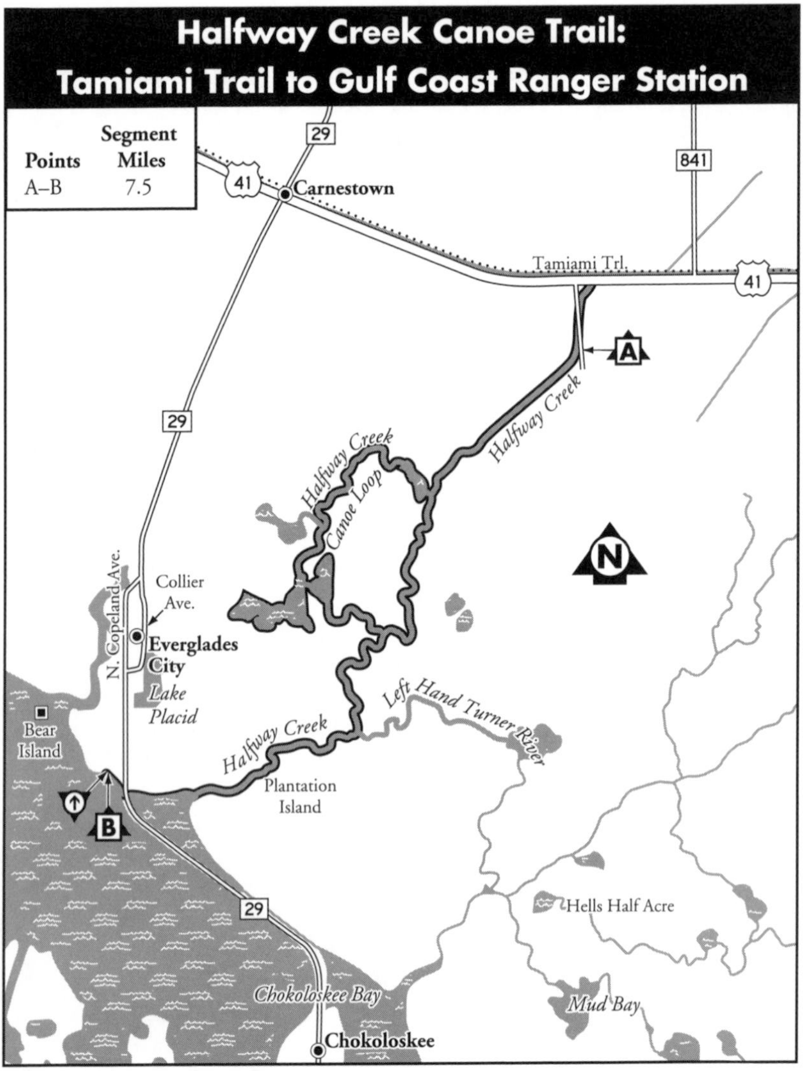

Halfway Creek Canoe Trail: Tamiami Trail to Gulf Coast Ranger Station

Points	Segment Miles
A–B	7.5

An Everglades shoreline made of shells

River. To your right, west, Halfway Creek widens and continues toward Chokoloskee Bay. Stay with Halfway Creek.

Leave the Everglades National Park boundary and pass a few houses on your right. Notice the Australian pine, Brazilian pepper, and other exotic vegetation. The Plantation Island community is on your right before opening into a bay. Keep southwest to reach the Halfway Creek bridge. Watch for strong tides flowing through here. Once through the bridge, turn northwest, passing a tour boat landing and two brown park service buildings to the Gulf Coast Ranger Station, ending your route.

SHUTTLE: The takeout is in Everglades City at the Gulf Coast Ranger Station (off of CR 29, Copeland Avenue). To reach the put-in from Everglades City, drive north on CR 29 for 3 miles to US 41. Turn right, east, on US 41 and drive 2 miles to Sea Grape Drive. Turn right on Sea Grape Drive and follow it a short distance to the Halfway Creek landing.

GAUGE: Visual, phone. If in doubt, check with the rangers at the Big Cypress Visitor Center at (239) 695-1201 for the latest creek conditions.

TURNER RIVER CANOE TRAIL

This may be the most biologically diverse paddle in the Everglades. It starts on the Tamiami Trail in the Big Cypress National Preserve amid a freshwater environment dominated by towering cypress trees. It opens into saw grass broken with occasional tree islands, makes a tight squeeze through eerie tree tunnels, then transforms to classic mangrove zone environment before reaching Hurddles Creek. Continue down the Turner River as the river opens up and passes a tall historic Calusa Native American mound before arriving at civilized Chokoloskee Island.

Be apprised that the paddling on this trail can be tough. At first shallow water and hydrilla, an underwater plant, combine for slow going. Next the tunnels are very constricted, making steering and paddling difficult at best. Sea kayaks are untenable here; a double-bladed paddle simply can't work in the tight tunnels and sharp turns. To best enjoy this trail, take a canoe and consider getting an outfitter to provide a shuttle for a one-way trip.

MAPS: Big Cypress National Preserve map, Everglades National Park map, Ochopee, Chokoloskee (USGS)

class	I
length	8.5
time	5
gauge	Visual, phone
level	Mostly tidal
gradient	Mostly tidal
scenery	A

US 41 TO CHOKOLOSKEE ISLAND

DESCRIPTION: Put in at the landing adjacent to the bridge over the Turner River, and begin paddling south. The channel soon constricts to less than 15 feet. Your immediate surroundings are freshwater species: cypresses, cattails, and willows. The saw grass displacing cattails have made a recent appearance due to fertilizer runoff from the farming region north of the Everglades National Park.

This river was named for a guide, Richard B. Turner, who led U.S. forces up the waterway in search of Seminoles in 1857. The force, commanded by John Parkhill, went upriver and destroyed some Native villages. Later Parkhill was killed in an ambush, and the bluecoats retreated to the Gulf.

Come to the first mangrove tunnel just a short distance into the paddle—here, the roots of red mangrove form a gauntlet for your craft. Overhead the leaves and branches of the trees crowd out the sun, leaving scanty room for your canoe. Notice the profusion of epiphytes, or air plants, that grow on the mangrove branches. The water is shallow and crystalline. The going is slow.

Briefly emerge into a pond. Stay right and reenter the mangrove tunnel finally to enter another environment—here, cattails, saw grass, and willows provide an open and bright contrast to the cool, shady tunnel.

Intersect an old canal and turn right; the canal is blocked off to the left. Continue in the open, occasionally passing saw grass–ringed tree islands. One of these islands of palm, on river left, provides a dry spot to take a break. The river here varies in width, but stays deep enough to paddle with ease as you enter a very brief second mangrove tunnel. There will be mangrove on river right and saw grass on the left. Pay close attention here and

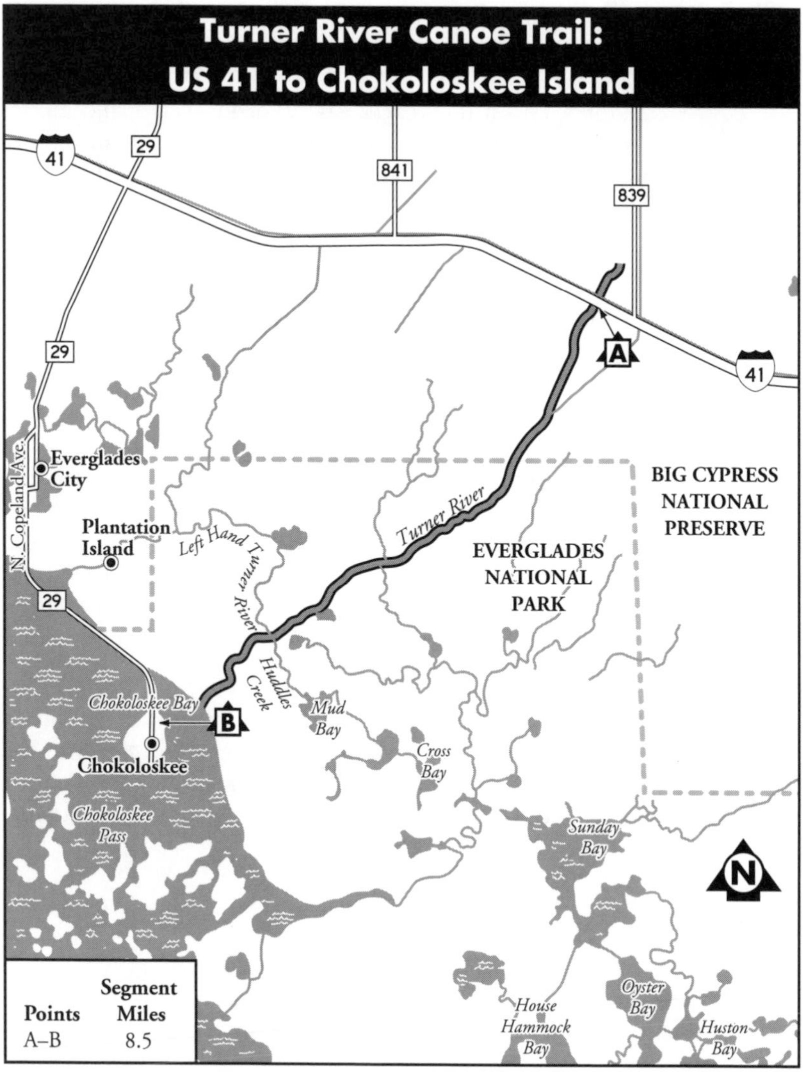

Turner River Canoe Trail:
US 41 to Chokoloskee Island

Points	Segment Miles
A–B	8.5

look for another tunnel diverging right. This tunnel is marked by an orange stake.

Take this tunnel to the right, soon passing an Everglades National Park boundary sign at 3.5 miles. This third tunnel is a little roomier than the first but is still a challenging paddle. After this tunnel opens, the vegetation becomes more typical of the park paddling zone: red and black mangrove, buttonwood, with a few palms thrown in. The Turner twists and turns and continues to vary in width. Keep your eyes peeled for orange tape tied to tree branches to help distinguish the main river from side streams. Otherwise watch for the stronger tidal flow.

The banks become higher as you come to a large bay on river left; stay right and paddle a bit farther to intersect Hurddles Creek on your left. To your right the Turner River becomes much wider.

Paddle west on the Turner River, passing Left Hand Turner River on your right. Stay with the left hand bank, looking for the nearly vertical bank of shell, indicating a Calusa shell mound reaching 19 feet at its highest elevation. Come to the mouth of the Turner River. The mouth is guarded by a few mangrove isles near Wilderness Waterway marker #129. Paddle westerly toward the park service boat ramp on the north end of Chokoloskee Island, near the Outdoor Resort, ending your route at 8.5 miles. It is 3 miles north along the CR 29 causeway to the Gulf Coast ranger station.

SHUTTLE: The takeout is on Chokoloskee Island, on CR 29 south of Everglades City. Outdoor Resorts has a private landing with a fee access. To avoid this fee, you can paddle on the east side of the CR 29 causeway and through the Halfway Creek bridge and takeout at Gulf Coast ranger station in Everglades City, adding 3 miles to your route. To access the put-in from Everglades City, drive north on CR 29 to US 41. Drive east on US 41 for 6 miles to the Turner River.

GAUGE: Visual, phone. If in doubt, check either with the rangers at the Gulf Coast ranger station in Everglades City or with the rangers at Big Cypress Visitor Center on US 41. Or call Big Cypress Preserve at (239) 695-1201 for the latest river conditions.

NINE-MILE POND CANOE TRAIL

This loop trail is located within Everglades National Park. The name Nine-Mile Pond leads you to believe this paddle is 9 miles, but it is actually 5 miles of multiple Everglades environments packed into one loop. It received its name because the pond was 9 miles from the original park visitor center at Coot Bay Pond. This trail is marked with sequentially numbered poles to help you navigate among the mangrove islands, prairies, and tree islands of the region. Prairies here are vastly different than in the Midwest. The Everglades' prairies are open, treeless wetlands, with saw grass emerging from atop the water. The water levels of these prairies change, depending on the wet or dry season, and can dry up completely at times. The water here is clear and very shallow; check with the park visitor center to see if there is enough water to float your boat. In some areas you will be paddling through saw grass that can slow your craft down a bit. Be advised that there is no easily accessible dry land on which to stretch your legs.

MAPS: Everglades National Park map, Mahogany Hammock (USGS)

NINE-MILE POND LOOP

class	I
length	5
time	3.5
gauge	Phone
level	N/A
gradient	None
scenery	A

DESCRIPTION: Start your trip at Nine-Mile Pond, which can be a little cloudy, and head directly across the water from the parking area to the farthest inlet of the pond. This inlet lies east and is between two saw grass stands. Here begins sequentially numbered poles that mark the paddling trail. Keep your eyes peeled because Nine-Mile Pond is a good place to see alligators. Pass through a mangrove tunnel and emerge onto a small prairie. The mud bottom casts a brownish tint to the otherwise clear water, where you can see small fish and minnows darting from your path.

The mangrove and saw grass environments alternate. Here the saw grass on the trail is sparse and doesn't affect your travel. Enter a wide-open prairie of saw grass just beyond marker #42. Saw grass is the most common plant in the Everglades; to many people, saw grass *is* the Everglades. Across the prairie are palm-topped tree islands, also known as bayheads.

Just after entering the prairie follow the numbered poles sharply to the right into a mangrove tunnel to continue the entire loop. If you want to shorten your loop, do not take the sharp right turn, but continue forward past marker #44 to #44A

and across the prairie to marker #82. Then turn left and complete your shortened loop.

The complete trail opens into another prairie where the saw grass is thicker and can slow you down. Take time to examine the microcosm of life that flourishes below you. Your direction has been primarily east and north until marker #73. Here the trail turns sharply to the left and begins heading westward back toward Nine-Mile Pond. Tall hammocks tinged with palm extend beyond the saw grass on both sides of the trail, though you'll pass closely by a few palms at marker #80. Leave the saw grass behind and enter small mangrove islands leading to a few dense palm patches.

Emerge onto a murky alligator pond and veer left through an opening in a line of saw grass onto another pond. Beyond this pond is yet another opening in the saw grass through which you can see the parking area. Paddle through this opening and the parking area is on your right across Nine-Mile Pond, completing your loop.

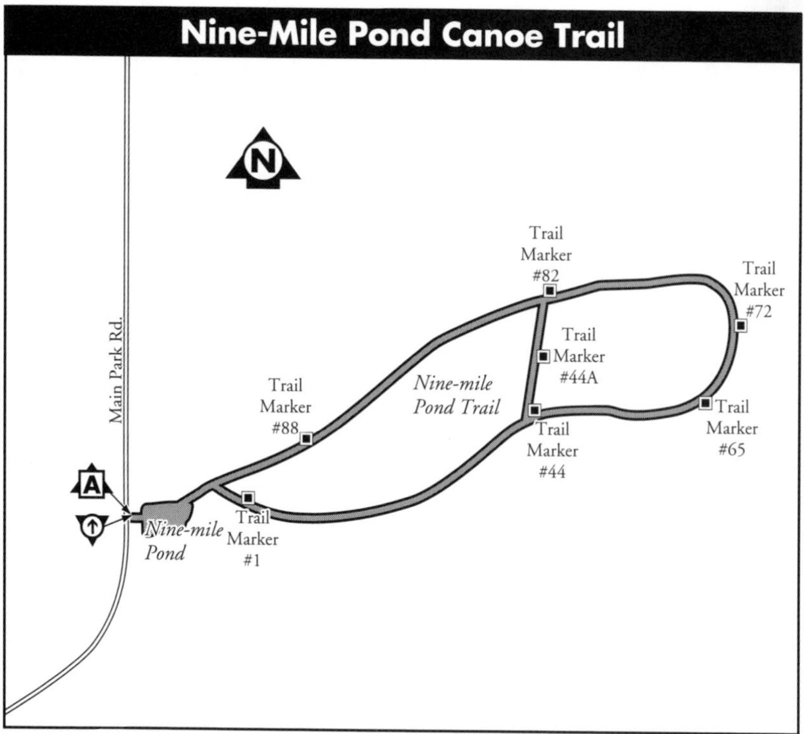

SHUTTLE: From the Flamingo Visitor Center, drive east on Main Park Road to the Nine-Mile Pond parking area at 11.2 miles. This loop is 27 miles east of the park entrance on Main Park Road.

GAUGE: Phone. Call Everglades National Park at (305) 242-7700 for the latest water conditions.

NOBLE HAMMOCK CANOE TRAIL

This is one of my favorite short paddles in Everglades National Park. This marked trail offers quiet quality once you leave Main Park Road behind. An intimate narrow canoe path winds through a mangrove maze, looping around past Noble Hammock, once a haven for moonshiners in the early twentieth century. You will also encounter many fish that will stir the waters on your arrival. Take this trail if the wind is howling, or if you only have time for a short trip. And paddle slowly here—the sudden twists and turns of the trail demand it. Full-size sea kayaks are not maneuverable enough to enjoy this trail. A canoe and excellent cooperation between bow and stern paddlers will maximize your pleasure here. Bring insect repellent along with you in these covered waters.

MAPS: Everglades National Park map, West Lake (USGS)

class	I
length	2
time	2
gauge	Visual, phone
level	N/A
gradient	None
scenery	A

NOBLE HAMMOCK CANOE TRAIL

DESCRIPTION: Depart from the small dock away from Main Park Road and shortly turn right, following the first of 124 sequentially numbered poles. Don't let these poles detract from the scenery, for you would soon be lost in the scenery if it weren't for the upright white PVC pipes. The waters of the Noble Hammock Trail have a coffee-colored tint to them due to the decomposition of plant matter at its bottom.

Passageways barely wide enough for a canoe give way to tiny bays where openings draw you toward them—but don't go in them, follow the poles. Then just as quickly the trail leads into tiny creeks over which hang shade-giving mangroves. And so it goes. After marker #45, pass a clump of paurotis palms where you can get out and stand for a moment. There is very little dry land around here.

Continue on through the dense growth. Soon on your right is a sign marking Noble Hammock. There is a small landing where you can get out, but exploring Noble Hammock and maybe finding the remains of Bill Noble's Prohibition-era moonshining brick furnace requires some serious bushwhacking. But it was this very growth and available buttonwood for burning that led to this tree island, among many others, becoming a moonshiner's asylum.

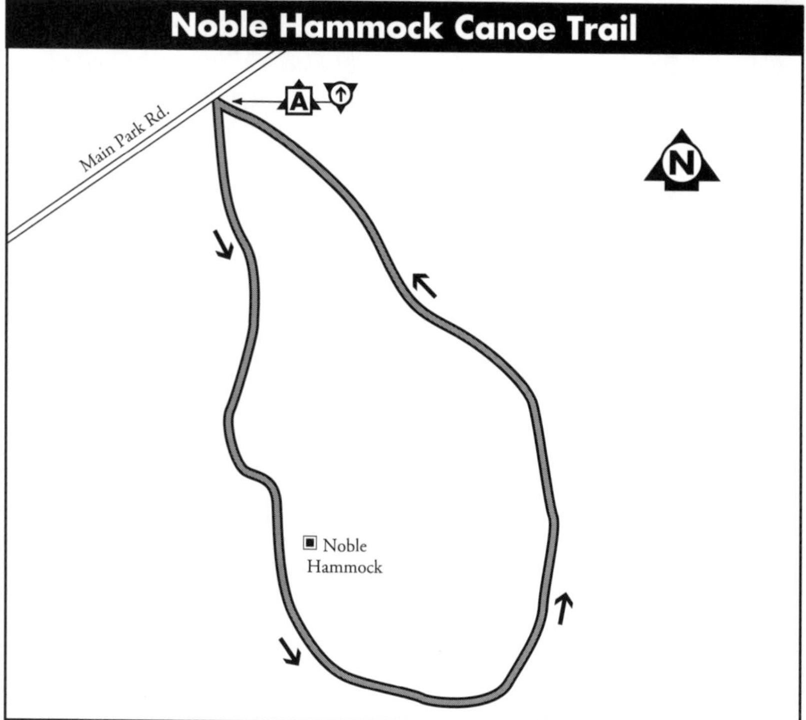

Don't be surprised when the water stirs as you round a corner on this trail. Many fish ply these waters, including such native species as bluegill, largemouth bass, and the distinctive long-snouted Florida gar. Unfortunately, you will also see tilapia, an exotic bream-like fish that is successfully reproducing here.

SHUTTLE: This loop does not require a shuttle. From Flamingo, drive east on Main Park Road for 10 miles to the Noble Hammock put-in, on the right side of the road. The trail is 28 miles from the park entrance station on Main Park Road.

GAUGE: Visual, phone. If in doubt, consult with the rangers at the Flamingo Visitor Center at (305) 242-7700.

MUD LAKE LOOP TRAIL

This loop paddle inside Everglades National Park gives you a good taste of some open water, some confined water, and, more important, quiet water. Four miles of this loop is for hand-propelled craft only. There is a price to pay for this solitude, however: one leg of your loop requires a portage between waterways. I recommend this route for canoers only—the narrow creeks, downed trees, and the portage make sea kayaking downright troublesome. The following description starts at Coot Bay Pond on Main Park Road. However, if you want to make a shorter loop, paddlers can begin at the end of Bear Lake Road, making it a 4.8-mile adventure. Also be apprised that insects can be troublesome, especially on the Bear Lake Canoe Trail portion of this loop.

MAPS: Everglades National Park map, Waterproof Chart #39, NOAA Chart #11433, Flamingo (USGS)

class	I
length	7
time	4
gauge	Phone
level	Tidal
gradient	Tidal
scenery	A

MUD LAKE LOOP TRAIL

DESCRIPTION: Start your paddle on Coot Bay Pond and then pass beneath a mangrove tunnel to Coot Bay. Connect briefly to the Wilderness Waterway and the Buttonwood Canal Route before paddling a small creek to Mud Lake, which is a more appealing place than its name suggests. Enjoy the quiet of Mud Lake, then take another creek to the Bear Lake Canoe Trail, where you will trace an old drainage canal to the newer Buttonwood Canal. But getting to Buttonwood Canal requires a portage of 160 yards. Head back to Coot Bay Pond via the Buttonwood Canal and Coot Bay.

Set out from one of the small landings on Coot Bay Pond, paddling north to a small tunnel-like opening. From a distance it seems there is no passage, but this man-made cut barely wide enough for a canoe will lead you to Coot Bay. The spoils of the cut create land areas on which grow drier plant species, such as palm. Open up into Coot Bay and paddle west for Coast Guard marker #3 and the Buttonwood Canal Route. Continue to follow the channel markers north for the shortcut to Whitewater Bay, but for this loop stay with the south shore of Coot Bay to a PVC pipe marker at 2 miles, signaling the creek leading to Mud Lake.

Enter a shady slender waterway, which is made even more closed-in by hundreds of fallen trees, sawn just enough for your passage. Expect to slide over a few logs. Live mangrove hovers over

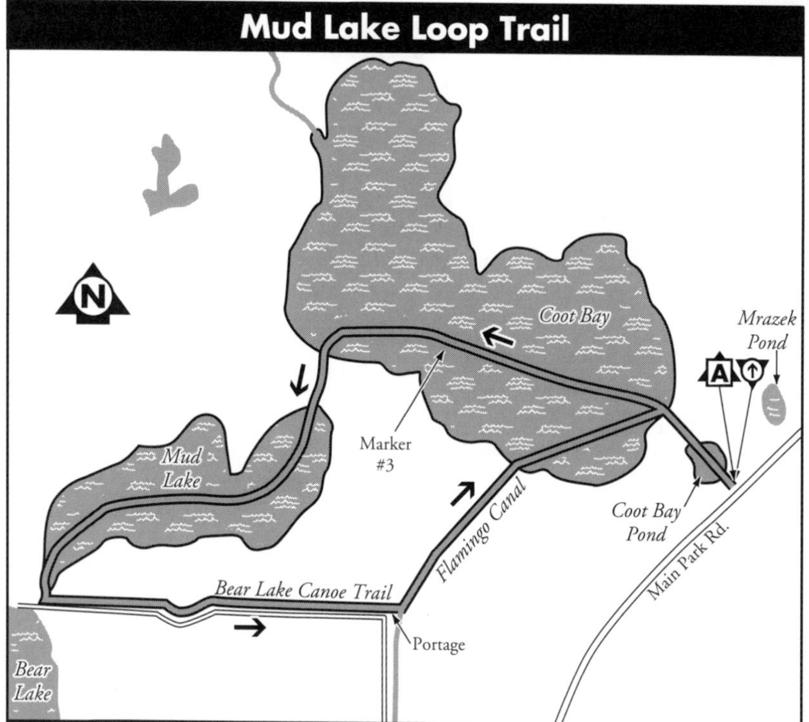

you until emerging onto Mud Lake and a group of small circular islands. Follow the PVC pipe markers south and west across this pretty lake. Its reddish-copper–colored waters contrast well with the green shores. The markers lead to the most southwesterly corner and a short creek connecting to the Bear Lake Canoe Trail. Follow this short creek to the Bear Lake Canoe Trail.

Once on the canoe trail, make sure to turn left (east). The pungent waters here are rich with the smell of decay, as vegetation continues its never-ending cycle of life and death. It is about 200 hundred yards east to Bear Lake. The Bear Lake Canoe Trail traces the old Homestead Canal, built in the 1920s alongside a road attempting to connect Florida City to Cape Sable. The road has reverted to a trail, and the canal is now silting in, making for very shallow paddling. Roots of mangrove grow into the water and branches hang overhead. Insects can be bothersome on the nearly 2 miles of paddling until the dock and ground landing at the portage.

Once at the portage, take your canoe on the foot trail to your left, then left again toward two wooden posts to a landing on the

Buttonwood Canal. Head left (north) up the waterway, which will seem like the Mississippi River after the Bear Lake Canoe Trail. Come to Coot Bay at mile 6 and paddle east toward a PVC pipe marker to the small channel to Coot Bay Pond. Head back through the tunnel to Coot Bay Pond, completing your loop at mile 7.

SHUTTLE: This loop trail does not require a shuttle. Coot Bay Pond is 34 miles east from the Florida City area park entrance station and 4 miles west of Flamingo on Main Park Road.

GAUGE: Phone. Call Everglades National Park at (305) 242-7700 for the latest water conditions.

part Ten

appendixes

Appendix A: Outfitters

THE WESTERN PANHANDLE

Adventures Unlimited
8974 Tomahawk Landing Road
Milton, FL 32570
(800) 239-6864
www.adventuresunlimited.com
This group has an elaborate outpost that serves Coldwater, Sweetwater, and Juniper Creeks as well as the Blackwater River and the Perdido River. They provide shuttle service, canoe and kayak rentals, catered meals, cabins, campsites for individuals and large groups, and outdoor challenge courses.

Bob's Canoe Rental and Sales
7525 Munson Highway
Milton, FL 32583
(850) 623-5457
In business since 1971, Bob's operates exclusively on Coldwater Creek. They offer shuttle services and rent canoes and kayaks. Call ahead for reservations between October 1 and April 1.

Scott's Ferry General Store
6648 FL 71 South
Blountstown, FL 32424
(850) 674-2900
This store and campground rents canoes on the lower Chipola River and has cabins and a campground. They do not provide shuttles, however.

Blackwater Canoe Outpost and Rental
10274 Pond Road
Milton, FL 32583
(850) 623-0235
www.blackwatercanoe.com
This outfit, located near Blackwater River State Park, is open

year-round and rents canoes, kayaks, and tubes for use on the Blackwater River. They will provide shuttles for private boats. Reservations are recommended. They also have a camp store.

THE CENTRAL PANHANDLE

Econfina Canoe Livery
5641-A Porter Pond Road
Youngstown, FL 32466
(850) 722-9032
www.canoeeconfinacreek.com
Located on the beautiful Econfina Creek, this friendly group rents canoes and kayaks and provides shuttles for their boats and private boats as well. Reservations are recommended.

Sopchoppy Outfitters
106 Municipal Avenue
Sopchoppy, FL 32358
(850) 962-2220
www.SopchoppyOutfitters.com
This quality outfit offers varied trips on the Sopchoppy River, both guided and unguided. Visit their restored shop in downtown Sopchoppy.

THE BIG BEND

Lighthouse Central Canoe & Bait
7996 Coastal Highway
Newport, FL 32327
(850) 925-9904
These folks rent canoes and kayaks for use on the St. Marks River and Wakulla River.

Steinhatchee Outpost
P.O. Box 48
Perry, FL 32348
(800) 589-1541
www.steinhatcheeoutpost.com
Located on the Steinhatchee River in the tiny town of Tenmile, this group rents canoes and kayaks, as well as providing shuttle service to private boats with a day's advance notice.

THE NORTHERN PENINSULA

American Canoe Adventures
10610 Bridge Street
White Springs, FL 32095
(386) 397-1309
www.aca1.com
This outfit primarily operates on the upper Suwannee River, but serves the entire Suwannee from the Okefenokee Swamp to the

Gulf of Mexico. They also sell and service canoes. Reservations are recommended.

Canoe Outpost–Santa Fe River
P.O. Box 592
High Springs, FL 32655
(386) 454-2050
www.santaferiver.com
Jim Wood and company are located on the Santa Fe River near US 441. They rent canoes and kayaks and offer shuttles for private boats. They also work the Ichetucknee River and Suwannee River.

Canoe Outpost–Suwannee
2461 95th Drive
Live Oak, FL 32060
(800) 428-4147
Located on the Suwannee River, this group rents canoes and kayaks, and shuttles private boats and backpackers hiking nearby portions of the Florida Trail. They service not only the Suwannee but also the Withlacoochee north and the Alapaha.

Dragonfly Watersports
20336 East Pennsylvania Avenue
Dunnellon, FL 34432
(800) 919-9579
www.dragonflywatersports.com
These folks rent canoes, kayaks, tubes, and more for use on the Rainbow River and Withlacoochee River south. They also offer guided trips and paddling instruction as well as selling boats and boating supplies. Reservations are recommended.

Ichetucknee Family Canoe & Cabins
8587 S.W. Elim Church Road
Fort White, FL 32038
(866) 224-2064
www.ichetuckneecanoeandcabins.com
Located near Ichetucknee River, they rent tubes, canoes, and kayaks, and offer shuttle service to and from the Ichetucknee, Santa Fe, and Suwannee rivers. They also have cabins and a campground for overnighting.

THE CENTRAL PENINSULA

King's Landing Canoe Rental
5714 Baptist Camp Road
Apopka, FL 32712
(407) 886-0859
http://members.aol.com/kingslndng
Conveniently located at the head of Rock Springs Run and

Wekiva River, these folks rent canoes and kayaks and provide shuttles for private boat owners.

Nobleton Boat Rental
29196 Lake Lindsay Road
Nobleton, FL 34661
(800) 783-5284
www.nobletoncanoes.com
Located on the middle portion of the Withlacoochee River south, this outfit rents canoes, pontoon boats, and fishing boats. They also rent bikes and provide shuttles for private boats.

Ocklawaha Canoe Outpost & Resort
15260 N.E. 152nd Place
Fort McCoy, FL 32134
(352) 236-4606
www.outpostresort.com
Based on the Ocklawaha River, this outfit rents canoes and kayaks and offers overnight trips. They have an on-site camp store, as well as a campground and cabins for rent. They do shuttle private boats.

Withlacoochee River RV Park and Canoe Rental
P.O. Box 114
Lacoochee, FL
(352) 583-4778
www.gatorstyle.com
Located on the upper part of the Withlacoochee River south, this friendly outfit rents canoes as well as shuttles private vehicles. They have a campground that caters to RVs and tents.

THE CENTRAL HIGHLANDS

Canoe Outpost–Peace River
2816 NW CR 661
Arcadia, FL 34266
(800) 268-0083
www.canoeoutpost.com
Run by friendly folks, this outfit rents canoes and kayaks, shuttles private boats, and has a campground on the Peace River. They are conveniently located near Arcadia but service the entire Peace.

Canoe the Peace River
2555 US 17 South
Wauchula, FL 33873
(888) 977-7878
www.zwkoa.com
Located at the KOA Kampground in Wauchula, this group rents

canoes and kayaks and provides shuttles on the upper Peace River.

Fisheating Creek Outfitters
7555 US 27 Northwest
Palmdale, FL 33944
(863) 675-7855
www.fisheatingcreek.com
These folks are the concessionaires for the state-owned campground and outfitter on Fisheating Creek. They rent boats and provide shuttle service for paddlers on the entire creek. You must use these outfitters to access certain parts of the river. Reservations are required, so call well ahead of time.

Hidden River RV Park
15295 East Colonial Drive
Orlando, FL 32826
(407) 568-5346
Hidden River Park offers trips between FL 50 and Snowhill Road on the Econlockhatchee River. These include guided trips. They rent canoes and kayaks as well.

THE ATLANTIC COAST

Canoeing & Kayaking on the Loxahatchee River
9060 West Indiantown Road
Jupiter, FL 33478
(888) 272-1257
www.canoes-kayaks-florida.com
These folks have been in business for over 20 years and offer canoe and kayak rental and sales on the Loxahatchee River. Reservations are recommended.

Spruce Creek Outfitters
6996 Ridgewood Avenue
Port Orange, FL 32127
(386) 763-9417
www.sprucecreekkayaks.com
These energetic people rent canoes, a wide variety of kayaks, and other boats for adventures on Spruce Creek. They offer guided trips and have a restaurant/bar on the premises, which borders Strickland Bay.

THE SOUTHWEST GULF COAST

Alafia River Canoe Rentals
4419 River Drive
Valrico, FL 33594
(813) 689-8645
This outfitter, the oldest livery on the Alafia, primarily runs trips

on the Alafia River between Alderman's Ford Park and Lithia–Pinecrest Road, where its base is located. They rent boats and will shuttle private boats.

Canoe Escape
9335 East Fowler Avenue
Thonotosassa, FL 33592
(813) 986-2067
www.canoeescape.com
Canoe Escape operates on the Hillsborough River. They offer trips of varying lengths through the Hillsborough. They rent canoes and kayaks and provide shuttles for private boats.

Canoe Outpost–Little Manatee River
18001 US 301 South
Wimauma, FL 33596
(813) 634-2228
www.canoeoutpost.com
This outfit offers trips of varied lengths along the Little Manatee River, including canoe camping. They rent canoes and kayaks, as well as shuttle private boats. A camp store is conveniently located on site in case you forgot anything.

Estero River Outfitters
20991 South Tamiami Trail
Estero, FL 33928
(239) 992-4050
www.esteroriveroutfitters.com
Estero Outfitters operates on US 41 on the Estero River. They rent canoes and kayaks for use both on and off the Estero. They offer guided tours and local trip information, have saltwater bait and tackle, and engage in monthly moonlight paddles.

Oak Haven River Retreat
12143 Riverhills Drive
Tampa, FL 33688-4072
(813) 988-4589
www.oakhavenriverretreat.com
Oak Haven River Retreat, located on the Hillsborough River, offers canoe and kayak rentals on Saturday and Sunday from 9 a.m. until 5 p.m. and weekdays by appointment. They provide tandem canoes and both solo and tandem kayaks.

Ray's Canoe Hideaway and Kayak Center
1247 Hagle Park Road
Bradenton, FL 34212

(941) 747-3909
www.rayscanoehideaway.com
Tucked away on the upper Manatee River, Ray's offers canoe and kayak rentals as well as boat launching from their facility. They also have a camp store.

Weeki Wachee Canoe Rental
6131 Commercial Way
Spring Hill, FL 34606
(352) 597-0360
www.floridacanoe.com
These people operate inside the old Weeki Wachee Springs tourist attractions. They rent canoes and kayaks and provide shuttles for private boats on the Weeki Wachee River.

THE EVERGLADES

North American Canoe Tours
P.O. Box 5038
Everglades City, FL 34139
(239) 695-3299
www.evergladesadventures.com
These folks rent canoes, kayaks, and gear; lead tours; and provide shuttles at Everglades National Park, Wilderness Waterway, Turner River, and Halfway Creek. They also offer showers and overnight lodging at their Ivey House, which is located adjacent to North American Canoe Tours in Everglades City.

Everglades International Hostel
20 SW Second Avenue
Florida City, FL 33034
(305) 248-1122
www.evergladeshostel.com
This outfit provides inexpensive lodging and kayak and canoe rentals for Everglades National Park and the Wilderness Waterway. It's only 15 minutes from the east entrance to Everglades National Park.

Appendix B: Paddling Clubs

Emerald Coast Paddlers
2 SW Miracle Strip Parkway
Fort Walton, FL
(850) 837-1577
ecpaddlers@yahoo.com

Florida Sea Kayaking Association
www.fska.org

Coconut Kayakers
P.O. Box 3646
Tequesta, FL 33469

Tampa Bay Sea Kayakers
765 24th Avenue North
St. Petersburg, FL 33704
(727) 898-2907

Seminole Canoe and Kayak Club
4619 Ortega Farms Circle
Jacksonville, FL 32210
(904) 388-6733

Space Coast Paddlers
P.O. Box 360193
Melbourne, FL 32936
(407) 773-4664

Florida Canoe and Kayak Association
P.O. Box 20892
West Palm Beach, FL 33416
(407) 686-8800

West Florida Canoe Club
P.O. Box 17203
Pensacola, FL 32522
(904) 932-3756

Silent Otters Paddle Club
High Springs, FL
(904) 454-1082
obladi4me@aol.com

Wilderness Trekkers
3225 San Miguel Avenue SE
Palm Bay, FL 32909
www.wilderness-trekkers.org

Appalachia Canoe Club
P.O. Box 4027
Tallahassee, FL 32315
(904) 224-9668

Citrus Paddling Club
Route 1, Box 415
Floral City, FL 32636

Central Florida Paddlemasters
9335 East Fowler Avenue
Thonotosassa, FL 33592
(813) 986-0997

Clearwater Beach Outrigger Canoe Club
2708 First Street
Indian Rocks Beach, FL 33785
(813) 593-9854

Coconut Kayakers
P.O. Box 3646
Tequesta, FL 33469

Florida Competition Paddlers
4546 Huntington Street NE
St. Petersburg, FL 33703
(813) 823-8000

King's Landing Canoe Club
5714 Baptist Camp Road
Apopka, FL 32712
(407) 886-0859

Jupiter Outdoor Center Outrigger and Canoe Club
18095 Coastal A1A
Jupiter, FL 33477
(877) SIT-ON-TOP
(561) 747-9666

Marion County Aquaholics Paddlers Group
P.O. Box 1138
Citra, FL 32113
(352) 347-1994
mcaquaholids@aol.com

Mugwump Canoe Club
9025 Sunset Drive
Miami, FL 33173

The Persistent Paddlers Kayak Klub
P.O. Box 281
Placida, FL 33946
(942) 697-8825

Lanakila'iki Outrigger Canoe Club
100 NW 55th Street
Ft. Lauderdale, FL 33309
(954) 491-5147

Nature Coast Paddle Club
2300 South Suncoast Boulevard
Homosassa, FL 34448
(352) 621-4972

Palm Beach Pack & Paddle Club
P.O. Box 16041
West Palm Beach, FL 33416
(800) 947-7717
(407) 683-2851

Paradise Paddlers/Florida Keys Paddling Club
104050 Overseas Highway
Key Largo, FL 33037
(305) 451-3018
kayak@terranova.net

Peninsula Paddling Club
8571 Shady Glen Drive
Orlando, FL 32619
(407) 352-1711

Seminole Canoe and Kayak Club
4619 Ortega Farms Circle
Jacksonville, FL 32210
(904) 778-8621
paddlejax@hotmail.com

Florida Riverine Ecosystem Explorers
4085 Forest Hill Drive
Cooper City, FL 33026
(954) 258-8605

Appendix C: Safety Code of American Whitewater

Adopted 1959, Revision 1998
Lee Belknap, *Safety Chairman*
Charlie Walbridge, *Safety Vice Chairman*
Mac Thornton, *Legal Advisor*
Rich Bowers, *Executive Director*

This code has been prepared using the best available information and has been reviewed by a broad cross section of whitewater experts. The code, however, is only a collection of guidelines; attempts to minimize risks should be flexible, not constrained by a rigid set of rules. Varying conditions and group goals may combine with unpredictable circumstances to require alternate procedures. This code is not intended to serve as a standard of care for commercial outfitters or guides.

I. PERSONAL PREPAREDNESS AND RESPONSIBILITY

1. Be a competent swimmer, with the ability to handle yourself underwater.
2. Wear a life jacket. A snugly-fitting vest-type life preserver offers back and shoulder protection as well as the flotation needed to swim safely in whitewater.
3. Wear a solid, correctly-fitted helmet when upsets are likely. This is essential in kayaks or covered canoes, and recommended for open canoeists using thigh straps and rafters running steep drops.
4. Do not boat out of control. Your skills should be sufficient to stop or reach shore before reaching danger. Do not enter a rapid unless you are reasonably sure that you can run it safely or swim it without injury.
5. Whitewater rivers contain many hazards which are not always easily recognized. The following are the most frequent killers.
   a. **High water.** The river's speed and power increase tremendously as the flow increases, raising the difficulty of most rapids. Rescue becomes progressively harder as the water rises, adding to the danger. Floating debris and strainers make even an easy rapid quite hazardous. It is often misleading to judge the river level at the put in, since a small rise in a wide, shallow place will be multiplied many times where

the river narrows. Use reliable gauge information whenever possible, and be aware that sun on snowpack, hard rain, and upstream dam releases may greatly increase the flow.

b. **Cold.** Cold drains your strength and robs you of the ability to make sound decisions on matters affecting your survival. Cold water immersion, because of the initial shock and the rapid heat loss which follows, is especially dangerous. Dress appropriately for bad weather or sudden immersion in the water. When the water temperature is less than 50 degrees F, a wetsuit or drysuit is essential for protection if you swim. Next best is wool or pile clothing under a waterproof shell. In this case, you should also carry waterproof matches and a change of clothing in a waterproof bag. If, after prolonged exposure, a person experiences uncontrollable shaking, loss of coordination, or difficulty speaking, he or she is hypothermic, and needs your assistance.

c. **Strainers.** Brush, fallen trees, bridge pilings, undercut rocks or anything else which allows river current to sweep through can pin boats and boaters against the obstacle. Water pressure on anything trapped this way can be overwhelming. Rescue is often extremely difficult. Pinning may occur in fast current, with little or no whitewater to warn of the danger.

d. **Dams, wiers, ledges, reversals, holes, and hydraulics.** When water drops over a obstacle, it curls back on itself, forming a strong upstream current which may be capable of holding a boat or swimmer. Some holes make for excellent sport. Others are proven killers. Paddlers who cannot recognize the difference should avoid all but the smallest holes. Hydraulics around man-made dams must be treated with utmost respect regardless of their height or the level of the river. Despite their seemingly benign appearance, they can create an almost escape-proof trap. The swimmer's only exit from the "drowning machine" is to dive below the surface when the downstream current is flowing beneath the reversal.

e. **Broaching.** When a boat is pushed sideways against a rock by strong current, it may collapse and wrap. This is especially dangerous to kayak and decked canoe paddlers; these boats will collapse and the

combination of indestructible hulls and tight outfitting may create a deadly trap. Even without entrapment, releasing pinned boats can be extremely time-consuming and dangerous. To avoid pinning, throw your weight downstream towards the rock. This allows the current to slide harmlessly underneath the hull.

6. Boating alone is discouraged. The minimum party is three people or two craft.

7. Have a frank knowledge of your boating ability, and don't attempt rivers or rapids which lie beyond that ability.

a. Develop the paddling skills and teamwork required to match the river you plan to boat. Most good paddlers develop skills gradually, and attempts to advance too quickly will compromise your safety and enjoyment.

b. Be in good physical and mental condition, consistent with the difficulties which may be expected. Make adjustments for loss of skills due to age, health, fitness. Any health limitations must be explained to your fellow paddlers prior to starting the trip.

8. Be practiced in self-rescue, including escape from an overturned craft. The eskimo roll is strongly recommended for decked boaters who run rapids Class IV or greater, or who paddle in cold environmental conditions.

9. Be trained in rescue skills, CPR, and first aid with special emphasis on the recognizing and treating hypothermia. It may save your friend's life.

10. Carry equipment needed for unexpected emergencies, including foot wear which will protect your feet when walking out, a throw rope, knife, whistle, and waterproof matches. If you wear eyeglasses, tie them on and carry a spare pair on long trips. Bring cloth repair tape on short runs, and a full repair kit on isolated rivers. Do not wear bulky jackets, ponchos, heavy boots, or anything else which could reduce your ability to survive a swim.

11. Despite the mutually supportive group structure described in this code, individual paddlers are ultimately responsible for their own safety, and must assume sole responsibility for the following decisions:

a. The decision to participate on any trip. This includes an evaluation of the expected difficulty of the rapids

under the conditions existing at the time of the put-in.

b. The selection of appropriate equipment, including a boat design suited to their skills and the appropriate rescue and survival gear.

c. The decision to scout any rapid, and to run or portage according to their best judgment. Other members of the group may offer advice, but paddlers should resist pressure from anyone to paddle beyond their skills. It is also their responsibility to decide whether to pass up any walk-out or take-out opportunity.

d. All trip participants should consistently evaluate their own and their group's safety, voicing their concerns when appropriate and following what they believe to be the best course of action. Paddlers are encouraged to speak with anyone whose actions on the water are dangerous, whether they are a part of your group or not.

II. BOAT AND EQUIPMENT PREPAREDNESS

1. Test new and different equipment under familiar conditions before relying on it for difficult runs. This is especially true when adopting a new boat design or outfitting system. Low volume craft may present additional hazards to inexperienced or poorly conditioned paddlers.
2. Be sure your boat and gear are in good repair before starting a trip. The more isolated and difficult the run, the more rigorous this inspection should be.
3. Install flotation bags in non-inflatable craft, securely fixed in each end, designed to displace as much water as possible. Inflatable boats should have multiple air chambers and be test inflated before launching.
4. Have strong, properly sized paddles or oars for controlling your craft. Carry sufficient spares for the length and difficulty of the trip.
5. Outfit your boat safely. The ability to exit your boat quickly is an essential component of safety in rapids. It is your responsibility to see that there is absolutely nothing to cause entrapment when coming free of an upset craft. This includes:

    a. Spray covers which won't release reliably or which release prematurely.

b. Boat outfitting too tight to allow a fast exit, especially in low volume kayaks or decked canoes. This includes low hung thwarts in canoes lacking adequate clearance for your feet and kayak footbraces which fail or allow your feet to become wedged under them.

c. Inadequately supported decks which collapse on a paddler's legs when a decked boat is pinned by water pressure. Inadequate clearance with the deck because of your size or build.

d. Loose ropes which cause entanglement. Beware of any length of loose line attached to a whitewater boat. All items must be tied tightly and excess line eliminated; painters, throw lines, and safety rope systems must be completely and effectively stored. Do not knot the end of a rope, as it can get caught in cracks between rocks.

6. Provide ropes which permit you to hold on to your craft so that it may be rescued. The following methods are recommended:

a. Kayaks and covered canoes should have grab loops of ¼" + rope or equivalent webbing sized to admit a normal sized hand. Stern painters are permissible if properly secured.

b. Open canoes should have securely anchored bow and stern painters consisting of 8–10 feet of ¼" + line. These must be secured in such a way that they are readily accessible, but cannot come loose accidentally. Grab loops are acceptable, but are more difficult to reach after an upset.

c. Rafts and dories may have taut perimeter lines threaded through the loops provided. footholds should be designed so that a paddler's feet cannot be forced through them, causing entrapment. Flip lines should be carefully and reliably stowed.

7. Know your craft's carrying capacity, and how added loads affect boat handling in whitewater. Most rafts have a minimum crew size which can be added to on day trips or in easy rapids. Carrying more than two paddlers in an open canoe when running rapids is not recommended.

8. Car top racks must be strong and attach positively to the vehicle. Lash your boat to each crossbar, then tie the ends

of the boats directly to the bumpers for added security. This arrangement should survive all but the most violent vehicle accident.

III. GROUP PREPAREDNESS AND RESPONSIBILITY

1. **Organization.** A river trip should be regarded as a common adventure by all participants, except on instructional or commercially guided trips as defined below. Participants share the responsibility for the conduct of the trip, and each participant is individually responsible for judging his or her own capabilities and for his or her own safety as the trip progresses. Participants are encouraged (but are not obligated) to offer advice and guidance for the independent consideration and judgment of others.
2. **River conditions.** The group should have a reasonable knowledge of the difficulty of the run. Participants should evaluate this information and adjust their plans accordingly. If the run is exploratory or no one is familiar with the river, maps and guidebooks, if available, should be examined. The group should secure accurate flow information; the more difficult the run, the more important this will be. Be aware of possible changes in river level and how this will affect the difficulty of the run. If the trip involves tidal stretches, secure appropriate information on tides.
3. **Group equipment should be suited to the difficulty of the river.** The group should always have a throw line available, and one line per boat is recommended on difficult runs. The list may include: carbiners, prussick loops, first aid kit, flashlight, folding saw, fire starter, guidebooks, maps, food, extra clothing, and any other rescue or survival items suggested by conditions. Each item is not required on every run, and this list is not meant to be a substitute for good judgment.
4. **Keep the group compact, but maintain sufficient spacing to avoid collisions.** If the group is large, consider dividing into smaller groups or using the "buddy system" as an additional safeguard. Space yourselves closely enough to permit good communication, but not so close as to interfere with one another in rapids.
   a. **A point paddler sets the pace.** When in front, do not get in over your head. Never run drops when you cannot see a clear route to the bottom or, for advanced

paddlers, a sure route to the next eddy. When in doubt, stop and scout.

b. **Keep track of all group members.** Each boat keeps the one behind it in sight, stopping if necessary. Know how many people are in your group and take head counts regularly. No one should paddle ahead or walk out without first informing the group. Paddlers requiring additional support should stay at the center of a group, and not allow themselves to lag behind in the more difficult rapids. If the group is large and contains a wide range of abilities, a "sweep boat" may be designated to bring up the rear.

c. **Courtesy.** On heavily used rivers, do not cut in front of a boater running a drop. Always look upstream before leaving eddies to run or play. Never enter a crowded drop or eddy when no room for you exists. Passing other groups in a rapid may be hazardous: it's often safer to wait upstream until the group ahead has passed.

5. **Float plan.** If the trip is into a wilderness area or for an extended period, plans should be filed with a responsible person who will contact the authorities if you are overdue. It may be wise to establish checkpoints along the way where civilization could be contacted if necessary. Knowing the location of possible help and preplanning escape routes can speed rescue.

6. **Drugs.** The use of alcohol or mind altering drugs before or during river trips is not recommended. It dulls reflexes, reduces decision making ability, and may interfere with important survival reflexes.

7. **Instructional or commercially guided trips.** In contrast to the common adventure trip format, in these trip formats, a boating instructor or commercial guide assumes some of the responsibilities normally exercised by the group as a whole, as appropriate under the circumstances. These formats recognize that instructional or commercially guided trips may involve participants who lack significant experience in whitewater. However, as a participant acquires experience in whitewater, he or she takes on increasing responsibility for his or her own safety, in accordance with what he or she knows or should know as a result of that increased experience. Also, as in all trip formats, every participant must realize and assume the risks associated with

the serious hazards of whitewater rivers. It is advisable for instructors and commercial guides or their employers to acquire trip or personal liability insurance:

a. an "instructional trip" is characterized by a clear teacher/pupil relationship, where the primary purpose of the trip is to teach boating skills, and which is conducted for a fee.

b. a "commercially guided trip" is characterized by a licensed, professional guide conducting trips for a fee.

IV. GUIDELINES FOR RIVER RESCUE

1. Recover from an upset with an eskimo roll whenever possible. Evacuate your boat immediately if there is imminent danger of being trapped against rocks, brush, or any other kind of strainer.

2. If you swim, hold on to your boat. It has much flotation and is easy for rescuers to spot. Get to the upstream end so that you cannot be crushed between a rock and your boat by the force of the current. Persons with good balance may be able to climb on top of a swamped kayak or flipped raft and paddle to shore.

3. Release your craft if this will improve your chances, especially if the water is cold or dangerous rapids lie ahead. Actively attempt self-rescue whenever possible by swimming for safety. Be prepared to assist others who may come to your aid.

a. When swimming in shallow or obstructed rapids, lie on your back with feet held high and pointed downstream. Do not attempt to stand in fast moving water; if your foot wedges on the bottom, fast water will push you under and keep you there. Get to slow or very shallow water before attempting to stand or walk. Look ahead! Avoid possible pinning situations including undercut rocks, strainers, downed trees, holes, and other dangers by swimming away from them.

b. If the rapids are deep and powerful, roll over onto your stomach and swim aggressively for shore. Watch for eddies and slackwater and use them to get out of the current. Strong swimmers can effect a powerful upstream ferry and get to shore fast. If the shores are obstructed with strainers or under cut rocks, however, it is safer to "ride the rapid out" until a safer escape can be found.

4. If others spill and swim, go after the boaters first. Rescue boats and equipment only if this can be done safely. While participants are encouraged (but not obligated) to assist one another to the best of their ability, they should do so only if they can, in their judgment, do so safely. The first duty of a rescuer is not to compound the problem by becoming another victim.
5. The use of rescue lines requires training; uninformed use may cause injury. Never tie yourself into either end of a line without a reliable quick-release system. Have a knife handy to deal with unexpected entanglement. Learn to place set lines effectively, to throw accurately, to belay effectively, and to properly handle a rope thrown to you.
6. When reviving a drowning victim, be aware that cold water may greatly extend survival time underwater. Victims of hypothermia may have depressed vital signs so they look and feel dead. Don't give up; continue CPR for as long as possible without compromising safety.

V. UNIVERSAL RIVER SIGNALS

These signals may be substituted with an alternate set of signals agreed upon by the group.

Stop: Potential hazard ahead. Wait for "all clear" signal before proceeding, or scout ahead. Form a horizontal bar with your outstretched arms. Those seeing the signal should pass it back to others in the party.

Help/emergency. Assist the signaler as quickly as possible. Give three long blasts on a police whistle while waving a paddle, helmet or life vest over your head. If a whistle is not available, use the visual signal alone. A whistle is best carried on a lanyard attached to your life vest.

All clear. Come ahead (in the absence of other directions proceed down the center). Form a vertical bar with your paddle or one arm held high above your head. Paddle blade should be turned flat for maximum visibility. To signal direction or a preferred course through a rapid around obstruction, lower the previously vertical "all clear" by 45 degrees toward the side of the river with the preferred route. Never point toward the obstacle you wish to avoid.

I'm OK. I'm OK and not hurt. While holding the elbow outward toward the side, repeatedly pat the top of your head.

VI. INTERNATIONAL SCALE OF RIVER DIFFICULTY

This is the American version of a rating system used to compare river difficulty throughout the world. This system is not exact; rivers do not always fit easily into one category, and regional or individual interpretations may cause misunderstandings. It is no substitute for a guidebook or accurate first-hand descriptions of a run.

Paddlers attempting difficult runs in an unfamiliar area should act cautiously until they get a feel for the way the scale is interpreted locally. River difficulty may change each year due to fluctuations in water level, downed trees, recent floods, geological disturbances, or bad weather. Stay alert for unexpected problems!

As river difficulty increases, the danger to swimming paddlers becomes more severe. As rapids become longer and more continuous, the challenge increases. There is a difference between running an occasional Class IV rapid and dealing with an entire river of this category. Allow an extra margin of safety between skills and river ratings when the water is cold or if the river itself is remote and inaccessible.

Examples of commonly run rapids that fit each of the classifications are presented in the document "International Scale of River Difficulty—Standard Rated Rapids" (at **www.americanwhitewater.org/archive/safety/bnchmark.htm**). Rapids of a difficulty similar to a rapids on this list are rated the same. Rivers are also rated using this scale. A river rating should take into account many factors including the difficulty of individual rapids, remoteness, hazards, etc.

THE SIX DIFFICULTY CLASSES:

Class I: *Easy.* Fast moving water with riffles and small waves. Few obstructions, all obvious and easily missed with little training. Risk to swimmers is slight; self-rescue is easy.

Class II: *Novice.* Straightforward rapids with wide, clear channels which are evident without scouting. Occasional maneuvering may be required, but rocks and medium sized waves are easily missed by trained paddlers. Swimmers are seldom injured and group assistance, while helpful, is seldom needed. Rapids that are at the upper end of this difficulty range are designated "Class II+".

Class III: *Intermediate.* Rapids with moderate, irregular waves which may be difficult to avoid and which can swamp an open canoe. Complex maneuvers in fast current and good boat control in tight passages or around ledges are often required; large waves or strainers may be present but are easily avoided. Strong eddies

and powerful current effects can be found, particularly on large-volume rivers. Scouting is advisable for inexperienced parties. Injuries while swimming are rare; self-rescue is usually easy but group assistance may be required to avoid long swims. Rapids that are at the lower or upper end of this difficulty range are designated "Class III–" or "Class III+" respectively.

Class IV: *Advanced.* Intense, powerful but predictable rapids requiring precise boat handling in turbulent water. Depending on the character of the river, it may feature large, unavoidable waves and holes or constricted passages demanding fast maneuvers under pressure. A fast, reliable eddy turn may be needed to initiate maneuvers, scout rapids, or rest. Rapids may require "must" moves above dangerous hazards. Scouting may be necessary the first time down. Risk of injury to swimmers is moderate to high, and water conditions may make self-rescue difficult. Group assistance for rescue is often essential but requires practiced skills. A strong eskimo roll is highly recommended. Rapids that are at the upper end of this difficulty range are designated "Class IV–" or "Class IV+" respectively.

Class V: *Expert.* Extremely long, obstructed, or very violent rapids which expose a paddler to added risk. Drops may contain large, unavoidable waves and holes or steep, congested chutes with complex, demanding routes. Rapids may continue for long distances between pools, demanding a high level of fitness. What eddies exist may be small, turbulent, or difficult to reach. At the high end of the scale, several of these factors may be combined. Scouting is recommended but may be difficult. Swims are dangerous, and rescue is often difficult even for experts. A very reliable eskimo roll, proper equipment, extensive experience, and practiced rescue skills are essential. Because of the large range of difficulty that exists beyond Class IV, Class 5 is an open ended, multiple level scale designated by 5.0, 5.1, 5.2, etc. Each of these levels is an order of magnitude more difficult than the last. Example: increasing difficulty from Class 5.0 to Class 5.1 is a similar order of magnitude as increasing from Class IV to Class 5.0.

Class VI: *Extreme and exploratory.* These runs have almost never been attempted and often exemplify the extremes of difficulty, unpredictability and danger. The consequences of errors are very severe and rescue may be impossible. For teams of experts only, at favorable water levels, after close personal inspection and taking all precautions. After a Class VI rapids has been run many times, its rating may be changed to an appropriate Class 5.x rating.

glossary

Boil line Located immediately downstream of a hole, the point (or area) at which current begins passing downstream again instead of rushing upstream into the hole.

Boof To launch over and off of a rock at the top lip of a drop. A successful boof lifts the bow so that the angle of the boat is more shallow than the angle of the water falling off the drop.

Bow The forward end of the boat.

Brace Paddle stroke used to prevent the boat from flipping over.

Breaking wave A wave that intermittently curls back on itself, falling upstream.

By-pass A channel cut across a meander that creates an island or oxbow lake.

Chock-stone A stone that the current flowing over a falls lands onto.

Chute A channel between obstructions that has faster current than the surrounding water.

Curler A wave with a top that is curled over onto the face of the wave.

Deadfall Trees or brush that have fallen into the stream totally or partially obstructing it.

Decked boat A kayak (usually) or canoe that is completely enclosed and fitted with a spray skirt that keeps the hull from filling with water.

Downstream V A river feature often marking the best route through obstacles, with the point of the V facing downstream. Formed by the eddy lines resulting from two obstacles bracketing a faster channel of water, or by turbulent water bracketing a smooth tongue.

Drop-and-pool Term used to describe a river characterized by rapids separated with long, placid stretches. The rapids act as natural dams that still the current preceding the drop.

Eddy The water downstream of an obstruction in the current or below a river bend. The water in the eddy may be relatively calm or boiling, and will flow upstream.

Eddy line The boundary at the edge of an eddy separating two currents of different velocity and direction.

Eddy-out Exit the downstream current into an eddy.

Eddy turn Maneuver used to enter or exit an eddy.

Ferry A maneuver for moving laterally across a stream, executed facing upstream or downstream.

Flood stage The point at which a river is out of its banks. The level associated with flood stage is location-specific and depends on the depth of the river bed, height of the banks, and flow.

Gradient A river's change in altitude over a fixed distance, usually expressed in feet per mile.

Hair Turbulent, foamy whitewater.

Haystack A pyramid-shaped standing wave caused by deceleration of current from underwater resistance, commonly found at the end of a chute where the faster current collides with the slower moving water pooled below the rapid.

Hole A river feature created where water flows over an obstacle with sufficient flow and velocity to create a wave that violently and continuously breaks (recirculates) upstream against its face.

Hydraulic General term for souse holes and holes.

Keeper Any hole that is difficult to exit. Can take the form of a hole whose right and left edges curve upstream and fold back into the hole, or a very large hole whose boil line is found more than a boat-length downstream.

Ledge The exposed edge of a rock stratum that acts as a low, natural dam creating a falls or rapid as current passes over it.

Line A viable route through a rapid.

Low-head dam A usually man-made obstacle that laterally spans a river from the left to the right bank, creating a pool upstream and a keeper hydraulic immediately below. Grimly referred to as the "perfect killing machine" for their lack of exit points once a boater is caught in the hydraulic.

Meander A large loop in a river's path through a wide floodplain.

Oxbow A U-shaped lake formed when a river's meander is bypassed by the main channel.

Peel-out A maneuver for exiting an eddy and quickly entering

the downstream current.

Pencil in When a boat pierces the water below a drop in a vertical position.

PFD Personal flotation device. Better term for "lifejacket." The Coast Guard recognizes five classes of PFDs. The ACA recommends U.S. Coast Guard–approved Class III PFDs.

Pile The frothy whitewater on top of a wave or in a hole.

Pillow Bulge on the surface of the river created by water piling up against an underwater obstruction, usually a rock.

Pinning When an object (usually a boat) is pushed onto an obstacle (usually a rock) and held there forcefully by the pressure of the current.

Pool A section of river where the prevailing current has been stilled, and the water is usually deep and quiet.

Portage To avoid an obstacle, hazard or rapid by exiting the river, carrying boat and gear downstream, and re-entering the river below the obstacle.

Pot-hole Formed by erosion, a depression in the river bed at the base of a steep drop.

Pour-over A sticky hole formed by water flowing over an abrupt drop.

Punch Approaching and passing through a hole aggressively, boat perpendicular to the hole, to reach the current moving downstream beyond the boil line.

Rapids Portion of a river where there is appreciable turbulence usually accompanied by obstacles.

Riffles Slight turbulence with or without a few rocks tossed in, usually found where current is swift and very shallow.

River left The left side of the river as determined when facing downstream.

River right The right side of the river as determined when facing downstream.

Rock garden Rapids that have many exposed or partially submerged rocks necessitating intricate and technical maneuvering.

Roll The technique of righting a capsized kayak or canoe with the paddler remaining in the paddling position.

Scout To evaluate a rapid (either from the shore or while your boat is in an eddy) to decide whether or not to run it, or to facilitate selection of a suitable route through it.

Shuttle Using vehicles to transport people and boats on land between river access points prior to or after a run.

Sieve A hazard formed by channels of swift water flowing through menacingly tight spaces between and underneath boulders, usually accompanied by undercuts. Water can flow freely through, but debris and paddlers are easily pinned underwater by the forceful currents.

Slide rapid An elongated ledge that descends or slopes gradually rather than abruptly, usually covered by shallow water.

Sneak An alternative route through a rapid that avoids the main flow. Usually, but not always, an easier route than the main channel.

Souse hole *See* Hole.

Spray skirt A hemmed piece of neoprene or nylon clothing that resembles a short skirt, having an elastic hem fitting around the boater's waist and an elastic hem fitting around the cockpit of a decked boat.

Standing wave A wave that does not move in relation to the riverbed. *See* Haystack.

Stern The rear end of the kayak or canoe.

Strainer Branches, trees, or vegetation partially or totally submerged in the river's current. A serious hazards for paddlers, they only allow water to pass through freely. The current will pull anything else down, plastering it into place, similar to the action of a kitchen colander.

Surfing The technique of situating your boat on the upstream face of a wave.

Swamp To fill a canoe or kayak with water.

Tongue *See* Chute.

Undercut rock A hazard in which the river has eroded a boulder below the surface of the water, creating a cavity with potential for entrapment not visible above the surface.

About the Author

Johnny Molloy is an outdoor writer based in Johnson City, Tennessee. A native Tennessean, he was born in Memphis and moved to Knoxville in 1980 to attend the University of Tennessee. In Knoxville Molloy developed his love of the natural world, which has since become the primary focus his life.

It all started on a backpacking foray into the Great Smoky Mountains National Park. That first trip, though a disaster, unleashed an innate love of the outdoors that has led to Molloy spending over 110 nights in the wild per year, over the past 25 years, backpacking and canoe-camping throughout our country and abroad. In 1987, after graduating from the University of Tennessee with a degree in Economics, he continued to spend an ever-increasing time in natural places, becoming more skilled in a variety of environments. Friends enjoyed his adventure stories, and one even suggested he write a book. Soon Molloy parlayed his love of the outdoors into an occupation.

The results of his efforts are 27 books, ranging from hiking guides to paddling guides to camping guides to true outdoor adventure stories. Molloy's books primarily cover the Southeast but range to Colorado and Wisconsin. He has written several Florida guidebooks, including *A Paddler's Guide to Everglades National Park, Best in Tent Camping: Florida, Beach & Coastal Camping in Florida, The Hiking Trails of Florida's National Forests Parks and Preserves,* and a true adventure story titled *From the Swamp to the Keys: A Paddle through Florida History,* in addition to updating and rewriting this guidebook.

Today Molloy spends his winters in Florida, enjoying the best of what the Sunshine State has to offer in the outdoors. He has also written numerous magazine articles for magazines such as *Backpacker* and *Sea Kayaker,* as well as for Web sites such as **gorp.com.** Molloy continues to write to this day and travels extensively to all four corners of the United States pursuing a variety of outdoor activities.

index